Banks and Finance in Modern Macroeconomics

A Historical Perspective

Bruna Ingrao

Department of Social and Economic Sciences, Sapienza University of Rome, Italy

Claudio Sardoni

Department of Social and Economic Sciences, Sapienza University of Rome, Italy

 Edward Elgar
PUBLISHING

Cheltenham, UK • Northampton, MA, USA

Published by
Edward Elgar Publishing Limited
The Lypiatts
15 Lansdown Road
Cheltenham
Glos GL50 2JA
UK

Edward Elgar Publishing, Inc.
William Pratt House
9 Dewey Court
Northampton
Massachusetts 01060
USA

A catalogue record for this book
is available from the British Library

Library of Congress Control Number: 2018962948

This book is available electronically in the **Elgar**online
Economics subject collection
DOI 10.4337/9781786431530

ISBN 978 1 78643 152 3 (cased)
ISBN 978 1 78643 153 0 (eBook)

Contents

Preface

Some years ago – when the profession was discussing the reasons why macroeconomics had failed so badly to understand, let alone foresee, the crisis of 2007–2008 – a group of master students of our university, highly interested in economic theory and policy, asked us to organize an extra-curricular short course on macroeconomic theory and its evolution over time, which could help them put what they were studying in other courses in a more general context as well as better understand the current economic situation. Since in our university, like in most universities over the world, courses in the history of economics are no longer on offer, we promptly answered their request in the positive.

Together with the students, we decided to focus the lectures on the way in which mainstream macroeconomics had dealt with a number of problems strictly connected to financial and economic crises, topics on which we had already done some research in the past. A crucial issue to deal with was, of course, how different economists with different theoretical backgrounds had approached the problem of the interrelation between the financial and the real sectors of the economy. But equally, if not more important was to try to understand and explain why, at least since the late 1930s until the late 1980s, mainstream macroeconomics had almost completely ignored, or amply downplayed, the importance of the financial sector and its interplay with the real side of the economy.

After the more tentative experience of the first year, we repeated the course for two more years by extending the number of economists and topics covered in the lectures. This book is largely the result of our work to prepare our lectures.

Over the years, we have been studying and discussing the topics and issues with which the book is concerned with many colleagues and in several seminars and conferences. It would be difficult to make an exhaustive list of all the people with whom we had the benefit to discuss our ideas. Therefore, here we limit ourselves to thank only a few people who have commented on the book or some of its chapters more recently. First of all, we want to thank the students attending the lectures mentioned above for their enthusiasm and intellectual curiosity, which stimulated us to improve on our work.

The book has been presented in a mini-course at the University of São Paulo (USP) and in two seminars at the University of Brasilia in May 2018.

We would like to thank, in particular, Pedro Garcia Duarte, who organized the mini-course at USP and stimulated us to improve and clarify our treatment of several topics with his questions and suggestions, and Mauro Boianowsky, who organized our seminars in Brasilia and participated in the discussion with very interesting comments and observations. Chapters of the book have been also presented and discussed in various seminars; we would like to thank the participants in these events for their helpful observations and comments. Finally, we wish to thank Geoff Harcourt, who read a first draft of our book and made a number of useful suggestions. To the best of our capacity, in writing the book we have tried to take account of all the comments that we received. Naturally, the responsibility for any remaining errors is exclusively ours.

1. Introduction

Should one ask the layman whether banks and finance are important to understand the working of the economy, the answer would be immediate and straightforward: Yes! In fact, the importance of financial markets and banks for the working of market economies is at the centre stage in popular discussion, as well as in current debates on economic policy. Yet, as it is generally recognized (see, e.g., Gertler, 1988; Goodhart, 2005–2006), for a large part of the 20th century, spanning from the late 1930s to the 1980s, mainstream macroeconomics put banks and the financial system to backstage, or even expelled them completely from its theoretical representations of the economy.[1]

In the meantime, the financial system has expanded enormously in its complex interaction with the real side of the economy. Banks too big to fail trade on global markets, marketing innovative financial products; a whole shadow banking industry has emerged, with complex and non-transparent links to the banking industry; financial institutions of various sizes and definitions trade in derivatives or other non-standard contracts involving massive financial flows; firms' and families' budgets take advantage of getting credit from the global financial system, whose poor transparency in terms of capital requirements and indebtedness suddenly became so evident since 2007.

1.1 THE DISTURBING PUZZLE OF BANKS AND FINANCE

An explanation of such an evolution of macroeconomic theory could be that, during the period when banks and finance were essentially ignored, the financial side of market economies worked in a relatively smooth way and, thus, economists tended to be concerned with different issues and topics, regarded as more urgent and challenging. Such an explanation, though containing an element of truth, cannot be regarded as fully satisfactory. The theoretical interest, or its vanishing, in the working of the financial side of the

---

[1] We define mainstream economics as the evolving set of theories, prominent in academic communities at the research and teaching levels, during a certain historical period. For the idea of mainstream economics as a flexible, evolving core of theories, see Colander et al. (2004).

economy and its interactions with the real side cannot be simply related to the occurrence, or absence, of serious disturbances like the Great Depression of the 1930s and the crisis of the late 2000s. Finance and credit always play such a vital role in modern capitalism that they cannot be the concern of economic theory only at critical times. There must be, in our view, deeper and more general reasons why macroeconomics evolved in the way it did. Our book aims to explain such a puzzling evolution.

The dominant families of macroeconomic models in mainstream macroeconomics substantially avoided incorporating banks and finance in their basic analytical structures. As a related and intertwined question, the debt structure within the private sector was also cancelled, either by aggregating the private debts of heterogeneous agents, or by simply assuming that the macroeconomic behaviour of the economy could be effectively represented by models with a single representative agent. It was only in the last 30 years or so that the interest in the study of credit and financial markets and their interrelation with the 'real' economy grew significantly. We propose an explanation of all this which is essentially based on the analysis of the way in which banks and financial markets have been conceptualized in mainstream economics, not only in Monetarism and New Classical macroeconomics, but also in Keynesian and Neo-Keynesian macroeconomics (the post-war Keynesianism of the Neoclassical Synthesis).[2]

Our historical narration reconstructs the state of affairs in contemporary macroeconomics by considering the historical context in which macroeconomists elaborated their theories, the evolution of the research technologies which they explored as effective analytical tools, and finally the vision of the market economy that different scholars had in mind when looking for operational models to be assumed as reference standards. We deal with these aspects by focusing our narration on the evolution of core theories. Given the long-term historical perspective of the book, we cannot deal in any detail with economic history, changing economic policies, or the sociology of research in academic communities. We write a history of ideas, and we focus on selected authors and selected works without any pretence of exhaustiveness. Our aim is to critically explore the threads and issues in the evolution of ideas that we regard as most relevant.

In doing so, we try to provide elements that can help answer some critical questions: do banks and finance really make a fundamental difference for our understanding of macroeconomic events, so that 'forgetting' them means missing crucial aspects of phenomena like fluctuations and growth,

---

[2]   For brevity, here we adopt the conventional label 'Neoclassical Synthesis'; in Chapters 6 and 7 below, we address in some detail the differences among the various scholars, notably Patinkin, Modigliani and Tobin.

macroeconomic stability or macroeconomic policies? Can macroeconomists ignore banks and finance in their modelling and interpretative strategies with only a minor cost to bear? Should macroeconomists stick to models and theories deprived of any explicit reference to banking and finance, or even to money?

By calling attention to these issues, the book aims at restoring a view of financial markets and banks as primary actors in the functioning, or malfunctioning, of market economies, to capture a more realistic vision of the 'visible hands' at work, rather than the impersonal operation of 'invisible' and impersonal market forces. In monetary market economies, the entrepreneurial activities in banking and finance are among the visible hands, which operate within a complex system of institutional settings to promote the inter-temporal coordination among millions of heterogeneous, independent agents. Financial networks may be exposed to major shocks and be severely disrupted, with the consequence of blocking growth or amplifying business fluctuations. Notwithstanding the recent developments mentioned above, in our view, macroeconomic theory has still a long way to go to reach a satisfactory account of the complexities of financial markets in models and theories which the profession uses in education, in conceptual analysis, and in policy advice.

In the following sections of this chapter, we briefly outline the main issues, topics and economists that will be considered in detail in the successive chapters; but before proceeding it is worth reminding that our historical reconstruction is concerned only with mainstream macroeconomics. Although well aware of the fact that some important contributions to the topics with which the book deals come from economists outside the mainstream, a systematic and detailed consideration of their work is beyond the scope of the book. We limit ourselves to look only at some contributions by Minsky, one of the few non-mainstream economists whose analysis of recurrent episodes of fragility of economic systems with a well developed financial sector has attracted the attention of some mainstream economists especially after the recent crisis.

1.2   FROM THE 19TH CENTURY TO THE 1930s

In the 19th century, scholars addressing questions in the realm of economic theory from the systemic perspective of growth and fluctuations had again and again directed their attention to price adjustments and price instability, the regulation of the money supply, banking policy and the stability or the fragility of the financial system, the sequences of waves of credit expansion or contraction, the fluctuations of expectations and confidence in financial markets.

Thornton's early analysis of liquidity crises, Tooke's, J. S. Mill's or Lord Overstone's narrations of speculative booms and busts in the so called overtrading theories of recurrent financial crises, the banker John Mills's psychological explanation of speculative waves, Jevons's theory of recurrent business cycles, the two Marshall's interpretation of booms and depressions, are a few prominent interpretations of economic instability. All these scholars evoked speculative bubbles due to imitative expectations, followed by disappointed expectations of capital gains, with collective failures in the rational planning of budget constraints, the domino effects due to bankruptcies and the consequent out-of-equilibrium processes of adjustment. From various perspectives, these scholars analysed how in monetary economies, after some real or monetary shock, including shocks to the quantity of money, out-of-equilibrium adjustment processes take place. Their theories made recourse to observable phenomena of monetary illusion, due to either the outright mistaken expectations about future prices by many private agents or to the misalignment of monetary variables in the dynamic process that leads, eventually, to an adjustment to long-term equilibrium values.

In these various accounts of financial crises and business cycles, banks and their reckless financing of speculative investment had a prominent explicatory role. The overtrading interpretation of financial crises was intertwined with the 'cycle of credit' that fuelled immoderate speculation, and later accelerated the financial collapse, because of the credit crunch, the crises of confidence and the panic rush to liquidity that followed the bubble burst. Bankruptcies and their domino effects were an essential aspect in the picture of economic instability, both for their effect in influencing expectations and for their impact on spending and production.

During the 19th century, however, economic thought suffered a kind of schizophrenia: if monetary instability had a prominent role to account for historical events, price theory gave pride of place to equilibrium values in their various descriptions, be they classical or marginalist. The hardcore of economic theory focused on barter economies, where relative prices were transparently set in a non-monetary environment. The emphasis placed on dynamic disequilibrium phenomena in credit and financial markets ambiguously coexisted with the emphasis placed on the stability of 'natural' values in classical political economy, and it quite openly clashed with the focus on equilibrium exchange values in the so-called marginalist revolution.[3] In classical thought, out of equilibrium, price theory pointed to the smooth adjustment to long-term equilibrium values, established independently of the

---

[3]   We use the controversial expression 'marginalist revolution' for brevity, with no pretence to discuss here the problem of its continuity or break with respect to classical political economy, or the remarkable differences of approach among 'marginalist' scholars.

supply of money, finance and the banking system. Classical growth theory gave exclusive role to real variables. The schizophrenia became even more visible with the emergence of mathematical models of rational, maximizing behaviour within the new paradigm of maximizing equilibrium that various scholars explored in campaigning for a science of political economy grounded in rigorous mathematical language.

At the turn of the 19th century, the gulf between monetary theory and relative price theory appeared wide open to the innovative scholars actively involved in building mathematical models of competitive market equilibrium. The equilibrium analysis of consumers' and producers' rational, optimal choices was disconnected from the study of business fluctuations and the monetary economy. Both Jevons and Walras addressed the question, suggesting that it was the inevitable result of the two-stage construction of political economy as a science. Statics, the equilibrium theory of relative prices in a transparent barter economy, was the scientific foundation on which to build business cycle dynamics in the future (Ingrao, 2013, pp. 575-ff.).[4] Since the late 19th century, there was some uneasiness in such promises of future solutions. Wicksell addressed the thorny question as a major topic in his research; in 1898, in *Interest and Prices* he underlined the dichotomy between equilibrium exchange values and the absolute level of prices.[5] Marshall tried to bridge the gulf between the foundations of economics, dealt with in his *Principles of Economics*, and monetary theory, by devoting a late separate volume to money and credit (*Money, Credit and Commerce*, 1923).

Along the years, in the various editions of his major work *Eléments d'Économie Politique Pure ou Théorie de la Richesse Sociale*, Walras made an effort to coherently include a technology of monetary payments within the equilibrium construction of pure political economy, justifying (and indeed imposing) the demand for cash. He dealt, in particular, with the mathematical expression of the quantity theory of money. Whether he succeeded or whether the equilibrium frame of pure political economy is structurally an ideal barter economy, disconnected from any monetary description of transactions, has been the object of controversy to the present day.[6] Walras devoted considerable attention to monetary questions in his writings on applied political economy,

---

[4] On the distinction between statics and dynamics, see Walras (1900, pp. 259–260, 298 and 301–302).

[5] 'The exchange of commodities in itself, and the conditions of production and consumption on which it depends, affect only exchange values or *relative* prices: they can exert *no direct influence whatever on the absolute level of money prices*' (Wicksell, 1898[1936], p. 23).

[6] Bridel (1997) carefully scrutinizes Walras's attempts to put money into his general equilibrium construction; he concludes that they failed. Baranzini (2005) addresses the controversial relation of Walras's monetary theory in pure economics and in applied economics.

but the coherence of these with his pure theoretical construction is also the object of ongoing controversy.

The uneasiness about the open gap between static equilibrium theory, and monetary theory, the theory of the trade cycle or economic dynamics in general, fully came to light in the early 20th century, when it took front stage at the frontier of research. Since the early 20th century, many scholars signalled it, with reference to Walras's general equilibrium theory or to other neoclassical theories of relative prices in the context of a transparent barter economy. The question was addressed either from the perspective of how the quantity theory of money could be integrated into equilibrium theory or from the complementary perspective of how to reconcile static price theory with the explanation of dynamic phenomena in monetary economies.

Both perspectives involved new controversies about the quantity theory of money. There was a shared preoccupation with credit expansion or contraction via banks' loans. Since the early 20th century, and until the 1930s, a number of scholars (among whom were Wicksell, Fisher, Robertson, and Schumpeter) insisted on the role of private banks in creating money if not without limits, certainly within the movable limits set by highly elastic constraints. In the first quarter of the 20th century, macroeconomics as a discipline distinct from microeconomics had not yet emerged. Banks, as institutions that create money through credit, were studied within fluid disciplinary borders, dealing with monetary instability, investment and growth, or the explanation of business cycles. Their ability to create money was the object of concern, the transfer of bank deposits becoming the customary means of payment in the business community. In Europe, banks had been prominent in the financing of investment for development in France, Germany, Italy, and other countries; a highly decentralized banking system characterized the U.S. until the institution of the Federal Reserve system in 1913.

By the mid-1920s, both for dramatic historical reasons (the post-war instability) and for the inner logic of development of the equilibrium paradigm, which was taking the centre-stage in economic theory, the reconciliation of competitive market equilibrium and business cycles in a monetary economy became a major theoretical issue, which the most creative economists of the time addressed as an urgent and unsolved question. Hayek had dealt with it since the late 1920s; in 1933 he argued that the aim to unify coherently equilibrium price theory and dynamics was the task of his generation, since till then little advance had been done to bridge the gulf.[7] From a different

---

[7]   'The most characteristic feature of the work of our generation of economists is probably the general endeavour to apply the methods and results of the pure theory of equilibrium to the elucidation of more complicated "dynamic" phenomena. Perhaps one might have expected all generations of economists to have striven to approach nearer to reality by gradually relaxing the

perspective, Keynes complained that neoclassical theory was the theory of a barter economy, and that this prejudiced the understanding of unemployment, a theme to be found in his writings since the 1920s (Keynes, 1933[1973]). Myrdal wrote *Monetary equilibrium* (1939), published in Swedish in 1931, having in view the task to go further than Wicksell in reducing the gap between monetary theory and equilibrium theory;[8] Hicks had in mind the same purpose when writing *Value and capital*, published in 1939. In the midst of the turbulence following the first World War, in the early 1920s, or later during the contagion of the international financial crisis and the spreading of the depression, a variety of analyses emerged that focused on banks and financial markets in the macroeconomic scene, notably by Hawtrey (1919), Robertson (1926[1949]), Fisher (1922, 1932, 1933), Hayek (1933, 1939), Keynes (1931[1972]d, 1931[1972]a.)

On the distinction between monetary versus real theories of the business cycles a word of caution is in order. Whether the disturbances to full employment and market equilibrium arise from real forces in the economy (such as new investment, productivity shocks in agriculture, innovation and technological change, or 'sudden changes in the channels of trade', as Ricardo named them) or from monetary disturbances is a question debated since the 19th century. Different scholars from Thornton to Ricardo, from J.S. Mill to Marx, from Jevons to Wicksell and Marshall, underlined either the primary role that real forces play or the primary role of monetary disturbances, or some combination of both. Jevons, who introduced the study of business cycles based on the statistical analysis of time series in the mid-19th century, articulated the theory of business cycles as caused by shocks to agricultural crops due to the periodicity of solar spots. He was a real business cycle theorist *ante litteram*, arguing that the ultimate cause of fluctuations are productivity shocks, with no connection to money or finance; but he never dreamt of severing the analysis of real business cycle from monetary phenomena, and he explored how the shocks to agricultural crops finally affected British manufacturing markets, affecting expectations in the business world and credit markets. Also the other above-mentioned authors who pointed their finger towards real factors examined the transmission mechanisms via the links with the financial sector to explain fluctuations in prices, income and employment. Often they made recourse to speculative price bubbles to account for recurring commercial crises.

---

degree of abstraction of pure theory. Yet advance in this direction was not great during the fifty years preceding say 1920' (Hayek, 1933[1939], p. 135).

[8] Myrdal underlined the difficult coexistence of the theory of general economic equilibrium with dynamic analysis. He rejected the simplified dichotomy between equilibrium values in real terms and monetary variables.

According to the various theories, the links between the real and financial sectors were established by considering the expansion or contraction of credit by financial intermediaries, fluctuations in nominal interest rates, divergence between the market rate of interest and the real rate of return on investment, the delay of monetary wages to adjust to inflation or deflation, liquidity crises in the banking industry, the systemic bankruptcies of improvident investors, and so on. In the 20th century the Austrian school underlined how the divergence between the banking rate of interest and the real rate of return on investment put into motion a train of events that involved both real investment and monetary phenomena. Schumpeter, a proponent of real business cycles due to innovative change, did not fail to connect investment to bank credit. Whether the ultimate cause is real or monetary, or a mixture of both, the working of the system of payments, the credit structure, the degree of risk in the balance sheets of households or firms, the solidity of banks and financial institutions, affect the way in which market economies react to shocks. Markets could nurture inside shocks, progressively building up to disequilibria and financial fragility.

1.3   THE KEYNESIAN PARADIGM, THE MONETARIST COUNTER-REVOLUTION AND BEYOND

In the lively and controversial climate of the debates recalled above, since the late 1930s and during the 1940s, macroeconomic theory finally emerged as a separate field of research with the coming to dominance of the Keynesian paradigm. Unfortunately, under the dominance of Keynesianism from the late 1940s to the early 1970s, banks, financial intermediaries and financial markets faded away from macroeconomic models. Commercial banks came to play a merely passive role. Attention was focused on central banks, which were assumed to be able to implement effective policies to control the money supply and stabilize the economy.

The lack of attention to the financial system and its effects on the working of the economy may appear quite paradoxical, given the emphasis that Keynes, in the 1920s and 1930s, laid on the banking system and finance. In reality, however, Keynes himself in *The General Theory* had expunged banks from his analysis of the functioning of the economy; a choice that can be explained by his wish to stress the importance, in an uncertain world, of liquidity preference expressed as demand for (idle) money – something that cannot be easily done when the existence of bank loans make the supply of money endogenous – and his adoption of an equilibrium method, as opposed to the dynamic method of his earlier major work, *A Treatise on Money*.

As a consequence of Keynes's choice, in the post-war years, also the authoritative Keynesian scholars, who built the theoretical scaffolding of the so-called 'Neoclassical Synthesis', designed macroeconomic models, where the financial side of the economy is collapsed into the equilibrium equation between the demand and supply of money, and the money stock is an exogenous policy variable under the assumption of a stable money multiplier. The well-known Modigliani-Miller theorem (Modigliani and Miller, 1958) contributed to such an evolution of macroeconomic analysis as it stated that, under the hypothesis of perfect markets, the value of a firm is unaffected by how that firm is financed. In principle, the inside debt structure of firms in the private sector of the economy appeared to be irrelevant for macroeconomic stability.

The Keynesian dominance came to its end after the radical critique carried out by Milton Friedman and other scholars who promoted the so-called monetarist counter-revolution. Friedman criticized American Keynesians for having 'forgotten' money; but the new monetarist focus on the money stock did not bring with it a renewed attention to the financial system as a whole. Friedman pointed to the primary role of erratic monetary shocks affecting the stability of nominal income, under the assumption that the central bank could easily control the appropriate money aggregates, and, hence, promote long-term price stability. The use of simplified operational models, which Friedman and other monetarist scholars favoured, induced them to look at macroeconomic models as 'black boxes', into which the financial sector could be put with no long-term impact on the crucial relationship between the two operational macroeconomic variables, the money stock and nominal income.

Monetarism was followed by New Classical Macroeconomics (NCM), and inside money and finance were given an even less significant role to play. During the 1970s, in New Classical Macroeconomics the monetary aspects were essentially confined to considering the effects of 'monetary surprises' caused by unanticipated changes in the money stock controlled by the central bank (Lucas, 1972, 1981). The explicit choice to conceive of the macro-economy as a system of markets in full equilibrium, the equilibrium path being disturbed only by the transitory misconceptions of relative prices due to monetary surprises, implied the a priori exclusion of financial markets as a source of disturbances to equilibrium, failed adjustments, systemic collapse or low-growth traps.

Eventually, money disappeared altogether in the new generation of real business cycle models (RBC). Monetarism finally turned into 'Monetarism without money', as the point of arrival of such a paradoxical evolution has been named (Laidler, 2015, p. 19). Since the early 1980s, real business cycle models shifted their focus from monetary to technological shocks. Money, let alone financial markets, disappeared from the theory of business cycles, which were reduced to optimal responses to real shocks by the isolated representative agent. In one-agent economies, financial intermediation is redundant.

In due course, the ability of RBC models to explain the real world was chal-
lenged by the emergence of New Keynesian Economics (NKE), whose salient
feature is the importance that market imperfections have for the explanation
of the working of the economy. The conflict among NCM, RBC and NKE
in the late 1980s gave rise, some years later, to a sort of convergence among
macroeconomists on a number of topics and issues, which has been called the
'New Neoclassical Synthesis' (Goodfriend and King, 1997). The key features
of the new synthesis may be summarized as follows: i) macroeconomics has
to be based on rigorous inter-temporal general-equilibrium foundations; ii) the
agents' expectations are rational; iii) there exist imperfections and frictions that
are relevant for the working of the economy and they make policies (especially
monetary policy) effective; and iv) the most advanced analytical tools are
dynamic stochastic general equilibrium (DSGE) models.[9]

Thus, the most significant New Keynesian contribution to the New Synthesis essentially is the emphasis on imperfections. Initially, NKE mostly
concentrated on imperfections in the goods and labour markets; banks and
financial markets remained outside the mainstream analytical picture. They
were missing in most DSGE models, based on the fictional hypothesis of a
single representative agent. Over the years, and especially after the 2007–2008
financial crisis, there has been a growing number of writings concerned with
credit and financial markets.

1.4   BANKS, FINANCE AND GENERAL EQUILIBRIUM

In reconstructing the crucial passages briefly outlined above, our focus will
be on how different authors and different theoretical strands dealt with two
separate, but highly intertwined problems: the nature of banks and other
financial firms as active agents in monetary market economies; the visible
coordination activities, which make monetary market economies work.

In the first perspective, we shall underline the distinction between banks
seen as mere intermediaries between savers and borrowers, and banks seen as
institutions that create money through credit or, more in general, on the role of
banks and other financial firms as strategic players in contested, non-perfectly
competitive markets, where they fight for market spaces through product
innovation, innovative approaches to risk management, oligopolistic strategies,

---

[9]   Another important aspect of the New Neoclassical Synthesis, on which we do not dwell in
the book, is that monetary policies are no longer based on the control of the money supply but
on 'inflation targeting': central banks fix the policy interest rate and, consequently, the supply of
money is endogenous (on inflation targeting, see e.g. Bernanke et al., 1999b).

or even sheer fraudulent behaviour. The money supply is endogenous via credit creation by banks, which is not perfectly controlled by the central bank.

Keynesians of the Neoclassical Synthesis still saw banks as able to create money through credit, but in a passive way. The quantity of money in circulation was conceived as essentially determined by the central bank. In fact, it was assumed very often that the quantity of money created by commercial banks was a fixed multiple of the hard money issued by the central bank (the money multiplier). In the 1960s, the prevailing view of banks underwent a further change: they came to be regarded as institutions that are not essentially different from any other financial intermediary (Tobin, 1963).

The monetarist counter-revolution did not bring about any significant change in the conceptualization of the banking system, if not for signalling the systemic risk of banks' runs intrinsic to a less that 100 per cent reserve banking system. The crucial role of central banks and the passive role of commercial banks were theorized by Friedman, who campaigned to impose 100 per cent reserve requirements in deposit banking. If banks are passive intermediaries, or if specific legislation constrains them to be passive intermediaries, it is reasonable to abstract from their role, when analysing the macro-economy. Essentially this same line was followed by most of the earlier New Keynesian literature. Taking banks into account appears to be only a complication to avoid without any relevant theoretical consequence, especially at the textbook level.

In the macroeconomic literature, it is certainly well known that in a decentralized market society financial markets promote the inter-temporal coordination of spending and saving decisions among different agents. And yet it is not so often recognized that banks are strategic actors in financial markets, and, as a consequence, in market economies at large. Far from being passive, their role as intermediaries between lenders and borrowers is linked with their role as competing innovators. They competitively create the money contracts which they sell, tailoring them to the clients, anticipating the emerging needs on the demand and the supply side. They design, and market, new financial products to capture aggressive investors, to convince prudent lenders, to encourage potential borrowers. The mechanical reading of the money multiplier forgets that the banks generate financial innovation that is a major engine promoting growth, or it may be a major factor of financial fragility and macroeconomic instability, if not accompanied by effective regulations, or sound new practice, to deal with transparency and solvency.

In the second perspective, we shall advance a straightforward critique of the auctioneer metaphor that dominated mainstream macroeconomics because optimal inter-temporal equilibrium was the assumption adopted in modelling strategies, or because these were conceived under the dominant, theoretical influence of neo-Walrasian general equilibrium models. The ambiguous, monetary technology that Walras had tried to build was left aside in the evolution of the general-equilibrium theory. The image of competitive markets developed into a dichotomous frame, which left a durable imprint in post-war macroeconomic theory. The conception of an equilibrium system of competitive markets turned out to be logically split into the set of equations setting relative prices in goods and services markets, where neither money nor financial intermediation play any role, and the added quantity theory equation needed to set the general price level, and eventually anchor the system to monetary values. If the quantity theory equation appears to solve the problem of intregrating monetary values into the pure price theory, the two complementary sets of equations are deeply disconnected with regard to their analytical foundations.

The efforts to integrate monetary theory and general equilibrium theory (the 'peak of neoclassical thought' according to Samuelson) clashed again and again with this structural, theoretical difficulty. Notwithstanding the efforts that the best minds in economics had devoted to the task in the years of high theory from the 1920s to the late 1930s, the thorny question was still open in the 1960s. In 1967, Arrow noted that the failed relation between macroeconomics and microeconomics was a scandal in price theory (Arrow, 1967, pp. 734–735). Arrow's scandal was so much of a challenge that it was worthwhile pointing to it almost fifty years later. The 'Arrow's scandal', as Thomas Sargent called it in 2015 quoting Arrow's passage, was still relevant for macroeconomics at the opening of the 21st century. It was exceedingly difficult to explain why money should be there, or how it could be put there following a stringent line of research.

Why had the task to unify value theory and monetary theory, which was to be the primary aim of theoretical economists in the 1920s, so dramatically failed in the 1960–1970s? Lucas's disheartening 2013 summing up acknowledges that in contemporary mainstream macroeconomics, money is not there (Lucas, 2013, pp. xxvi–xxvii). Not only it is not there; it is a puzzle, and a difficult one to solve.[10] The difficulty, or more precisely the theoretical impossibility, to include money in neo-Walrasian general equilibrium models is acknowledged by a large specialized literature.[11] As Sargent noted in his review of Lucas's monetary essays, in the neo-Walrasian world money as cash makes no sense, since there are no bilateral exchanges, and thus no need of a generally accepted

---

[10] 'Beliefs aside, a successful policy to deal with a monetary or liquidity crisis will need to be based on some understanding of how real effects of monetary shocks come about, some kind of theory. This has been a central unresolved issue for economists at least since David Hume addressed it in the eighteenth century. This is the theme of my Nobel Lecture, Chapter 16 here, but no resolution is offered in that essay' (Lucas, 2013, p. xxiv).

[11] As for general equilibrium theorists, Debreu explicitly recognized that money is absent from his *Theory of Value* (Debreu, 1959). Hahn repeatedly discussed the issue with a negative answer; he convincingly argued that money has no place in the Arrow-Debreu model (see, e.g., Hahn, 1965, 1982, 1987).

medium of exchange.[12] In the multi-lateral system of complete spot and forward markets, where transparent transactions are perfectly coordinated ex ante for the whole horizon of exchanges, there is no need for money as a means of payment. The system of payments is mimicked as if it were a perfectly centralized, coordinated system of mutual credits, none of which is at risk of insolvency or default. The fictional auctioneer, calling equilibrium spot and forward prices at infinite speed of adjustment, guarantees that no agent defaults, or fails to accomplish what is stated in contracts. The rationality assumption guarantees that each planned budget is balanced over the relevant horizon. In principle, there are no financial or credit markets: each and every trader is simply adjusting his or her own optimal inter-temporal plan balancing present with future sales and purchases. In perfectly competitive markets, moreover, each and every bond or share, if any are conceivable in these fictional markets, would be perfectly transparent in terms of expected risk and returns to all traders.[13]

There is no need for money even as a unit of account, since every single good or basket of goods may be chosen as numeraire, provided its price is by assumption chosen to be equal to one. In market economies the need of money as a unit of account is related to the convenience in the standardization of computations, to facilitate communication among communities of traders, the collection of taxes or other payments, the setting of price tags in various locations. It helps because of the limited cognitive abilities of traders in processing and comparing lists of prices and values in different units. *A fortiori*, in the fictional Arrow-Debreu markets there is no need for money to transfer general purchasing power from the present to the future, as the liquidity component of portfolios. Every good is perfectly liquid at the prevailing equilibrium price, once general equilibrium is instantaneously achieved.[14] No risk is run that your neighbour will cheat you by deferring payment, or failing to pay according to commitment; no sanctions are required to impose compliance with signed contracts. If risks arise, they are fully covered by contingent forward exchanges, according to the states of the world.

---

[12] 'A major source of Arrow's "scandal" was that in the Arrow-Debreu model of general equilibrium, all trades are multilateral; they are accomplished through a credit system that comprehensively nets out claims. There is no role for cash because there are no bilateral transactions' (Sargent, 2015, p. 47).

[13] In a recent review essay, Lagos et al. (2017, p. 372) motivate the emergence of New Monetarism on the plain evidence that in the Arrow-Debreu model agents do not trade with each other, but 'they merely slide along budget lines'. They add: '...money is not essential in standard theories' (p. 375).

[14] The horse that Marshall compared to money to discuss the relative utility of a real good versus an inventory of general purchasing power, such a horse is as liquid as an ounce of gold or a skyscraper in Manhattan.

The absence of money in modelling the economy implies *a fortiori* the absence of finance and credit, apart from the spurious multilateral credit system of neo-Walrasian markets mentioned above. Theoretically, it is conceivable that some intermediaries might supply credit to their debtors in terms of stocks of goods, that is to say, loans in kind,[15] but the essence of a modern credit system is to supply purchasing power that is not constrained in terms of the goods to be acquired with it. There are restrictions on the transactions approved for each credit line or instrument, or open to each specific borrower, such as investment goods, housing or durable consumer goods, if the purchased goods stay as a guarantee to the creditor; but the nature of credit is to supply general purchasing power that borrowers will be free to use according to their best knowledge of their specific circumstances and purposes. Credit and finance are structurally linked to monetary values, and embedded into a monetary economy using a medium which is representative of general purchasing power.

Moreover, since the 1970s, and notably after the radical turn that expelled money from business cycle theory since the 1980s, the research technology most widely adopted in mainstream macroeconomics refrained from going through explicit aggregation procedures. These were bypassed by making the assumption of a strict equivalence between the macroeconomic behaviour of the economy and the behaviour of an ideal, representative household. In real business cycles models, there is not even a barter economy, as we reminded above, and no possible asymmetric information (Mishkin, 2011, pp. 13–4). The research technology based on the representative agent postulates the irrelevance of heterogeneous agents for the dynamic macroeconomic outlook. The cultural roots of this approach date back to Pigou's welfare economics, and the development that followed through Ramsey's aggregate model of the national household which optimally allocates saving through time.

In the last quarter of the 20th century a large theoretical literature on business cycles was based on Ramsey's optimal saving model and the Solow-Swan aggregate growth model, more than on neo-Walrasian general equilibrium models with heterogeneous agents and goods. Those who introduced this shortcut argued that a general equilibrium system with a multitude of consumers is perfectly equivalent to an economy with a single representative household, pretending that such equivalence has been demonstrated. They bypassed all the radical questions that the technical literature on general

---

[15] Wicksell contemplated credit in kind in describing an ideal exchange economy. Historically, in the share-cropping system in agriculture, landlords advanced seeds or nourishment to their poor farmers. In the cottage system in pre-industrial revolution times, merchants advanced cotton or wool to cottage weavers. Credit in kind is obviously not the main character of the contemporary banking or financial industries.

equilibrium had raised since the late 1970s on the poor results to be reached within the original Arrow-Debreu model. Their pretence has been criticized in highly technical general-equilibrium literature, but criticisms were ignored or regarded as irrelevant.[16]

We cannot deal here with these technical debates, the importance of which, however, must not be underestimated. Whatever the theorems, it is easy to see that the single household assumption erases a priori heterogeneous borrowers and lenders from the macro economy, including the constellation of diverse banks and financial bodies. The rational, single household optimally adjusting inter-temporal choices cannot enter into borrowing and lending with itself; it cannot be exposed to any risk of illiquidity or insolvency; it runs no risk of not complying with its own optimal choices, or not knowing its own patrimonial solidity. The single household moves along its optimal path whatever the exogenous shocks that might hit it. The choice of this research technology was justified by the aim to demonstrate theorems within the sophisticated but still tractable macroeconomic models that it permitted to build. The choice was replete with implications concerning what such simplified lenses allow us to see of the real world around.

1.5 WHY SHOULD BANKS AND FINANCE COME BACK TO MACROECONOMICS?

Since the 18th century, market economies worldwide work within the setting of a fully developed monetary system; financial institutions form an articulated system of markets, regulated both by private contracts and public regulations. In the network of markets which form the skeleton of our economies, financial institutions play a crucial role.

In the historical development of market economies, the monetary system and the network of financial markets have undergone decisive changes in terms of their extension and pervasiveness, and in terms of variety of organization, radical innovation in contracts, technologies of transactions, working practices and public regulations. From the first industrial revolution to the present, the smooth functioning or the maladjustment and crises of market economies have gone hand in hand with radical changes in the financial system. Innovations in financial regulations and/or in the functioning of financial institutions and their accepted business practices have marked epochal changes in the history of market economies.

---

[16] Research on aggregation demonstrates that no one-to-one mapping may be established between a properly general equilibrium economy and a single agent's economy, unless very strong restrictions are introduced (Kirman, 1992, 2006; Hendry and Muelbauer, 2018).

Banks and specialized firms in financial markets emerged and acted as Schumpeterian entrepreneurs, introducing radical innovations. They opened the way to the diffusion of new means of payments, new loan contracts, new insurances, new ways of raising funds for investment and innovation, new ways of hedging, a new world of transactions and business practices creating opportunities for enhanced coordination, but also for enhanced risks of systemic collapse, due to their becoming deeply ingrained into the current management of the consumers' and non-financial firms' balance-sheets. Notwithstanding the recurrent cases of malignant speculation in financial markets, nobody could conceive the development of contemporary market economies all over the world separately from the intertwined development of payment systems, credit contracts, mortgages, insurance policies, hedging funds, stock exchanges, and so on. It is so much so that today it is even problematic to draw a neat dividing line between finance and the real economy when dealing with large corporate businesses.

In the light of the historical experience of capitalist economies, the need for embodying banks and finance into theoretical reasoning and modelling is obvious. The issue, however, requires more elaborated theoretical consideration. The starting point is clear: no auctioneer exists to make the complex system of markets on which our society depends work smoothly. There is no a priori, inter-temporal coordination of people's decisions in market transactions; no central authority which might collect the appropriate information and impose whatever optimal allocation in real time. The working of markets depends on a set of norms, social practices, and institutions to regulate the production and allocation of resources in decentralized, bilateral transactions taking place in societies undergoing continuous innovation and change. Markets include systems of partial coordination, which require trained staff operating within the constraints of law, norms and shared conventions. Trained staff work daily to smooth arising disequilibria, which generate endogenous innovation and change. Markets work, more or less effectively, thanks to visible persons, visible logistics and communication systems, visible monetary arrangements and financial contracts.

Systems of law, social norms, or shared conventions are the foundations of the trust that permits the encounter in bilateral exchanges of private people or organizations, having in principle no reason to trust each other with respect to their reciprocal commitment to sign contracts and to not violate them. People trading in markets trust and rely on visible conventions which are shared by the other agents too. Money is a social, shared, convention regarding the common standard of value, in which bilateral partners denominate their contracts. Money is no veil; it is the instrument by which millions of transactions are expressed in a common language of value that permits mutual understanding and trust in exchange. The objects traded in financial markets are essentially present and future flows of purchasing power denominated in money. By their nature, financial markets deal in contracts defining trades in abstract flows of purchasing power denominated in some currency or package of currencies. These contracts might be backed up by some real goods, or anchored to some real goods, but not necessarily so. In any case, collaterals have to be priced in money values.

In the decentralized markets of contemporary societies no transparent information is fully available a priori, and no inter-temporal equilibrium prevails in complete, forward markets. No central authority covers the risks of each and every contingency over the whole planning horizon. Markets work thanks to the dynamic strategies of busy agents, who take care of partial coordinating activities within changing institutional settings, and under changing conditions. Financial institutions, be they banks or other private agencies (or even government agencies), are among the busy bodies whose strategic investment in human capital, effectiveness in communication and accumulated wealth help the coordination of bilateral monetary transactions in a global world of radical uncertainty and asymmetric information. They exist because information about creditworthiness and risk of default is asymmetric and costly, in the same way as acquiring the proper expertise to evaluate expected returns and risks of investments is time-consuming and costly. They exist because financial intermediation operates within regulations by law and custom that impose high transactions costs, due to the necessity to impose sanctions to protect traders in an environment of asymmetric information, and radical uncertainty governing the future money value of the assets in people's portfolios.[17]

Banks and other financial intermediaries work as visible hands to allocate money flows to potential buyers, or to sell investment products to potential savers, coordinating choices not only in financial markets, but at the junction of these with the markets for goods, services, or properties. They may succeed or fail, like other visible bodies and brains at work in market economies. They bet on making choices today that are compatible with uncertain future flows of income, pricing assets whose future prices are volatile, assessing risks, smoothing possibly emerging imbalances, providing for buffers, and so on. They produce innovative change in conventional practices and rules, opening improved opportunities for welfare and growth, or increasing the risks of disequilibria, imbalances, or conflicts.

---

[17] In some societies people could directly trade in bilateral transactions their present wealth against future flows of consumption, or acquire their present consumption against flows of future labour services. The debtor could settle the debt for present consumption by enslaving himself/herself for future forced work due to the lender. Against the present payment of a dowry the family could enslave the daughter into a monastery, which promised her lifelong consumption. In our societies these contracts are luckily forbidden.

Banks manage the system of payments, that is, the accounting technology to support legal, bilateral transactions in the commonly accepted means of payment. As accountants, banks monitor the solvency of traders, who pay through the payment instruments having their mark, such as credit cards or deposit transfers. The collapse or the malfunctioning of the system of payments has severe consequences in terms of higher transaction costs and loss of confidence; it implies the more or less extensive paralysis of transactions and, hence, of the market economy. Bilateral transactions require trust in the currency that is exchanged against goods or services, in terms of its purchasing power and liquidity. As the historical experience has proven, the collapse of the system of payments drastically reduces the opportunities for otherwise useful and welfare improving transactions; it drastically shrinks the real economy.

Credit creation by banks accompanies macroeconomic fluctuations through the financing of real investment or consumers' spending, or through the swelling of price bubbles. Banks inject flows of purchasing power into the balance sheets of borrowers, who channel it into the property markets, the stock exchange, the markets for consumer durables or investment goods,[18] with differential effects on prices or production in the markets where they are channelled. In extending loans, banks perform an allocative function: they evaluate creditworthiness and risks of default. In market environments dominated by imperfect, asymmetric information and volatile asset prices, banks provide the human capital to assess for each liquidity constrained buyer the capability for inter-temporal substitution. Their role in asserting creditworthiness is crucial as regards potential borrowers who, because of the modest size of their business and wealth, cannot provide guarantees to potential lenders;[19] banks assess their ability to incur debt today to be repaid with future income.

Under prudential practices, information gathering and public regulations, banks eventually manage their auctioneer's job, and help rationed borrowers get their sustainable financing. If the perception of the systemic risk of default

---

[18] 'The bulk of money is in the form of commercial bank liabilities, and banks can behave very differently over time. The form of their liabilities, their capital base, their confidence and their risk appetite can and does alter over time, both cyclically and more permanently. The whole question of whether certain segments of the economy can access funds beyond their current income depends crucially on the behaviour of the banks. If there is a supply shock to money, with certain groups now getting more, or less, access to funding, for example when banks provide mortgages to a wider group of households on easier terms, will this not feed back into the IS curve? Of course it will' (Goodhart, 2007, p. 58).

[19] Notably, they finance the middle or small size firms, which have no access to the stock exchange or alternative channels of finance. By financing their current activities, they help them to balance through time, flows of sales against flows of costs; they help finance their investment expenditures, or their buying of properties. Similarly, they provide purchasing power to households to buy consumer durables or enter mortgage markets.

increases, inducing banks to be selective in lending, their prudential behaviour cuts out from access to expenditure potential borrowers, with effects of credit rationing, or credit crunches. Banks' role at the junction with real markets is partially blocked; they no more provide buffers to smooth disequilibria. The allocative function requires competent staff and organization, and it cannot be easily substituted for.

If the fictional hand of the auctioneer is removed from the macroeconomic picture, coordination failures evidently show up. Some firms or consumers may become insolvent, or go bankrupt. The relevance of single bankruptcies, and their spillovers into other balance sheets, with real effects on spending, are related to the complex structure of the financial system. The systemic spreading of insolvency among the heterogeneous firms acting in the economy depends on the existing buffer stocks in both the real and the financial sectors of the economy, which are linked to the financial structure with respect to the distribution of debts and financial wealth. The wealth's basis of balance sheets are money values, which depend on volatile prices of properties, shares and other real or financial assets. Bankruptcies in the banking and financial industry, if and when they happen, create systemic effects in the macro-economy via expectations and confidence, and the reduction in the velocity of circulation of money.

The above are only a few aspects and features of modern sophisticated market economies, but they are sufficient to show how taking account of the financial sector and its interaction with the real sector should necessarily be a fundamental constituent part of an economic theory aiming to understand, and possibly improve, the world in which we live. Other questions, of course, are open and in need of more satisfactory answers. Should the economists' attention concentrate on banks or other financial institutions? Which is the difference, and which is the relation between them? Which financial flows are provided by bank credit and which by issues at the stock exchange or other funds channelled in financial markets? How is shadow banking related to banking properly?

To accomplish such a task, we argue, requires to go beyond the analytical and methodological strictures that still characterize the current mainstream. More specifically, we need to reject the pretension that an exclusive recourse to models, as sophisticated as they may be, can provide a fully satisfactory understanding of banks and finance in their complex interrelation with the real economy. It is necessary to mobilize a wide range of available cognitive instruments, including historical knowledge, the critical exploration of economic ideas and their evolution over time, the consideration of the complexity of human behaviour as well as the complexity of paths and trajectories that depend on crucial events, institutions and the social and political context. It is the lesson we draw from the great scholars whose ideas we examine and discuss in the book. 'Giants' of the past like Wicksell, Fisher, Schumpeter, Robertson, Keynes, Hicks and Tobin developed their theories, carried out their analyses and formulated their policy prescriptions in the context of wide cultural horizons, where historical explanations, the knowledge and understanding of the evolution of economic concepts played a crucial role together with the elaboration of new views and interpretations.

1.6   PLAN OF THE BOOK

The book is divided into two parts. Part I (Chapters 2 to 6) is concerned with the period spanning from the early years of the 20th century to the years immediately following World War II, when banks and their functioning enticed the attention of many scholars even though, at the same time, there emerged views and positions that can explain the subsequent theoretical developments that led to the fading into 'oblivion' of banks and other financial institutions.

Chapter 2 looks at how Wicksell and Fisher, acknowledging the growing importance of banks, took account of them in their attempts to elaborate what they regarded as a more satisfactory quantity theory of money. Chapter 3 is devoted to considering Schumpeter's and Robertson's contributions. They were not particularly interested in the analysis of the general price level per se and focused on the role of credit and banks as fundamental factors in capitalist processes of change. The Great Depression of the 1930s was, of course, a major concern of many economists; in Chapter 4 we examine Fisher's and Keynes's viewpoints on the effects of the bank and financial crises and, in particular, their deflationary effects, a topic that returned to interest several in the aftermath of the late 2000s crisis.

Finally, Chapters 5 and 6 are devoted to Keynes's major theoretical contributions in the 1930s and the debates following the publication of *The General Theory*. More specifically, Chapter 5 looks at the evolving of Keynes's views of banks from *A Treatise* to *The General Theory*. We argue that the well known fact that, in passing from one book to the other, Keynes let banks virtually disappear, can be explained by two crucial factors: his focus on liquidity preference expressed as a demand for money and his abandonment of a dynamic/sequential approach in favour of an equilibrium method. Part of Chapter 5 and the whole of Chapter 6 are concerned with criticisms of Keynes's *General Theory*. We concentrate on criticisms of the liquidity preference theory of the interest rate, to which a modern loanable funds theory was opposed, and the debate on the so-called wealth (or Pigou) effect.

Part II (Chapters 7 to 9) is concerned with macroeconomic theory from the post-war years to the recent developments of the late 20th and early 21st centuries. Since the early debates on *The General Theory*, one of the claims of the critics of Keynes was that his major results did not stand, or they had to be significantly qualified, when the analysis is carried out by taking account of all the relevant interrelations among markets. In due time, this criticism became a claim for the adoption of a proper Walrasian general-equilibrium framework to deal with macroeconomic phenomena. In Chapter 7, we look at how this problem was tackled by the economists of the Neoclassical Synthesis, though from different perspectives and points of view. We look in particular at the contributions of Patinkin, who was one of the earliest and most important representatives of the general-equilibrium approach to macroeconomics, but who also perceived the difficulties of introducing money into such a framework. Attention is also paid to the innovative approach to money and finance followed by Gurley and Shaw, who significantly influenced Tobin and his attempt to introduce financial markets into a general-equilibrium framework. Tobin's work was interesting and original, but his research project encountered significant difficulties and remained at the margins of the mainstream.

Chapter 8 deals with the main exponents of the 'anti-Keynesian counter-revolution', starting with Friedman's new monetarism and ending with the Real Business Cycle (RBC) approach. With the partial exception of Friedman, who essentially remained a Marshallian, all the major anti-Keynesian economists of the time emphasized their commitment to develop macroeconomics within an alleged modern Walrasian, or Arrow-Debreu, framework. But they encountered great difficulties in dealing with money, let alone financial markets, within such an environment. These difficulties, however, were underrated or, more prosaically, put under the carpet and the solution to them essentially was to abandoning any pretension to give money and financial markets any significant role to play in standard macroeconomic models.

Both Lucas's monetary surprises and RBC technological shocks proved largely unable to give a reasonable account of economic fluctuations experienced by actual economies. Chapter 9 explores the developments following these failures, which ended up with the confluence of mainstream macroeconomics to the so-called New Neoclassical Synthesis, with the concurrence of New Keynesian Economics (NKE), characterized by the central role that it gives to market imperfections. Thanks to the abandonment of the hypothesis of perfectly competitive markets, and notably thanks to the emphasis on informational imperfections, there emerged a new generation of macroeconomic models that make some steps forward in including banks or finance in their interaction with the real economy.

However, these models encounter a number of difficulties, which essentially derive from their still close and strong connection with the previously dominant paradigms of the New Classical Macroeconomics. We look at some such difficulties and the issues and questions that still remain open and in need of more satisfactory answers. More in particular, we concentrate on the difficulties inherent in the very notion of imperfection and those that the analysis of financial and credit markets encounters when carried out by using models that are structured on the coexistence of steady states and exogenous random shocks, relegating economic change and innovation to the sphere of unexplained phenomena and underrating, if not ignoring altogether, the crucial role of the endogenous dynamics of financial markets in the evolution of crises and phases of severe depression.

Finally, the chapter examines some contributions from behavioural economics which, by relying also on psychological research, offer analyses of the functioning of financial markets far from those of the efficient markets hypothesis and closer to Keynes's approach. Human behaviour, at the individual as well as collective level, cannot be fully explained by the assumption of well-informed agents optimizing over infinite horizons.

The concluding Chapter 10 summarizes the main results of our research and outlines a number of critical issues and topics that require further developments by approaching them in a novel and richer way than has been done so far.

PART I

From the 1920s to the early post-war period

2. Banks and the quantity theory: Wicksell and Fisher

At the opening of the 20th century, with the marginalist approach emerging as the dominant paradigm in economic theory, there were two problems that most concerned economists both in Europe and the U.S.: the need for a more satisfactory theory of the general price level and the search for satisfactory explanations to account for monetary instability and economic fluctuations. The debates on these issues, often almost inextricably intertwined with one another, kept on going until the 1930s, when Keynes's novel approach to economic theory and analysis took the centre stage and diverted the focus of the theoretical as well as practical economic debate.[1]

At the beginning of the century, many scholars, exponents of differing versions of the neoclassical theory of value, tackled the problem of the relation between the static equilibrium theory and monetary theory. It was an open question, since price theory pointed to the smooth adjustment to long-term equilibrium values, established independently of the supply of money, finance and the banking system. Price theory focused on barter economies, where relative prices were transparently set at equilibrium values, and the quantity equation to set the price level had to be connected to this static core. Wicksell addressed these problems in his *Lectures*, and he set out to develop a more satisfactory theory of the general price level in which the banking system plays a crucial role (Wicksell, 1901[1934], 1906[1935]). Also Fisher, one of the 'fathers' of the modern quantity theory of money, dealt with the problem of the general price level by giving banks a central role. He was more interested in the problem of economic fluctuations than Wicksell, and credit relations and banks were of crucial importance for his explanation of economic depressions.

In this chapter we look at Wicksell's and Fisher's contributions on these issues. We do so with no pretence to provide a full and exhaustive survey of their works and the tremendous amount of secondary literature on them. We concentrate on the question of how, and to which extent, the existence

---

[1] For more comprehensive examinations of the economic debates during this period, see, for example, Patinkin (1982) and Laidler (1991, 1999). See also Lucas (1977), who complains about the negative effects of the Keynesian shifting of attention.

of banks and other financial institutions characterize both Wicksell's and Fisher's versions of the quantity theory of money as well as their explanations of fluctuations. Fisher's analysis of deflation and depressions will be more extensively considered in Chapter 4 below.

2.1 WICKSELL'S SOLUTION TO THE PROBLEM OF THE GENERAL PRICE LEVEL

Most of Wicksell's scientific production belongs to the last part of the 19th century and the first years of the 20th, but he came to be best known in the English-speaking world only in the 1930s, when his most important works were translated into English. Thus, it is quite natural that Wicksell's theoretical contribution was a point of reference in many of the debates on monetary theory that took place in that period.[2]

Here we focus on the role that the banking system plays in Wicksell's analysis. We do so by referring particularly to the second volume of his *Lectures on Political Economy* (Wicksell, 1906[1935]).[3] Wicksell's monetary theory is centred on his attempt to provide a more satisfactory version of the quantity theory of money, which he regarded as the most satisfactory theory of the general price level (Wicksell, 1906[1935], p. 141). In this attempt, credit relations and the banking system play a central role. In fact, Wicksell devotes attention to the banking system only in so far as it influences monetary phenomena and, in particular, the velocity of circulation of money.

Once banks enter the analytical picture, the simple immediate relation between the quantity of money and the general price level, postulated by the traditional quantity theory, ceases to exist. Given the simplest formulation of the quantity theory, i.e. $P = \frac{MV}{Q}$, the existence of credit affects the general price level because it affects V, the velocity of circulation of money:

> ...credit is a very powerful, indeed the most powerful, means of quickening the circulation of money. (...) So long as the credit obligation lasts, the need for money is actually less than it would have been because, if the purchase had been made for cash, the seller, other things being equal, would have had the money lying in his safe until he himself wished to make a purchase; whereas now the same amount of money can circulate elsewhere. (Wicksell, 1906[1935], p. 65)

---

[2] On Wicksell's theory and his heritage, see, e.g., Chiodi (1991), Laidler (1991, pp. 119–152) and Leijonhufvud (1981, 1997).

[3] Other fundamental works by Wicksell on the topics dealt with in the *Lectures* are *Interest and Prices* (Wicksell, 1898[1936]) and his concise but very clear 1907 article in the *Economic Journal* (Wicksell, 1907).

Wicksell's considerations above refer to credit in general; i.e. both 'simple' credit (between individuals) and 'organized' credit, in which banks and the stock exchange play a central role. He mainly dealt with organized credit and focused his attention on banks which, differently from the stock exchange, specialize in short-term borrowing and lending (Wicksell, 1906[1935], p. 80).

Banks and the credit relations they create are fundamentally different from 'simple' credit relations between individuals. The existence of banks makes credit relations more stable and permanent;[4] but, more importantly, the amount of bank loans is in general larger than the amount of funds that their customers deposit with them (the assembled credit). It is so for two reasons.

> In the first place there is the Law of Large Numbers. Even if the bank's customers were entirely independent of each other, the simultaneous withdrawals of their funds by all of them, or by the majority of them, would be one of the rarest of occurrences. (...) In the second place, and if possible to an even greater extent, there is the operation of the fact that the customers of a bank frequently have direct or indirect business with each other, so that a withdrawal by one of them for the purchase of goods necessarily leads within a short time to a deposit by another after the sale. (Wicksell, 1906[1935], pp. 83–84)

The impact of banks on the working of the economy can be better understood by considering the case of a pure credit economy, that is to say an economy in which there is only one bank in the economy and bank accounts are largely used to make payments. In this case the total existing amount of money would be kept with banks and payments would be made through transfers from the buyers' accounts to the sellers' accounts. In such a context,

> ...the bank cannot lend *in concreto* a farthing of the money deposited with it, because it would flow back to the bank in the form of deposits as soon as it had been used. The lending operations of the bank will consist rather in its entering in its books a fictitious deposit equal to the amount of the loan, on which the borrower may draw, whilst the actual documents, e.g. a discounted bill, will be added to the bank's securities (...). Or it might open against real security or sureties a direct credit on which the borrower may draw cheques at will up to a maximum amount (...). Thus in both cases payments will be made by successive drawings by the borrower upon his credit in the bank, and every such cheque must naturally lead to a credit with another person's (seller's) account, either in the form of a deposit paid in or of a repayment of a debt. The obligation of the bank to the public will thus still exceed its claims by the whole amount of these cash holdings, less the bank's own capital. (Wicksell, 1906[1935], pp. 84–85)

---

[4]   Banks 'prolong' credit as they transform their short-term liabilities into 'more stable credit in the interests of borrowers and producers' (Wicksell, 1906[1935], p. 80).

In this world, a bank's ability to lend is not constrained by the amount of deposits with it, so that its lending could be unlimited. The velocity of circulation of money, therefore, becomes 'virtual' (Wicksell, 1906[1935], p. 67) and the very notion of the interrelation between demand for and supply of money is essentially meaningless. Demand for and supply of money are about the same thing (Wicksell, 1907, p. 215).

Although Wicksell was convinced that there was a tendency for actual economies towards the 'ideal' economy of pure credit, he was well aware that there existed (internal as well external) obstacles to its realization, to the examination of which he devoted a considerable number of pages (Wicksell, 1906[1935], pp. 87–126). In an economy in which multiple non-perfectly co-ordinated banks operate, customers of different banks would have relations with one another and the cheques drawn by them would inevitably imply the existence of credit and debit relations among banks (Wicksell, 1906[1935], p. 86). It is in this more realistic context that Wicksell set out to develop his theory of the general price level, that is to say the determination of the exchange value of money.

As mentioned above, Wicksell regarded his theory as a more adequate version of the quantity theory, which he first considered in its pure form, i.e. in a context in which credit does not play a significant role.[5] But his most original contributions reside in his analysis of an economy with well developed credit relations, which is preceded by his criticism of alternative theories of money and by his reconstruction of the 19th century debate between the currency school and the banking school (Wicksell, 1906[1935], pp. 168–190).[6]

Wicksell's analysis is centred on the relationship between the real[7] and the monetary (or loan) interest rates. The interest rate on loans depends on the profits generated by the use of the capital borrowed and not on the quantity of money (Wicksell, 1906[1935], p. 191). The interest rate so determined is what Wicksell calls the 'normal' interest rate: 'The rate of interest at which the demand for loan capital and the supply of savings exactly agree, and which more or less corresponds to the expected yield on the newly created capital, will then be the normal or natural real rate' (Wicksell, 1906[1935], p. 193).

---

[5] Wicksell's analysis of the pure form of the quantity theory can be regarded as more thorough and precise than those carried out by Fisher and the Cambridge School, but it does not offer any really original and innovative contribution (Laidler, 1991, p. 127).

[6] 'This matter had of course occupied every monetary economist from Adam Smith onwards, not least Wicksell's contemporaries in England and the United States, but none of them dealt with it with the depth and care which marked his work' (Laidler, 1991, p. 127).

[7] In his works, Wicksell used the terms 'normal', 'neutral' and 'real' interest rate, of which he gives different definitions (see Laidler, 1991, p. 130). Here we refer to Wicksell's definition in his *Lectures*.

This relation is easy to understand in the case of simple credit. The picture becomes more complicated when organized credit is taken into consideration. Because of the existence of banks, which are not the same as individual lenders, there is no longer an immediate and obvious link between the loan rate and the real interest rate. The link, however, exists and is established through variations of the price level.

> Banks are not, like private persons, restricted in their lending to their own funds or even to the means placed at their disposal by savings. By the concentration in their hands of private cash holdings, which are constantly replenished by in-payments as fast as they are depleted by out-payments, they possess a fund for loans which is always elastic and, on certain assumptions, inexhaustible. With a pure credit system the banks can always satisfy any demand whatever for loans and at rates of interest however low, at least as far as the internal market is concerned. (Wicksell, 1906[1935], p. 194)

Changes in the general price level can be caused by the banks lending at a rate different from the normal rate. In particular, a lower interest rate induces less saving and a consequent increase in the demand for consumer-goods. Moreover, the firms' profit opportunities will increase by giving rise to a larger demand for inputs and labour for future production, which in turn causes a further rise of the prices of consumer-goods, and so on. The inflationary process so started will not stop until the loan rate remains below the normal rate. The increase in demand and the consequent price increase could be partially offset by an increase in the aggregate supply, but this for Wicksell is a secondary consideration, as he assumes an initial condition of full employment (Wicksell, 1906[1935], p.195).

Thus, there exists a fundamental difference between the equilibrium of relative prices and that of the general price level:

> ...the former is usually stable and is to be likened to a freely suspended pendulum, or a ball at the bottom of a bowl. If by an accident they are driven out of the position of equilibrium they tend themselves, i.e. through the force of gravity, to resume their former position. The general price level on the other hand is, on the assumption of a monetary system of unlimited elasticity, in a position of, so to speak, indifferent equilibrium of the same kind as that of a ball or cylinder on a plane, though somewhat restricted, surface: the ball does not move itself further, but from inertia and friction remains where it has been placed; if forces of sufficient strength to drive it from its position of equilibrium are brought into play, it has no tendency to resume that position, but if the forces which set it in motion – i.e. in this case the difference between the normal or real rate and the actual loan rate – cease to operate they will remain in a new and also indifferent position of equilibrium. (Wicksell, 1906[1935], pp. 196–197)

There can be offsetting forces at work, but they are inevitably dominated by the tendency for prices to rise caused by the gap between the loan and the normal interest. In fact, the counteracting factors operate only once, whereas the price rise is a cumulative process (Wicksell, 1906[1935], p. 197). A low interest rate on loans can induce agents to keep a larger amount of money idle rather than to lend it, so that the velocity of circulation of money is reduced with a consequent depressive effect on prices.[8] However, although a low loan rate can produce such an effect, it 'could only exercise a pressure on prices up to a certain point, whereas the pressure we are now discussing tends to raise prices without limit, so long as the difference between the bank and the normal rate continues' (Wicksell, 1906[1935], p. 197). A process of opposite sign would take place if banks keep the loan interest rate above the normal rate.

Wicksell then concludes,

> If we take as our starting point the view that a lowering of the loan rate below the normal rate (...) in itself tends to bring about a progressive rise in all commodity prices, and a spontaneous rise in loan rate a continuous fall in prices, both of which would go beyond all limits in practice, then all monetary phenomena would be extraordinarily clear and simple and at the same time the obligation of the banks to maintain the rate of interest in agreement with the normal or real rate of interest would be obvious. (Wicksell, 1906[1935], p. 201)

Such a conclusion, however, clashes with what is observed in reality, where rising prices are generally associated with rising monetary interest rates and, vice versa, declining prices go together with monetary interest rates lower than the real interest rate. Wicksell believed that these observed facts can be readily reconciled with his theory. His solution is based on the idea that the cumulative processes are mostly started by the banks being unable to immediately adjust the rate on their loans to variations in the real rate. This, in turn, depends on the fact that 'there predominates in the field of banking (...) a procedure built up upon custom and tradition, in a word – routine. It may, indeed, be said that the banks never alter their interest rates unless they are induced to do so by the force of outside circumstances' (Wicksell, 1906[1935], p. 204). Banks affect the general price level because of their passivity.[9]

There are several reasons why the real interest rate changes over time and, therefore, the fact that the money rate does not follow suit gives rise to price variations, which in due time bring the realignment of the two rates. The cumulative processes of price variation triggered by the gap between the real and money rates keep on going until banks are induced to alter their rate and

---

[8] See also Wicksell (1906[1935], pp. 198–199) for other possible offsetting factors.

[9] Wicksell analyses also the effects on the bank rate due to changes in the quantity of gold in the economy (Wicksell, 1906[1935], pp. 204–205). In particular, he deals with the problem in the contest of a gold-standard regime (Wicksell, 1906[1935], pp. 200-ff.). Here, for brevity, we do not deal with this issue.

re-establish its equality with the real rate. In particular, when the bank rate is lower than the real rate, banks will eventually be induced to raise their rate because the increasing demand for loans would not be matched by an increase in their deposits and/or reserves.[10]

> Our conclusion is that rising prices are accompanied by high and rising rates of interest, and falling commodity prices by low rates of interest – which is in full agreement with our theory (...) It might therefore be supposed that the fluctuations in the bank or money rate of interest are sometimes the cause of fluctuations in commodity prices and sometimes, more frequently, caused by them. (...) The primary cause of price fluctuations in both cases is the same, namely the difference arising no matter how, between the normal and actual money or loan rates. (Wicksell, 1906[1935], pp. 207–208)

Wicksell's reformulation of the quantity theory in the context of an economy with organized credit can be questioned from several viewpoints and it can be argued that he ultimately weakened rather than strengthened the theory (Laidler, 1991, p. 147). Here, we limit ourselves to a few considerations on Wicksell's analysis of credit relations and the problems that it leaves open. First, as we saw, Wicksell focuses his attention only on banks and short-term loans and does not carry out any detailed analysis of the financial institutions that manage long-term loans. As a consequence, his analysis of interest rates is limited to short-term rates.[11]

Second, Wicksell does not offer any satisfactory explanation of the factors that determine the public's demand for bank deposits. In particular, he does not contemplate the possibility that part of the public's deposits with banks can be motivated by the desire to hold at least a portion of their wealth in a highly liquid form. In Wicksell's context, the amount of deposits with banks depends on the amount of the medium of exchange that the public demand. In other words, Wicksell considers only the demand for money due to the 'transactions motive' (on this, see also Laidler, 1991, pp. 148–149).

The amount of deposits in the economy also depends on the amount of loans that the banking system wishes to make. But Wicksell's analysis of the banks' lending decisions is far from thorough. In so far as banks regard their amount of reserves adequate they lend as much as possible and no attention is paid to the possibility that they do not want to lend for other reasons like, for example, an unsatisfactory creditworthiness of the potential borrowers or an increase in their aversion to illiquidity. As we shall see in Chapter 5 Keynes, in *A Treatise on Money* (1930[1971]), took up and dealt with some of these issues.

---

[10] Notice that this offsetting factor would not be operating in a pure credit economy with a single bank or a co-ordinated system of banks.

[11] Only a few observations are devoted to the relation between the short and the long-term rates. See, e.g., Wicksell (1907, pp. 215–216) and Wicksell (1906[1935], pp. 191–192).

2.2 TRADE CYCLES AND THE ROLE OF BANKS IN WICKSELL

The analysis of trade cycles was not Wicksell's main concern and he never managed to arrive at a well developed theory of cycles. Here, we devote some attention to the topic because of the evident relation between cyclical fluctuations and price movements and the role that banks play.[12]

For Wicksell, the nature and causes of trade cycles, which are connected to price movements, are essentially of a real nature.[13] Banks' behaviour is an exacerbating factor at work both during booms and depressions (good and bad times). Wicksell does not question that good and bad times are associated with rising and declining prices respectively and that price variations intensify fluctuations, but he rejects the idea that price variations are the driving factor of trade cycles.[14]

After having criticized also the idea that price variations can be explained only by real factors, Wicksell concludes: 'On the whole it is vain here, as in the general theory of prices, to explain any particular movement without regard to the one thing which constitutes a basis of comparison in all price-formation, namely money and its substitutes, or the means of hastening its velocity of circulation, credit' (Wicksell, 1906[1935], p. 210). The velocity of circulation of money changes over the trade cycle. It is banks that affect the velocity of circulation in the most important way:

> The general tone of confidence produced by a boom no doubt has the effect of considerably expanding the volume of claims and debts on ordinary current account between merchants – and vice versa in times of depression – but in the main and especially nowadays it is probably the banks who by their discounting of bills

---

[12] For a thorough analysis of Wicksell's position on trade cycles, see Boianovsky (1995). See also Laidler (1991, pp. 143–146), who makes a comparison between Wicksell's and Fisher's positions on cycles, and Leijonhufvud (1981, pp. 151–160), who provides a rigorous exposition of Wicksell's analysis of cumulative processes as distinct from the analysis of business cycles.

[13] Cycles are caused by real factors 'independent of movements in commodity price, so that the latter become of only secondary importance, although in real life they nevertheless play an important and even a dominating part in the development of crises' (Wicksell, 1906[1935], p. 209).

[14] The fundamental cause of cyclical fluctuations is to be found 'in the fact that in its very nature technical or commercial advance cannot maintain the same even progress as does, in our days, the increase in needs (...) but is sometimes precipitate, sometimes delayed. It is natural and at the same time economically justifiable that in the former case people seek to exploit the favourable situation as quickly as possible, and since the new discoveries, inventions, and other improvements nearly always require various kinds of preparatory work for their realization, there occurs the conversion of large masses of liquid into fixed capital which is an inevitable preliminary to every boom and indeed is probably the only fully characteristic sign, or at any rate one which cannot conceivably be absent'. (Wicksell, 1906[1935], pp. 211–212). On the relation between real and monetary variables see also Wicksell (1907[2001]).

and other credit facilities regulate the amount of circulating medium. (Wicksell, 1906[1935], p. 211)

The amount of bank credit is determined by the ratio of the loan rate to the real rate. Therefore, 'changes in the purchasing power of money caused by credit are under existing conditions certainly ultimately bound up with industrial fluctuations and undoubtedly affect them, especially in causing crises, though we need not assume any necessary connection between the phenomena' (Wicksell, 1906[1935], p. 211).

In a context in which the fundamental determinants of fluctuations are real, a greater price stability could be ensured by better management of the bank interest rate on loans, which should be raised during a boom and lowered in a depression.[15] Thus, even in this 'real' context, the banks' inability to adequately adjust their interest rate to the real rate affects price variations.

Prices, however, would vary to a larger extent if there was not another offsetting force at work. Such a force is the countercyclical variations of stocks.[16] Additionally, with respect to stocks banks can play an important role. If, in a situation in which prices decline, banks offer sufficient cheap credit, it would be profitable for firms to increase their stocks without waiting for a decrease in wages and prices of raw materials (Wicksell, 1906[1935], p. 213).

2.3   FISHER'S 'MYSTERY OF BANKING' OR 'CIRCULATING CREDIT'

Fisher extensively dealt with bank money and the credit cycle in his treatise *The Purchasing Power of Money*, published in 1911 and revised in 1922 (Fisher, 1922). As he wrote in the 1911 Preface, the main subject of the book was a restatement of the old quantity theory of money, which he regarded as the proper theoretical frame to understand monetary instability and to find remedies to the evils it entails (Fisher, 1922, p. ix).

---

[15] If banks operated in this way, 'presumably the real element of the crisis would be eliminated and what remained would be merely an even fluctuation between periods in which the newly formed capital would assume, and, economically speaking, should assume, other forms' (Wicksell, 1906[1935], p. 212).

[16] 'Since the demand for new capital in an upward swing of the trade cycle is frequently much too great to be satisfied by contemporaneous saving, even if it is stimulated by a higher rate of interest, and since, on the other hand, in bad times this demand is practically nil, (...) the rise in rates of interest and commodity prices in good times and their fall in bad times would presumably be much more severe than now, if it were not that the replenishment and depletion of stocks in all branches of production producing durable goods, acted as a regulator or "parachute"' (Wicksell, 1906[1935], pp. 212–213).

For Fisher, monetary instability is intrinsically linked to the credit cycle. The theoretical focus on the quantity theory has the double purpose to set equilibrium principles and explain fluctuations.[17] Fisher sees the quantity theory of money as a general scientific principle asserting the proportionality of the general price level to the quantity of money in a hypothetical long term. The principle refers to the abstract comparison of theoretical equilibrium positions before and after changes in the quantity of money, all other variables being given (Fisher, 1922, p. 159). But he cautiously adds that the permanent effects of a change in the supply of money will realize only when the new position of equilibrium is finally established, 'if indeed such a condition as equilibrium may be said ever to be established' (Fisher, 1922, p. 56).

Dynamic processes of change are always at work in a monetary economy, which never is in a state of equilibrium as it always moves along transition paths or it is hit by shocks. The quantity theory is a scientific theoretical proposition under ideal conditions, not a short-term empirical regularity. Within this general framework, money is primarily seen as a means of exchange (Fisher, 1922, p. 8) and a large role is attributed to banks' deposits as part of the 'currency' or 'circulating media'. Bank deposits are not classified as money properly, although they are for all purposes means of payment (Fisher, 1922, p. 10). They appear in the equation of exchange, with their own velocity of circulation,

$$Cv_{ct} + Dv_{dt} \equiv PT$$

(where C denotes the amounts of coins plus notes in circulation and v_{ct} is their velocity of circulation; D is the amount of bank deposits and v_{dt} is their velocity of circulation; P is the general price index, T is the index of the general level of transactions.)

The exchange equation, as an accounting identity, implies no causal relation between the stock of money and the price level, or between any of the other variables. In principle, each variable might affect the others or they might be all causally interlinked. Fisher enters into a detailed discussion of the causality nexuses to argue that the primary direction of causality goes from money to the general price level: the price level 'normally' varies in direct proportion with the amount of notes and coins in circulation plus the amount of bank deposits, under the assumption that the respective velocities of circulation and the general level of transactions do not vary and taking the degree of development of the banking system as given with a stable relation between money proper and bank money (Fisher, 1922, p. 14, pp. 156–157).

---

[17] On Fisher's theory of the business cycle and its relation to monetary instability see Laidler (1991, pp. 91ff.). See also Laidler (1999); Pavanelli (1997); Dimand (2003, 2005).

In dealing with bank money, Fisher addresses the controversial issue of what amount of means of payment banks can create and whether they have the power to create purchasing power *ex nihilo*. He strongly denies this last interpretation: the means of payment created through credit are anchored to real wealth. Wealth is the collateral that firms and private persons offer, on which banks open new deposits by making loans against the issue of promissory notes to be repaid by the borrowers. Banks have the capacity to convert illiquid wealth into liquid means of payments: 'To put it crudely, banking is a device for coining into dollars land, stoves, and other wealth not otherwise generally exchangeable' (Fisher, 1922, p. 41). This is, unveiled, the mystery of banking.

For its regular working, such a device for coining real wealth into dollars requires the adoption of prudential strategies. There exist upper limits to the amount of deposits that banks can create; they are set by reserves and by the strategic behaviour of banks when extending loans. The value of the banks' capital is the safeguard against the risk of insolvency; the ratio of cash reserves to deposits is the safeguard against the risk of insufficient cash, or illiquidity risk.

> So far as anything has yet been said to the contrary, a bank might increase indefinitely its loans in relation to its cash or in relation to its capital. If this were so, deposit currency could be indefinitely inflated. There are limits, however, imposed by prudence and sound economic policy, on both these processes. Insolvency and insufficiency of cash must both be avoided. Insolvency is that condition which threatens when loans are extended with insufficient capital. Insufficiency of cash is that condition which threatens when loans are extended unduly relatively to cash. Insolvency is reached when assets no longer cover liabilities (to others than stockholders), so that the bank is unable to pay its debts. Insufficiency of cash is reached when, although the bank's total assets are fully equal to its liabilities, the actual cash on hand is insufficient to meet the needs of the instant, and the bank is unable to pay its debts on demand. (Fisher, 1922, p. 43)

Insufficiency of cash, an exceedingly dangerous condition for a bank, depends on opinion. In the case of a panic, if 'a large percentage' of the bank's depositors should simultaneously withdraw cash, the bank could not escape its failure (Fisher, 1922, p. 44). In runs to withdraw deposits, expectations of bank failures become self-fulfilling.

Fisher has a clear perception of the risks inherent in banking: the capital requirements necessary to provide a buffer to bail in unexpected losses on loans; the inherent imbalance in banks' balance sheets between deposits that are liabilities on demand, and the illiquid nature of their assets (loans). Deposit currency cannot be indefinitely inflated. This firm statement marks Fisher's distance from extreme fictional cases such as the pure credit economy imagined by Wicksell.

In his conclusion, Fisher suggests that the ratio of deposits to money proper (i.e. the money multiplier in later terminology) is stable, as it is determined by a 'more or less definite' ratio of reserves to deposits according to the banks' prudential strategies and a 'more or less definite' ratio of cash money to deposits according to firms' and consumers' preferences.[18] But these 'more or less' definite ratios are subject to many caveats in the discussion of banks' strategies and in the study of 'transitions periods' after monetary shocks. Throughout his book, Fisher maintains a precarious balance between the quantity theory and the vagaries of fluctuations observed in history. The notion of the quantity theory as both an ideal law and a long-term stable relationship lives side by side with the often asserted, transitory volatility of what occurs during messy processes of change in 'transition periods'.

2.4   TRANSITION PERIODS AND THE CREDIT CYCLE

A large part of Fisher's book is devoted to the theory of price indexes and the study of price fluctuations in historical time series, since his aim is to analyse the causes and remedies of business fluctuations as due to price instability. In Fisher's diagnosis, price fluctuations have been the main cause of crises and depressions throughout the 19th century and up to the beginning of the 20th century. The transitory reactions to a monetary shock before the new equilibrium is established are predominantly cyclical, although the fluctuations may be more or less severe or persisting. The credit cycle dominates the transition periods, independently of the ultimate effects, which remain consistent with the quantity theory.

Chapter 4 of the book is devoted to the study of transition periods. The chapter offers an updated version of the explanation of business cycles based on credit cycles, whose roots are to be found in the overtrading tradition of the 19th century.[19] Without pretending to offer a full-fledged explanation of business cycles, Fisher looks at the sequence of inflationary, speculative

---

[18] 'But the fact is that the quantity of circulating credit, M', tends to hold a definite relation to M, the quantity of money in circulation; that is, deposits are normally a more or less definite multiple of money. Two facts normally give deposits a more or less definite ratio to money. The first has been already explained, viz. that bank reserves are kept in a more or less definite ratio to bank deposits. The second is that individuals, firms, and corporations preserve more or less definite ratios between their cash transactions and their check transactions, and also between their money and deposit balances. (...) Hence, both money in circulation (as shown above) and money in reserve (as shown previously) tend to keep in a fixed ratio to deposits. It follows that the two must be in a fixed ratio to each other' (Fisher, 1922, pp. 50–52).

[19] In the book Fisher does not deal with what, in contemporary terminology, is called a 'corridor of stability', as he does in later writings (Dimand, 2005). Laidler (1991, pp. 89–94) deals extensively with the classical analysis of credit cycles and Fisher's refinements of the monetary analysis of the cycle. In comparing Pigou's and Fisher's accounts of banks in the cycle, Laidler

booms and deflationary depressions linked to the expansion or, reversely, the contraction of bank credit, and the associated changes in the velocity of circulation of deposits.

In Fisher's analysis, the adjustment process following an initial shock, which increases the money stock, is characterized by a sequence of phenomena: an initial inflationary boom that culminates in a crisis and a deflationary depression. In the expansionary phase of the credit cycle, the increase of short-term bank loans and the creation of new deposit accounts play a major role. The relation between deposits and money properly becomes flexible; the money multiplier is no longer stable, but variable (Fisher, 1922, p. 55).

The cyclical effects of monetary instability are created primarily by the delay in the adjustment of nominal interest rates to inflation or deflation, with a temporary fall of the real cost of credit in inflationary phases and reversely a temporary increase of it in deflationary phases (Fisher, 1922, p. 56). The low cost of credit due to the partial adjustment of nominal interest rates to inflation encourages businessmen to ask for further loans, which convert themselves into demand for goods. Borrowed money does not stay idle: '...whenever a man borrows money, he does not do this in order to hoard the money, but to purchase goods with it' (Fisher, 1922, p. 56).

The following period of expansion, which Fisher (1922, p. 62) calls 'unhealthy', will end up in a depression. The expansionary phase has the nature of a cumulative spiralling of prices and inflationary expectations fuelled by the parallel increase in loans and deposits.[20] The expectations of expanding profits fuel the demand for loans by businessmen, whose collateral meanwhile appears to be more valuable.

> As prices rise, profits of businessmen, measured in money, will rise also, even if the costs of business were to rise in the same proportion. (...) But, as a matter of fact, the business man's profits will rise more than this because the rate of interest he has to pay will not adjust itself immediately. Among his costs is interest, and this cost will not, at first, rise. Thus the profits will rise faster than prices. Consequently, he will find himself making greater profits than usual, and be encouraged to expand his business by increasing his borrowings. These borrowings are mostly in the form of short-time loans from banks; and, as we have seen, short-time loans engender deposits. (...) More loans are demanded, and although nominal interest may be forced up somewhat, still it keeps lagging below the normal level. Yet nominally the rate of interest *has* increased; and hence the lenders, too, including banks, are led to become more enterprising. (Fisher, 1922, pp. 58–59)

(1991, p. 100) underlines 'Fisher's detailed treatment of the creation and destruction of bank money and induced changes in velocities which accompany the cycle'.

[20] 'In other words, a slight initial rise of prices sets in motion a train of events which tends to repeat itself. Rise of prices generates rise of prices, and continues to do so as long *as the interest rate lags behind its normal figure*' (Fisher, 1922, p. 60).

Banks, which regulate nominal rates, are important actors in transition periods. They flexibly accommodate the increased demand for loans by businessmen. According to Fisher, banks, like other agents, are subject to some degree of money illusion.[21] Banks are 'beguiled' to misconceive higher nominal rates for higher returns, and easily satisfy higher demands by borrowers. Variations in bank money act as an amplifier of business fluctuations, through the expansion or contraction of banks' loans to firms. Deposits 'abnormally' expand as a component of the total currency available (Fisher, 1922, pp. 60–61). The inflationary expansion stops when the nominal rate of interest is fully adjusted to inflation, or when loans and deposits hit the ceiling set by bank reserves or other constraints. When interest rates finally rise, the value of collateral falls, some firms go bankrupt and confidence in banks declines; depositors run to cash their deposit accounts. The 'collapse of bank credit brought about by loss of confidence' is the culminating event of the commercial crisis ending the expansionary boom (Fisher, 1922, p. 66). The economy experiences cycles of 'prosperity' and 'depression' marked by financial crises.

> When interest has become adjusted to rising prices, and loans and deposits have reached the limit set for them by the bank reserves and other conditions, the fact that prices no longer are rising necessitates a new adjustment. Those whose business has been unduly extended now find the high rates of interest oppressive. Failures result, constituting a commercial crisis. A reaction sets in; a reverse movement is initiated. A fall of prices, once begun, tends to be accelerated for reasons exactly corresponding to those which operate in the opposite situation. (Fisher, 1922, p. 73).

Fisher is ambiguous about the extent to which the inflationary boom stimulates production, or whether the monetary phenomenon of the speculative swelling of prices, expected profits and indebtedness have effects on real quantities.[22] He assumes a state of the economy of quasi-full employment, but he does not exclude a limited expansion of production through over-employment or the cut of residual unemployment. 'Profits increase, loans expand, and the Q's increase' (Fisher, 1922, p. 63).

However, the speculative bubble of prices prevails; production is constrained by real factors such as population, productivity and invention, which cannot be increased in the short term. In Fisher's analysis bank credit does not affect the rate of invention; the expansion of short-term loans by banks that fuels the

---

[21] Laidler (1991, p. 92-ff) underlines that 'information asymmetries and learning lags' figures prominently already in Fisher's study of the secular relation between the price level and the rate of interest in his book *Appreciation and Interest* (1896). They later became a crucial aspect of his cycle theory. See also Pavanelli (1997).

[22] It is the duplicity of the quantity theory since Hume's early formulation of the transitional effects.

'unhealthy' bubble of prices, does not affect productive capacity, technological innovation or productivity. As we shall see in Chapter 4, consideration of the experience of the 'roaring twenties' induced Fisher to partially change his mind and connect the expansion of finance and debts to the entrepreneurs' perception of 'real opportunities to invest lucratively'; a 'very real base' linked to the pace of invention and technological change (Fisher, 1932, 1933, pp. 71–72 and p. 349 respectively).

Dealing with the effects of inflation on real incomes, Fisher downplays the importance of the distributional effects of inflation as a possible brake to the swelling of booms. Although he does not cancel out a priori the effects of gains and losses by different agents because of monetary variations, in his picture the positive or negative effects of monetary instability on profits (be they in ex-post real terms or as perceived in businessmen's expectations) are the main factors that determine price and quantity variations.[23] Although 'the creditor, the salaried man, or the labourer' may be suffering because of higher prices, the ordinary businessman is the 'enterpriser-borrower' who sets in motion trade on the hope of profits that apparently are increasing. However, being deceived by money illusion, enterprisers-borrowers are unable to anticipate the full adjustment of the rate of interest to inflation.

> The reason many people spend more than they can afford is that they are relying on the dollar as a stable unit when as a matter of fact its purchasing power is rapidly falling. The bond-holder, for instance, is beguiled into trenching on his capital. He never dreams that he ought to lay by a sinking fund because the decrease in purchasing power of money is reducing the real value of his principal. Again, the stockholder and enterpriser generally are beguiled by a vain reliance on the stability of the rate of interest, and so they overinvest. It is true that for a time they are gaining what the bondholder is losing and are therefore justified in both spending and investing more than if prices were not rising; and at first they prosper. But sooner or later the rate of interest rises above what they had reckoned on, and they awake to the fact that they have embarked on enterprises which cannot pay these high rates. (Fisher, 1922, p. 66)

---

[23]   'Trade (the Q's) will be stimulated by the easy terms for loans. This effect is always observed during rising prices, and people note approvingly that "business is good" and "times are booming." Such statements represent the point of view of the ordinary businessman who is an "enterpriser-borrower." They do not represent the sentiments of the creditor, the salaried man, or the laborer, most of whom are silent but long-suffering, paying higher prices, but not getting proportionally higher incomes (...) The surplus money is first expended at nearly the old price level, but its continued expenditure gradually raises prices. In the meantime the volume of purchases will be somewhat greater than it would have been had prices risen more promptly. In fact, from the point of view of those who are selling goods, it is the possibility of a greater volume of sales at the old prices which gives encouragement to an increase of prices. Seeing that they can find purchasers for more goods than before at the previously prevailing prices, or for as many goods as before at higher prices, they will charge these higher prices' (Fisher, 1922, pp. 61–62).

If in the upturn businessmen over-invest because of their myopic faith in the stability of the rate of interest, a form of money illusion, in the downturn they are sunk by the contracts previously signed in nominal terms that cannot be changed in the short run. The resulting bankruptcies paralyze the credit market both on the supply and the demand side.

> Borrowers now find that interest, though nominally low, is still hard to meet. Especially do they find this true in the case of contracts made just before prices ceased rising or just before they began to fall. The rate of interest in these cases is agreed upon before the change in conditions takes place. There will, in consequence, be little if any adjustment in lowering nominal interest. Because interest is hard to pay, failures continue to occur. There comes to be a greater hesitation in lending on any but the best security, and a hesitation to borrow save when the prospects of success are the greatest. (Fisher, 1922, pp. 67–68)

The spreading of bankruptcies paralyses both borrowers and creditors, and the credit market shrinks. The inside debt structure, i.e. the network of loans which links enterprisers-borrowers to banks and finances expenditures coining real wealth into dollars, is fragile in conditions of monetary instability, inflation and deflation being poorly understood and poorly anticipated. Trust and the stable value of money are the pillars on which the debt structure stands; but both pillars are shaky in the event of shocks, unless appropriate stabilization policies are adopted. This theme will become dominant in Fisher's macroeconomic analysis in the 1930s.

2.5 FROM THE REFORMULATION OF THE QUANTITY THEORY TOWARDS NEW CONCERNS

Both Wicksell's and Fisher's main theoretical concern was a satisfactory reformulation of the quantity theory of money, that is to say to provide a rigorous determination of the general price level and its dynamics. Wicksell as well as Fisher acknowledged that the quantity theory is fully valid only in the long period, when equilibrium is established, and they were interested in the transition from an equilibrium position to another and set out to study such dynamic processes. Within their analytical framework, banks, which characterize modern economies, play an important role. Banks are at the core of their interpretation of the quantity theory of money. The existence of credit affects the velocity of circulation of money and, hence, prices. Regarding the nature and working of banks, not only is Fisher's analysis more detailed and multifaceted than Wicksell's, he also resolutely denies the banks' ability to create money *ex nihilo*, anchoring credit to real wealth, whereas Wicksell maintains a certain degree of ambiguity when not considering a pure credit economy, in which the banks' ability to create money through lending is obviously unconstrained.

There are also other significant differences between the positions of the two economists. Wicksell concentrates on monetary instability in cumulative processes of inflation or deflation and does not deal extensively with business cycles. He is firmly convinced that in the trade cycle, as distinguished from cumulative processes, the ultimate causes of fluctuations are real. Conversely, Fisher concentrates on fluctuations originated by monetary shocks, although not denying the possibility of real shocks. He underlines that the sequences of events that monetary shocks put in motion follow a somewhat cyclical pattern, with the economy going through booms and busts. Both scholars maintain some ambiguity with respect to the fluctuations of real income during the trade cycle or the transition period following a monetary shock. They give priority to monetary fluctuations over changes in real income, though not excluding real effects. They are essentially concerned with monetary instability and give banks a significant degree of responsibility for it, since their behaviour can exacerbate or lessen the severity of fluctuations.

Most of the topics and issues with which Wicksell and Fisher were concerned remained central for many economists of the 1920s and 1930s, even though the focus progressively moved from the defence and refinement of the quantity theory to other concerns. The quantity theory of money was still central in Keynes's research in *The Treatise on Money*, although his aim is critical: the old quantity theory is rejected because it oversimplifies the relation between the quantity of money and the general price level. In the book banks still play a prominent role, but in subsequent works, and especially in *The General Theory* Keynes's attention to the determination of prices and the role and importance of banks tends to vanish.

The link between the quantity equation and the equilibrium equations determining relative prices was at the centre of discussions during the 1940s: in the controversy over the relation between Keynes and the Classics and in the debate on Walras Law. The reconciliation of the quantity theory with Walrasian general equilibrium was the task that Patinkin put for himself since the late 1940s, culminating in the publication of *Money, Interest and Prices* in 1956. In the assessment of the neutrality of money in the Neoclassical Synthesis, banks and the financial structure are no longer relevant.

Outside the Keynesian positions, the interest in the quantity theory remained alive during the 20th century, but also in this case the attention to the banking system progressively declined. Friedman, who vindicated the restatement of the quantity theory against neoclassical Keynesians, was attentive to banks, and the phenomena of monetary instability due to a fragile and uncontrolled banking system. Banks and bank money are still crucial in Friedman's and Schwartz's historical reconstruction of the Great Depression. These aspects disappear from the 1970s New Classical explanations of business cycles based on monetary surprises. In 1996, Robert Lucas's Nobel Lecture, extensively devoted to the quantity theory of money, contains no reference at all to banks and almost no reference to the financial structure of the economy.

We shall return to the problem of the relation between the quantity theory, banks and the financial structure of the economy on several occasions in the following chapters. The next chapter, however, deals with a different key question: how and if banks play a significant role in dynamic processes of change through their financing of capital formation. This was a major theme of Schumpeter's and Robertson's writings.

3. Money and banking in the process of change: Schumpeter and Robertson

As we saw in the previous chapter, both Wicksell's and Fisher's analyses of banks, though different in several respects, were set in the context of their attempts to develop a more satisfactory quantity theory of money. During the same period, others looked at banks and their role in market economies from a different perspective. In this chapter, we focus on the contributions of Schumpeter and Robertson who devoted considerable attention to the role of banks in capitalist processes of change. Schumpeter was concerned both with growth generated by innovation and with economic fluctuations. Robertson mainly focused on trade cycles which, however, he saw as inherently connected to innovation and growth (Goodhart, 1992). For both of them, such processes of change cannot be properly understood without taking banks and their role into account.

Schumpeter's and Robertson's approaches to banks show some important analytical similarities. For them, banks are not mere intermediaries between savers and borrowers; they are able to create additional money through credit. This is of key importance in processes of change: without bank loans, firms could not obtain the necessary means to finance the required amounts of circulating and fixed capital to promote change.

3.1 SCHUMPETER'S ATTEMPTS AT DEVELOPING A THEORY OF MONEY

Schumpeter planned to publish a treatise on money and banking, to which he was making reference as a forthcoming book in *Business Cycles*, and on which he worked until the end of his life. He did not succeed in accomplishing his project.[1] In a letter of 1949 (quoted in Swedberg, 1991, pp. 237–238), Schumpeter complained to have never written systematically on monetary economics. For him, *The Theory of Economic Development* (1934[1983])

---

[1]   The first twelve chapters of the treatise, written in German, were posthumously published under the title *Das Wesen des Geldes*. Berti and Messori (1996) have published, in Italian, three additional chapters.

and *Business Cycles* (1939) were the works in which he had exposed his thoughts on money more clearly. As a further contribution, although not fully satisfactory in his own judgement, Schumpeter mentioned his article on money and the social product (Schumpeter, 1917–1918[1956]). The *History of economic analysis* (Schumpeter, 1954[2006]) is rich in references to monetary theories and debates.

Schumpeter's work gave rise to several controversies about the significance of its achievements in the field of monetary economics (see Messori, 1996, 1997; Tichy, 1984). Since he was a most prolific scholar, it is impossible to discuss here the evolution of Schumpeter's monetary thought thoroughly.[2] However, it is worth mentioning the major reason for Schumpeter's failure to complete his planned *Theory of Money and Banking*.[3]

The hope nurtured by Schumpeter was to integrate money into a dynamic Walrasian general equilibrium framework. Although he always was a staunch admirer of Walras and regarded his equilibrium theory as the backbone of the economic science, Schumpeter well knew Walras's limits especially with respect to monetary theory.[4] More specifically, he was dissatisfied with Walras's theory of money in 'Statics', that is the monetary general-equilibrium model presented in the later editions of the *Éléments d'Économie Politique Pure*. Like other scholars in the 1920s and 1930s, though on different lines, Schumpeter aimed at integrating the monetary analysis into the dynamic theory of business cycles, without giving up the Walrasian equilibrium foundations. This project was doomed.[5] With the wisdom of hindsight, Messori (1997, pp. 647–648) argues that Schumpeter's attempt at integrating money into 'the more complex field of dynamics led Schumpeter to tiring and inconclusive work.' Notwithstanding this negative judgement on the overall coherence of Schumpeter's monetary theory, Messori (1997, pp. 668–669) underlines the importance of two points with which the unfinished *Theory of Money and Banking* was concerned: i) the micro-foundations of banks' behaviour in the context of different monetary regimes; ii) and the coordinating and accounting role of the banking system, conceived as a system of social accounting

---

[2] The literature on the evolution of Schumpeter's ideas and theories is correspondingly ample. On Schumpeter's view of banks, see the important contributions by Tichy (1984); Berti and Messori (1996); Festré (2002).

[3] This is the title Schumpeter mentioned in November 1949, when he was still thinking of publishing the book, before his premature death in January 1950 (Messori, 1997, p. 645).

[4] Berti and Messori (1996) highlight Schumpeter's criticism of Walras's monetary theory.

[5] Even today it is highly controversial whether money as a means of exchange and reserve of value makes any sense within the ex-ante perfectly coordinated, perfect foresight economy of neo-Walrasian equilibrium models. Hahn gave a negative answer to the possibility to have money, other than as a numeraire, in neo-Walrasian models. On the static character of Walras's monetary theory and the difficulty to introduce money into the Walrasian equilibrium theory, see also Bridel (1997).

based on a standard of value. Both points are important for our historical reconstruction.

With remarkable continuity since the early 1910s, banks and their role were at the core of Schumpeter's theoretical analysis. Moreover, the evolution of the banking system and its activities, institutional changes or mismanagement, were an outstanding subject in the historical narration that fills so many pages of *Business Cycles*. We shall follow Schumpeter's own suggestion and concentrate on his two above-mentioned books and add some relevant references to a few other works and to his unfinished *History of economic analysis*.

3.2   THE CREATION OF MONEY *EX NIHILO*

Schumpeter fundamentally was a 'real' business cycle theorist. He was mainly concerned with the endogenous real forces that generate development and fluctuations. Innovations, which are the driving force of development, are endogenous to the capitalist system in his various historical phases.[6] Schumpeter, however, did not confine his analysis to a barter economy and did not put investment and credit into two separate compartments. He denied the neutrality of money;[7] banks and their social accounting function in fabricating means of payment are an integral part of his theory (Tichy, 1984, p. 133). Against Fisher's vision of banks that convert illiquid real wealth into liquid means of payments, Schumpeter attributes to bankers the ability of creating purchasing power *ex nihilo* when they finance the entrepreneurs' plans to buy resources for projects not yet realized (Schumpeter, 1934[1983], p. 101). Bank money created by credit is a capital fund that is anticipated to finance investment for growth; it provides new purchasing power to innovative entrepreneurs, to

---

[6] 'By "development", therefore, we shall understand only such changes in economic life as are not forced upon it from without but arise by its own initiative, from within' (Schumpeter, 1934[1983], p. 63). Schumpeter's innovative technology shocks are endogenous to a historical form of social and economic organization.

[7] '...the problem arises of defining how money would have to behave in order to leave the real processes of the barter model uninfluenced. Wicksell was the first to see the problem clearly and to coin the appropriate concept, Neutral Money. In itself, this concept expresses nothing but the established belief in the possibility of pure "real analysis". But it also suggests recognition of the fact that money need not be neutral. So its creation induced a hunt for the conditions in which money is neutral. And this point eventually led to the discovery that no such conditions can be formulated, that is, that there is no such thing as neutral money or money that is a mere veil spread over the phenomena that really matter – an interesting case of a concept's rendering valuable service by proving unworkable' (Schumpeter, 1954[2006], pp. 1054–1055).

buy the required resources for innovative projects in competition with existing firms in the market.[8]

In the capitalist process of growth, bankers perform a social role of direction and monitoring. They allow new comers devoid of resources ('entrepreneurs' properly) to enter markets by diverting existing resources from routine utilization towards new combinations that produce economic change. Far from simply transferring savings from savers to borrowers, bankers play the essential role of socially sanctioning the access to resources for innovative entrepreneurs. They finance new projects not yet realized but potentially profitable not out of existing, accumulated saving, but out of the expansion of their liabilities on demand against promises for future repayments out of the future sales. Interests will be paid as a quota of the forthcoming entrepreneurial profits. By credit creation *ex nihilo*, banks promote the reallocation of resources that finance new investment for economic growth. The risk inherent in the banking activity to this purpose, together with the domestic and international monetary regimes in which banks operate, set limits to the expansion of credit. The amount of bank credit is flexibly anchored to the strategic or prudential criteria adopted by profit-maximizing banks that take into consideration their size and market share within the more or less competitive environment in which they operate. Finally, the amount of credit is flexibly anchored to the reserve requirements or other domestic regulations imposed by the Gold Standard or other monetary regimes.

In *The Theory of Economic Development*, Schumpeter sketches the process of creative destruction in competitive capitalism, that is to say, the discontinuous, dynamic process of growth triggered by radical innovations that change the previously established use of resources and bring about major productivity gains. Such discontinuous, dynamic process is endogenous to the capitalist economy, because it is driven by active entrepreneurs, who conceive and realize innovative transformations of the circular flow of resources and break the established circulation on which reproduction depends.[9] The entrepreneur, as defined by Schumpeter, is neither the inventor nor the capitalist providing capital.[10] The entrepreneur is a charismatic leader who is able to

---

[8]   In the 1934 edition of *Theory of Economic Development* (Schumpeter, 1934[1983]), which is a revised version of the 1912 German edition, Schumpeter pointed out that his view of banking as already expounded in the 1912 edition had received 'valuable substantiation and improvement' from the work of L. A. Hahn in his book *Economic Theory of Bank Credit* (2015[1920]). On the relationship between Hahn and Schumpeter, see Hagemann's 'Introduction' to Hahn's book (Hagemann, 2015, pp. v–xxiv).

[9]   'Circular flow' is the expression that Schumpeter uses to indicate the Walrasian equilibrium of prices and quantities in a substantially 'static' economy, i.e. not experiencing major changes.

[10]   'Enterprise' is the specific term that Schumpeter uses to indicate the effective act of producing radical innovations, as opposed to inventions that do not create economic change or to the management of current, routine activities (Schumpeter, 1934[1983], pp. 74ff.). In the last

effectively promote and bring to completion one of the five types of radical changes to which the circular flow can be subjected: producing and marketing new products; introducing innovative processes that change the technologies currently in use; opening new markets; accessing new sources of primary and energy goods; revolutionizing management, organization and the market structure (Schumpeter, 1934[1983], p. 66). After having experienced such radical changes, the economy converges to a new equilibrium circular flow. New firms have displaced old ones, and the new technologies have settled into a smooth cycle of production and marketing. The new circular flow lasts until there are new radical changes.

In Schumpeter's theory of development and business cycles, which are strictly intertwined, the endogenous flow of innovative investment that discontinuously changes the use of resources with major productivity gains, is financed by the creation of bank credit. In the long-term process of growth specific to the historical phase of competitive capitalism, banks play a primary role: they create new means of payment by extending credit to innovative entrepreneurs. Innovative entrepreneurs receive newly created flows of bank money, which allow them to compete with old firms by buying the resources they need to innovate.

The elasticity of bank money via credit expansion, or contraction, is at the core of Schumpeter's theories of growth and business cycles, which are strictly intertwined. In the ascending phase of fluctuations when innovations, appearing in swarms, create prosperity, credit expansion in the form of additional bank money supports and permits the activities of new firms. When the price of investment goods rises because of the competition in resources, when the old products are displaced by the new ones available at more competitive prices, when the new firms are finally able to reap profits from their sales and repay the loans initially received by banks, the economy enters into its descending phase. In the recession, there is a contraction of liquidity, since the stock of bank money is reduced; meanwhile, the firms unable to innovate go bankrupt and are expelled from the market.

In the circular flow money plays a social accounting role. Ideally, the monetary transactions may be imagined as settled within a 'central settlement bureau, a kind of clearing house or bookkeeping centre for the economic system' (Schumpeter, 1934[1983], p. 124). But a radically different view of credit markets has to be adopted when dealing with processes of development. Schumpeter carries out his analysis by considering the 'money market', in

---

part of Chapter II of the book, Schumpeter sketched the traits of the entrepreneur as a leader, and inquired into the motives, which drive entrepreneurs to promote innovative change (Schumpeter, 1934[1983], pp. 88ff.).

which the present purchasing power fabricated by banks is traded against the entrepreneurs' promises to repay it in the future.

> The kernel of the matter lies in the credit requirements of new enterprises. (...) only one fundamental thing happens on the money market, to which everything else is accessory: on the demand side appear entrepreneurs and on the supply side producers of and dealers in purchasing power, viz. bankers, both with their staff of agents and middlemen. What takes place is simply the exchange of present against future purchasing power. In the daily price struggle between the two parties the fate of new combinations is decided. (Schumpeter, 1934[1983], p. 125)

He is aware that in actual money markets the funds to finance innovation are allocated together with those to finance the monetary payments relative to the settled circular flow (Schumpeter, 1934[1983], p. 125), but he drastically simplifies his analysis by collapsing all sorts of credit into his notion of the money market.[11]

In the 1920s and 1930s Schumpeter elaborated on his theory of development in a number of articles.[12] In 1927, in 'The explanation of the business cycle', he examines in some detail the creation of credit by banks as part and parcel of the core banking activity and 'not by way of mistake or aberration from sound principles' (Schumpeter, 1927, p. 301). To the process of credit creation he devotes a long note (Schumpeter, 1927, p. 301, footnote 1). Banks are not simple intermediaries between savers and investors; they systematically create credit beyond the amount of savings which are deposited with them.

The expansion of bank money via credit creation creates inflation as in the Wicksellian cumulative process, but inflation has also real effects because the new firms add their production to the already existing supply (Schumpeter, 1927, p. 302). Moreover, the inflationary process will not go on indefinitely. The process of 'manufacturing' money by banks will be reversed as soon as the innovators are able to pay back their credits thanks to the realized sales. After the peak of prosperity has been reached, 'self-deflation' will take place and the purchasing power created by banks automatically vanishes (Schumpeter, 1927, p. 303).

---

[11]   He describes the working of actual markets by explaining how past saving out of innovation profits or parts of current profits could enter the great reservoir of purchasing power managed by the banks, jointly with a variety of other financial flows. The intricacy of the funds flowing in and out of the money market might well obscure the fundamental phenomenon (Schumpeter, 1934[1983], pp. 198–201). Here we do not enter into the discussion of how Schumpeter derived a monetary theory of interest from these premises.

[12]   He also introduces his sketchy distinction between long cycles (Kondratieff), nine-year cycles (Juglar) and short cycles (Kitchin), an articulation that was still missing in *The Theory of Economic Development*.

In 1928, Schumpeter looks at credit in a more general perspective. Banking and credit are core aspects of the conceptual definition of the economic system. Credit distinguishes contemporary competitive capitalism from other economic systems similarly characterized by private property and production for the market. Both from a theoretical and a historical perspective, a capitalist system is a market economy based on free enterprise that operates with a credit system (Schumpeter, 1928, p. 362).[13] Without the new means of payments created *ex nihilo* by banks, the competition of innovative firms versus the old ones already well established in the circular flow could not take place. New innovative investment requires payments, which have to be anticipated before the radical innovators reap entrepreneurial profits. The required flows of means of payments cannot be generated by previous savings in the circular flow.

Schumpeter does not deny the role of banks as financial intermediaries, but this is definitely not their primary role in the processes of change and growth.

> The role of credit would be a technical and a subordinate one in the sense that everything fundamental about the economic process could be explained in terms of goods, if industry grew by small steps along coherent curves. For in that case financing could and would be done substantially by means of the current gross revenue, and only small discrepancies would need to be smoothed. (...) As, however, innovation, being discontinuous and involving considerable change and being, in competitive capitalism, typically embodied in new firms, requires large expenditure previous to the emergence of any revenue, credit becomes an essential element of the process. And we cannot turn to savings in order to account for the existence of a fund from which these credits are to flow. For this would imply the existence of previous profits, without which there would not be anything like the required amount – even as it is, savings usually lag behind requirements – and assuming previous profits would mean, in an explanation of principles, circular reasoning. 'Credit-creation,' therefore, becomes an essential part both of the mechanism of the process and of the theory explaining it. (Schumpeter, 1928, p. 381)[14]

At the same time, Schumpeter underlines that credit creation by banks is not the ultimate impulse generating the process of change. The 'propelling force of the process' is the innovative activity by creative entrepreneurs. As in other writings of his, Schumpeter is crystal clear that to give a crucial role to the banking system in growth processes and in fluctuations does not imply supporting a monetary theory of business cycles.

---

[13]   In *Business Cycles* Schumpeter (1939, pp. 223–224) again defines and dates capitalism with reference to credit creation.

[14]   As we shall see below (section 3.8), Robertson also points out the different role of banks and finance in economies experiencing an orderly and smooth process of growth and in economies subject to discontinuous changes.

3.3 THE MANUFACTURING OF CREDIT IN PROSPERITY AND DEPRESSION

In 1931, in the article 'The present world depression: a tentative diagnosis' (Schumpeter, 1931), Schumpeter refers to his refined vision of the periodicity of cycles and suggests that the severity of the world depression was due, besides other contingent historical events, to the conjunction of the troughs of the three long, medium and short cycles (Schumpeter, 1931, pp. 179–180). In the mid 1930s, in the article 'The analysis of economic change' (Schumpeter, 1935), he deals with the four phases of the cycle (prosperity, recession, depression and revival) and the role that bank money plays in them (Schumpeter, 1935, pp. 6–7).[15]

Finally, in 1939, Schumpeter published the two volumes of *Business Cycles*, where banks and their complex functions and activities are examined both at the theoretical (first volume) and the historical (second volume) level. The most interesting aspects of Schumpeter's analysis of banking are in Chapter 3 of the first volume of *Business Cycles*, in the section 'The role of money and banking in the process of evolution', where he critically compares his own approach to other theories of banking. He first criticizes and rejects the 'commercial', or 'classical', theory of banking, according to which bank activities are restricted to supporting and smoothing production and trade by extending commercial credit to finance circulation, by intermediating saving and consumption or by intermediating saving and investment.

Without denying the importance of these routine credit activities, Schumpeter underlines how, in the daily practice, such activities mix or run parallel with the decisive banks' role in the creation of money to finance innovative investment. But, for Schumpeter, there is a radical theoretical divide between the 'commercial' functions of banks and the proper and crucial role of banks as financiers of entrepreneurial investment that creates radical economic change and promotes growth.[16] Having rejected the commercial theory of banking Schumpeter turns to the criticism of the 'investment theory of banking', according to which banks primarily operate as intermediaries between savers

---

[15]   He also favourably mentions Robertson's works on trade cycles. 'The first author to do this consciously was, as far as the present writer knows, Mr. D. H. Robertson (*A Study of Industrial Fluctuations*, published in 1915, and an earlier paper in the *Journal of the Royal Statistical Society*), which, equally independently, also developed a schema of the working of the credit mechanism, similar in many respects to the one implied above and developed in 1911, in his *Banking Policy and the Price Level* (1926)' (Schumpeter, 1935, p. 6, footnote 1).

[16]   In so far as the analysis is concerned with the circular flow, it could even be possible to ignore credit and finance altogether. For Schumpeter, if we exclude radical innovation and change, the ideal model of a barter economy with no financial sector might well approximate the Walrasian circular flow in equilibrium, even if in historical reality banks are effective engines to smooth the routine production and circulation processes and facilitate the intermediation of savings.

and investors. In particular, he criticizes the mechanical definition of the limits to credit that this view of banks offers.

For Schumpeter, these theories of banking do not perceive the essential role that banks play in the process of growth triggered by innovation, even though, he recognizes, such a role can be incorporated into the 'familiar' vision of banking. The loans made to innovative entrepreneurs do not have to be necessarily repaid; they can be renewed, so that the corresponding amount of means of payment permanently becomes part of the circulating medium in existence.

> In the disequilibria caused by innovation other firms will have to undertake investments which cannot be financed from current receipts, and hence become borrowers also. Whenever the evolutionary process is in full swing, the bulk of bank credit outstanding at any time finances what has become current business and has lost its original contact with innovation or with the adaptive operations induced by innovations, although the history of every loan must lead back to the one or the other. (Schumpeter, 1939, p. 114, Vol. 1)

If the consumers' borrowing and saving are also introduced into the picture, not only do we have all the aspects of banks' normal activities taken into due consideration, but also

> ...the explanation of the fact that current, or 'regular' business has been emphasized to the point of giving rise to a theory of banking which recognizes nothing else but the financing of current commodity trade and the lending of surplus funds to the stock exchange, and to a canon of the morals of banking by which the function to which we assign logical priority is almost excluded from the things a banker might properly do. (Schumpeter, 1939, p. 114, Vol. 1)

The commercial theory of banking correctly captures the customary activities of banks, but it fails to see their role in processes of innovation and growth. This theory, moreover, 'obscures the relation which even "classical" credit creation for short-time purposes bears to innovation – best exemplified by loans to the stock exchange, which help to carry new issues – and leads to a narrow view about the function of finance bills and of credits in current account' (Schumpeter, 1939, p. 116, Vol. 1). The investment theory of banking, by exclusively emphasizing the quantity of bank credit outstanding as the variable regulating growth, fails to see 'enterprise' as the force producing development. For Schumpeter, these criticisms are important to clarify the prudential rules as well as the professional ethics that bankers should follow in their behaviour.

The 'classical' theory of banking rightly points to the behavioural norms of transparency and honesty which should rule banking practices, but it fails to see the importance of the assessment of creditworthiness of innovative investment. To play the role of financiers of growth and support innovative changes in the proper way, bankers should maintain full independence from the business world and politics. Their judgement should be free from outside pressures and based on accurate information.[17] The effectiveness of the assessment and monitoring activities depends on the characteristics of the banking industry, which in turn depend on innovation in organization, logistics and management. But it also depends essentially on the breadth of vision and clear insight of the single banker.

The banker is a peculiar 'entrepreneur', whose charisma is complementary to his deep knowledge of the business world, the personal contact with his customers, and the clear-sightedness. These qualities are acquired both by long training and by personal intelligence; they should be daily absorbed from the working environment. Their deep roots are in the high standards of behaviour that the banking industry should customarily practice. If banks finance innovation, all these features of proper banking become 'incommensurably more important'. If the banking system suffers a shortage of resourceful and independent staff, if it lacks a solid tradition of honesty and independence of judgement in the assessment of creditworthiness, if its management is at the service of the private interests of the business world or, worse, of politicians, it will bring disasters involving the whole economy (Schumpeter, 1939, pp. 117–118, Vol. 1).

The chapter ends with a discussion of how far banks can go in the creation of credit not covered by reserves in gold or legal tender. Besides the 'brake' imposed by the gold standard in the monetary regimes which adopt it, Schumpeter recalls prudential considerations due to risk management in the banking industry, the specific knowledge of customers by bank managers, the size of the banking firm, the standards adopted by the whole banking system in terms of risk management, the possible pressure that competition imposes to limit the reckless behaviour of competitors, the technicalities of loans, and of course the framework created by regulatory laws.

For Schumpeter, however, all such constraints are flexible. They can be circumvented or relaxed thanks to innovations in banking practices, a growing number of more sophisticated customers who learn to deal with finance, the progressive abandonment of the use of cash in transactions, the more or less lax atmosphere that may capture the hearts and minds of managers and staff in the banking world (Schumpeter, 1939, pp. 121–123, Vol. 1).

---

[17] In assessing creditworthiness, the banker should be absolutely free from the pressures of businessmen as well as from the influences of politicians. 'It should be observed how important it is for the functioning of the system of which we are trying to construct a model that the banker should know, and be able to judge, what his credit is used for and that he should be an independent agent. To realize this is to understand what banking means' (Schumpeter, 1939, p. 116, Vol. 1).

It is interesting also to look at Schumpeter's views concerning the way in which the economists' approach to banks and finance evolved in time. In Chapter 8 of *The History of Economic Analysis*, especially in section 6 devoted to banks' credit and deposits creation, Schumpeter observes that in the period under examination (1870–1914), the ample literature on the banking system and central banking formed 'a separate compartment' within the literature on money and credit. The complaint, which other scholars had made about the theoretical gap between monetary economics and barter equilibrium, or business cycle research, here turns into a complaint about the gap between the widespread interest in credit, banking and banking policy, and a deeply rooted conservative approach to the theory of banking. Still, at the beginning of the 20th century, the idea of credit creation by banks was misunderstood by the majority of economists (Schumpeter, 1954[2006], p. 1080).[18]

For Schumpeter, the erroneous view of the nature of banks has much to do with the notions of saving and investment, and thus with real changes and the non-neutrality of credit money in the capitalist society.

> Banks do not, of course, 'create' legal tender money and still less do they 'create' machines. They do, however, something (...) which, in its economic effects, comes pretty near to creating legal-tender money and which may lead to the creation of 'real capital' that could not have been created without this practice. But this alters the analytic situation profoundly and makes it highly inadvisable to construe bank credit on the model of existing funds being withdrawn from previous uses by an entirely imaginary act of saving and then lent out by their owners. (...) The theory of 'credit creation' not only recognizes patent facts without obscuring them by artificial constructions; it also brings out the peculiar mechanism of saving and investment that is characteristic of full-fledged capitalist society and the true role of banks in capitalist evolution. With less qualification than has to be added in most cases, this theory therefore constitutes definite advance in analysis. (Schumpeter, 1954[2006], p. 1080).

Schumpeter credits Robertson and Pigou as the innovators turning the tide towards the right track, but he laments that economists soon went astray

---

18   For those economists, credit essentially is '...quite independent of the existence or non existence of banks and can be understood without any reference to them. If, as a further step in analysis, we do introduce them into the picture, the nature of the phenomenon remains unchanged. The public is still the true lender. Bankers are nothing but its agents, middlemen who do the actual lending on behalf of the public and whose existence is a mere matter of division of labour. The depositors become and remain lenders both in the sense that they lend ('entrust') their money to the banks and in the sense that they are the ultimate lenders in case the banks lend out part of this money. (...) As the depositors remain lenders, so bankers remain middlemen who collect 'liquid capital' from innumerable small pools in order to make it available to trade. They add nothing to the existing mass of liquid means, though they make it do more work' (Schumpeter, 1954[2006], p. 1079). Schumpeter polemically mentions Cannan's article on bank deposits (Cannan, 1921) as an example of this view of banks.

and substantially abandoned the concept of credit creation by banks, mostly because of the bad influence of Keynesianism (Schumpeter, 1954[2006], p. 1082), an issue to which we return in Chapter 5.

3.4　SCHUMPETER'S HISTORICAL ANALYSIS

The two volumes of *Business Cycles* are rich in references to financial history, with which we shall not deal in detail but for a few comments to underline the complexity of Schumpeter's approach to the subject. Private banks and central banks are prominent characters of his narration, but neither is the main protagonist; Schumpeter, in fact, firmly denied that banking activity could be the endogenous or exogenous prime mover of business fluctuations. In his historical narration, he looks at the malfunctioning of banking or finance in various episodes, with nuanced judgements and attention to the institutional structure, the financial depth, the nature of loans and mortgage contracts, reckless practices or morality standards.[19]

Schumpeter (1939, pp. 250–251) portrays John Law as the ambitious entrepreneur, who failed for having pretended to be the banker of his own ventures. On the occasion, he comments on 'the possibilities and weaknesses of the capitalist machine and of all the rules that apply to its handling' (Schumpeter, 1939, p. 252). Secondary expansionary waves, following the primary ones induced by major innovations, are portrayed as often opening the way to imprudent investment, excesses of speculation, or frauds. In specific cases, the banks' poor performance contributed to maladjustments or even catastrophes in the economic history of Western nations.

Already in the last chapter of *The Theory of Economic Development* Schumpeter (1934[1983], p. 236) had distinguished the 'normal' process of liquidation taking place in a depression from the 'abnormal process of liquidation', i.e. the severe disruption, that can occur in specific episodes of recession.[20] He judges 'the losses and destruction which accompany the abnormal course of events', aggravated by abnormal panics and financial collapse, as useless sufferings to be avoided by appropriate policies whenever possible (Schumpeter, 1934[1983], pp. 251–253).[21]

---

[19]　See e.g. Schumpeter's mixed evaluation of 'reckless banking' in the context of deteriorated standards of morality in the United States at the beginning of the 19th century (Schumpeter, 1939, pp. 294–295, Vol. 1); see also his evaluation of mortgage practices in financing housing in Germany (Schumpeter, 1939, p. 438, Vol. 1).

[20]　See Dal-Pont Legrand and Hagemann (2016) on this aspect of Schumpeter's thought.

[21]　In these passages Schumpeter hints at the possibility of multiple equilibria, depending on the normal or abnormal trajectory that events follow (Schumpeter, 1934[1983], pp. 251–252).

In *Business Cycles* Schumpeter deals again with 'abnormal liquidation' during the Depression (Schumpeter, 1939, pp. 149-ff., Vol. 1). The structural weaknesses of the U.S. banking and financial system were decisive to explain the severity of the depression. In 1946, in an article on 'The decade of the Twenties', Schumpeter points out three main factors, specific to the U.S. economy, which explain why the recession precipitated into 'disaster' by going well beyond the evolution of other episodes of recession: the 'specifically American mass psychology' that nurtured the speculative mania with 'wild excesses' in 1927–1929; the 'three banks epidemics' in the context of a fragmented banking industry; the 'reckless borrowing and lending' in mortgages in both the urban and rural environment (Schumpeter, 1946, p. 9). He also underlined the heavy psychological effects of banking panics that 'spread paralysis through all sectors of the business organism', and of farms' foreclosures in the agricultural sector (Schumpeter, 1946, p. 9).

On the role of money, banking and finance in economic history, Schumpeter suggests the adoption of a long-term perspective. As a scholar with deep knowledge of the history of economic thought and economic history, he does not fail to take account of the evolution of banking and finance along with the long-term processes of development of Western societies. Being well aware of financial history, and the institutional changes in financial practice, he puts money and monetary institutions among the pillars of the institutional settings of historical societies and their evolution. In addressing questions related to the history of development in France, Germany, or Great Britain, Schumpeter deals with the evolution of banking practices and policies since the late Middle Ages or the early Renaissance.[22] In Schumpeter's overall picture of the economic history of the Western World, banking and finance are of crucial importance for the changes that innovative entrepreneurs promote, but still they do not have the same importance as manufacturing or transport in the process of creative destruction.

We cannot discuss the complex transformation in the process of creative destruction that according to Schumpeter marks the passage from competitive to trustified capitalism. In *Capitalism, Socialism and Democracy* (Schumpeter, 1950[1994]), he ends up with the controversial diagnosis of the euthanasia of capitalism that metamorphoses from trustified capitalism into socialism. In the book, dealing with the composition of the bourgeoisie, Schumpeter placed 'the bulk of what we refer to as industrialists, merchants, financiers and bankers' in a specific layer of the bourgeoisie, whose activities are in 'the intermediate stage' between 'entrepreneurial venture and mere current

---

[22]   In *Business Cycles*, he also discusses the controversial issue whether aspects of the financial practices in the Ancient World might be read as anticipations of modern credit systems. See e.g. Schumpeter (1939, pp. 225–226, Vol. 1).

administration of an inherited domain' (Schumpeter, 1950[1994], p. 134). In Schumpeter's vision, bankers and financiers, though not mere routine players, play their best role supporting and serving properly innovative entrepreneurs, but he also considered the possible role of bankers themselves as innovative entrepreneurs and active promoters of major changes in financial organization. In 1947, he explicitly mentioned banking and bankers when dealing with creative responses in the course of economic history (Schumpeter, 1947).[23]

In summary, Schumpeter clearly conceived how finance, if not the ultimate propelling force of investment for growth, is the essential social technology without which innovative entrepreneurs could not be set at work to produce economic change. In economics, Schumpeter's ideas stimulated research on the role of finance in the long-term process of economic development, questioning the adequacy of the dominance attributed to accumulation of capital, labour or productivity growth in neoclassical models (King and Levine, 1993).[24] Recent research in economic history has placed new emphasis on money and finance as major innovations in the world history, providing contributions that go beyond what Schumpeter explicitly considered in his historical analysis of the role of banks in development. In a long-term historical perspective, finance has been strictly intertwined with the world history of urban civilization in the last five millennia, in ancient China or ancient near East as well as in modern Europe. Finance is a technology of civilization that 'has vastly improved our species' ability to reduce existential risks and to allocate resources through time to foster growth' (Goetzmann, 2016, p. 3). All these fascinating subjects are, however, beyond the scope of this book.

3.5 PRICES, MONEY AND BANKS IN ROBERTSON

A large part of Robertson's most relevant contributions to the analysis of trade cycles and the role of banks belongs to the first two decades of the 20th century, a period characterized by his intense collaboration and partnership with Keynes, which ended in the 1930s (see, e.g., Hicks, 1966; Presley, 1978). The book *Banking Policy and the Price Level* (Robertson, 1926[1949]) can be regarded as the culmination of Robertson's analytical effort in that period. Here we concentrate on this work and Robertson's 1928 summary of its main

---

[23] He wrote: 'Financial institutions and practices enter our circle of problems in three ways: they are "auxiliary and conditioning"; banking may be the object of entrepreneurial activity, that is to say the introduction of new banking practices may constitute enterprise; and bankers (or other "financiers") may use the means at their command in order to embark upon commercial and industrial enterprise themselves (for example, John Law)' (Schumpeter, 1947, p. 153, n. 8). This aspect is emphasized by Festré and Nasica (2009) .

[24] King and Levine (1993, p. 735) also refer to the literature on endogenous growth as 'incorporating key roles for financial intermediaries'.

aspects (Robertson, 1928[1966]). We shall return to consider other aspects of Robertson's work in subsequent chapters (5 and 6).[25]

In the preface to the 1949 edition of *Banking Policy*, Robertson indicated the two main objectives of his book: i) to present again part of the analytical framework of his *Study of Industrial Fluctuations* (Robertson, 1915); ii) to connect the mainly non-monetary analysis carried out in that work to the discussion of the relation between saving, credit creation and capital growth (Robertson, 1926[1949], p. vii). Some of the topics considered in *Banking Policy* had already been dealt with by Robertson in the first edition (1922) of *Money*, although not satisfactorily in his view.[26]

More specifically, *Banking Policy* deals with the problem of price stability that, according to the mainstream view of the time, should be a desirable objective to realize. Without distancing himself excessively from the orthodoxy, Robertson questions such a position (see also Robertson, 1928[1966]). The book, however, attracted most attention for Robertson's attempt to clarify the interrelation between credit creation, capital formation and saving. In this respect, Robertson's most significant contributions are related to his analysis of economies characterized by the existence of a modern well-developed banking system, which creates money, i.e. the amount of bank deposits existing at a certain time.[27] A relevant question is how banks determine the amount of money they create. For Robertson, the general principle that regulates the total amount of deposits created by banks is their objective to maintain a certain proportion between their deposits (loans) and their reserves. [28]

To fully understand Robertson's analysis of the banking system two preliminary steps are required. First, to see how he approaches the problem of quantity and price stability. Second, to understand his terminology and classification with respect to the key concepts of capital and saving. Robertson begins his

[25]   For a thorough exposition of Robertson's contributions see Presley (1978). See also Laidler (1995), for a critical survey of Robertson's work in the 1920s and its relation to the Austrian School; Costabile (2005) for the differences between Robertson and the Austrian School; Bridel (1987) and Boianovsky (2018) for studies of Robertson's theoretical contributions in relation to Cambridge economics.

[26]   He had written the book without knowing the works of Wicksell, Schumpeter, Mises and Hahn. In 1928, Robertson published a second edition of *Money* with relevant changes and then two successive editions with minor revisions (Robertson, 1928[1962]).

[27]   Bank money 'is created not by the public but by the bankers, when they accord to the holders of cheque-books the right to draw cheques' (Robertson, 1928[1962], pp. 41–42).

[28]   The banks' reserves 'consist partly (...) of common money in their possession, partly of a chequery at the Bank of England' (Robertson, 1928[1962], pp. 42–43). See also Robertson (1928[1962], pp. 43–44) on the ratio of banks' common money to their deposits with the central bank. Common money is what is universally accepted as a means of payment within a certain political area (Robertson, 1928[1962], p. 34).

analysis by considering barter economies.[29] In such economies there exist rational incentives for producers to vary their output. Such rational incentives are of three types: i) changes in operating costs; ii) changes in the desire for the goods that producers obtain in exchange for their output; iii) changes in the 'real demand price' for the producers' output (Robertson, 1926[1949], pp. 6–33). Then, Robertson lifts the hypothesis of barter to analyse a monetary economy, that is to say an economy in which the government or the banking system have the power to inject money into it. The money injections 'are not free gifts, but are made by way of loan' (Robertson, 1926[1949], p. 23). Initially, Robertson does not consider the time-element of loans and regards them simply as currency issues.

The conclusions reached in such analytical context are two: i) like in the case of barter, there exist rational and justifiable fluctuations of the output that policies should not try to prevent; ii) fluctuations of the output are accompanied by price variations and it is not necessarily sound to implement monetary policies aiming to restore the original price level. The latter conclusion is reinforced when time is taken into account, that is to say when the fact that 'production takes *time* and requires the aid of *saving*' is taken into account (Robertson, 1926[1949], p. 34).

Robertson considers also what he calls 'inappropriate' fluctuations of output, i.e. fluctuations that exceed the rational fluctuations mentioned above. For him, the main reason of inappropriate output fluctuations is 'the stress of competition, aggravated by the length of time which is required to adjust production to a changed demand' (Robertson, 1926[1949], p. 37). Competition and the existence of independent competing firms induce each single firm to produce a larger output than it would be rational to produce.[30] Competition per se does not necessarily ensure the realization of optimal aggregate outcomes.

3.6 SAVING, CAPITAL FORMATION AND CREDIT

Robertson's analysis is based on his complex and very articulate definitions and classifications of capital and saving. In 1926, Robertson adopted a terminology that, later on, he defined 'strange and barbarous' (Robertson, 1928[1966], p. 24) and turned to using more standard terms (see also Laidler, 1995). Here, we retain Robertson's original terminology to follow and

---

[29] Robertson considers two types of barter economy: one in which each industry is in the hands of a group of co-partners, so that there is no conflict between capital and labour; another in which crucial decisions are made by entrepreneurs who employ workers.

[30] See Robertson (1926[1949], pp. 34–37 and 38–39) for other causes of excessive output fluctuations.

understand more easily his analysis as expounded in the 1926 book, but all unconventional terms are accompanied by the corresponding terms used in 1928.

The activity of providing capital is necessarily based on abstention from current consumption, which Robertson calls 'lacking' (saving) and, therefore, 'the things in the provision of which Lacking eventuates I propose to call Capital.' Capital, in turn, can be divided into fixed, circulating and imaginary, to which three classes of lacking correspond: long, short and unproductive lacking (Robertson, 1926[1949], p. 41).

Long lacking is devoted to the provision of fixed capital (factories, machinery, etc.). Short lacking is for the provision of circulating capital:[31] 'the essence of Short Lacking is seen to lie in some persons going without consumable goods in such wise that other persons, who are engaged in a lengthy productive process, consume them' (Robertson, 1926[1949], p. 43). Unproductive lacking is abstinence from consumption by some people in favour of others who want to anticipate their income but do not produce any marketable goods (Robertson, 1926[1949], pp. 44–45).[32]

Lacking can also be divided into applied and abortive (hoarding). Applied lacking can be used directly or indirectly, i.e. through lending. If, instead, an individual's unspent income is kept in money form to increase her/his money stock, we have hoarding (Robertson, 1926[1949], pp. 45–46). When hoarding takes place, if the equilibrium between aggregate demand and supply has to be guaranteed, the hoarders' abstinence from consumption must be matched by an equal increase in consumption by others (Robertson, 1926[1949], p. 46).

Finally, Robertson provides a further classification of lacking, which he regards as 'troublesome'. First, he defines 'spontaneous lacking', which corresponds to the ordinary notion of voluntary saving; second, he introduces the notion of 'automatic lacking' (forced saving). Automatic lacking, in turn, requires the introduction of the notion of 'automatic stinting', which occurs 'whenever an increase in the stream of money directed on to the market prevents certain persons from consuming goods which they would otherwise have consumed.' The increase in the stream of money can be due to the decision of some to dis-hoard or to the spending of additional money created in the economy. In both cases, the additional quantity of money brought to the market 'competes with the main daily stream of money for the daily stream of marketable goods, secures a part of the latter for those from

---

[31]   For Robertson (1926[1949], pp. 42–43) circulating capital includes finished goods ready for immediate consumption but kept in stock as well as goods that will never be consumed because they are used as intermediate goods.

[32]   The most important form of unproductive lacking is taxes which transfer purchasing power to a government to finance a war.

whom the additional stream of money flows, and thus deprives the residue of the public of consumption which they would otherwise have enjoyed.' Automatic stinting does not necessarily imply automatic lacking. It implies automatic lacking only when 'the consumption of those who undergo it is reduced both below what they intended and below the value of their current output' (Robertson, 1926[1949], p. 48). Robertson calls the opposites of automatic stinting and automatic lacking 'automatic splashing' and 'automatic dislacking' respectively.

The basic important point made by Robertson in dealing with lacking and stinting can be expressed as follows. From the viewpoint of an individual, the decision to increase (decrease) his/her money hoard corresponds to the decision to increase (decrease) his/her saving, but this is not necessarily the eventual outcome when the economy as a whole is considered. The effect of the individual decision to hoard on his/her saving can be assessed only by taking account of the effect of the other individuals' decisions induced by the hoarding itself. The easiest way to understand this point, concerning the possible inconsistency between individual decisions and collective outcomes, is to consider cases in which all individuals simultaneously decide to dis-hoard or to hoard.

> If *all* members of the public simultaneously dis-hoarded to an appropriate extent, they might impose on one another Automatic Stinting which in each case exactly cancelled the intended Dis-lacking involved in the process of Spontaneous Dis-hoarding, so that on the balance neither Lacking nor Dis-lacking would be done by anyone. Conversely, if all members of the public increased their Hoarding to an appropriate extent, the real income of each might suffer no diminution; for the intended Lacking involved in his Spontaneous Hoarding might be exactly cancelled by the Automatic Splashing in which the Spontaneous Hoarding of his neighbours enabled him to indulge. (Robertson, 1926[1949], pp. 48–49)

Finally, Robertson introduces the notions of induced and imposed lacking. Induced lacking occurs when the same process that generates automatic lacking also reduces the value of the money stock of the affected people, who then reduce their consumption to restore the value of their money stock (Robertson, 1926[1949], p. 49).[33] Imposed lacking is the sum of induced lacking plus automatic lacking.

On the grounds of the definitions above, Robertson turns to consider the expansion of fixed and circulating capital in relation to lacking. As for fixed capital, although not entirely, its expansion occurs through spontaneous

---

[33] See Laidler (1995, p. 158) on the relationship between Robertson's induced lacking and Keynes's inflation tax in *A Tract on Monetary Reform* (Keynes, 1923[1971]).

long lacking by individuals and/or firms (Robertson, 1926[1949], p. 50).[34]
As for the expansion of circulating capital, it comes about in three ways:
i) spontaneous short lacking (voluntary saving) by entrepreneurs; ii) the
transformation of spontaneous (voluntary) new hoarding into applied lacking;
iii) 'the infliction upon individuals of Imposed Lacking.' In the second and
third case the expansion of circulating capital occurs thanks to the operations
of the banking system (Robertson, 1926[1949], p. 50).

In a regime of metallic money and 'old-fashioned' banks,[35] the relation
between saving and capital is transparent. Unspent money is brought to banks
that lend it to firms which 'pay increased wage-bills to productive workers,
who on the one hand buy increased quantities of goods and, on the other add
to the stock of Circulating Capital' (Robertson, 1926[1949], p. 51). In this
case, there is no automatic lacking (forced saving), because the additional
expenditure generated by the increased wage-bills is exactly matched by the
reduced spending of the savers. In other words, in the markets for goods there
is no more competition than if the saved money were directly spent by its
original holders.

The picture changes when one turns to consider the modern banking system.
The basic process illustrated above is 'obscured' because a modern banking
system 'not only itself creates the most important forms of money (...) but
creates them mainly by way of loan to the business world. By expending these
loans businessmen procure practically the whole of that part of the expansion
of Circulating Capital which they are not willing to provide by Direct Lacking'
(Robertson, 1926[1949], p. 51).

The injection of new money into the market through lending generates a
price rise and automatic stinting, i.e. some are prevented from consuming
goods by the increase in the price level. It follows that, in a modern economy
with a well developed banking system, a large part of the newly created
circulating capital is not the result of voluntary saving. Robertson, however,
tries to avoid any confusion about the delicate issue of the relation between
saving ('waiting') and capital formation. Since the creation of new money by
banks gives rise to automatic stinting, it could be tempting to infer that capital
formation is not the product of waiting but of forced saving, or that the new
capital is the product of the hoarding of the owners of the new deposits, first in
the hands of borrowers and then in the hands of those from whom borrowers
buy goods and services (Robertson, 1926[1949], pp. 51–52).

---

[34]   We return to this issue in the next section.
[35]   Old-fashioned, or 'cloak-room', banks operate as mere intermediaries between depositors
and borrowers and are unable to create additional money through credit. See, e.g., Cannan (1921)
and Machlup (1965).

To test the validity of such 'temptations', Robertson considers a pure credit economy, in which the money supply entirely consists of the inconvertible issues of a 'single giant bank', and examines three possible cases: i) a change in the public's propensity to hoard; ii) an increase in productivity with constant population; iii) an increase in population with constant productivity (Robertson, 1926[1949], pp. 52–58). In the case in which there is an increase in the public's propensity to hoard and a corresponding decrease in the flow of money to the market, if the bank does nothing, the necessary outcome would be a price fall. If, instead, the bank makes additional loans, the price fall can be prevented (Robertson, 1926[1949], p. 53). Considered alone, the action of the bank generates automatic stinting; but considered jointly with the new hoarding

> ...it nips in the bud the Automatic Splashing which would otherwise occur as a by-product of the New Hoarding. The bank, therefore, while imposing Automatic Stinting is *not* imposing Automatic Lacking, but is in effect transforming Spontaneous New Hoarding into Applied Lacking very much as a 'cloak-room' bank does when it accepts cash from the public and lends it out to entrepreneurs. (Robertson, 1926[1949], p. 54)

If there is an increase in productivity with a constant population and the bank does nothing, there will be a decrease in prices and an increase in the value of the public's money stock, which is not the result of any new spontaneous lacking. The supply of circulating capital increases while its total value remains constant. If the bank makes additional loans, the decline of prices can be prevented and it can extract from the public an amount of (automatic and induced) lacking, whose value is equal to the increase in the value of the public money stock if there were no new loans. Such lacking is available to increase the supply of circulating capital not only in physical terms but also in value terms (Robertson, 1926[1949], pp. 54–55). In conclusion, 'owing to the increase in productivity the bank has been able, without causing a rise in the price-level, to impose upon the public a quantity of Lacking whose imposition would have necessitated a rise in the price-level if there had been no increase in productivity' (Robertson, 1926[1949], p. 55).

Finally, Robertson analyses the case in which the output grows because of an increase in population while productivity stays constant. The increase in output can be realized if there has been a previous increase in circulating capital, which in turn implies an initial imposed lacking during the period in which the additional capital is being produced. The successive effect of the increased output on the price level depends on the saving decisions of the new population. If the new population, at some stage, wants to build up a money stock on a similar scale to that of the rest of the population and the bank does nothing, there would be a fall in the price level, and 'Spontaneous New Hoarding of the new population would be counterbalanced by Automatic and Induced Dis-lacking on the part of the old population' (Robertson, 1926[1949], p. 56). If the bank makes additional loans, the price fall can be prevented.

Thus, any amount of capital that the economy wants to produce is necessar-ily and inevitably associated with an equal amount of lacking (more precisely, applied lacking). This, however, does not mean that banks are ultimately unimportant or mere intermediaries between savers and borrowers ('cloak-room banks'). Through their operations, which affect the price level, banks put in motion those processes that lead to the generation of the required amount of applied saving. In principle, moreover, it is possible to define bank policies that ensure price stability in every situation, even though Robertson is sceptical about the actual possibility to always implement such policies with success: 'The conclusion of certain writers that it is the unambiguous duty of the bank to render itself the agent for the procural of just so much Short Lacking that the level of prices is kept stable, seems to rest on too easy an assumption of the fulfilment of economic harmonies' (Robertson, 1926[1949], p. 58).

Banks are, on the one hand, the instrument through which the expansion of capital can take place and, on the other hand, they can implement policies ensuring the stability of prices. But this twofold responsibility of banks can become the source of serious difficulties: 'In short period of rapid change, the incompatibility between a banking policy designed to promote a stable price-level and a banking policy designed to secure appropriate additions to the quantity of Circulating Capital may ... become a serious source of trouble' (Robertson, 1926[1949], p. 58).

In Robertson's analysis of the relation between saving and capital formation banks play the important role we saw because production takes time and, consequently, he analyses the process by adopting a sequential methodology (a 'step-by-step method'). In his preface to the 1949 edition of *Banking Policy*, Robertson (1926[1949], pp. xi–xii) observes that nobody who had understood his methodology '... need have been puzzling his head in 1930 over the problem of "where the saving went to", or have stood in need of the crowning revelation that "saving" and "investment", if defined so as to be identical, are indeed always necessarily equal – a phenomenon which was the starting-point, not the culmination, of the analysis attempted in this little book!' Robertson's polemic is evidently against Keynes and his younger followers. We shall return to this issue in Chapter 5.

3.7   THE BANKING SYSTEM IN THE TRADE CYCLE

The above-mentioned difficulties caused by the twofold responsibility of banks are dealt with by Robertson in the context of his analysis of the trade cycle. He starts by considering an upward swing, whose crucial feature is that there is a large and discontinuous increase in the demand for circulating capital that calls for additional short lacking. Since the supply of short lacking is not sufficiently elastic, the responsibility for satisfying the larger demand rests almost entirely on the banking system (Robertson, 1926[1949], p. 72). In this situation, 'it seems unreasonable to expect the banking system *both* to ensure that appropriate additions are made to the quantity of Circulating Capital *and* to preserve absolute stability in the price-level' (Robertson, 1926[1949], p. 72).[36]

Banks can mitigate the price rise through the interest rate. An increase in both passive and active interest rates would diminish the depositors' willingness to dis-hoard and the borrowers' demand for loans. But banks can mitigate the price rise also by selling government securities which are the public's unproductive lacking.[37] Finally, banks could ration credit. In any case, the weapons that banks can use affect both the demand for and the supply of saving.

Robertson concludes that certain discontinuous expansions of the output are desirable and socially beneficial. Given the relative rigidity of the supply of lacking, banks must intervene and provide additional loans to finance the necessary increase of the circulating capital. Therefore, in general, the expansion of the output must be accompanied by a certain rise in the price level (Robertson, 1926[1949], pp. 78–79). There is no guarantee that this is a smooth and orderly process. It is undeniable that 'the expansion of industrial output is liable to be carried beyond the point justified by the underlying conditions of utility and cost' and that 'the demand for Short Lacking is likely to be inflated out of proportion to the expansion of industrial output' (Robertson, 1926[1949], p. 79). In other words, there can be 'inappropriate' variations of output and prices. Banks, in principle, could prevent or check such 'secondary' expansion of trade expansion, but this is not an easy task. If they fail, the only possible 'remedy' is the reduction of the demand for short lacking through the liquidation of stocks of goods and the curtailment of swollen productive capacities (Robertson, 1926[1949], p. 80).

The analysis is similar in the case of a downward swing, which as a rule should be accompanied by a decline in the price level. Falling prices put in motion forces that stimulate new hoarding and reduce the demand for short lacking on banks. This tends 'to beget a further fall in the price-level which in turn begets a further and "unjustifiable" decline in the scale of industrial

---

[36] We have already seen why the banks' intervention would cause the price level to rise, but Robertson (1926[1949], pp. 72–76) provides additional reasons of why the equality between the supply of and the demand for short lacking requires that prices should rise even more.

[37] The sale of these securities, however, would have the desired effect only if the public's inducement to unproductive lacking increases (Robertson, 1926[1949], p. 77).

output' (Robertson, 1926[1949], p. 81). However, for banks it is harder to check a price fall than to prevent a price rise. In fact, first of all, while it is always possible to fix the interest rate at a sufficiently high level to curb the demand for loans, it might be impossible to sufficiently stimulate the demand for loans because of the 'zero lower bound' of the interest rate (Robertson, 1926[1949], p. 81).[38]

The last chapter of *Banking Policy* is concerned with long lacking or, more precisely, with the relation between short and long lacking. The mechanism through which long lacking is provided to support the formation of fixed capital is different from that relative to short lacking and circulating capital. In an economy experiencing a process of steady growth, 'the new supplies of Long Lacking are provided, as the outstanding supply has already been provided, by Investors' (Robertson, 1926[1949], p. 85).[39] In such a context, the banking system does not play a crucial role.[40] It might seem that this same conclusion can be drawn also when considering an economy out of its steady-growth path and subject to cyclical fluctuations; but this is not the case.

First, a discontinuous increase in the demand for capital goods requires a reduction in hoarding and, hence, a rise in the price level.[41] In other words, the process turns to be essentially the same as that considered for short lacking. Secondly, it is likely that the demand for and supply of long lacking do not proceed at the same pace. Instead, it is probable that, during a boom, the demand exceeds the supply and the banking system has to intervene to fill the gap. Banks can provide long lacking in exactly the same way as they provide short lacking, that is to say 'by extorting it from the general public through the multiplication of currency' (Robertson, 1926[1949], p. 89) with a consequent price rise.[42] Robertson also deals with the problem of the complementarity between short and long lacking and the need for banks to

---

[38]   The final section of the chapter (Robertson, 1926[1949], pp. 82–83) is concerned with the analysis of the behaviour of stocks over the cycle. For Robertson, as for Wicksell, stocks decrease during a boom and increase in a depression, but he points out that the relevant variable to take into account is the ratio of stocks to short lacking rather than the absolute amount of stocks.

[39]   The investors are: i) entrepreneurs who reinvest their profits; ii) managers of corporations who reinvest the company's profit; iii) the public who buy securities issued by companies (Robertson, 1926[1949], pp. 85–86).

[40]   'It is true that the purchase of instruments, in which the act of Long Lacking consists, is conducted with bank-money, and requires on the part of each several investor a more or less prolonged period of Hoarding followed by a discontinuous act of Dis-hoarding; but in a "steady" society such individual rhythms would be merged in a general move of advance. Long Lacking would not, like Short Lacking, be provided in appearance by the Banks and in reality by the consuming community, but would both be, and be seen, the outcome of voluntary decisions on the part of individuals or corporations' (Robertson, 1926[1949], p. 86).

[41]   The prices to rise first are those of capital goods, then followed by the other prices (Robertson, 1926[1949], p. 87).

[42]   The situation can be even more complicated if there arises a substitution of hoarding for investment (Robertson, 1926[1949], p. 89).

ensure a certain balance between them. The expansion of fixed capital implies an expansion of circulating capital as well. The short lacking for circulating capital is provided through banks and a price rise. The pace of the expansion of fixed capital is set by investors and, therefore, banks must be able to ensure that the corresponding adequate amount of short lacking is created (Robertson, 1926[1949], p. 92).

Thus, when considering trade cycles and discontinuous processes of change, banks inevitably play a decisive role, which in turn implies that

> the crisis may occur at a moment dictated by the general state of strain upon the banking-system rather than by the stage which has been reached in the true constructional cycle. It may, that is to say, occur *before* the moment at which the increasing cost of instruments, or the decline in their desirability caused by their increasing numbers, would, even if unexhausted supplies of Long Lacking were available, prescribe a revaluation of the net advantage of acquiring instruments and a consequent decline in the quantity of them demanded. (Robertson, 1926[1949], pp. 90–91)

As acknowledged by Robertson himself, his 1926 book was conceptually difficult and used an awkward terminology. It can then be helpful to expound again the key aspects of his analysis by extensively quoting from his 1928 article, which is a concise account of the book.

> First, (...) we (...) concentrated our attention on bank deposits. Secondly, we decided that the magnitude of these bank deposits lies mainly within the discretion of the banking system, though it is not certain that in all conceivable circumstances the system will find it easy to create as much of them as it might have reason for desiring to create. Thirdly, the real value of these bank deposits, which must balance the real value of bank assets held against them, lies within the discretion of the public and not of the banking system; so that there is a broad apparent correspondence at any time between the amount of saving which the public has been willing to do in monetary form and the power of the banks to assist industry and trade. But there are two things which make this correspondence more apparent than real: the first is the power of the banks to extract forced saving from the public over a period of time by the creation of new money (...). The second is the possibility that the banks, by failing to create *sufficient* new money, will permit individuals to increase the real value of their bank balances without transforming this new saving into new real industrial assets (Robertson, 1928[1966], p. 33)[43]

When analysing market economies, banks and credit relations must be taken into consideration not simply for realism, but because it is necessary to take

---

[43] On the real value of bank deposits, i.e. money, see also Robertson (1928[1966], p. 26). The value of money, i.e., the general price level, is determined by the public's decisions about spending and hoarding in response to what banks decide about the amount of loans they make, i.e. the amount of money they create.

account of the inescapable truth that production takes time, so that permanent relations of credit and debt must be established in the economy. With the introduction of the banking system into the analytical framework, a disturbing factor enters the picture. It is likely that the operation of the banking system brings with it a certain degree of instability, in the sense that it can produce undue amplifications of the processes of change. Change, however, remains a crucial feature of the working of the economy. The stability of output as well as prices is not necessarily always a sound policy objective. Changes can be rational and beneficial. Policy, therefore, should not be always aimed at ensuring stability but rather aimed at limiting as much as possible those undue amplifications.[44]

3.8   THE CENTRALITY OF CREDIT IN THE PROCESS OF CHANGE

Both Schumpeter and Robertson paid great attention to the economic process of change and growth, intrinsically characterized by its proceeding along a cyclical path. For both, but especially for Schumpeter, technological innovations are a prime driver of such a process. In their analyses, credit and banks play a key role and there are several similarities and points of contact between them. Banks create additional money *ex nihilo* through credit, and without bank loans, firms, which promote growth, could not obtain the necessary means to finance the required amounts of circulating and fixed capital. Banks, however, operate in such a way that they can upset the orderly working of the economy. However, despite their importance, banks are not the prime movers of change. The fundamental factors in the processes of growth and economic fluctuations are indisputably real. Both Schumpeter (e.g. 1954[2006], p.1087) and Robertson (e.g. 1913) were critical of the 'monetary' interpretation of trade cycles put forward, for example, by Hawtrey (1913, 1919) and Hahn (2015[1920]).

Robertson dealt extensively with banks' loans to finance short-term investment in circulating capital, and the associated fluctuations. Schumpeter gave priority to bank loans for longer-term investment in fixed capital, though recognizing that this requires also investment in circulating capital. Notwithstanding these differences, Robertson and Schumpeter share the attention to finance as instrumental to economic change. In Schumpeter the theme is intertwined

---

[44]   Robertson ends his book with some considerations on the best policies to face an industrial depression. He deals with three issues: i) capital development by public authorities; ii) the provision of consumer goods to unemployed workers by the government; iii) the firms' price policies.

with a keen interest in human capital and the institutional settings that are required for the banking industry to perform their role effectively in supporting economic change.

The interest in the relation between finance, trade cycles and growth almost disappeared from mainstream macroeconomics after the Keynesian paradigm came to dominance. Since the mid-1930s, the macroeconomic models of growth and trade cycles inspired by Keynesian ideas dealt almost exclusively with the real side of the economy (see, e.g., Harrod, 1936, 1939; Samuelson, 1939; Domar, 1946).[45] In the following years, the exclusive accent on the real side of economic processes prevailed both in the expanding literature on growth and in the later real business cycle models. Under the prevailing assumption of perfect capital markets, the interest for finance and change was not a priority. In Chapter 7, we consider some lines of research on finance and growth that failed to gain prominence in mainstream macroeconomics and ended up as specialized research niches in development economics. Why all this occurred is the question that we try to answer in the following chapters.

---

[45]   In his book on trade cycles, Harrod (1936, p. 110) recognizes that monetary factors (the interest rate and monetary policy) play a role in the explanation of economic fluctuations, but only 'a subordinate one'.

4. Banks, debt and deflation in the Great Depression

The monetary instability of the early 1920s and, most of all, the phenomena of depression and deflation following the 1929 Wall Street crash were naturally issues to which many paid attention. In this chapter, we look at the positions of two eminent economists of the time, Keynes and Fisher, with special attention to the connections between deflation and the financial structure of the economy that they explored.

Keynes devoted considerable attention to the risks of deflation and its effects on the financial system in relation to Britain's return to the Gold Standard in the 1920s and in relation to the 1929 crash. However, although he repeatedly dealt with these issues in articles and other publications, Keynes never really embodied his views on deflation in connection with financial structure and credit into his major theoretical works, *A Treatise on Money* (Keynes, 1930[1971]) and *The General Theory* (Keynes, 1936[1973]). An explanation of this peculiarity can perhaps be found in Keynes's conviction that the financial crisis that spread in the U.S. and Europe in the early 1930s, with all its ensuing effects, essentially was a very exceptional event, not very likely to occur often and regularly. Therefore, ignoring the problem of the combination of severe depression and deflation could be justified in the context of more general theoretical works.

There is, however, an aspect of Keynes's work that connects his theoretical work, in particular *The General Theory*, to his less academic contributions. In all cases, Keynes is firmly convinced that deflation is a wrong medicine to heal the economic diseases of the time. It produces large economic and social costs without ensuring that the economy is able to recover from the crisis. Deflation can be forced upon the economy mainly through wage cuts. Keynes's aversion to deflation therefore means his aversion to wage cuts, realized through increasing unemployment. This conviction remains strong throughout Keynes's intellectual life from the 1920s to *The General Theory*.

Fisher's ideas, already examined in Chapter 2, were very much affected by the events that characterized the U.S. slump and the recurring banking crises of the early 1930s. In fact, the early years of the Great Depression produced a significant break in the evolution of Fisher's economic theorizing and policy views. From the relative optimism of the period of the 'roaring twenties', he turned to an analysis of the effects of the crisis and the ensuing deflation that leaves much less room to optimism and the belief in the market economies to overcome crises quickly and painlessly without some form of 'exogenous' intervention. Differently from Keynes, Fisher tried to embody his observation of historical events into his theoretical contributions, namely in his book *Booms and Depressions* (Fisher, 1932) and the article 'The debt-deflation theory of great depressions' (Fisher, 1933).

4.1 KEYNES ON THE COSTS OF DEFLATION IN THE 1920s

The risks of monetary instability, especially deflation, had been discussed in the tradition of monetary thought on which Keynes was trained as an economist in Cambridge. Keynes dealt with the real effects of monetary instability since 1919, in *The Economic Consequences of the Peace* (Keynes, 1919[1971]). In the 1920s and 1930s, he returned again and again to the destabilizing effects of severe monetary instability. The depressive effects of deflation were emphasized in the *Tract on Monetary Reform* (Keynes, 1923[1971]).

In the mid-1920s, the perverse effects of severe deflation came to the forefront. The subject received special emphasis again in 1931, at the peak of the European financial crisis. In all these writings, contracts denominated in money were conceived of as the daily language of economies operating within the institutional framework of free enterprise and freedom of contract. In Keynes's vision, monetary transactions are a central trait of contemporary market economies, monetary contracts being a typical feature of their decentralized organization of economic activity. People enter into contracts denominated in money, the flows of which take place in time; no central authority exists to coordinate simultaneous changes of nominal prices.

In a decentralized market economy, where bilateral transactions denominated in money take place at different moments of time, inflation and deflation are not symmetric in terms of how they affect relative prices. Inflation or deflation affect private persons or social groups differently according to their opportunities to change their money contracts in response to price changes, or to their ability to perceive how the contracts they have signed will be affected by the ongoing changes in the value of money. Uncertainty and misconceptions about relative prices when nominal values change are the result of an economic organization in which all economic activities take place through a set of uncoordinated, sequential transactions in money units, on the underlying assumption of a fundamentally stable standard of value.[1]

It might seem that banks and the financial system should obviously appear in this picture, but banks and other credit institutions have a comparatively minor role in Keynes's diagnosis of depression, with the major exception of a few writings in 1931. Keynes mainly focuses on the policy of the central bank. The assumption that the central bank is able to regulate the money supply, fully controlling the extent of bank credit to the economy is a cornerstone in the policy message that Keynes puts forward in *A Tract on Monetary Reform*. In later writings during the 1920s until *The General Theory*, notwithstanding the changing theoretical framework, Keynes mainly will follow the same line.

In a long excerpt from *A Tract on Monetary Reform*,[2] Keynes argues that it is impossible to quickly change, in a coordinated and simultaneous way, all money values and money contracts in a market economy. As a consequence, inflation and deflation have asymmetric redistributive effects and upset the ex ante planning of inter-temporal balances. Keynes (1931[1972]c, p. 59) is perfectly aware of the neutrality of money under the ideal condition of the instantaneous adjustment of all monetary values to perfectly transparent changes in the value of the established standard, but he denies that such perfectly simultaneous adjustment can take place in societies where monetary transactions are not centrally coordinated and take place in time.

In 1923, in analysing the real effects of deflation, Keynes explains a slackening aggregate supply by giving pride of place to the expectations of falling prices rather than to the augmented burden of debt, increasing financial fragility, or credit crunches.[3] Keynes emphasizes the direct effects of deflation on aggregate real output. Deflation discourages production by reducing the value of inventories in the hands of producers, while the expected, future returns become uncertain or negative.

Expected deflation is more relevant than actual deflation. The fear of deflation negatively influences the expectations of future profits.

> Now it follows from this, not merely that the *actual occurrence* of price changes profits some classes and injures others (which has been the theme of the first section of this chapter), but that a *general fear* of falling prices may inhibit the productive process altogether. For if prices are expected to fall, not enough risk-takers can be

---

[1]   Keynes does not need to place fictional agents in imaginary islands to account for possible misconceptions of relative prices: the very technology of bilateral payments in a free market economy implies radical uncertainty about real values, when society is exposed to changes in the value of the monetary standard.

[2]   Reprinted in 1931 in *Essays in Persuasion* with the title 'Social Consequences of Changes in the Value of Money'.

[3]   The augmented burden of debt was then only mentioned, but it was dealt with in more detail in later writings (Keynes, 1931[1972]b, p. 213).

found who are willing to carry a speculative 'bull' position, and this means that entrepreneurs will be reluctant to embark on lengthy productive processes involving a money outlay long in advance of money recoupment, – whence unemployment. The *fact* of falling prices injures entrepreneurs; consequently the *fear* of falling prices causes them to protect themselves by curtailing their operations; yet it is upon the aggregate of their individual estimations of the risk, and their willingness to run the risk, that the activity of production and of employment mainly depends. (Keynes, 1931[1972]c, pp. 73–74)

No ex ante adjustment to the anticipated or current changes in the value of money can occur in the market because the flows of monetary payments take place in time. In a regime based on monetary contracts and lengthy processes of production, the business world is forced 'to carry a big speculative position; and if it is reluctant to carry this position, the productive process must be slackened' (Keynes, 1931[1972]c, p. 73). Finance may reduce the risk of the entrepreneurs' speculative positions when facing deflation, but it cannot cover it completely.

In the mid-1920s, in the debate on the return of Great Britain to the Gold Standard at the pre-war parity, Keynes took a strong stance against the social cost of deflation. In 1925 he wrote the polemical essay *The Economic Consequences of Mr Churchill* to stigmatize the depressive impact of the return to the old parity because of its contractionary effects on British exports and, via exports, on real output.[4] In the meantime, the United States had emerged as a major manufacturing country in the world economy, and Keynes reckoned that the old parity, at post-war prices, was too high to protect the British competitiveness. Deflation, then, would be deliberately engineered by the Treasury and the Bank of England to compensate for the excessive revaluation of the pound and keep the real exchange rate at a value that would not be disastrous for the British balance of payments.

According to Keynes, this policy required to deliberately subject the economy to a negative monetary shock. To maintain the new parity, the Bank of England was forced to impose a higher cost of credit and a credit crunch, which determined a recession. The only way to force deflation on the economy was to induce a recession and increase unemployment to force down monetary wages, so that the consequences of the adjustment were to be mainly felt by wage earners.[5] Since no economic or political 'machinery' existed to engineer the fair, simultaneous change of all nominal incomes, there would occur a war

---

[4] The return to the old parity was finally deliberated in 1925, under Winston Churchill as prime minister.

[5] With the consequence of strikes and lock-outs, unequal effects on the stronger and weaker groups, economic and social waste.

among social groups, whose winners were uncertain, the weaker groups being surely condemned to be the losers (Keynes, 1931[1972]b, pp. 211–212).

In the mid-1920s, the problem of the social costs of deflation was central in Keynes's criticism of the contention that the Gold Standard was a self-adjusting monetary system and the ultimate foundation of international stability. However, although he rejected managed deflation on the grounds of the 'economic and social waste' it brought about, Keynes did not question the effectiveness of the credit crunch that the Bank of England could produce, 'soundly' following the rules of the Gold Standard. The 'visible hand' of the Bank of England behind the credit restriction, was 'an incredibly powerful instrument, and even a little of it goes a long way' (Keynes, 1931[1972]b, p. 220).

4.2   DERANGING THE FINANCIAL STRUCTURE: KEYNES ON THE 1931 GLOBAL CRISIS

At the beginning of the 1930s, deflation became a dramatic evidence of the ongoing economic events in the world economy. In the U.S., there had been the precipitous fall of stock prices from October 1929, coupled with the persistent fall of property prices and agricultural prices. In the Summer of 1931 in Europe, a dramatic financial crisis followed the collapse of the Credit-Anstaldt in Austria.[6] Later in 1931, the crisis extended to financial institutions in Germany; in September 1931 Great Britain was forced to abandon the Gold Standard.[7] In the U.S., after the local banks' difficulties, in December 1930 a major bank, the Bank of United States, had to shut, after a run on deposits and the refusal by the Clearing Bank of New York to help (Eichengreen, 2015, p. 131).

Between 1931 and 1933, the US economy was ravaged by a sequence of runs and banks' bankruptcies that brought the payments system near to collapse, until in March 1933 F. D. Roosevelt declared a Bank Holiday to stop the run from deposits.[8] Banks were closed; withdrawals and almost all banking activities were suspended for a few days (from the 6th of March to the 10th of March 1933).[9] An emergency legislation was hurriedly passed by the

---

[6]   Credit-Anstaldt suspended payments in May 1931, and its bankruptcy had devastating effects on Germany and central European countries. There was a run to withdraw funds from banks in Hungary, Czechoslovakia, Romania, Poland, and Germany.

[7]   See Bernanke (1983, pp. 274–275) and Eichengreen (2015, p. 152).

[8]   The Bank Holiday was declared soon after the president elected had taken his oath; it was an emergency measure in a climate of national disaster.

[9]   For the reconstruction of evolution of the events, see Eichengreen (2015, Chapters 10 and 15 (especially pp. 164-ff. and 228-ff.). See also Rauchway (2015), especially Chapters 2 to 6.

Congress, and Roosevelt devoted his first fireside chat to a memorable speech to restore confidence in the banking system.[10]

In *An Economic Analysis of Unemployment*, a series of three lectures given in June 1931 in the U.S., Keynes extensively addresses the risks of deflation and denies that falling prices and wages might help to return to prosperity (Keynes, 1931[1973]).[11] Again, he takes a strongly polemical stance against the economists in favour of deflation. He points to the risks of increasing economic and social instability in deflationary conditions and takes a firm position against policies predicating the opportunity of deflating wages and prices as a way to recovery (Keynes, 1931[1973], p. 349).[12]

In his lectures, Keynes also denounces the iniquity of increasing the 'burden of monetary indebtedness' for debtors and the related risk of a collapse of the banking system. He points out the systemic risk of bankruptcies: liquidation is but a 'polite phrase for general bankruptcy' (Keynes, 1931[1973], p. 349). Moreover, he underlines the ineffectiveness of deflation to help profits recover in manufacturing industries; profits being the clue to the recovery of investment that in turn is the clue to the revival of growth (Keynes, 1931[1973], pp. 360–361). Keynes advances a specific argument to explain the possible paralysis of the credit market during a slump. The crisis of confidence undermines the trust between lenders and borrowers. The lender 'must have sufficient confidence in the credit and solvency of the debtor', otherwise an additional margin ('a crushing addition') would be added to the pure interest rate to protect the loans from the risk of insolvency. The debtor, to be ready to borrow at this higher interest rate should have sufficient confidence that the expected sales and returns will cover the heavier interest costs. It is then possible that the economy enters a vicious circle, with the paralysis of the credit market and the financing of investment (Keynes, 1931[1973], p. 363).

As we shall see in the next section, Keynes's interpretation of the worldwide slump in June 1931 has more than one point of contact with Fisher's reading of the Great Depression. Keynes sees the positive effects of the investment boom

---

[10]   See, e.g., Hiltzik (2011) and Eichengreen (2015, pp. 229-ff.).

[11]   Dimand points out Keynes's considerations on debt deflation in his lectures and in the article of which more below (Dimand, 2005, pp. 190–191). He suggests that these 1931 writings of Keynes might have influenced the positions taken later on by Minsky (1975).

[12]   Keynes is against the 'austere and puritanical souls' making appeal to 'what they politely call a "prolonged liquidation" to put us right'. Sprague, a professor at Harvard and advisor to the Bank of England and the Federal Reserve, is Keynes's straw man (Keynes, 1931[1973], p. 361). Sprague had argued that the U.S. economy should reach a new equilibrium at lower wages and prices (Meltzer, 2010, pp. 277–278). Meltzer underlines that the idea that, after the inflationary boom of the late 1920s, deflation was the natural way to re-establish the economy was an authoritative, shared opinion at central banks.

of the second half of the 1920s[13] and the parallel huge expansion of debts. Also for Fisher the U.S. boom of the late 1920s originates in the expansion of real opportunities to invest, which is accompanied by over-indebtedness. Fisher, however, concentrates on the subsequent speculative boom that turned into a severe financial crisis, due to the spiralling of debt and deflation. Keynes does not subscribe to Fisher's focus on booms and busts to explain the severity of the slump. He attributes the fall of investment that originated the slump to a combination of causes, including the mismanagement of monetary policy by the Federal Reserve that forced up interest rates to check the boom, just when investment was turning unprofitable at high interest rates, even though he believed that it would have anyhow gone down because 'borrowers could not really hope to earn on new investment the rates which they had been paying' (Keynes, 1931[1973], p. 350). Rather than view mistaken judgements due to speculative manias, Keynes seems to look at the real exhaustion of high return opportunities.[14]

In sketching the sequential analysis of the depression, Keynes hints at the spiralling down of profits, prices and investment (Keynes, 1931[1973], p. 351). He argues that aggregate supply would spiral down to stop at a lower floor: 'a sufficiently low level of output which represents a kind of spurious equilibrium' (Keynes, 1931[1973], p. 356). In terms of policies for the recovery, Keynes advocates for construction works sponsored by state agencies and 'a drastic fall in the long term rate of interest' to support investment.[15]

Keynes's 1931 work shows his perceptive attention to the complexity of the interactions between the financial structure and the macro-economy. But the complexity of this picture is somewhat lost when Keynes addresses the remedies for the recovery. In his final remarks, talking about the measures to force down the long-term interest rate that might brake investment, Keynes mentions the responsibility of the banking system, but he essentially means the central bank and its policies.[16] Indeed, Keynes recommends central bank

---

[13]   He goes as far as to envisage that if investment and technological change proceed at the same pace for a few more quinquennia, the world economy could come near 'the economic Eldorado, where all our reasonable economic needs would be satisfied' (Keynes, 1931[1973], pp. 347–348).

[14]   The speculative mood is brought into the picture by reminding that the Stock Exchange speculation on the domestic market drew funds of American investors back home and away from investment in foreign bonds, leaving highly indebted foreign borrowers deprived of the previous abundant financing.

[15]   He, however, is well aware of the difficulties to restore entrepreneurs' confidence or to timely and efficiently start public works (Keynes, 1931[1973], p. 359).

[16]   On the central question 'How is the banking system to affect the long term rate of interest?', Keynes observes: 'The practical means by which investment can be increased is, or ought to be, the bankers' business, and pre-eminently the business of the central banker' (Keynes, 1931[1973], pp. 359 and 363).

open-market operations to curb the long rate and bring the short rate near to zero (the 'vanishing point') (Keynes, 1931[1973], p. 366).

Meanwhile, both in the U.S. and in Europe, in the summer of 1931 the financial crisis reached a peak that was to deeply influence the later evolution of the depression. During summer 1931, in the short article 'The Consequences to the Banks of the Collapse of Money Values',[17] Keynes points out the risk that deflation could undermine the stability of banks in even more dramatic tones than those used a couple of months before. Keynes comments on the international financial crisis from the perspective of the disruptive effects that the severe deflation of patrimonial prices was having on banks' balance sheets. He sees banks as intermediaries between savers and final borrowers; but he also underlines the service that banks supply by interposing their guarantee between depositors and borrowers. In their double role of intermediaries and security providers, banks ask borrowers a security margin on the value of the collateral offered by the borrower.[18]

Until the deflation of commodities and property prices is well below such a margin, banks are not affected. The value of the collateral protects their loans from the risk of insolvency, and their balance sheets remain solid. But this is no longer true in a severe deflation, like that experienced at the peak of the international financial crisis, which simultaneously hit raw materials and foodstuff commodities and, hence, the value of the inventories financed by bank credit; the prices of shares and bonds purchased on short-term bank credit or held by banks; the prices of properties bought on mortgages.[19]

However, Keynes remains convinced that the ruinous 1930–1931 deflation was a rare event.[20] It had determined an unfair, painful redistribution of income and wealth, but possibly with no permanent consequences on future growth (Keynes, 1931[1972]a, p. 157). For Keynes, the frail pyramid of debts that had been built up against any sound rule of prudent management by bankers is at the origin of the financial disaster. Bankers are stigmatized for their lack of rationality, being slaves to myopic calculations and conventional thinking

---

[17]   The article, originally written for the magazine *Vanity Fair* in August 1931, was published in a later, revised version. It was finally reprinted in *Essays in Persuasion* (Keynes, 1931[1972]a).

[18]   In conventional practice, the margin was between 20 and 30% on the more marketable assets; according to Keynes, a margin up to 50% of collateral was considered to be very prudent practice.

[19]   Keynes observes that the ruinous impact of such a severe deflation on the banking system went well beyond what was usually recognized as the increased burden of debt on debtors, that is the effect of shifting wealth from debtor to creditor (Keynes, 1931[1972]a, p. 156).

[20]   'Fortunately, this is a very rare, indeed a unique event. For it had never occurred in the modern history of the world prior to the year 1931' (Keynes, 1931[1972]a, p. 153). It was a 'black swan', an event at the extreme tail of the probability distribution, but with disastrous consequences if it happens.

even when on the verge of disaster.[21] There had been in the banking system a collective failure of rationality, which makes banks 'the weakest element in the whole situation' (Keynes, 1931[1972]a, p. 157). Thus, for Keynes, in conditions of exceptional deflation, the entire financial system could collapse, though temporarily. He, however, does not proceed to explore the channels through which the paralysis or the crash of the credit system might affect aggregate demand and output.

The alarm for the 'widespread insolvencies and defaults and the collapse of a large part of the financial structure' in the 1931 articles almost disappears in Keynes's later works and especially in *The General Theory*.[22] More in general, for reasons that we try to explain in the next chapter, credit and the banking system are given a minor, if any, role to play. An important role, instead, is given to the vagaries of Stock Exchange prices and the behaviour of professional speculators.

However, in continuity with his diagnosis of the mid-1920s and 1931, in *The General Theory* Keynes remains firmly convinced of the ineffectiveness of wage and price deflation as a self-adjusting mechanism to bring back recovery and full employment (Keynes, 1936[1973], p. 267). In Chapter 19, applying his new theoretical scaffolding, Keynes argues in terms of the possible effects of deflation on the propensities to spend and the effects on aggregate demand through consumption and investment. He concludes that 'a moderate reduction in money wages may prove inadequate, whilst an immoderate reduction might shatter confidence if it were practicable' (Keynes, 1936[1973], p. 267). In this chapter, only a couple of passages evoke the financial themes dealt with in 1931, when the paralysis and collapse, though temporary, of the financial system were at stake, not just the propensities to expenditure of the debtors or creditors.

> On the other hand, the depressing influence on entrepreneurs of their greater burden of debt, may partially offset any cheerful reactions from the reduction of wages. Indeed, if the fall of wages and prices goes far, the embarrassment of those entrepreneurs who are heavily indebted may soon reach the point of insolvency, -with severely adverse effects on investment. Moreover the effect of the lower price-level on the real burden of the National Debt and hence on taxation is likely to prove very adverse to business confidence. (Keynes, 1936[1973], p. 264)

---

21 'The present signs suggest that the bankers of the world are bent on suicide. At every stage they have been unwilling to adopt a sufficiently drastic remedy. And by now matters have been allowed to go so far that it has become extraordinarily difficult to find any way out' (Keynes, 1931[1972]a, p.157–158).

22 In particular in *The General Theory*, business cycles occupy a minor space. The explanation of the persistence of involuntary unemployment essentially relies on the chronically low level of private investment that cannot support aggregate demand at its full-employment level.

The destabilizing effect of wage deflation on social relations is expounded along a line similar to that followed in the 1920s: there is no central authority to engineer a simultaneous change; there are no criteria of fairness, but violation of social justice and 'wasteful and disastrous struggles' (Keynes, 1936[1973], p. 267). Keynes concludes on the recommendation to anchor the price level to stable money wages, a kind of new anchor to the monetary standard in a closed economy, to avoid the uncertainty and possible disruptions brought about by violently unstable prices: '...a great instability of prices, so violent perhaps as to make business calculation futile in an economic society functioning after the manner of that in which we live' (Keynes, 1936[1973], p. 269).

The apocalyptic tones, though firmly rooted in the background of Keynes's arguing, do not enter the analytic skeleton of Chapter 19, which relates to the controversy on the wealth effect on aggregate demand in post-war macroeconomics; a discussion that was quite blind to the importance of inside finance and the banking system.

4.3 THE OUT-OF-EQUILIBRIUM SPIRALLING OF DEBT AND DEFLATION

After the short recession of 1922–1923, throughout the 'roaring twenties' the U.S. economy had experienced high rates of growth, with technological change and productivity gains, and a stock exchange boom. The expansionary phase, after an earlier slowdown, abruptly ended with the the fall of Wall Street and the forthcoming depression, neither of which Fisher had anticipated. On the contrary, soon before the collapse of stock prices in October 1929, he had forecast the stabilization of assets' prices at the high plateau they had reached. He had supported the diffusion of investment in stocks by U.S. households as a measure to protect real savings from financial mistakes due to money illusion, which people not properly trained in economics could easily make.[23]

In December 1929, Fisher sent to print the pamphlet *The Stock Market Crash – and After* (Fisher, 1930a) to explain the sound grounds on which he had formulated his mistaken forecasts. In a short paper published in March 1930, anticipating his interpretation of the stock market crash in 1929, he argued that the bull market had a substantial justification in the investment opportunities open by the mass production of inventions based on science, and the resulting increase in productivity due to labour saving innovations (Fisher, 1930b, pp. 94–95). If the healthy fundamentals justified a bull market,

---

[23] Fisher thought that investing in equities was safer than investing in bonds (Goetzmann, 2016, pp. 471–472). He had himself invested a large part of his wealth in shares (Pavanelli, 2004, p. 290).

speculation was stimulated by the swelling of brokers' loans and a 'great credit structure beyond anything that had previously been erected' (Fisher, 1930b, p. 94). Financial innovations, such as the tendency to buy assets on borrowed money, the flight from bonds to stocks and the diffusion of investment trusts, had nurtured the building up of a shaky credit pyramid. The speculative wave that had swelled the 'justified bull market' was inflated by the 'unjustified going into debt' (Fisher, 1930b, p. 96). Thus, in this early Fisher's interpretation, the crash was due to the 'unsound financing of sound prospects' (Fisher, 1930b, p. 96).

Fisher remained mildly optimistic till 1931, but from then on he became increasingly involved in the attempt to explain the recession, and why the financial crisis had precipitated. In his writings of 1932 and 1933, he put forward a general interpretation of major depressions in history by looking at the dynamic spiralling of debts and deflation.[24] Fisher dealt with deflation, banks' prudential strategies, the asymmetric burden of debt, the spreading risk of insolvencies, the instability of the financial system. The most dramatic phases of the Great Depression between 1929 and 1933 were decisive to drive Fisher towards an interpretation of financial crises and persisting depressions more radical than the milder view of transition periods presented in *The Purchasing Power of Money* ten years earlier (Fisher, 1922).[25]

In 1932, Fisher fully developed his new ideas in the book *Booms and Depressions* (Fisher, 1932), which he summarized a year later in the article 'The Debt-Deflation Theory of Great Depressions' (Fisher, 1933). In his explanation of the severity and long duration of the depression, Fisher regards monetary instability as strictly connected with firms' indebtedness and unbalanced private budgets. His analytical focus is on disequilibrium trajectories.[26] He distinguishes 'economic statics', or the study of 'imaginary ideal equilibrium' with the related stability conditions, from 'economic dynamics', conceived as the study of disequilibrium processes. The study of economic dynamics can be conducted either from a historical perspective by focusing on specific historical cases or from a theoretical perspective by focusing on 'tendencies', that is to say, abstract disequilibrium phenomena occurring and combining among themselves in each specific evolution of historical events. 'Economic history' and 'economic science' are thus complementary in the study of dynamics.

---

[24]   Fisher had presented his ideas in lectures at Yale in 1931 and then in a presentation in January 1932 (Fisher, 1933, p. 350, n. 4).

[25]   Following the dynamics of events, Fisher's theory and policy proposals evolved as well. Pavanelli provides a detailed reconstruction of the evolution of Fisher's views of business cycles and stabilization policies (Pavanelli, 1997, 1999, 2004).

[26]   The so called cycle theory is merely one part of the study of economic disequilibria (Fisher, 1933, p. 337).

In the 1933 article Fisher deals with disequilibrium processes as the normal condition of market economies.[27] Attention is paid to sequences of events in time. However, the crucial issue is the correct identification of the conditions that make severe disequilibria occur without adjustment processes taking place in reaction, so that there is no return to the previous equilibrium and they become persistent.

> There may be equilibrium which, though stable, is so delicately poised that, after departure from it beyond certain limits, instability ensues, just as, at first, a stick may bend under strain, ready all the time to bend back, until a certain point is reached, when it breaks. This simile probably applies when a debtor gets 'broke', or when the breaking of many debtors constitutes a 'crash,' after which there is no coming back to the original equilibrium. (Fisher, 1933, p. 339) [28]

Long and severe depressions arise from the firms' and other subjects' high leverage during a speculative boom. Their risky exposure becomes more and more burdensome, when the deflationary process sets in. The two diseases of 'over-indebtedness' and deflation 'act and react on each other' (Fisher, 1933, p. 344). The 'starters' are the factors accounting for the original building-up of over indebtedness.[29] Moreover, financial fragility is also related to the short maturity of the outstanding debts (Fisher, 1933, p. 345).

While deeply sceptical about the historical existence of regular cycles, Fisher still puts the 'boom-depression' sequence at the core of historical fluctuations, each of which has a specific evolution, depending on the 'starters', the 'tendencies' at work and how policies interact (Fisher, 1933, p. 338).[30]

> While any deviation from equilibrium of any economic variable theoretically may, and doubtless in practice does, set up some sort of oscillations, the important question is: Which of them have been sufficiently great disturbers to afford any substantial explanation of the great booms and depressions of history? (...) in the great booms and depressions, each of the above-named factors has played a

---

[27] 'Theoretically there may be – in fact, at most times there must be over-or under-production, over- or under-consumption, over- or under-spending, over- or under-saving, over- or under-investment, and over or under everything else. It is as absurd to assume that, for any long period of time, the variables in the economic organization, or any part of them, will "stay put," in perfect equilibrium, as to assume that the Atlantic Ocean can ever be without a wave' (Fisher, 1933, p. 339).

[28] Dimand (2005) extensively examines these passages, suggesting that Fisher anticipated the idea of 'a corridor of stability' later advanced by Leijonhufvud (1973).

[29] Among which, in the late 1920s, there was the combination of lucrative investment opportunities and easy money (Fisher, 1933, p. 348).

[30] As noted in Chapter 1, the roots of this vision of booms and busts are in the tradition of the credit cycle or 'overtrading' literature of the 19th century. In the early 1930s, however, Fisher was much more radical in underlying the destabilizing effects of deflation than Mill or Marshall. Fisher called the credit cycle 'the Debt Cycle (or cycle tendency)'. See Fisher (1932, p. 41).

subordinate role as compared with two dominant factors, namely *over-indebtedness* to start with and *deflation* following soon after; also that where any of the other factors do become conspicuous, they are often merely effects or symptoms of these two. In short, the big bad actors are debt disturbances and price level disturbances. (Fisher, 1933, pp. 340–341, emphasis in the original)

High debt and severe deflation make a dangerous mix, which can give rise to a destabilizing spiral. Firms cut fixed investment spending, save on inventories and try to forcefully liquidate assets to abate their debt burden. Such measures are apparently coherent with sound managerial practice as they aim to improve the firms' financial viability; but, when taken simultaneously by many firms, their outcome is a curtailment of monetary demand, with the consequence of a further decline of prices. Deflation, by reducing the value of assets and the flow of monetary sales, aggravates the burden of past debt, whose monetary value is fixed. Thus, firms remain highly leveraged, notwithstanding the efforts to repay their debt and improve their financial resiliency.

According to Fisher, the destabilizing spiral of high leverage and price deflation, which spreads the systemic risk of insolvency through the economy, is the dynamic process that explains why major recessions become so severe and persistent. There is no self-adjusting process at work, until past debts have been cancelled out after a long and painful process of price deflation, output losses and bankruptcies. If deflation proceeds at a quick pace, the burden of debts cannot be curbed, notwithstanding the firms' joint efforts to curtail expenditure and desperately liquidate assets to repay loans. Deflation, far from being stabilizing, is severely destabilizing, and the 'adjustment' process pushes the economy into a prolonged depression. Fluctuations of output and employment are also brought into the picture: 'Idle men and idle machines spell lessened production and lessened real income, the central factor in all economic science. Incidentally this under-production occurs at the very time that there is the illusion of over-production' (Fisher, 1933, p. 345).

In his book, as in previous works, Fisher assumes that many economic agents, including businessmen and bankers and even some economists, are prone to money illusion (Fisher, 1932, p. 24). Even able businessmen and bankers are driven to liquidate their debts or call back their loans, being forced by competition to do what other people in the market are doing. Debtors or creditors, be they firms or banks, are deeply aware that the riskiness of their own position depends on the economy-wide risk of insolvency and they adapt their expectations and reactions to the perceived expectations and reactions of other agents in the economy.

The pessimism of highly leveraged debtors is contagious and affects also economic agents not immediately at risk of insolvency, pushing them to rush for liquidity. When trust is falling, pessimism affects also those not directly in trouble. They anticipate the spreading risks of the ongoing deflation and its effect on their own balance sheets (Fisher, 1932, p. 26).

4.4 OVER-INDEBTEDNESS, FINANCIAL INTERMEDIARIES AND BANKS IN THE DEFLATIONARY SPIRAL

In Fisher's narration, financial institutions and banks are outstanding characters from several viewpoints: the elasticity of credit and bank money as a component of the money supply; the financial innovations, introduced and aggressively marketed by banks and other institutions, which promote improvident indebtedness; the mistaken regulations of financial markets; the asymmetric information of lenders and borrowers; the imitative expectations spreading in the market.

Fisher's explanation of the deflationary spiral largely depends on the elasticity of bank money, since repaying banks' loans means the destruction of bank money and thus a contractionary pressure.[31] The general rush to liquidity means a drastic decrease in the velocity of circulation of money. The cumulative destruction of bank money occurs through the calling back of loans. Whereas the previous cumulative expansion during the boom had resulted from expanding loans, which were not 100 per cent covered by bank reserves. In the crisis, banks are forced by competition to call back their loans and rush to liquidity: 'When a bank calls a loan, it helps deflate the credit currency; but other banks, equally scared, would deflate it anyhow; and if one bank stayed out, its debtors would go insolvent before they could be dunned. In a word, the banks, too, are forced into cut-throat competition for cash or "liquidity"' (Fisher, 1932, p. 26).

At the core of Fisher's analysis of deflationary processes there is the denial of symmetric wealth effects on expenditure, which might cancel out in the aggregate. He explicitly denies that the gains of creditors can compensate the losses of debtors. Borrowers and debtors are conceived as chained to each other in the rush to distress selling and the search for liquidity. When firms or banks begin to go bankrupt, there are domino effects in the economy that act both through direct links and through imitative expectations. These domino effects are especially relevant for banks, since banking activity depends on trust. The perceived risk of banks turning illiquid further reduces the velocity

---

[31] '...disturbances of deposit currency disturb the price level far more than do the very considerable disturbances of the gold supply' (Fisher, 1932, p. 22).

of circulation of bank money; bank runs follow and precipitate the conditions of insolvency in the banking industry with further bankruptcies.[32]

In Part II of his book, Fisher develops a thorough analysis of the Great Depression in the light of the theoretical framework expounded in Part I. It is a complex and articulate interpretation of the depression which takes into account also international factors (Pavanelli, 2004, p. 992). We only focus on the passages where Fisher deals with the behaviour of the banking system in relation to the dramatic U.S. financial crisis.[33]

Chapter 7 is entirely devoted to the over-indebtedness of the U.S. economy that, for Fisher, was a disease that, between 1921 and 1929, progressively hit both the financial markets and the real economy with disastrous effects. In the domestic markets, the building-up of farmers' debts had created the conditions for the later increased foreclosures of agricultural firms, while the debts of insurance companies as well as the debts incurred by public bodies such as municipalities and states had increased.[34] These were 'ominous signs' (Fisher, 1932, p. 74), which he himself had not clearly perceived. Fisher also laments the excessive expansion of various types of American loans abroad to private firms and local municipalities or to cover the German reparation payments or other intergovernmental debts left as a heritage of the war. In his concluding evaluation, the extension of domestic debts and foreign loans had been such as to menace the stability of the gold base, on which the U.S. monetary system rested (Fisher, 1932, p. 84).

In Fisher's narration considerable space is given to the banks' and other financial institutions' strategic behaviour in promoting financial innovation, with marketing strategies to aggressively sell financial products in search for profits, and unprincipled behaviour in dealing with potential customers. Fisher analyses, in particular, the U.S. boom of the second half of the 1920s, with special attention to the years 1926 to 1929. He observes that larger corporations reduced their debts by placing substantial amounts of new issues of their shares in the market, thus reducing their leverage (Fisher, 1932, p. 72). Debts were transferred from firms to private investors in a remarkable phenomenon of collective change of the composition of private portfolios. People transferred wealth from bonds to shares. The stocks placed in the market were often subscribed by financing the purchase with short-term debts. This had a positive

---

[32] Fisher briefly lists the sequence of events, though admitting more intricate interactions: Hoarding. Runs on Banks. Banks Curtailing Loans for Self-Protection. Banks Selling Investments. Bank Failures. Distrust Grows. More Hoarding. More Liquidation. More Distress Selling. Further Dollar Enlargement (Fisher, 1933, p. 343).

[33] Notice that the book was published in 1932, before the peak of bank runs that drove the banking system near to collapse early in 1933.

[34] Fisher elaborates a whole apparatus of graphics and tables to give evidence on the phenomena of increasing indebtedness in the U.S. economy.

effect on the firms' budgets in the early 1930s, after the Wall Street collapse, which however was more than offset by the fact that the burden of the debt was shifted from corporations to stockholders. Moreover, the debts incurred to buy shares, being short-term, were most dangerous ('largely margin accounts with brokers, whose loans were call loans') (Fisher, 1932, p. 72).

The innovation of investment trusts and their spreading in the market gave impulse to more risky behaviour. Investment bankers, through their bank affiliates or their high-pressure salesmen, actively encouraged their customers to over-indebtedness. During the stock exchange boom preceding the recession, a pyramidal castle of risky stocks of uncertain fundamental value was built, whose trading ultimately depended on complex and frail debt structures (Fisher, 1932, p. 73).

For Fisher, the diffusion of investment in bonds and stocks among American households was also a consequence of the familiarity with investing savings in bonds that even common people had acquired by buying government bonds to finance the war. This was a major financial innovation, originally promoted by the government, which later on spread thanks to the active strategies of major firms, banks and other financial intermediaries. But these new investors were not so trained or sophisticated as to be able to properly perceive and evaluate the risks of portfolios containing a high proportion of shares with an unstable fundamental value.[35]

Fisher, like Schumpeter, thinks that frauds are a systemic phenomenon that typically emerges in the last stage of a speculative boom (Fisher, 1932, p. 74).[36] Moreover, he underlines the perverse effect of the tax on capital gains. The tax had induced savers with a part of their portfolios invested in shares not to sell their stocks during the bull market, fearing that the heavy burden of the tax would have cut their assets' value when sold. These joint phenomena had sustained the stock exchange boom. When speaking of the perverse effects of excessive indebtedness, Fisher deals specifically with rising Stock Exchange prices and with the speculative bubble that was swelling in the financial markets. He conjectures that there had been no comparable inflation

---

[35]   This is a subject with which also Keynes will deal in Chapter 12 of *The General Theory*. Fisher quotes a letter received from a financial expert explaining how the reckless marketing of risky assets had gone on. The letter, denouncing the prevailing climate in financial markets before the 1929 panic, clearly pointed out the asymmetric information between financial promoters and savers, the imprudence and reckless behaviour of promoters, the forecasting mistakes committed by both expert professionals and common people, or the evidence of plain frauds.

[36]   In the 1933 article, Fisher (1933, p. 349) briefly deals with the 'psychology of going into debt for gain', identifying various stages, from the original search for long-term profits based on genuine investment opportunities to the later lure for immediate capital gains, to the mania for 'reckless promotions', or finally to 'downright fraud, imposing on a public which had grown credulous and gullible.'

in wholesale prices because of the simultaneous development of technical progress and increased productivity during the boom of the 1920s.

In the 1929–1932 depression, Fisher sees all the nine main factors at play, which in Part I of the book he had analysed and singled out as the 'tendencies', which may operate in single historical episodes. In his summary, he mentions the liquidation of brokers' debts; the growth of pessimism that reduces the velocity of circulation of money and brings a substantial reduction of bank deposits; the heavy fall of prices of industrial stocks and the declining commodity price level; the record number of commercial failures and bank suspensions, which he interprets as a loss of net worth; the negative net profits of both industrial and miscellaneous corporations; the fall of industrial production from October 1929 to January 1932 and the earlier and heavier fall of construction works; the various interest rates that rose with the boom and fell with the depression.

Once the collapse of Wall Street had started the vicious cycle of debt liquidation, deflation and bank collapses, the burden of debt became heavier with the effect of slowing down the recovery.

> . . . it matters little which factor in the vicious spiral (. . .) started first nor what factor, remote or near, started either of them. They could even start together. But once started, they were doomed to continue in a vicious spiral, each accelerating the other. What seems sure is that the crash of the stock market helped to force the rest of our debt structure into liquidation, and that it was the hopeless magnitude of the debt burden which made it so difficult for the economic organism to right itself. (. . .) It is this growth of *real* debt burden, despite huge efforts at liquidation, which, in my opinion, constitutes the master fact of the depression of 1929–32. (Fisher, 1932, pp. 92, 110)[37]

In the 1933 article, Fisher acknowledged the importance of the 'artificial respiration' that Roosevelt had implemented in March 1933 to stop the financial crisis, without which 'we would soon have seen general bankruptcies of the mortgage guarantee companies, savings banks, life insurance companies, railways, municipalities, and states'. The spiral debt-deflation could have stopped only after an almost universal bankruptcy, if left to what Fisher (1933, p. 346) ironically calls the 'natural' way out from a depression. But, later on in the 1930s, he became suspicious of the 'artificial respiration' and even of his own plans to stabilize the dollar. The 'mystery of banking', as Fisher had called it in 1922, appeared so intractable and so poorly managed that he finally

---

[37]   Fisher also underlines how the mismanagement of the regulation of the rediscount rate had real effects due to the divergence that arose between nominal and real interest rates, the nominal rates completely losing their signalling power to borrowers (Fisher, 1932, p. 106).

joined the group campaigning for the imposition of 100 per cent reserves to commercial banks.[38]

4.5 FINANCE, DEBT AND DEFLATION IN THE HISTORY OF THE GREAT DEPRESSION

The role of the banking crises in the evolution of the international recession of the 1930s is emphasized by the historical literature on the Great Depression. An ample historical literature addresses the role of deflation, domestic and international debt and the financial crises during the depression years, specifically in connection with the institutional frailties of banks and the financial system or with the unsettled issues of war debts (see, e.g., Kindleberger, 2000). Here, we cannot survey the historical controversies on monetary non-neutrality in the Great Depression but for a reminder of a few issues directly related to Keynes's and Fisher's contributions.

In 1983, Bernanke, then a professor at Stanford University, years later Chairman of the Federal Reserve, acknowledged excessive debt, the increasing debt burden and insolvencies in the early 1930s, with direct reference to Fisher's debt-deflation theory. Excessive indebtedness and insolvencies were pervasive in the housing markets and in the agricultural markets; they affected local governments too. Deflation of agricultural prices aggravated the American farmers' difficulties to repay their debts; insolvencies ruined both the farmers and the local banks, which had supplied mortgaged loans to them.[39] The small and medium size firms were more severely affected.

> The second major aspect of the financial crisis (one that is currently neglected by historians) was the pervasiveness of debtor insolvency. Given that debt contracts were written in nominal terms, the protracted fall in prices and money incomes greatly increased debt burdens. (...) The resulting high rates of default caused problems for both borrowers and lenders. (...) The seriousness of the problem in the Great Depression was due not only to the extent of the deflation, but also to the large and broad-based expansion of inside debt in the 1920's. (...) Like the banking crises, then, the debt crisis of the 1930's was not qualitatively a new phenomenon; but it represented a break with the past in terms of its severity and pervasiveness. (Bernanke, 1983, pp. 260–261)

---

[38] For more details on Fisher's stabilization plans at various stages see Pavanelli (1999, 2004, pp. 296-ff.) and Boianovsky (2013).

[39] 'Because of the long spell of low food prices, farmers were in more difficulty than homeowners. At the beginning of 1933, owners of 45 percent of all U.S. farms, holding 52 percent of the value of farm mortgage debt, were delinquent in payments ...' (Bernanke, 1983, p. 260).

The U.S. banking system comprised many independent small banks also because of the legislation against banking concentration. For this institutional reason, the banking system was especially exposed to runs, followed by dramatic crises due to the Federal Reserve's failure to adopt policies to stop the runs (Bernanke, 1983, p. 260). In credit markets the recovery after the 1933 Bank Holiday was slow; in the emergency, firms had made recourse to whatever financial resources they had access to, including commercial credit, accumulated liquidity or the liquidation of assets (Bernanke, 1983, pp. 272–273).

> Although the government's actions set the financial system on its way back to health, recovery was neither rapid nor complete. Many banks did not reopen after the holiday, and many that did open did so on a restricted basis or with marginally solvent balance sheets. Deposits did not flow back into the banks in great quantities until 1934, and the government (through the Reconstruction Finance Corporation and other agencies) had to continue to pump large sums into banks and other intermediaries. Most important, however, was a noticeable change in attitude among lenders; they emerged from the 1930–33 episode chastened and conservative. Friedman and Schwartz (pp. 449–62) have documented the shift of banks during this time away from making loans toward holding safe and liquid investments. The growing level of bank liquidity created an illusion (as Friedman and Schwartz pointed out) of easy money; however, the combination of lender reluctance and continued debtor insolvency interfered with credit flows for several years after 1933. (Bernanke, 1983, pp. 272–273)

Bernanke, sharing the emphasis on the contraction of bank money among the primary causes of the severity of the depression, recognizes the active role of financial intermediaries in assessing creditworthiness and evaluating the risk of insolvency in conditions of uncertainty and asymmetric information, where debtors may be prone to moral hazard behaviour. At the root of his interpretation, there is a vision of the credit system that denies the assumption of perfectly efficient financial markets *à la* Eugene Fama. The banking crises, with the increased risk of bankruptcy due to the spreading of insolvencies, brought the credit system to a collapse, paralyzing its allocative function. A credit squeeze aggravated the recession.

> The present paper builds on the Friedman-Schwartz work by considering a third way in which the financial crises (in which we include debtor bankruptcies as well as the failures of banks and other lenders) may have affected output. The basic premise is that, because markets for financial claims are incomplete, intermediation between some classes of borrowers and lenders requires nontrivial market-making and information-gathering services. The disruptions of 1930–33 (as I shall try to show) reduced the effectiveness of the financial sector as a whole in performing these services. As the real costs of intermediation increased, some borrowers (especially households, farmers, and small firms) found credit to be expensive and difficult to

obtain. The effects of this credit squeeze on aggregate demand helped convert the severe but not unprecedented downturn of 1929–30 into a protracted depression. (Bernanke, 1983, p. 257)

After his contribution in 1983 with explicit focus on inside debts and deflation, in later comparative research Bernanke (1995, p. 24) argues that there is strong evidence of the real effects of deflation through the burden of non indexed debt contracts, which induce wealth redistribution and financial crisis. Both the operational rules of the inter-war Gold Standard and the weaker financial conditions of banks favoured financial distress, panics and runs on banks, with a relevant impact on output and the macro-economy (Bernanke, 1995, pp. 7–8 and 18–20). In his history of the New Deal, Hiltzik (2011) emphasizes the dramatic situation of American farmers and the social unrest created by foreclosures, and how the legislation for the reshaping of the banking system was among the first emergency measures of the New Deal. He deals with the institutional aspects of mortgage finance that precipitated the mortgage crises in conditions of monetary instability, as much as contemporary historians deal with the institutional aspects of subprimes, the mortgage market and shadow banking in explaining the Great Recession. Eichengreen (2015, p. 166) polemically writes of the U.S. banking crises: 'The banking system was allowed to disintegrate over the misplaced priority attached to moral hazard.'

These topics came forcefully back in the debates about the Great Recession. The effects of deflation have been notably discussed by researchers, notably C. Borio, at the Bank of International Settlements (BIS), who took a polemical stance against the effectiveness of the quantitative easing programme adopted by the ECB. In 2015 Borio and others published a paper in the *BIS Quarterly Review* that deals with the costs of deflation in a historical perspective. They distinguish the real effects of deflation in the general price level of goods and services (proceeding at higher or lower rates and more or less persistent or transitory), from the costs of deflation due to the fall of prices of patrimonial assets, such as shares sold at the Stock Exchange or housing. According to their interpretation, the real effects of a fall of patrimonial assets' prices are more relevant than a fall of the general price level in checking aggregate demand. They may be associated to bankruptcies and financial crises with further real effects. The main link would thus be from severe deflation of patrimonial assets (primarily houses and properties) to debt crises (Borio et al., 2015, p. 46). In the perception of wealth owners, the net value of wealth is reduced more through this channel than by the fall of the general price level, whose real effects act mainly through redistributive asymmetries (Borio et al., 2015, p. 47). The financial crisis of the 1930s was interpreted within this theoretical frame (Borio et al., 2015, p. 38, Box 1). Although these authors do not subscribe to Fisher's debt-deflation theory, they are inspired by the idea of sequences of speculative booms followed by depressions and financial crises, an idea shared in the 1920s and 1930s by Fisher and Austrian economists.

4.6   WHY DID DEBT AND DEFLATION DISAPPEAR FROM MACROECONOMICS SINCE THE 1950s?

In the *Treatise*, as we shall see in the next chapter, Keynes devoted much attention to the banking system in general terms, without going into a detailed analysis of how credit relations can exacerbate deflation or how deflation, in turn, affects creditors and debtors in different ways. In *The General Theory*, the problems of banks and credit are not crucial pillars of the main line of argumentation. Only sporadic attention is paid to credit and the banking system, which are dealt with in a number of specific passages, mostly confined to lateral lines of arguing. Deflation is dealt with in Chapter 19, where Keynes explains why the mechanism of deflation may fail to generate the expansion of aggregate demand necessary to sustain full employment. Once again, he warns that severe deflation is dangerous because of its social costs, the uncertainty it spreads in lowering the expectations for future profits, the knock-on effects in spreading bankruptcies. Although the analysis of deflation in Chapter 19 is not fused into the main line of arguing in the book, the theoretical construction in *The General Theory* stands on it.

Like Keynes, Fisher regards a severe deflation as a destabilizing dynamic process that does not bring the macro-economy to stable full-employment equilibrium. However, differently from Keynes, the destabilizing debt-deflation process is conceived as the rupture of a previous, unstable condition of systemic financial fragility in the economy, built up after firms have accumulated excessive debts in the frenzy of a speculative boom. In Fisher's later diagnosis the policy prescription was to drastically abolish the freedom of commercial banks to expand or contract deposits by changing their reserve coefficients. As we point out in Chapter 8, this measure will again be prominent in Milton Friedman policy prescriptions in the late 1950s.

The themes with which Keynes and Fisher dealt in the early 1930s are present in the historical literature on the Great Depression, and they are again debated in the diagnoses of the Great Recession, following the financial crisis in the first decade of the 20th century. They have been almost absent in macroeconomic theory and models for more than fifty years after World War II, both in the case of the Keynesians of the Neoclassical Synthesis and in the case of the modelling strategies adopted by the New Classical Macroeconomics. From a theoretical point of view, the line followed by Keynes in his 1936 book together with the later exclusive emphasis on equilibrium models can be seen as at the origin of this major turn. Also the relative monetary stability during the so-called Great Moderation did not encourage exploring disequilibrium debt-deflation spirals. Notably, the disruptive effects of financial crises were absent in the equilibrium macroeconomic models to which academic economists referred to advise central bankers until the end of 20th century and in the econometric models that central banks adopted to devise their monetary policies and forecasts. In commenting on the subprime crisis and the lack of transparency in the financial markets with which it intermingles, Eichengreen (2015, p. 171) observes: 'Nor were these complex financial structures incorporated into the Federal Reserve's model of the economy.'

Both Keynes's and Fisher's reasoning on deflation and financial distress was merely discursive, though attentively argued according to the standards accepted in academic economics of the time. In more recent years, there have been some attempts to build dynamic models of debt and deflation spirals and strive to incorporate their effects into conventional macroeconomic models (see, in particular, Tobin 1975 or, for later works, King 1994 and Goetz 2005).

5. Keynes on banks in *A Treatise*, *The General Theory* and after

In his *History of Economic Analysis* Schumpeter mentions the evolution of Keynes's view of banks from *A Treatise on Money* (Keynes, 1930[1971]) to *The General Theory* (Keynes, 1936[1973]): 'There is, however, a sequel to Lord Keynes's treatment of the subject of credit creation in the *Treatise* of 1930 of which it is necessary to take notice in passing. The deposit-creating bank loan and its role in the financing of investment without any previous saving up of the sums thus lent have practically disappeared in the analytic schema of the *General Theory*, where it is again the saving public that holds the scene' (Schumpeter, 1954[2006], p. 1080, n. 5).[1] Also Leijonhufvud, by referring more directly to the problem of the determination of the interest rate, points out a significant difference between Keynes's two works: 'The *Treatise* has a *stock-flow* treatment where the interest rate must clear a market that trades not only in new issues but also in outstanding securities. In the *General Theory*, Keynes goes to a pure stock-analysis of interest determination. This last step would be retrogressive in itself. But, on top of that, it is the excess stock demand, not for securities, but for money that – he argues – governs the interest rate. Not an appealing doctrine!' (Leijonhufvud, 1981, p. 170). With Keynes's concentration on stock-analysis the role of banks, which affect the flows of funds, becomes irrelevant.

This chapter is an attempt to explain why Keynes's ideas evolved in such a way. Soon after its publication in 1930, Keynes's *Treatise* gave rise to a lively debate that started the process that, in a few years, led to *The General Theory*, which, in several respects, represents a break from his previous theoretical and analytical positions. We look at the relationship between Keynes's two works only with respect to a particular issue,[2] that is to say the reasons that might have

---

[1] For Schumpeter, orthodox Keynesians have followed Keynes along the same path: 'Orthodox Keynesianism has in fact reverted to the old view according to which the central facts about the money market are analytically rendered by means of the public's propensity to save coupled with its liquidity preference. I cannot do more than advert to this fact. Whether this spells progress or retrogression, every economist must decide for himself' (Schumpeter, 1954[2006], p. 1080, n. 5).

[2] For useful reconstructions of the process leading from the *Treatise* to *The General Theory*, see for example Moggridge (1992, pp. 511–571), and Skidelsky (1992).

induced Keynes to develop his analysis in *The General Theory* without giving banks any significant role to play, whereas they played quite an important role in the *Treatise*. Considering this topic makes it necessary also to look at the evolution of Keynes's position after 1936. When trying to defend and better expound his book, Keynes returned to give banks a role to play.

Keynes's general treatment of money and banks in the *Treatise* raises an interesting issue. In the initial chapters of Volume 1, Keynes clearly rejects the view of banks as mere intermediaries between depositors (savers) and borrowers, but later in the book, when dealing with the problem of liquidity preference, he seems to go back to a more traditional notion of banks as mere intermediaries. As intermediaries between savers and borrowers, banks can affect the overall degree of liquidity preference and, hence, the prices of securities. For example, a high liquidity preference of savers, which induce them to have deposits with banks rather than buy securities, can be totally or partially offset by a low liquidity preference of banks, which buy securities and/or lend their deposits. In such a situation, the prices of securities are unaffected, or less affected than it would be the case if only the savers' liquidity preference were at work. However, within a framework in which the main concern is liquidity preference and its effects on the economy as a whole, the role of banks, seen as intermediaries, can be assumed away to simplify the analysis without any relevant implication. This, in our opinion, was Keynes's 'tactical' choice in *The General Theory*.

There is another important aspect that can help explain why the role of banks is downplayed, if not totally ignored, in *The General Theory*. It has to do with Keynes's methodological and analytical approach to the problem of the relation between saving and investment. In 1936, Keynes concentrates on the relation between saving and investment and their necessary equality; he does so without paying attention to the process in time through which such equality is realized. Instead, as we saw in Chapter 3, the analysis of this dynamic process was a problem to which Robertson had paid most attention by giving banks and credit a key role to play: it is through bank credit that the equality between saving and investment is brought about. If, instead, Keynes's approach is accepted, it is evident that the concern for the role of banks and credit tends to disappear.

If banks are largely ignored in *The General Theory*, it is however true that in the book Keynes pays significant attention to financial markets, and the Stock Exchange in particular. For Keynes, the very nature of financial markets in an uncertain environment is such that they can represent a disturbing factor for the economy as a whole as they are prone to speculation, volatility and instability. Keynes's approach to the analysis of the working of financial markets did not attract much attention either in the 1930s or in the post-war period. Only recently, Keynes's ideas have been revived by a number of financial economists, particularly those who advocate the behavioural approach to the study of finance. We shall return to these topics in Chapter 9.

After the publication of *The General Theory*, Keynes wrote three important articles to better expound and defend the essential points he had made in his book. In these works, Keynes reasserted the key importance of the demand for liquidity as a defence from uncertainty, but he also returned to give banks and credit a role to play. Keynes, however, was not fully successful in his attempt to integrate the notion of liquidity preference into an analytical context in which banks' activity is significant and the money supply is endogenous.

5.1   MONEY AND BANKS IN *A TREATISE*

Keynes's main objective in the *Treatise* was to provide a general theory of money and, more in particular, an analysis of the relationship between the quantity of money and the general price level. Keynes saw his own approach to this issue as an advancement with respect to the old quantity theory of money, which focused only on equilibrium relations. He wanted '...to find a method which is useful in describing, not merely the characteristics of static equilibrium, but also those of disequilibrium, and to discover the dynamical laws governing the passage of a monetary system from one position of equilibrium to another' (Keynes, 1930[1971], p. xvii).

Like Wicksell and Fisher, Keynes also set out to deal with the problem of the general price level within the framework of a market economy characterized by the existence of a modern banking system. It is then not surprising that there are several points of contact and similarities in their works. It is, of course, even less surprising to find commonalities between Keynes's and Robertson's analyses, given their deep and intense intellectual collaboration up to the publication of the *Treatise*.[3]

The Treatise begins with a chapter that emphasizes the crucial importance of money as unit of account, the fundamental concept of monetary theory (Keynes, 1930[1971], p. 3). Money through which contracts are discharged is what Keynes calls 'money proper', which is strictly related to the state and its role:[4] contracts necessarily imply a role for the state, which enforces their delivery and establishes which instrument must be used to discharge

---

[3]   As already mentioned earlier (Chapter 3, section 3.6), the publication of the *Treatise* marked a break in their intellectual partnership, which became more drastic after the publication of *The General Theory*.

[4]   Keynes defines three different types of money proper (commodity money, fiat money and managed money), but he concentrates on managed money, which is similar to fiat money, i.e. a representative money, but, like commodity money, it has a determinate value in terms of a certain standard (Keynes, 1930[1971], p. 7).

them. Transactions, however, can be settled by using some form of debt acknowledgement as a substitute for money proper. In other words, money proper need not necessarily be the economy's medium of exchange. The debt acknowledgements functioning as substitutes for money proper are called 'bank money'. Money proper together with bank money constitute 'current money'.

Money proper is partly held by the public and partly held by commercial banks in the form of deposits with the central bank. The banks' deposits with the central bank are the reserves they hold against the public's deposits with them. The deposits plus the amount of money proper held by the public constitute the money supply (Keynes, 1930[1971], pp. 8–9).[5] What is relevant in the present context is Keynes's analysis of banks and the process through which they create money. Keynes draws an interesting distinction between past and modern banks: 'Historically a bank may have been evolved from a business which dealt in the precious metals or in the remittance of money from one country to another, or which offered its services as an intermediary to arrange loans or for the safe custody of valuables, or which borrowed the savings of the public on the security of its reputation and then invested them at its own discretion and at its own risk. But we shall be concerned in what follows with banks of the fully developed modern type existing as going concerns' (Keynes, 1930[1971], p. 20).

Modern banks create money, i.e. deposits which are claims against themselves in two ways. On the one hand, they create deposits by accepting the public's money proper; in other words, they operate like 'old' banks. On the other hand, they create deposits either by purchasing assets and paying for them by creating a claim against themselves or by lending (Keynes, 1930[1971], p. 21). Banks, in one way or the other, continually create deposits and, at the same time, cancel deposits because claims against them are exercised, in cash or through transfers from one bank to another. This raises the banks' need for reserves: 'the rate at which the bank can, with safety, actively create deposits by lending and investing has to be in a proper relation to the rate at which it is passively creating them against the receipt of liquid resources from its depositors.' (Keynes, 1930[1971], pp. 21–22).

The banks' passive deposits can obviously be used as reserves, but this does not imply that such deposits represent a constraint to the banks' ability to create active deposits, i.e. to lend. To make this point clear Keynes considers a closed economy in which no cash is demanded and in which banks do not hold reserves but settle their inter-bank indebtedness by using some other asset, i.e.

---

[5]   Keynes's determination of the supply of money is more elaborate than the one adopted here, which is however adequate for our present purposes.

a pure credit economy. In this world, 'there is no limit to the amount of bank money which the banks can safely create *provided that they move forward in step*' (Keynes, 1930[1971], p. 23, emphasis in the original).

Every loan made by a bank and then used by the borrower to make payments 'weakens' the lending bank and 'strengthens' the bank with which the recipient of the payments has an account. However, if all banks behave in the same way ('move in step'), i.e. they lend at the same pace, no bank is weakened and, therefore, banks as a whole can extend their lending indefinitely. Such a system would be inherently unstable. Any factor that pushes the whole banking system in the same direction would face no constraint or obstacle and, hence, give rise to explosive or implosive processes. A certain tendency to instability is always present in actual economies (Keynes, 1930[1971], p. 23), but it is checked essentially by the fact that banks wish to maintain a certain proportion between the amount of their loans and the amount of their reserves with the central bank (Keynes, 1930[1971], pp. 24–25).[6] Keynes's view of a modern banking system is clearly expounded in the following passage.

> There can be no doubt that, in the most convenient use of language, all deposits are 'created' by the bank holding them. It is certainly not the case that the banks are limited to that kind of deposit, for the creation of which it is necessary that depositors should come on their own initiative bringing cash or cheques. But it is equally clear that the rate at which an individual bank creates deposits on its own initiative is subject to certain rules and limitations; – it must keep step with the other banks and cannot raise its own deposits relatively to the total deposits out of proportion to its quota of the banking business of the country. Finally, the 'pace' common to all the member banks is governed by the aggregate of their reserve resources. (Keynes, 1930[1971], pp. 26–27)

The banks' ability to lend – and, hence, to create deposits (money) – is not contingent on the amount of passive deposits that the public wish to hold with them. The amount of bank lending, however, is not unconstrained: the banks' need for reserves puts a limit to it.

Keynes's view of banks as firms that are capable to create money *ex novo*, or *ex nihilo*, is not too different from the analyses developed by Schumpeter and Robertson. In some respects, Keynes's analysis is even more detailed and accurate. However, in the subsequent analytical developments in the *Treatise*, Keynes concentrates on the role of banks as creators of 'passive' deposits, i.e. those deriving from accepting the public's proper money, so that their lending activity essentially reduces to intermediation. In Chapter 3, Keynes divides

---

[6]   The aggregate amount of banks' reserves is ultimately under the control of the central bank, provided that it can control and determine the amount of deposits with it. If it is so, 'the central bank is the conductor of the orchestra and sets the tempo' (Keynes, 1930[1971], p. 26).

passive deposits into two main classes: 'cash deposits' and 'saving deposits'. Cash deposits are held to have a certain amount of liquidity required to make transactions both by households and firms.[7] The households' deposits are called 'income deposits' and the firms' deposits are called 'business deposits'.[8] Saving deposits, instead, are generated by the public when they want to hold part of their wealth in a liquid form: 'a bank deposit may also be held … as a means of employing savings, i.e., as an investment.' (Keynes, 1930[1971], pp. 31–32). The public's demand for cash deposits is related to (real and financial) transactions, whereas the demand for saving deposits is related to the public's liquidity preference, as they are seen as an alternative to holding some other less liquid assets.[9] Saving deposits, as an expression of liquidity preference, play a central role in the determination of the general price level.

5.2 THE DETERMINATION OF THE PRICE LEVEL AND LIQUIDITY PREFERENCE: THE ROLE OF BANKS

Keynes starts his analysis of prices by considering the flows of money earnings and arrives at the three 'fundamental equations' of prices: the price level of consumer-goods (P), the general price level (Π) and the price level of investment-goods (P'). His analysis is based on the distinction, on the one hand, between incomes earned through the production of consumer-goods and those earned through the production of investment-goods and, on the other hand, between income spent on consumer-goods and saving.

With a number of transformations and simplifying hypotheses, Keynes obtains his first fundamental equation of the price level of consumer-goods,

$$P = \frac{E}{O} + \frac{I' - S}{R} \qquad (5.1)$$

---

[7] Keynes considers both real and financial transactions (Keynes, 1930[1971], pp. 38–43). It is interesting to look at his considerations on the relative stability of income deposits as opposed to the larger volatility of business deposits held for financial transactions.

[8] To a certain extent, the banks' ability to provide the economy with the required amount of medium of exchange is not contingent on the public's willingness to hold deposits with them. Banks have the possibility to concede overdrafts, which can be used as the instrument to effect transactions. Therefore, 'it is not in the least essential to the efficient working of the cheque-money system that any of those who have cheque books should also have deposits. The resources of the bank might consist entirely of its own capital or they might be drawn from a class of customer, namely from those who run fixed savings accounts with the bank, quite distinct from the customers who run cash accounts; in which case the cash accounts would consist entirely of debit accounts (i.e. overdrafts) and not at all of credit accounts (i.e. cash deposits)' (Keynes, 1930[1971], pp. 36–37).

[9] In the *Treatise*, Keynes does not use the terms 'liquidity preference' but the term 'bearishness'. Here, for simplicity, we use the two terms indifferently, even though they are not perfect synonyms. See Keynes (1936[1973], pp. 173–4), on the differences between them.

where E is total money income, O is total output, I' is the cost of production of investment-goods, S is total saving and R is the output of consumer-goods.

By denoting the rate of earnings per 'unit of human effort' with W (the wage rate) and the rate of earnings per unit of output with W_1, equation 5.1 can be written as

$$P = \frac{1}{e}W + \frac{I' - S}{R} \qquad (5.2)$$

with $W = eW_1$, where e is a coefficient of efficiency.[10]

The first term on the right-hand side of (5.2) is the cost of production of a unit of consumer-good. The second term is equal to zero, positive or negative according to whether the cost of production of investment-goods is equal to, larger or smaller than saving. Thus, the prices of consumer-goods deviate from their cost of production when the division of the output between investment-goods and consumer-goods is not the same as the division of the income between savings and consumption (Keynes, 1930[1971], pp. 122–23). To arrive at the equation of the general price level Π it is necessary to consider also the price level of investment-goods P', which Keynes initially takes as given. After some substitutions, he obtains his second fundamental equation:

$$\Pi = \frac{PR + P'C}{O} = \frac{1}{e}W + \frac{I - S}{O} \qquad (5.3)$$

where C is the output of investment-goods and $I = P'C$ is the value of the output of investment goods (Keynes, 1930[1971], p. 123).

Keynes then turns to the determination of the price level of investment goods, P'. For individuals, saving amounts to deciding to increase their wealth, but this decision must be followed by a second one about the form in which wealth is held. The two alternatives between which individuals choose are holding money ('hoarding') or some other asset ('investing'), which can be expressed also as a choice between bank deposits and investing in securities (Keynes, 1930[1971], p. 127). The public's decisions depend on the expected returns of the two alternatives, which are affected by their prices and the rate of interest.[11]

Banks, which collect saving deposits from the public, enter the picture and they can affect the prices of investments. The public may have a high

---

[10] $W = \frac{E}{L}, W_1 = \frac{E}{O}$ and $e = \frac{O}{L}$, where L is total human effort. Therefore $W = eW_1$.
[11] The decision between hoarding and investing regards the current flow of saving, but it also regards the form in which the stock of wealth is to be held. This latter decision, for Keynes, is far more relevant. (Keynes, 1930[1971], p. 127).

preference for saving deposits (a high liquidity preference), but banks may behave in the opposite direction, i.e. to have a high preference for holding assets, so that they employ the public's saving deposits to buy the securities that the public do not wish to hold. The public's low propensity to lend (by buying securities) can be, totally or partly, counterbalanced by the banks' high propensity to lend.

A change in the public's liquidity preference would imply a change in the price of assets (investments), but this need not occur if such a change is fully compensated for by a change in the banks' preferences in the opposite direction. Therefore, a fall in the price level of securities indicates that the 'bearishness' of the public is not completely offset by the banks' creation of savings deposits, or that the public's 'bullishness' is more than offset by the contraction of savings deposits (Keynes, 1930[1971], p. 128).

Thus, the actual price level of investments is the result of the public's sentiment and the banks' behaviour. A higher liquidity preference of the public expresses itself in a larger demand for money in the form of saving deposits, which should imply a fall in the price of other assets alternative to money. But it is not necessarily so if banks have a lower liquidity preference than the public:

> Since the price level of consumer-goods depends on the public's decisions concerning the proportion of their income devoted to saving and the entrepreneurs' decisions on how much of investment-goods to produce, we have that the general price level depends on the following factors: (1) the rate of saving, (2) the cost of new investment, (3) the 'bearishness' of the public, (4) the volume of savings deposits; or, if you like, on the two factors – (1) the excess of saving over cost of investment, and (2) such excess of bearishness on the part of the public as is unsatisfied by the creation of deposits by the banking system. (Keynes, 1930[1971], p. 129)

Keynes's conclusions are functional to his confutation and rejection of the traditional quantity theory of money. The relationship between the quantity of money and the general price level is more complex than that postulated by the old quantity theory (Keynes, 1930[1971], pp. 131–32). In equilibrium, there exists a unique relation between the quantity of money and prices, which change proportionally with it. Out of equilibrium, however, if $S \neq I'$ and/or there is a change in the liquidity preference in the economy, 'the fundamental price levels can depart from their equilibrium values without any change having occurred in the quantity of money or in the velocities of circulation' (Keynes, 1930[1971], p. 132).

Keynes, like Robertson, studies the dynamics of prices in an economy characterized by the existence of a modern banking system. For both, banks enter the analytical framework and their behaviour affects prices. However, there is also an important difference between them. In analysing banks,

Robertson concentrates on the creation of active deposits while Keynes focuses his attention on the banks' use of passive deposits with them. In Robertson's analysis, the creation of bank money is pivotal in the determination of the price level, whereas what is crucial in Keynes is the liquidity preference of the economy as a whole, i.e. the public's and the banks'.

In Keynes's perspective, considering banks can be regarded as a sort of analytical refinement. In fact, his main conclusions, as expounded above, can be reached by abstracting from the banking system altogether and rendering the analysis simpler. Although the bank's liquidity preference can differ and offset the public's, it is still true that it is the liquidity preference of the system as a whole (so to speak the aggregate liquidity preference) that affects the price level.

This feature of Keynes's analysis of the general price level can help explain why he virtually ignores banks a few years later in *The General Theory*. In so far as it is liquidity preference that plays a fundamental role, to take account of banks and their role is not crucial. In *The General Theory*, Keynes is no longer concerned with the determination of the price level like in the *Treatise*, but liquidity preference still plays a decisive role in his explanation of the working of the economy. It is reasonable to think that, to stress the importance of liquidity preference, Keynes might have decided to make the drastic simplification of ignoring banks.

There is also another similarity between Robertson and Keynes of the *Treatise*. Both admit the possibility that saving and investment diverge. In *The General Theory*, however, Keynes came to reject this possibility: the two variables are always equal. Keynes (1936[1973], pp. 77–79) held that in the *Treatise* saving could diverge from investment because of the particular definition of income adopted there. But there is a deeper and more fundamental methodological reason why in *The General Theory* saving and investment are regarded as always equal. We look at this issue in the next section.

5.3   INVESTMENT, SAVING, BANKS AND FINANCE IN *THE GENERAL THEORY*

Banks are hardly mentioned in *The General Theory*. For example, in Chapter 13, concerned with the theory of the interest rate, Keynes deals with decisions to save almost in the same terms as in the *Treatise* (Keynes, 1930[1971], p. 127), but without considering banks and the demand for money in the form of saving deposits. He mainly refers to the demand for cash as the expression of the individuals' preference for liquidity. The individuals' decision to save in order to increase their wealth must be followed by a second one concerning the form in which wealth is held (Keynes, 1936[1973], p. 166). Therefore, argues

Keynes, the interest rate cannot be determined by saving as such, because if saving is held in cash there is no interest to be earned. Instead, the interest rate is the price 'which equilibrates the desire to hold wealth in the form of cash with the available quantity of cash' (Keynes, 1936[1973], p. 167).

Although very briefly, Keynes considers banks and credit in Chapter 7, where his effort is directed to show that saving and investment must necessarily be equal and to confute others who argued contrarily. Keynes objects to the idea that the existence of a banking system and credit can imply that the equality $I = S$ is not necessarily true. In particular, he criticizes the idea that 'the banking system can make it possible for investment to occur, to which no saving corresponds' (Keynes, 1936[1973], p. 81). Keynes's analysis is carried out by considering both cases in which saving is devoted to the purchasing of existing assets and cases in which new investment-goods are bought. In the first case, it is obvious that saving and investment must coincide.[12] Things are different when dealing with the demand for new assets.

The idea that credit allows investment to which no 'genuine' saving corresponds is the consequence of 'isolating one of the consequences of the increased bank-credit to the exclusion of others.' The new investment financed by credit determines an increase in income 'at a rate which will normally *exceed* the rate of increased investment.' The proportion in which the additional income is consumed and saved depends on the public's 'free choice', but 'it is impossible that the intention of the entrepreneur who has borrowed in order to increase investment can become effective (. . .) at a faster rate that the public decide to increase their savings.' Thus, Keynes concludes that 'the old-fashioned view that saving always involves investment, though incomplete and misleading, is formally sounder than the newfangled view that there can be saving without investment or investment without 'genuine' saving' (Keynes, 1936[1973], p. 83).[13]

In dealing with the relation between saving and investment in this way, Keynes has in mind the notion of multiplier, $\Delta Y = \frac{1}{s}\Delta I$. Considering the way in which he uses this notion provides a reason why credit and banks can be safely ignored in the analytical framework of *The General Theory*, where the attention is focused on the final equilibrium produced by a larger investment, i.e. 'on the logical theory of the multiplier which holds good continuously without time-lag, at all moments of time' (Keynes, 1936[1973], p. 122). Keynes is not concerned with the analysis of the dynamic process

---

[12] '[N]o one can acquire an asset (. . .) unless (. . .) someone else parts with an asset of that value which he previously had' (Keynes, 1936[1973], pp. 81–82).

[13] This, however, does not justify the inference that an individual decision to save implies an equal increase in aggregate investment. It is the other way around: any decision to invest a certain amount gives rise to an equal amount of saving (Keynes, 1936[1973], p. 83).

triggered by an initial increase in investment and, hence, with the transition from the old to the new equilibrium. Once Keynes's methodological approach is accepted, it is obviously true that saving and investment are always equal, but is also evident that the problem of how investment is initially financed becomes irrelevant.

Robertson, as we saw in Chapter 3, followed a different line of analysis and was severely critical of Keynes. For him, Keynes's multiplier 'forgets' the period of transition between the initial increase in investment and the realization of the final equilibrium, at which investment is necessarily equal to saving. He felt uneasy about ignoring the transition period. In recollecting his relationship and differences with Keynes at the time of the publication of *Banking Policy*, Robertson wrote: 'While Keynes must at the time have understood and acquiesced in my step-by-step method, it is evident that it never, so to speak, got under his skin; for in his two successive treatments of the saving-investment theme in his two big books he discarded it completely' (Robertson, 1926[1949], p. xi).[14]

Presley (1978, p. 86) clearly expounds the differences between Robertson and Keynes on the relation between saving and investment and the role of credit: 'The finance required for investment to take place is instantaneously provided by voluntary saving, so there is no need either for the banks to create credit to finance the investment or for forced saving to be imposed on the public. Indeed, in Keynes' thesis there is no such thing as forced saving. Even if credit is created by the banks, prices need not rise significantly so long as unemployed resources exist. In the forced saving doctrine prices rise even at less than full employment. Given the multiplier, and a static approach, the equality of saving and investment is guaranteed.'

Also others have pointed out the methodological difference between Robertson and Keynes. Hicks (1942, p. 55) illustrates it by referring to Kaldor's theory of the trade cycle as presented in 1940. Kaldor's analysis is based on the proposition that the economy always tends to the equality between saving and investment, which he regards as Keynesian (Kaldor, 1940, p. 78). But Hicks (1942, p. 55) questions the Keynesian nature of such an idea: 'this proposition is not Keynes at all – it is pure Robertson.' Kahn, the 'inventor' of the multiplier, pointed out some of the limitations of Keynes's approach and that, had Keynes taken account of the time element in his analysis, 'he would have had largely to rewrite the book' (Kahn, 1984, p. 125).[15] Leijonhufvud (1981, p. 170) remarks: 'If household saving and business investment are necessarily and therefore continuously equal, then it would seem that the banking system

---

[14] The two 'big books' obviously are the *Treatise* and the *General Theory*.

[15] On this issue, see also Ohlin (1937c), Pigou (1950, p. 64) and Hicks (1979, pp. 73–102). On the implications of Keynes's methodology for his theory of investment, see Sardoni (1996).

cannot possibly be doing anything else but simply serving as an obedient go-between. So we can just as well erase it and adopt the simplified picture of the circular flow that goes with the Keynesian cross.'[16]

The publication of *The General Theory* aroused numerous discussions and debates that were also concerned with some of the issues considered above. We deal with these discussions, which led Keynes to a partial change of mind, in section 5.5 below; before we look at another aspect of Keynes's analysis, that is to say his considerations about financial markets in Chapter 12 of *The General Theory* ('The state of long-term expectation', Keynes, 1936[1973], pp. 147–164).

5.4   THE WORKING OF FINANCIAL MARKETS

Modern financial markets play an important role in an uncertain context in which firms have to make irrevocable investment decisions. Organized financial markets offer the possibility to render such decisions 'less irrevocable'. Thanks to the existence of well-developed financial markets, it is possible to revert decisions to become illiquid at any time in the future (Keynes, 1936[1973], pp. 150–151). In other words, the existence of well developed financial markets makes investment, so to say, less illiquid and, hence, less risky for the investor.

In an uncertain environment, expectations about a relative distant future are based on extremely precarious knowledge.[17] This makes investment the most hazardous sort of decision, as they are based on precarious knowledge and they cannot be easily and promptly revised and corrected; they are largely irrevocable. There is, however, an important difference between the past and the present reality of market economies. In the past, decisions to invest were irrevocable to a very large extent, for individuals as well as for the community as a whole (Keynes, 1936[1973], p. 150). In contemporary economies, investment decisions remain irrevocable for the economic system as a whole, but not for individuals.

With the separation between ownership and management which prevails to-day and with the development of organized investment markets, a new factor of great importance has entered in, which sometimes facilitates investment but sometimes adds greatly to the instability of the system. In the absence of security markets,

---

[16] In a footnote, Leijonhufvud (1981, p. 171, note 58) adds: 'as far as I can understand, Robertson was consistently right on every aspect of the interest rate controversy between himself and Keynes' Cambridge followers'.

[17] 'The outstanding fact is the extreme precariousness of the basis of knowledge on which our estimates of prospective yield have to be made' (Keynes, 1936[1973], p. 149).

there is no object in frequently attempting to revalue an investment to which we are committed. But the Stock Exchange revalues many investments every day and the revaluations give a frequent opportunity to the individual (though not to the community as a whole) to revise his commitments. (Keynes, 1936[1973], pp. 150–151)

The revaluations that occur in financial markets are essentially finalized to the transfer of old investments, but they inevitably affect also decisions about new investment.[18] Keynes then analyses the way in which such revaluations are carried out and points out the instability of financial markets due to the flimsy bases on which revaluations are made. In this respect, conventions play a key role. In an uncertain context, for Keynes, agents fall back on the convention of assuming that 'the existing state of affairs will continue indefinitely, except in so far as we have specific reasons to expect a change' (Keynes, 1936[1973], p. 152). This, in turn, amounts to assume that the existing market valuation of assets is uniquely correct in relation to our existing knowledge.[19]

This conventional method is compatible with a 'considerable measure of continuity and stability in our affairs, *so long as we can rely on the maintenance of the convention*'. In fact, if the convention holds, 'an investor can legitimately encourage himself with the idea that the only risk he runs is that of a genuine change in the news *over the near future*, as to the likelihood of which he can attempt to form his own judgement, and which is unlikely to be very large'. But the assumption that the market valuation is uniquely correct is unwarranted because our knowledge does not provide sufficient grounds for the calculation of mathematical expectations and, therefore, it is precarious. Its precariousness 'creates no small part of our contemporary problem of securing sufficient investment' (Keynes, 1936[1973], pp. 152–153; emphasis in the original).

The precariousness of the convention depends on several factors: i) a growing proportion of shares is owned by people with little knowledge of business; ii) short-term variations of profits have an excessive influence on financial markets; iii) a convention that is the outcome of the psychology of many ignorant subjects is prone to change violently in consequence of changes of opinion due to factors that are not really important for the prospective

---

[18] '…there is no sense in building up a new enterprise at a cost greater than that at which a similar existing enterprise can be purchased; whilst there is an inducement to spend on a new project what may seem an extravagant sum, if it can be floated off on the Stock Exchange at an immediate profit. Thus, certain classes of investment are governed by the average expectation of those who deal on the Stock Exchange as revealed in the price of shares, rather than by the genuine expectations of the professional entrepreneur' (Keynes, 1936[1973], p. 151).

[19] In other words, asset prices correctly reflect the state of our knowledge and they are expected to change for no other reason than changes in information. As we shall see, this is the basic assumption on which the modern theory of efficient markets is based.

yield of investments; iv) professional operators in financial markets are not concerned with making well founded long-term forecasts of the yield of investments, but rather with foreseeing before the general public variations of the conventional basis of valuation (Keynes, 1936[1973], pp. 153–155). All the factors mentioned above have to do with the degree of confidence of speculators, with the tacit assumption that, if satisfied with their prospects, they have an unlimited 'command over money' at the market interest rate. But this is not true because 'we must also take account of the other facet of the state of confidence, namely, the confidence of the lending institutions towards those who seek to borrow from them, sometimes described as the state of credit' (Keynes, 1936[1973], p. 158). Keynes makes two important points: i) financial transactions largely take place by recourse to credit; ii) lenders are not passive agents that offer whatever amount of credit is demanded by the market. These aspects of his analysis of financial markets were largely ignored in the theoretical macroeconomic debate until very recently, but Keynes himself did not succeed in fully integrating these aspects into the rest of his analysis. More in particular, he overlooked the implications of considering credit and financial markets for his notion of liquidity preference, a topic that we consider in section 5.6.

5.5 AFTER *THE GENERAL THEORY*. CRITICISMS AND REJOINDERS

In 1937 Keynes wrote two important articles (Keynes, 1937a,b) to answer various criticisms of *The General Theory*.[20] In the articles, in the attempt to summarize and expound his theory in a clearer way, Keynes introduced some new analytical elements. In particular, he returned to devote attention to banks and credit. In replying to his critics, Keynes mainly referred to Ohlin. It is therefore useful to briefly present Ohlin's viewpoint, which can be regarded as largely representative of the Stockholm School of Economics.

Ohlin published two articles on the Stockholm School's theory of saving and investment and its relation to Keynes and other theoretical approaches (Ohlin, 1937b,c). Ohlin is convinced of the existence of 'surprising similarities as well as striking differences' between Keynes's theoretical apparatus and the Stockholm School (Ohlin, 1937b, p. 53). He expounds the Stockholm theory of processes of contraction and expansion, which deals with changes in employment, prices and output. The analysis is carried out by carefully distinguishing between cases in which the variables taken into consideration

---

[20] In 1937, Keynes also wrote another article (Keynes, 1937c) to argue against some of his critics. We briefly consider this article later on in the chapter.

refer to expectations and cases in which they refer to a period of time already elapsed; in other words, by distinguishing between ex ante and ex post analysis, a method that is similar to Robertson's (Ohlin, 1937b, p. 58).

In the ex ante analysis, which is about psychological causation, expectations of course are to be taken into account. Entrepreneurs, on the basis of expectations and knowledge, make plans to carry out.[21] Investment is planned on the basis of expected profits. But not all planned investments are carried out, depending on the credit conditions faced by the firm:

> Of all the possible investments which seem profitable, only some are planned for the next period and actually begun. This may be due to the fact that the present cash and credit resources of the firm are not large enough to permit more, or that the expected cash and credit resources put a check on the investments. Sometimes, however, strong business firms which could easily borrow huge sums for profitable-looking investment prefer not to do so. They are averse to an increase of their indebtedness. (...) In any case it is clear that the cash and credit resources, which the firm has at its disposal at the beginning of a period and acquires during the period, provide an upper limit for its *ability to buy*, and that the expectations concerning them set a limit to its investment plans; while the profit expectations and the expectations with regard to future cash and credit resources influence the *desire to buy*. (Ohlin, 1937b, pp. 61–62, emphasis in the original) [22]

Ohlin then turns to consider the relation between saving and investment. Ex ante, there is no guarantee that investment and saving are equal, whereas they are necessarily equal ex post. The question is how the ex post equality is realized. An ex ante inequality between saving and investment triggers a process which makes the realized values of income, saving and investment diverge from their expected or planned values (Ohlin, 1937b, pp. 64–65). This is a very straightforward issue, which Keynes treats unsatisfactorily, because he does not always make a clear distinction between the notions of ex ante and ex post.[23]

Within this framework, the interest rate cannot 'be determined by the condition that it equalizes the supply of and the demand for savings, or, in other words, equalizes savings and investment. For savings and investment are equal *ex definitione*, whatever interest level exists on the market. Nor can one say that the rate of interest equalizes planned savings and planned investment, for it obviously does not do this' (Ohlin, 1937c, p. 221). The solution to the problem lies in the recognition that 'the rate of interest is simply the price of credit, and that it is therefore governed by the supply of and demand for credit.

---

[21] During the time period chosen by Ohlin, plans are not modified.

[22] For the consumption of durable and non-durable goods a similar line of analysis can be followed (Ohlin, 1937c, pp. 62–64).

[23] On Ohlin's criticism of Keynes's confusion on the two notions see also Ohlin (1937c).

The banking system – through its ability to give credit – can influence, and to some extent does affect, the interest level' (Ohlin, 1937c, p. 221).

This does not mean that the interest rate has nothing to do with the propensity to save and other elements in the price system: 'Given a certain disposition to save and certain income expectations, i.e. certain consumption and savings plans, the level of the rate of interest relatively to profit expectations, etc., determines the volume of investment and the way in which production, trade and prices develop' (Ohlin, 1937c, p. 221). Keynes's rejoinder concentrates on this aspect.

The discussion above is carried out under the assumption that the banking system alone fixes interest rates, but it is not so.[24] Again, the distinction between ex ante and ex post is crucial. To explain the determination of the interest rate, an ex ante analysis is required.

> The willingness of certain individuals during a given period to increase their holdings of various claims and other kinds of assets minus the willingness of others to reduce their corresponding holdings gives the supply curves for the different kinds of new credit during the period. Naturally, the quantities each individual is willing to supply depend on the interest rates (...) Similarly, the total supply of *new* claims *minus* the reduction in the outstanding volume of *old* ones gives the demand – also a function of the rates of interest – for the different kinds of credit during the period. The prices fixed on the market for these different claims – and thereby the rates of interest – are governed by this supply and demand in the usual way. (Ohlin, 1937c, pp. 224–225)

People's choices about holding different claims determine the supply of credit and the total supply of claims governs the demand for credit. Supply and demand are brought to equality through price variations, which determine the interest rate. In this respect, Ohlin makes an interesting criticism of Keynes's emphasis on the demand and supply of cash.

> It goes without saying, that the interest rates existing at any given moment fulfil the condition that they make people willing to hold as cash (...) the total amount outstanding. But the same is true of all other claims and assets. The total quantity of cash is not fixed by the banking system at a certain figure, but depends on the economic development and on the actions of a number of individuals just as does the quantity of bonds outstanding. The 'market' for cash has no key position in relation to the other markets. (Ohlin, 1937c, pp. 225–226)

---

[24] 'Only the discount rate is usually fixed by the central bank. As to the other rates, e.g. the bond yield, the banking system is only one of many factors which affect demand, supply, and price' (Ohlin, 1937c, p. 224).

Ohlin makes two important points: i) in a world with banks the total quantity of money is an endogenous variable; ii) the way in which demand and supply of money are analysed cannot be different from the way in which demand and supply of any other asset is studied. For Ohlin, his approach 'brings out the relation of the rates of interest to the other elements of the price system and to their movements, whereas Keynes' construction (...) seems to regard the rates of interest as determined largely "outside" the price system, or at least as having almost no connection with the system of mutually interdependent prices and quantities' (Ohlin, 1937c, p. 227). The second point made by Ohlin will be taken up also by other interpreters and critics of Keynes and we shall return to it in Chapter 6; for now we concentrate on the first point.

In 'Alternative theories of the rate of interest' (1937a), Keynes refers to Ohlin's, Hicks's and Robertson's theories of the interest rate, but he focuses on Ohlin's. Keynes argues that, in reality, the alternative theories of the interest rate are nothing but a reformulation of the old view, according to which the interest rate is the price that makes saving and investment equal. For him, instead, the interest rate is not determined by the supply of saving and the demand for investment; it is determined by the supply of and the demand for money.

Also for Ohlin, as we saw, the interest rate cannot depend on saving and investment, but it is determined by the demand for credit and the net supply of credit. Keynes's objection is that the net supply of credit, as defined by Ohlin, is nothing but saving and that the total demand for credit is nothing but net investment (Keynes, 1937a, p. 244). Thus, 'we are completely back again at the classical doctrine which Prof. Ohlin has just repudiated – namely, that the rate of interest is fixed at the level where the supply of credit, in the shape of saving, is equal to the demand for credit, in the shape of investment' (Keynes, 1937a, p. 245).

Keynes then takes into consideration two aspects that, in his view, might generate some confusion. He first considers bank loans, the demand for which, being demand for money, could be regarded as resembling his own approach; but this resemblance, for him, is only superficial because a variation of the demand for bank loans 'is concerned with changes in the *demand for bank borrowing*, whereas I am concerned with changes in the *demand for money*; and those who desire to hold money only overlap partially and temporarily with those who desire to be in debt to the banks' (Keynes, 1937a, pp. 245–246). Keynes's point is not very clear, but he is presumably arguing that the demand for loans is demand for money to be spent, which we call demand for 'active' money, but there is also the demand for money to be kept idle to be considered, which expresses the economy's degree of liquidity preference.

Another factor that might create confusion and make the credit theory plausible is that investment sometimes involves 'a temporary demand for money before it is carried out, quite distinct from the demand for active balances which will arise as a result of the investment activity whilst it is going on' (Keynes, 1937a, p. 246). To eliminate this source of confusion, Keynes modifies his definition of demand for money by including in it the so-called finance motive and by re-introducing banks into his analytical framework. Keynes recognizes that, although it is true that investment is equal to saving, in the sense that any new investment generates an equal amount of additional saving, it is true that with any new investment there arises the need for a bridge between the time when investment is decided and the time when the additional saving actually occurs. In other words, there is a gap to be filled (Keynes, 1937a, p. 246).

The investing firms can fill the gap either through bank loans or through the financial market by issuing new liabilities. In any case, 'the market's commitments will be in excess of actual saving to date and there is a limit to the extent of the commitments which the market will agree to enter into in advance'. This gives rise to an 'extra special demand for cash', which Keynes calls 'finance' and observes 'I should (I now think) have done well to have emphasized it when I analysed the various sources of the demand for money' (Keynes, 1937a, p. 246).[25] Finance has nothing to do with saving. At the stage of the investment process when finance is demanded there is no new net saving: finance and commitments to finance are just 'credit and debit book entries, which allow entrepreneurs to go ahead with assurance' (Keynes, 1937a, p. 247).

Keynes, however, remains convinced that his theory of the interest rate does not require any substantial change: '. . . finance is not the only source of demand for money, and the terms on which it is supplied, whether through the banks or through the new issue market, must be more or less the same as the terms on which other demands for money are supplied. Thus it is precisely the liquidity-premium on cash ruling in the market which determines the rate of interest at which finance is obtainable' (Keynes, 1937a, p. 248). Notice that Keynes

---

[25] 'If by "credit" we mean "finance", I have no objection at all to admitting the demand for finance as one of the factors influencing the rate of interest. For "finance" constitutes . . . an additional demand for liquid cash in exchange for a deferred claim. It is, in the literal sense, a demand for money' (Keynes, 1937a, pp. 247–248). Finance is crucial when investment increases: 'If investment is proceeding at a steady rate, the finance (or the commitments to finance) required can be supplied from a revolving fund of a more or less constant amount, one entrepreneur having his finance replenished for the purpose of a projected investment as another exhausts his on paying for his completed investment. But if decisions to invest are . . . increasing, the extra finance involved will constitute an additional demand for money' (Keynes, 1937a, p. 247).

regards all the firms' sources of finance, namely bank-loans and new market issues, as virtually perfect substitutes.[26]

Within this generalized analytical context, 'a heavy demand for investment can exhaust the market and be held up by lack of financial facilities on reasonable terms. ...Yet this is only another way of expressing the power of the banks through their control over the supply of money – i.e. of liquidity' (Keynes, 1937a, p. 248). Keynes acknowledges that banks play a role in the determination of the supply of money, but he does not seem to realize that this has implications for his theory of the interest rate. When banks create active deposits, the supply of money becomes an endogenous variable and the very notion of hoarding, i.e. holding 'idle' money, becomes ambiguous and misleading. In a world with banks able to create active deposits, a high degree of their liquidity preference does not amount to a high demand for hoards but rather to less lending, i.e. to a reduced supply of money.

Keynes does not seem to be aware of such analytical implications and, in the last section of his article, he returns to a line of argumentation which is compatible with the hypothesis of a given supply of money. For him, hoarding means holding idle money and the interest rate is the variable that equates the demand and supply of hoards. More precisely, the 'function of the rate of interest is to modify the money-prices of other capital assets in such a way as to equalize the attraction of holding them and of holding cash' (Keynes, 1937a, p. 250). And, continues Keynes, 'no amount of anxiety by the public to increase their hoards can affect the amount of hoarding, which depends on the willingness of the banks to acquire (or dispose of) additional assets-beyond what is required to offset changes in the active balances. If the banks stand firm, an increased propensity to hoard raises the rate of interest, and thereby lowers the prices of capital assets other than cash, until people give up the idea of selling them or of refraining from buying them in order to increase their hoards' (Keynes, 1937a, p. 251).

In conclusion, although in 1937 Keynes reintroduces banks into his analysis, he does not go beyond what he had already said in the *Treatise*, where the problem of demand for money and liquidity preference was dealt with by overlooking the banks' ability to vary the supply of money through credit. Introducing the finance motive and the banks' ability to respond to the demand for money through the creation of active deposits, i.e. through lending, implies that the money supply cannot be regarded as given but as

---

[26] This is a problem with which macro-economists will deal in subsequent years and to which we return in Chapters 6 and 7.

endogenously determined by banks.[27] Regarding the supply of money as an endogenous variable has implications for Keynes's liquidity-preference theory of the interest rate.

At the methodological level, Keynes remains critical of the sequential approach and, hence, of Ohlin's ex ante/ex post method. In a letter to him of January 1937, Keynes argues that his own method is preferable when 'something truly logical and properly watertight' has to be proved and that

> ...the *ex post* and *ex ante* device cannot be precisely stated without very cumbrous devices. I used to speak of the period between expectation and result as 'funnels of process', but the fact that the funnels are all of different lengths and overlap one another meant that at any given time there was no aggregate realised result capable of being compared with some aggregate expectation at some earlier date. (Keynes, 1973, p. 185)

At the end of the same year, Keynes published 'The "ex ante" theory of the rate of interest' (1937b), in which he returns to the criticism of the ex ante/ex post approach. He criticizes and rejects Ohlin's notion of ex ante saving, whereas he accepts and uses the notion of ex ante investment. Keynes questions the very notion of ex ante saving and, hence, the possibility that it is a crucial variable in the determination of the interest rate (Keynes, 1937b, pp. 663–664). For him, '...nothing is more certain than that the credit or "finance" required by ex-ante investment is not mainly supplied by ex-ante saving' (Keynes, 1937b, p. 664).[28]

In his response to Keynes's observations, Ohlin (1937a) admits that he had not been clear enough in expounding his credit theory of the interest rate and he presents it again in different terms. It is necessary to distinguish between the actual quantity of credit given and the demand and supply curves for credit, or claims. Such curves are ex ante concepts (Ohlin, 1937a, pp. 423–424). There is a unique interest rate that makes demand for and supply of claims equal and such rate cannot possibly be seen as determined by saving and investment: 'There is a credit market – or rather several markets – but there is no such market for savings and no price of savings' (Ohlin, 1937a, p. 424).

Although there exists a supply curve of saving and a demand curve for planned new investment, they do not coincide with the supply curve of claims and the demand curve for claims respectively. Ohlin (1937a, pp. 425–426) indicates a number of reasons of why it is so; in particular, he points out that the

---

[27] It would not be so if banks were regarded as mere intermediaries between the depositors and the borrowers. In that case they would simply transform idle money (Keynes's saving deposits) into active money used by the borrowers.

[28] Keynes acknowledges that ex ante saving might play a certain limited role but this cannot elude the crucial problem of finance and liquidity preference (Keynes, 1937b, pp. 664–665).

difference between the two sets of curves depends on the behaviour of banks, which can decide to increase or reduce credit with respect to the amount of saving.[29]

For Ohlin, the main difference between his own and Keynes's theories lies in the fact that

> Mr. Keynes gives to the quantity of cash a central place, whereas in my opinion the quantity of claims plays just as "fundamental" a rôle and *provides a direct link with saving, investment, and the whole economic process*. Mr. Keynes says that the rate of interest is determined by the available quantity of money and by the demand schedule for a present claim on money in terms of a deferred claim on money (p. 241). But is not this demand schedule directly dependent on the available quantity of deferred claims, which in turn is influenced by the willingness to borrow and to lend and, thereby, by the willingness to invest and save? (Ohlin, 1937a, p. 427, emphasis in the original)

The supply of money cannot be regarded as independent of the amount of loans that are made by banks. Lending amounts to creating additional money. Also, Robertson (1937) deals with this issue. For him, Keynes's 'concession' concerning the existence of the finance motive certainly is an advance with respect to *The General Theory* as it implies accepting, at least to a certain extent, his own sequential analytical method, but Keynes's analysis remains inconsistent. In commenting on Keynes's view that obtaining the money required for finance through banks or through the new issue market is essentially the same thing, Robertson points out

> We thought we knew that the 'demand for money' meant the amount of money which the public as a whole is willing to hold in the face of a given rate of interest, and that the 'supply of money' meant the amount of money which the banking system permits to exist. But now we read (p. 248, my italics) 'finance is not the only source of demand for money, and the terms on which it is supplied, whether through the banks or *through the new issue market*, must be more or less the same as the terms on which other demands for money are supplied.' If private persons can thus supply a demand for money, either a new and subtle distinction must be drawn between supplying a demand for money, and supplying money in response to a demand for it: or the supply of money has completely changed its meaning, and become indistinguishable, after all, from the supply of loanable funds! (Robertson, 1937, pp. 432–433)

Robertson and Keynes returned to discuss their differences one year later (Robertson and Keynes, 1938). In that occasion, Keynes tries to resolve the 'confusion' about the term 'finance' used in the 1937 article. The confusion

---

[29] Also, Robertson (1934, pp. 551–652) had pointed out the difference between the supply curve of credit and saving when banks are taken into consideration. See also Lindner (2015).

is due to thinking of finance in terms of bank loans, whereas Keynes by finance meant 'the *cash* temporarily held by entrepreneurs to provide against the outgoings in respect of an impending new activity' (Robertson and Keynes, 1938, p. 319). But, as we saw, Keynes himself recognizes that the entrepreneurs' need for cash can be satisfied also by bank loans, i.e. through the creation of additional money. Once bank loans are taken into consideration, the quantity of money cannot be taken as given.

5.6 KEYNES'S DILEMMA: UNCERTAINTY, LIQUIDITY PREFERENCE, MONEY AND BANKS

Throughout the works we considered, Keynes always manifests his keen interest in the problem of liquidity and its crucial importance. Liquidity is the alternative to holding other assets and in particular investment-goods, which are the most illiquid. Over time Keynes came to emphasize with growing strength that the individuals' demand for liquidity has to be seen essentially as their defence from uncertainty.

In our view, the major limit to Keynes's approach to the problem of liquidity preference and uncertainty is that, for him, the demand, and need, for liquidity takes the specific form of demand for money, sometimes as demand for bank money (saving deposits in the *Treatise*) and sometimes as demand for cash altogether (especially in the *General Theory*). The demand for liquidity translates itself into demand for money because of its special properties, as expressed by Keynes in Chapter 17 of *The General Theory* ('The essential properties of interest and money' Keynes, 1936[1973], pp. 222–244).

In 1937, in an article written to respond to reviews of the *General Theory* by Leontief, Robertson, Taussig and Viner (Keynes, 1937c), Keynes expounds his position in an extremely perspicuous way,

> ...partly on reasonable and partly on instinctive grounds, our desire to hold Money as a store of wealth is a barometer of the degree of our distrust of our own calculations and conventions concerning the future. ...The possession of actual money lulls our disquietude; and the premium which we require to make us part with money is the measure of the degree of our disquietude. (Keynes, 1937c, p. 216)

Keynes was convinced that the relation between uncertainty, liquidity preference and money could be dealt with essentially in the same way, independently of considering or not banks and credit. In fact, in *The General Theory* he largely ignored this 'complication'. But he was wrong. In so far as banks and credit are not taken into consideration, his notion of liquidity preference can be defined in terms of demand for money without any relevant loss of generality and consistency with respect to his major analytical conclusions and, in particular, his theory of the interest rate. But the introduction of banks and credit into Keynes's analytical framework does not leave it unaffected. The main reason why considering banks and credit alters the picture is that a high liquidity preference – or a high illiquidity aversion – cannot be readily translated into a high demand for money.

For Keynes, money is a defence from uncertainty because it allows agents to avoid, or postpone, their commitments to purchase illiquid assets with higher expected yields but riskier; in particular, it allows firms to defer their most crucial decisions, i.e. investment. Therefore, a high degree of liquidity preference can be expressed as a high degree of aversion to spending. A high degree of uncertainty, as well as a low state of confidence, can induce firms not to make investment for future production, or to produce less than they could. Firms have a high liquidity preference or, more correctly, they are highly illiquidity-averse. But the firms' 'prudent' attitude toward the future does not translate itself into a higher demand for money. It is the other way around.

If firms need external financing to carry out their activities and they decide not to invest or to produce less than they can, their demand for money declines. In modern market economies, production and investment decisions imply, first of all, an increase in the demand for credit. Decisions to carry out lower amounts of investment and/or production imply a decrease in the demand for loans and, hence, a decrease in the demand for money. If firms own internal funds to finance investment and/or production but they decide to abstain from transforming them into an illiquid form, this implies an equal reduction in the quantity of money in the hands of those who would have sold goods and services to firms.

Banks can certainly decide not to lend, or to lend to a smaller extent than that the economy as a whole requires. In other words, banks can decide not to become less liquid, but this does not mean that their demand for money, in the form of larger reserves, is high. They simply do not create all the money demanded by the economy. Banks' decisions not to lend cannot be merely reduced to decisions to keep the public's resources liquid. The banks' decision not to lend largely amounts to not increase the supply of money through the creation of active deposits.

Keynes's insistence on the demand for idle money as a defence from uncertainty leads him to 'forget' the demand for active money and, hence, for loans, which are demand for money to be spent. Robertson observed: 'Mr. Keynes was so taken up with the fact that people sometimes acquire money in order to *hold* it that he had apparently all but entirely forgotten the more familiar fact that they often acquire it in order to *use* it' (Robertson, 1940, p. 12).

A possible way out from the difficulties met by Keynes consists in separating the notion of demand for money from the notion of demand for liquidity, or liquidity preference, as a defence from uncertainty. The need for liquidity in economies with well developed financial institutions, can be satisfied by purchasing other assets rather than money strictly defined (on this, see also Sardoni, 2015a). Keynes himself had argued that the existence of organized financial markets is a response to the need for liquidity.

Keynes's insistence on the relation between money, liquidity preference and uncertainty also leads him, quite naturally, to give money a key central analytical role and treat the demand and supply of it separately from the demand and supply of other assets which, in turn, can affect the demand and supply of money itself. In other words, in dealing with money, Keynes tends to overlook the interrelation among all the relevant markets. An aspect that, as we saw, was pointed out and criticized by Ohlin in 1937 and that will be one of the topics discussed in the debates of following years, examined in the next chapter.

More in general, the critics of Keynes's view of money rejected his idea that money is the 'special' asset demanded as a store of value and as a defence from uncertainty: money is mostly demanded as a means of payment, i.e. to be spent. Although these criticisms can be regarded as essentially correct, they also had another more serious consequence: most of Keynes's insightful considerations on uncertainty, the defence from it in different ways from demanding money, and its effects on the working of financial markets and the whole economy were largely overlooked, if not ignored, for a long period of time.

6. Further discussions and criticisms of Keynes's *General Theory*

The debate on *The General Theory* continued in the years following 1937. Here, we focus on the prosecution of the discussion about the theory of the interest rate and on the nature and implications of the so-called wealth (or Pigou) effect. These topics were mainly discussed within an analytical framework in which the interrelations among all the relevant variables and markets is taken into account. Such a framework may be depicted as a general-equilibrium context, though not always in a proper Walrasian sense. In time, as we shall see in the next chapter, the Walrasian connection, became stronger and more explicit.

In these discussions the contributions by Hicks and Patinkin are of particular importance. Hicks set a general-equilibrium framework in which, he argued, Keynes's liquidity-preference theory of the interest rate and the loanable-funds theory are not alternative to one another, but only two possible different ways to approach the problem. Within the same framework Hicks also carried out the analysis of the structure of interest rates. Patinkin, who also contributed to the debate on interest rates, played a significant role in the discussion on the wealth effect, which was set in a general-equilibrium context and aimed to depotentiate Keynes's notion of underemployment equilibrium.

Both these debates have another feature in common. In both cases, the discussion took place without any significant reference to the banking system. The disregard for the role of banks can be, at least partly, ascribed to some developments in the analysis of banking, which led to the prevailing view that banks play an essentially passive role in the economy; the central bank is the ultimate controller of the supply of money.

6.1 TWO ALTERNATIVE THEORIES OF THE INTEREST RATE?

Hicks held that macroeconomic analysis has to be carried out within a general-equilibrium framework. His 'Mr. Keynes and the "Classics"' (1937) is an attempt to expound macroeconomic theory in the context of a general-equilibrium model, though highly simplified. Against Keynes's choice to focus on the main directions of causality when analysing money as well as other variables,[1] Hicks contends that the aggregate model should exhibit a coherent system of simultaneous equations encompassing all the real and monetary variables to deal with.[2] The 'Keynesian case' holds true only if the demand for money is assumed to depend exclusively on the interest rate (Hicks, 1937, pp. 150–154).[3] A hypothesis in which, for Hicks, Keynes himself did not believe.

Two years later, in *Value and Capital* (1939[1965]), Hicks developed his approach to macroeconomic analysis by concentrating on the interest rate.

> [I]t is evident that any treatment which pretends to deal with the economic system as a whole (...) cannot possibly regard the rate of interest in isolation. It is a price, like other prices, and must be determined with them as part of a mutually interdependent system. The problem is not one of determining a rate of interest *in vacuo*, but is really the general problem of price-determination in an economy where borrowing and lending are practised, and in which the rate of interest is therefore a constituent part of the general price-system. (Hicks, 1939[1965], p. 154) [4]

In this analytical context, the alternative between the liquidity-preference theory and the loanable-funds theory of the interest rate is essentially non-existent. They yield the same results. To take into consideration the demand and supply of money or, alternatively, the demand and supply of loans is a matter of convenience. Both approaches are monetary theories of the interest rate[5] and they are essentially interchangeable with one another,

---

[1]   Keynes's methodological approach is well described in Chapter 18 of the *General Theory*: 'The division of the determinants of the economic system into the two groups of given factors and independent variables is, of course, quite arbitrary from any absolute standpoint. The division must be made entirely on the basis of experience, so as to correspond on the one hand, to the factors in which the changes seem to be so slow or so little relevant as to have only a small and comparatively negligible short-term influence on our *quaesitum*; and on the other hand, to those factors in which the changes are found in practice to exercise a dominant influence on our *quaesitum*'. (Keynes, 1936[1973], p. 247). On Keynes's Chapter 18, see also Sardoni (1989–1990).

[2]   We examine Hicks's contributions to the debate on general equilibrium theory in more detail in Chapter 7 below.

[3]   In the article, Hicks mentions the role of banks in the variations of the quantity of money, but he thinks of banks 'as persons who are strongly inclined to pass on money by lending rather than spending it' (Hicks, 1937, p. 151).

[4]   Hansen (1951) explicitly accepted Hicks's general-equilibrium approach and argued that Keynes's theory of the interest rate is as indeterminate as the neoclassical and the loanable-funds theories (Hansen, 1951, pp. 429–430). Hansen (1951, p. 431) concludes that '[t]he neoclassical formulation and the Keynesian formulation, taken together in the context of an IS-LM model, do supply us with an adequate theory of the rate of interest.'

[5]   For Hicks (1939[1965], p. 153), most economists would agree with the fact that the interest rate depends on the supply and demand for capital, but they differ on the meaning of the term 'capital'. If by capital is meant real capital, then we have a theory *à la* Böhm-Bawerk; as an alternative, we have the 'monetary view', according to which by capital is meant money capital.

Is the rate of interest determined by the supply and demand for loanable funds (that is to say, by borrowing and lending); or is it determined by the supply and demand for money itself? This last view is put forward by Mr. Keynes in his *General Theory*. I shall hope to show that it makes no difference whether we follow his way of putting it, or whether we follow those writers who adopt what appears at present to be a rival view. (Hicks, 1939[1965], p. 153)

In an economy with n goods, one of which is taken as standard of value (*numeraire*), we are left with n prices to determine, i.e. the prices of $(n-1)$ goods plus the interest rate. At the same time, we have $(n+1)$ equations of supply and demand: those of the $(n-1)$ goods plus the supply and demand for money and the supply and demand for loans. In a general-equilibrium framework one of the $(n+1)$ equations can be eliminated because it follows from the other (Walras Law).[6] Therefore we have n equations to determine n prices.

From a formal point of view, which equation is to be eliminated is irrelevant. However, the choice to eliminate one equation instead of another has different implications from the economic point of view. First, Hicks considers the case in which the equation eliminated is relative to one of the n goods, which is taken as standard of value. In such a case, difficulties arise with the interest rate because the rate determined through the remaining n equations is not the true interest rate, which is a money rate,[7] but a 'real' (or natural) rate that expresses the value of future deliveries of the standard commodity in terms of current deliveries of the same standard. There is no reason why this natural rate should coincide with the monetary interest rate.[8]

Keynes's approach is obviously based on the determination of the monetary interest rate, but his rejection of the approach based on the real interest rate is not sufficient to establish the best way to determine the monetary interest rate, that is to say as determined by the supply and demand for loans or by the supply and demand for money. It is certainly possible to eliminate the money

---

[6]   On Walras Law, see also Patinkin (1956, pp. 32–61), Lange (1942[1959]) and Handa (2000, pp. 478–503).

[7]   Any exchange of present goods or services for a promise to deliver goods or services some time in the future essentially is a loan and it is constituted by a spot transaction and a money loan. 'Even a pure barter of present commodities for future commodities ...can be ...reduced to a spot transaction, a forward transaction and a money loan. Where forward markets exist, rates of interest in real terms are always implicitly established' (Hicks, 1939[1965], p. 141).

[8]   The two rates 'will be identical only if future prices of the auxiliary commodity are the same as spot prices. This condition will be fulfilled if the value of money (or the money value of the auxiliary standard commodity) is not expected to change at all, *and* if this expectation is absolutely certain, so that risk is absent' (Hicks, 1939[1965], p. 160).

equation and determine the *n* prices of the goods and the interest rate through the demand and supply of loans or, vice versa, to eliminate the loans equation.[9]

The problem tackled by Hicks was addressed and debated by many others in the 1930s to the 1950s, although not always in a general-equilibrium framework. Here, we briefly look at the positions taken by only a few contributors to the discussion: Lerner, Tsiang and Patinkin. Lerner (1938) holds that the two theories of the interest rate really say the same thing. To see their similarity it is sufficient to add (or subtract) hoarding, dis-hoarding and changes in the quantity of money to the functions of supply and demand for saving. In such a way, Lerner (1938, p. 213) concludes that the interest rate is the price that equates the supply of credit, which is equal to saving plus the net increase in the amount of money, to the demand for credit (investment) plus net hoarding (hoarding minus dis-hoarding). The difficulty with Lerner's analysis is that to sustain the equivalence of the two theories he introduces a very peculiar kind of borrowing. He defines net hoarding as 'the measure of that amount of saving that does not get invested but is "hoarded" either by the savers themselves or by people who borrow from them' (Lerner, 1938, p. 213).[10] There should exist agents who borrow to keep the loan in the liquid form of cash rather than to spend it on goods and/or services. All the following analysis and conclusions by Lerner are significantly affected by his notion of borrowing to hoard the loan.[11]

Also Tsiang (1956) believes that there is no real alternative between the two approaches to the interest rate. He, however, criticizes the recourse to Walras's Law and demonstrate their equivalence without relying on the law.[12] His analysis is based on the idea that what Keynes said about the finance motive applies to every kind of planned expenditure, so that the finance motive can be regarded as demand for money for transactions.[13] On these grounds,

---

[9] Hicks returned to consider the issue of loanable funds vs liquidity preference 50 years later in a short paper, where he makes some qualifications and specifications with respect to his 1939 position (Hicks, 1989a).

[10] See also Lerner (1938, p. 217) for a similar definition: hoarding indicates an excess of saving over investment or an excess of borrowing over investment.

[11] For Lerner, the demand for hoarding depends on an inequality between the marginal utility of the money stock and the interest rate; an inequality that can be eliminated quickly (Lerner, 1938, p. 218). In other words, money is borrowed to be hoarded to enjoy its marginal utility. Six years later, Lerner (1944) deals again with these topics. Being aware of the difficulties for the liquidity-preference theory when, in a general-equilibrium framework, supply and demand for money cannot be regarded as independent of one another, Lerner tries to preserve the simplicity of partial analysis and puts forward a solution based on his notion of borrowing money to keep it idle.

[12] For Tsiang, Walras's Law essentially is an ex post truism, with which the problems discussed by the proponents of the two theories of the interest rate cannot be tackled (Tsiang, 1956, pp. 539–545).

[13] It is so for the way in which Tsiang sets out his period analysis. In each period ('day'), expenditures cannot be financed by current income (Tsiang, 1956, pp. 546–547).

Tsiang shows that the two theories state the same thing in different ways. The supply of loanable funds is given by the sum of: i) current planned saving; ii) disinvestment of fixed or working capital; iii) net dis-hoarding; iv) net additional credit creation. The demand for loanable funds is given by the sum of: i) the demand for financing net investment; ii) the demand for funds to finance any other expenditure. The interest rate is the price that equates demand and supply (Tsiang, 1956, p. 548).

Patinkin's 1958 contribution can be regarded as conclusive of the debate on the two alternative theories. In an economy with $(n - 2)$ goods, bonds (perpetuities) and money, one of the n excess demand equations is redundant. If $(n - 1)$ excess demand equations are satisfied, also the nth equation must be satisfied. After a number of passages, Patinkin arrives at the following excess demand equation for money in a closed economy without a government sector

$$F^d - F^s = (S - D) + (B - L) \qquad (6.1)$$

where F^d is the demand for money; F^s is the supply of money; S is the inflow of money to agents deriving from their sales of goods; D is the agents' outflow of money deriving from their purchases of goods; B is the inflow of money deriving from the agents' borrowing; L is the outflow of money deriving from the agents' lending. Demand and supply of money are equal $(F^d - F^s = 0)$ if $(S - D) + (B - L) = 0$, which only occurs 'at the set of prices and interest rate which equilibrates the commodity and bond markets, respectively' (Patinkin, 1958, p. 302). Therefore, the set of prices that equilibrates the goods and the bond markets is also the set of prices that equilibrates the money market.[14]

Patinkin then considers possible objections to his demonstration. The first objection is that his analysis is carried out in terms of flows, whereas the liquidity-preference theory is expressed in terms of stocks. This objection, for him, is a *non sequitur*: the excess demand for money as a stock is identical with the excess demand for money as a flow. The excess demand equation for money in stock terms is

$$M^d = M_0 + (S - D) + (B - L) \qquad (6.2)$$

where M^d is the amount of money that the economy as a whole wants to hold at the end of the period and M_0 is the quantity of money held at the beginning

---

[14]   Alternatively, if $F^d - F^s = 0$, also the other markets must be in equilibrium.

of the period. It is evident that $M^d = M_0$ only if $(S - D) + (B - L) = 0$, which is exactly the same condition for the equilibrium between demand and supply of money in terms of flows (equation 6.1). Therefore, for Patinkin, '...any set of prices and interest which equilibrates the money market when viewed as consisting of flows, must also equilibrate it when viewed as stocks, and vice versa. In so far as equilibrium analysis is concerned, no difference can arise from this difference in viewpoints' (Patinkin, 1958, p. 304). The same line of analysis can be followed when considering stocks and flows of bonds instead of money.

Patinkin deals also with the objection according to which the liquidity-preference theory differs from the loanable-funds theory if the analysis is carried out in dynamic terms. He examines the argumentation according to which the distinction between the two theories of the interest rate corresponds to the distinction between the two following dynamic hypotheses: i) an excess supply of money makes the interest rate fall and an excess demand for money makes it rise; ii) an excess supply of bonds makes the interest rate rise and an excess demand for bonds makes it fall. These two hypotheses certainly represent two different dynamic theories of the behaviour of the interest rate, but their difference does not derive from considering the two different markets for money and bonds. Their difference derives from the fact that they imply a different dynamic behaviour of the same market, that is to say the money market (Patinkin, 1958, pp. 310–311).

Thus, concludes Patinkin, there do not exist two alternative theories of the interest rate and the debate on such a possibility belongs to a 'confused, transitory stage' in the development of economic theory, which should be relegated to the 'limbo of intellectual curiosa' (Patinkin, 1958, p. 317). From a formal point of view, Patinkin's analysis, which essentially is a refinement of Hicks's, can be regarded as conclusive, but it is important to point out that with Patinkin's approach to the determination of the interest rate, the analysis of credit markets and their role in market economies lost most of the richness and complexity that characterized, for example, Robertson's and Ohlin's positions in their critique of the liquidity preference theory. As we shall see in more detail in the next chapter, in Patinkin's world banks are almost totally ignored; the importance of credit in dynamic processes of change is not taken into consideration; the market for loans (bonds) is regarded as essentially the same as the market for goods.

6.2   SHORT- AND LONG-TERM INTEREST RATES

We do not consider the problem of the structure of interest rates in any detailed way; we look at the issue by concentrating on some aspects that are more relevant to the topics treated in the book.[15] First, the analysis of the structure of interest rates has implications for Keynes's notion of liquidity preference and his theory of the interest rate. Second, the way in which the problem of the term structure was tackled is an example of macroeconomic analysis carried out in a general-equilibrium framework. Finally, especially in Kaldor's case, the working of financial markets and speculation is analysed in a more detailed and complex way than in *The General Theory* and in most subsequent Keynesian contributions.

Before dealing with Walras's Law in relation to the determination of the interest rate in *Value and Capital*, Hicks had dealt with the problem of the interest rate on securities of differing maturity. Considering only the long and short-term rates, he argues that the long-term rate (R) is the arithmetic average between the current short-term rate (r_1) and forward short-term rates ($q_2, q_3, \ldots, q_n$). In his own words, 'every loan of every duration can be reduced to a standard pattern – a loan for the minimum period, combined with a given number of renewals for subsequent periods of the same length, contracted forward' (Hicks, 1939[1965], p. 145)

$$R_n = \frac{r_1 + q_2 + \cdots + q_n}{n} \tag{6.3}$$

where $q_2, q_3, \cdots, q_n$ are the forward short-term rates.[16]

Hicks takes into consideration the so-called 'bootstrap problem', which is related to the notion of money and the fundamental reasons why, differently from all other assets, it does not bear an interest. According to a view that Hicks attributes to Keynes, what distinguishes money from other securities is that the interest on it is nil. Money is the 'most perfect type of security' because its face value is equal to its present value. The interest rate on other securities is a measure of their imperfection, or their imperfect 'moneyness' (Hicks, 1939[1965], p. 163). A component part of the interest paid on securities is imputable to the risk of default and to uncertainty about the future price of the security itself. Thus, interest is nothing but a risk-premium, but 'to say that the rate of interest on perfectly safe securities is determined by nothing else than uncertainty of future interest rates seems to leave interest hanging by its own bootstraps; one feels an obstinate conviction that there must be more in it than that' (Hicks, 1939[1965], p. 164).

---

[15] For a more exhaustive examination of the structure of interest rates, see, e.g., Handa (2000, pp. 595–623).

[16] It is $q_i = r_i^e + \rho_i$, where r_i^e is the expected short-term rate at time i ($i = 2, 3, \cdots, n$) and ρ_i is the risk premium relative to time i. Hicks adopts a slightly different notation.

The problem is tackled by Hicks by looking at the relation between money and its closest substitute, i.e. perfectly safe, and highly liquid, very short-term bills. If one can understand why also those bills bear an interest, the 'boot-strap problem' is solved. If bills earn an interest, why should individuals not invest all their funds in them? If this were the case, money would have no superiority over bills and it could not stand at a premium relatively to them. But there are two problems with this possibility. The first has to do with costs of transaction when converting bills into money, which however is not sufficient to explain the existence of an interest rate on bills. If bills are perfectly safe, they could be used to make exchanges without any need to convert them into money (Hicks, 1939[1965], pp. 164–165). In a number of cases, in fact, such bills are actually used for exchanges, as they are accepted by the parties in the transaction. But it is acceptability that represents the crucial problem, '. . . general acceptability is something different from the mere absence of default risk (. . .) A class of bills may be regarded as perfectly safe by those who actually take them up, and yet these persons may be different from those to whom the borrower has to make payments. These latter would not accept his bills, so he has to pay *cash*; the former are perfectly willing to lend, but require interest to compensate for their cost of investment' (Hicks, 1939[1965], pp. 165–166).

Hicks sums up the results of his analysis as follows: 'Securities which are not generally acceptable in payment of debts bear some interest because they are imperfectly "money"' (Hicks, 1939[1965], p. 167). For very short-term bills, the interest rate corresponds to the cost of transaction; for longer-term securities, a positive interest rate is connected to the possibility of having to re-discount them on unfavourable terms, a cost that has to be added to their transaction cost. The bootstrap problem is solved. Short-term interest rates, which affect through forward markets the long-term rates do not depend on expectations. They ultimately depend on the costs of converting them into money, which is the security with unlimited acceptability, at least in normal situations.

Hicks's analysis is characterized by two important elements. The first is that the analysis is carried out by considering a complex set of markets, which includes both forward and spot transactions. In such a context expectations obviously play a decisive role, but they do so essentially through forward markets where they manifest themselves through market prices rather than being mere individual forecasts of future events. The second distinctive element of Hicks's approach is that the 'special' nature of money must be explained by taking account of aspects of social and historical nature. Money is special because it is the means of payment universally accepted within a certain economic system. How a specific asset comes to be recognized as money is a historical process that involves both individuals and the state. Such approach to money has distinguished Hicks's monetary theory throughout his scientific production. His last book, *A Market Theory of Money* (Hicks, 1989b), is a masterful logical-historical reconstruction of the processes through which certain assets become money. In the book, moreover, Hicks makes it clear that the use of an asset as money is strictly connected to its being the economy's standard of value (unit of account). Money appears in transactions in two ways: in the formation of contracts, when the value of the delivery has to be established and in the discharge of the buyer's debt. These two roles of money correspond to its functions of standard of value and means of payment respectively. The two functions of money are not independent of one another. A debt in money cannot be discharged unless money also plays the role of standard of value (Hicks, 1989b, p. 43). Money as a standard makes it possible to form price-lists, in which the values of commodities are reduced to a common measure.[17]

In 1939, the same year that *Value and Capital* came out, Kaldor published an article on speculation (Kaldor, 1939) which was, in several respects, significantly influenced by Hicks's analysis of interest rates and expectations.[18] Here we limit ourselves to consider those aspects of Kaldor's article that are more relevant in the present context.[19]

Kaldor has always been critical of Keynes's approach to money and liquidity preference, especially as expressed in *The General Theory*. In the 1980s, in expounding Keynes's theory as opposed to the 'old monetarism', Kaldor was quite dismissive of Keynes's innovations concerning the demand for money and the determination of the interest rate (Kaldor, 1989b).[20] For Kaldor, in *The General Theory*, 'Keynes invented some short-cuts through the maze of complications of a multi-market analysis and thereby reduced the essential aspects of the problem to manageable dimensions' (Kaldor, 1960a, pp. 3–4). The analytical foundations of Kaldor's view of Keynes's monetary theory can be found in his work on speculation. In retrospect, in 1960, Kaldor presented his article as an attempt to generalize Keynes on the basis of a general theory of speculation, i.e. a theory of the interplay between flow demand and supply curves and stock demand and supply curves. Kaldor studies the effects of speculation by considering spot and forward markets in which speculators,

---

[17] For Hicks, transactions carried out through contracts represent the most general form of exchange, while spot transactions are a particular case.

[18] Hicks, on the other hand, had a high opinion of Kaldor's article. In 1986, he wrote to Kaldor: 'I think that your paper was the culmination of the Keynesian revolution in theory' (as quoted in Thirlwall, 1987, p. 75n).

[19] We refer to a revised version of Kaldor's 1939 article published in 1960 (Kaldor, 1960c). For a more exhaustive illustration of Kaldor's contribution to monetary theory, see Sardoni (2007, 2017).

[20] Kaldor also held that his own analysis 'drew heavily' on Keynes's *Treatise* rather than *The General Theory*.

hedgers and arbitrageurs operate and distinguishes between cases of uniform and non-uniform expectations across the market.[21]

In so far as speculation is about producible goods, their normal price, i.e. the price to which they converge in the long period (Kaldor, 1960c, pp. 34–35), plays a crucial role as it is a sort of anchor which makes prices relatively stable in the long period. When speculation about financial assets, bonds in particular, is considered, there does not exist any notion of normal price and, however, the observed long-term rates are more stable than short-term rates. This can be explained by recourse to Hicks's approach to interest rates (Kaldor, 1960c, pp. 60–68). The long-term interest rate is influenced by changes in the current short-term rate only for a small proportion, even though this is strictly true only in the case of uniform expectations.

When the hypothesis of uniform expectations is lifted, speculators divide into 'bulls' and 'bears'. In a market where bulls predominate, the forward price tends to exceed the expected price and vice versa when bears predominate. Thus, Kaldor's conclusions about the long-term interest rate are not universally valid. In any case, the advantage of his approach is that it shows that there is a complex relationship between the long and the short-term interest rates; a relationship that Keynes did not consider in *The General Theory* (Kaldor, 1960c, pp. 68–69).

In Kaldor's analysis, the current short-term rate does not depend either on expected short rates or the long-term rate.[22] In a footnote, Kaldor gave his explanation of why the short-term rate is not dependent on either the current or the expected long-term rate.

> ...a change in the long-term rate (either the current or the expected rate) cannot react back on the short-term rate except perhaps indirectly by causing a change in the level of income and, hence, in the demand for cash. For, supposing the change in the long rate causes speculators to sell long-term investments, this could only affect the short rate if they substituted the holding of cash for the holding of long-term bonds, it cannot affect the short rate if the substitution takes place in favor of short-term investment other than cash (savings deposits, etc.). But there is no reason to expect, in normal circumstances at any rate, that the substitution will be in favour of cash. 'Idle balances' – i.e. that part of short-term holding which the owner does not require for transaction purposes – can be kept in forms such as savings deposits, which offer the same advantages as cash (as far as the preservation of capital value is concerned) and yield a return in addition. (Kaldor, 1960c, p. 39n)

---

[21]   Speculators assume risks and buy (sell) assets to sell (buy) them at a later date in the expectation of a capital gain. Hedgers enter the market in order to reduce the risk of their commitments. Arbitrageurs buy spot and sell forward when they can make a profit from the difference between the spot and the forward price. On their role in the determination of spot and forward prices, see Kaldor (1960c, pp. 23–28) and Sardoni (2007).

[22]   Expected short rates do not affect the current short rate because the duration of short-term bills is too short for expectations to be relevant (Kaldor, 1960a, p. 39n).

Since the elasticity of supply of cash with respect to the short-term rate is normally much larger than the elasticity of demand, the current short-term rate can be treated simply as a datum, essentially determined by the policy of the central bank, which controls the money supply (Kaldor, 1960c, pp. 38–39).

Kaldor makes the important point that, normally, the speculators' liquidity preference is not expressed as demand for idle money like in Keynes's analysis, but as an increased demand for other short-term liquid assets. Also in this respect, Kaldor's approach is close to Hicks's. For Hicks, money as a store of value can be dealt with by distinguishing non-voluntary and voluntary demand for money (Hicks, 1967b, p. 15). Non-voluntary demand is the demand for money as a means of payment to carry out transactions (to settle contracts); the voluntary demand for money is the demand for a store of value, which Hicks relates to Keynes's precautionary and speculative motives.[23] Investors choose the portfolio with the maximum yield. If they are risk-averse, their portfolio may contain a certain amount of money (Hicks, 1967a, pp. 17–27). This, however, does not imply that in the agents' portfolios there must always be a certain amount of money.[24] In other words, agents normally protect themselves from risk and uncertainty in ways different from holding idle money.

Kaldor (1960b) criticizes Keynes's notion of liquidity preference in relation to money also by referring to Chapter 17 of *The General Theory*,[25] where Keynes explains the crucial role of money (money 'rules the roost') in the determination of the macroeconomic equilibrium: the equilibrium quantity of all assets is determined by the asset yield that is fixed, or highly sticky, and the own interest rate on money is the most reluctant to decline. Keynes introduces the notions of own-rate of own interest and own-rate of money-interest of assets, which respectively are

$$R_i^o = q_i - c_i + l_i \tag{6.4}$$
$$R_i^m = a_i + q_i - c_i + l_i$$
$$(i = 1, 2, \cdots, n)$$

---

[23] Hicks's treatment of money as store of value relates to the theory of portfolio choice developed by Tobin (1958), which we discuss in Chapter 7 below. See also Hicks's article on a suggested simplification of the theory of money (Hicks, 1935).

[24] 'Keynes, I think, believed that it was always (or nearly always) the case – in an economy with developed financial markets – that there would be *some* money being held for a speculative motive (...) [R]isk aversion *may* induce the investor to hold some non-interest bearing money in his portfolio (...) but nothing has been said which would lead us to suppose that he must do so, unless he is feeling in a very poor state' (Hicks, 1967a, p. 46).

[25] Kaldor's criticism is expounded in a paper that was originally meant to be an appendix to his 1939 article, but the paper was not published until 1960.

where q_i is the yield of the $i - th$ asset in terms of itself, c_i is the asset's carrying cost, l_i is its liquidity premium (the amount of the asset itself that an agent is willing to pay for the potential convenience of the power of disposal of the asset) and a_i is the asset's appreciation or depreciation in terms of the economy's unit of account. Money (the $m - th$ asset) is characterized by the following properties: $q_m = 0, c_m = 0, a_m = 0, l_m = \bar{l}_m > 0$. Money is a non-producible asset (it has a zero elasticity of production) and the yield in terms of itself is nil. Money has also a nil carrying cost. Its appreciation (depreciation) is nil because it is the unit of account. Finally, money has a positive and constant liquidity premium (it has a zero elasticity of substitution). Therefore,

$$R_m^o = R_m^m = \bar{l}_m \qquad (6.5)$$

In equilibrium, it must be $R_m^m = R_i^m$ $(i = 1, 2, \cdots, n; i \neq m)$, that is to say,

$$\bar{l}_m = R_i^m \ (i = 1, 2, \cdots, n; i \neq m) \qquad (6.6)$$

which means that money 'rules the roost': its constant liquidity premium $(\bar{l}_m)$ determines the equilibrium quantities of all the other assets. The role of money could be played by any asset which has a constant liquidity premium. The functions of standard of value and means of payment are not sufficient to give money its crucial role.

Kaldor, instead, argues that money rules the roost because it is the standard of value and not because of its constant and positive liquidity premium. If the expected price of reproducible assets is given by their long-period supply price (their normal price), an asset is produced only if its current price is higher than its supply price, i.e., when a in (6.4) is positive. When, for an asset it is $a = 0$, its current price is equal to its normal price and, hence, the marginal efficiency of the asset,[26] its own-rate of own-interest and its own-rate of money-interest are all equal. The general level of the own-rates of money-interest is set by the greatest of the own-rates of own-interest among those assets whose own-rate of money-interest (R_i^m) cannot vary with respect to their own-rate of own-interest. The only asset with such a characteristic is money because it is the standard of value and, hence, $a_m = 0$.[27]

Years later, Hicks took a similar position to Kaldor's: it cannot be argued that money is the perfect liquid asset and, hence, its liquidity premium is positive and constant. Liquidity can be defined only in terms of exchangeability for money and, therefore, 'to define money as an asset with perfect liquidity is to

---

[26] The marginal efficiency of an asset is defined by Kaldor as the relationship of its future return to its present cost of production, i.e., its long-period supply price (Kaldor, 1960b, p. 59).

[27] '[A]ll assets other than money can adjust their own-rates of money-interest to that of money by a variation of their current price in terms of money; while the money-rate of money-interest can only be changed by varying money's own-rate of own-interest' (Kaldor, 1960b, p. 70).

argue in a circle. It is the other functions of money which are intrinsic; the liquidity property follows from them.' (Hicks, 1989b, p. 42).

Both Hicks and Kaldor carried out their analyses of interest rates within a more complex framework than that adopted by Keynes in *The General Theory*.[28] In their analyses expectations play a role in the determination of interest rates through forward markets. The agents' expectations reflect themselves onto actual market forward prices and it is in such a way that they affect the individuals' behaviour. In their analytical setting, the interest rate can no longer be seen as the price at which agents are willing to renounce to the perfect liquidity asset (money).

The critics of the Kaldor-Hicks approach essentially ignored the role of forward markets.[29] They concentrated on the idea that the short-term rate is not influenced by the long-term rate, whereas the opposite is true. Robertson (1952) rejected Kaldor's idea that there exists a one-way relation between the two rates (Robertson, 1952, p. 112). He questions the plausibility of Kaldor's description of the behaviour of interest rates by concentrating on the case of a rise in the long-term rate. In particular, if such a rise is due to an increase in the marginal productivity of investment funds, there will be an increased demand for money to make purchases of goods and securities and hence an increase in the short-term rate (Robertson, 1952, p. 113). Robertson is right in considering the effects that a change in the long rate might have on the demand for money, but he fails to take account of Kaldor's considerations on the behaviour of the supply of cash, which is more elastic than the demand and essentially is under the control of the central bank.[30] Kaldor's position regarding the supply of money is evidently related to the fact that in his analysis he had virtually ignored banks and their ability to create money. If banks can create money through lending, the ability of the central bank to control the money supply and the (short-term) interest rate is obviously lessened.[31]

Two of the closest economists to Keynes, Robinson (1951) and Kahn (1954[1972]), reacted to the Hicks-Kaldor approach in a much more critical

---

[28]   The simplifications in *The General Theory* were certainly not due to Keynes's ignorance of the complexity and sophistication of modern financial markets. For example, in the 1920s, in *A Tract on Monetary Reform* (Keynes, 1923[1971]), Keynes was one of the first economists to deal with forward markets. See also Tobin (1961, pp. 30–31) on Keynes's choice to deal with a single interest rate.

[29]   Also those who sympathized with the Hicks-Kaldor analysis of the term structure of interest rates did not pay much attention to the existence and role of forward markets (see, e.g., Kalecki, 1943[1991], 1954[1965]).

[30]   Kaldor responded to Robertson's criticism in his 1960 introduction to *Essays on Economic Stability and Growth* (Kaldor, 1960a, pp. 4–5n). On the discussion between Robertson and Kaldor, see also Kennedy (1948–1949).

[31]   The endogeneity of the money supply is something that, later on, Kaldor repeatedly pointed out in his critique of Friedman's monetarism (see, e.g., Kaldor, 1989a).

way. Although they both acknowledged that Keynes's theory of money and the interest rate was in need of further developments, Robinson and Kahn did not move appreciably in such a direction. Robinson, in developing her own theory, basically retains the same analytical framework as in *The General Theory*: speculators choose between holding idle money or assets.[32] A few years later, Kahn, in dealing with the distinction between the precautionary and the speculative demand for money, makes similar hypotheses about speculation and conducts his analysis by considering only the demand for long-term securities and the demand for money. Similar positions, as we shall see in the next chapter, were taken by many other Keynesians of the Neoclassical Synthesis in their use of various versions of the IS-LM model.

6.3   THE EVOLVING VIEW OF THE NATURE OF BANKING

Most of the authors considered in previous chapters – namely Wicksell, Schumpeter, Robertson and Keynes of the *Treatise* – viewed banks in a way that came to be described as 'old'. All these authors held that the modern banks' capacity to lend was not constrained by the amount of deposits they could attract. To use Schumpeter's terminology, banks can create money *ex nihilo*, which amounts to create (active) deposits through credit. However, none of these authors offered a fully fledged analysis of the relation between deposits and creation of bank money.

In the 1920s, there were some attempts at developing a more detailed analysis of banks which implied a criticism of the 'old view', even though Schumpeter, Robertson and others regarded their view of banks as new with respect to the previous. Here, we concentrate on Phillips's contribution (Phillips, 1921), which inspired other subsequent works. To argue that bank loans is an aggregate larger than bank deposits amounts to argue that banks can create money in excess of the quantity of money (currency) created and issued by the central bank and deposited with them, but such a statement can be interpreted in two different ways:

(i)   each single bank can create money in excess of the deposits with it, i.e. it can create money *ex nihilo*;
(ii)   no single bank can create money in excess of its deposits, but the *banking system as a whole* can.

---

[32]   Robinson also points out that Kaldor's theory strictly holds under the hypothesis of uniform expectations, something of which, as we saw, Kaldor himself was well aware.

Phillips defines these two interpretations of credit and money creation as the old and the new theory respectively.[33] According to Phillips (1921, p. 32), the old theory of banking is marred by the lack of a clear distinction between credit extension by a single bank and credit extension by the banking system as a whole. Once this distinction is neatly drawn, it becomes evident that statement (i) above is wrong. A single bank, argues Phillips, can extend its credit 'by a little more' than the amount of its 'primary' deposits, that is to say those deposits generated by the lodgement of cash, or an equivalent of it, with the bank (Phillips, 1921, p. 34). 'Derivative' deposits, by contrast, are those that the bank creates when it makes a loan.[34] According to the old incorrect theory, when a bank receives a cash deposit, it retains a certain amount with it as a reserve and lends out the rest and creates derivative deposits. Credit 'is called a deposit, and properly so, since the net purport of the transaction is that the banker has bought an interest-bearing security and the seller has deposited the money he received for it in the bank, to be drawn out at his pleasure'; but there is a difference between a primary and a derivative deposit, 'the one being of money and the other a bank credit' (Phillips, 1921, p. 35).

Holding that for a single bank it is possible to 'manufacture' credit to a significant larger extent than its deposits fails to take into due account the fact that such a large extension of credit would imply an unfavourable clearing house balance for the bank. The cheques drawn against the bank loans would, in large part, be deposited with other banks than the lending one. The other banks' claim for cash on the lending bank would reduce its amount of reserves (cash), with a consequent worsening of its clearing house balance. The loans made by the bank would largely '. . . represent cash that the bank would lose through unfavorable clearing house balances, an amount that would be scattered widely among the banks of the system. It is clear that an individual bank attempting to lend greatly in excess of the amount of an addition to its reserves would do so at its peril' (Phillips, 1921, p. 38). Cautious bankers do not extend their credit unlimitedly but tend to maintain a safe ratio of loans (derivative deposits) to reserves (primary deposits).

The picture would be different if there exists a single monopolistic bank. In this case, there would not be any loss of cash following the issuing of loans and their use for purchases. Therefore the bank's loans could be extended by an amount that is constrained only by its desired reserve ratio. What applies to the monopolistic bank can be immediately extended to a banking system

---

[33]   Phillips indicates Macleod as one of the most influential representatives of the old theory, but he does not mention either Hahn (2015[1920]) or the authors mentioned above. On the 'old view' see also Trautwein (2000) and Werner (2014a).

[34]   Phillips's distinction between the two types of deposits is clearly the same as Keynes's between passive and active deposits (see Chapter 5 above).

composed by many independent banks. By denoting the desired reserve ratio by R, the amount of primary deposits by c and the expansion of deposits through lending by D, Phillips (1921, p. 39) formulates the simplest version of what has come to be known as the money multiplier,

$$D = \frac{c}{R} \tag{6.7}$$

The factor that ultimately determines the amount of money created by banks through credit is the amount of reserves (cash) available to them. Crick (1927) clearly points out that the amount of cash available to banks is essentially determined by the policy of the central bank, which can change the volume of cash and in so doing it gives rise to 'multiple changes in the volume of deposits' (Crick, 1927, pp. 193–194).[35] Therefore, the central bank is the real controller of the money supply.

> The banks, except for short periods and so long as no permanent change in cash ratios is effected, have very little scope for policy in the matter of expansion or contraction of deposits, though they have in the matter of disposition of resources between loans, investments and other assets. But this is not to say that the banks cannot and do not effect multiple additions to or subtractions from deposits as a whole on the basis of an expansion of or contraction in bank cash. To say that a bank cannot in practice 'create' deposits to an indefinite extent is one thing; to say it cannot 'create' deposits at all is another. The first assertion is true (...) The second is untrue (Crick, 1927, p. 201)

In one of the most influential textbooks ever written, Samuelson (1948) expounds what he regards the correct interpretation of banking and deposit creation by using almost the same words as those used by Phillips and Crick more than twenty years earlier. For Samuelson, the explanation of how deposits are created is simple, but false ideas and explanations were still in circulation.

> According to these false explanations, the managers of an ordinary bank are able, by some use of their fountain pens, to lend several dollars for each dollar left on deposits with them. No wonder practical banks see red when such behavior is attributed to them. They only wish they could do so. As every banker well knows, he cannot invest money that he does not have; and any money that he does invest in buying a security or making a loan will soon leave his bank. (Samuelson, 1948, p. 324)[36]

As a consequence, 'practical bankers' go to the opposite extreme: the whole banking system cannot create any money. This idea is wrong as well, because

---

[35] Bank cash comprises currency held by banks to the credit of customers together with the banks' currency held at their credit by the central bank (Crick, 1927, p. 191).

[36] Samuelson carries out his analysis under the hypothesis that there exists a legal reserve ratio.

it is subject to the fallacy of composition. In reality, '[t]he banking system as a whole can do what each small bank cannot do!' (Samuelson, 1948, p. 324).

> Who creates the multiple expansion of deposits? Three parties do so jointly: the public by always keeping their money in the bank on deposit, the banks by keeping only a fraction of their deposits in the form of cash, the public and private borrowers who make it possible for the banks to find earning assets to buy with their excess cash. There is also a fourth party, the Central Bank, which by its activities makes it possible for new reserves to come to the banking system. (Samuelson, 1948, p. 329)

Samuelson develops his analysis further by making some important qualifications. First, the multiple expansion of deposits by banks is limited by the possibility that the public do not keep all their money with banks. Second, banks can keep some cash in the form of till money, which is something different from their reserves at the central bank but equally limits their ability to create deposits. Third, and most important, there is no reason why banks could not choose to lend less than the amount they are allowed by the legal reserve ratio; in other words, they can keep discretional reserves. Therefore,

> ...there is nothing automatic about deposit creation. Four factors are necessary: The banks must somehow receive reserves; they must be willing to make loans or buy securities; someone must be willing to borrow or to sell securities; and finally, the public must choose to leave their money on deposit with the banks. (Samuelson, 1948, pp. 332–333)

Samuelson's analysis can be expressed by using the well-known formula of the money multiplier. The total quantity of money M is

$$M = \frac{1}{[c + \theta(1 - c)]} H \qquad (6.8)$$

where c represents the share of money that the public wish to hold in cash, θ is the bank's reserve ratio (legal plus discretionary reserves) and H is the amount of hard money issued by the central bank.

Samuelson was cautious in his analysis of the money multiplier: the ratio of bank money (deposits) to cash (high-powered money) cannot be simply regarded as given and constant. From this it should follow that the money supply cannot be taken as a strictly exogenous variable, fully controlled by the central bank. In this sense, the criticism of the 'old view' of banks is less strong than it can appear. The advocates of the old view, as we saw, never held that each single bank can expand its loans unconstrained as it takes account of the risk of illiquidity and, hence, wants to maintain a certain (flexible) ratio of its loans to reserves.

Moreover, the critics of the old view seem to never contemplate the possibility that banks can borrow reserves from the central bank. If this possibility is admitted, the public, and their decisions to deposit or not money with the banks, play a less significant role in the determination of the possible amount of credit (deposits) that the banks can create. In so far as the central bank is ready to lend to commercial banks, deposits do not represent a constraint to lending. The role that the public play concerns the amount of loans (deposits) they demand from banks. In this world, banks operate in the economy as lenders and borrowers, both from the public (depositors) and the central bank. In the 'new world', banks apparently can borrow only from the public.

Notwithstanding Samuelson's caution, which makes his criticism of the old view less cogent, the approach to money and banks that prevailed at the time and later on is a mechanistic notion of the money multiplier and an essentially passive role for banks to play. These are important constituent parts of the so-called 'money view', in which the money supply is modelled as an exogenous variable fully controlled by the central bank.[37] A consequential implication of this approach to money is that the role of banks tends to be downplayed or ignored altogether. Trautwein (2000, p. 158) summarizes this aspect well: for the money view '...commercial banks do not require much attention in macro-economic analysis. Whatever the share of bank deposits in the relevant monetary aggregate, their supply is taken to be a stable function of the monetary base, expressed in money multipliers. ...Deposits (liabilities) play a role in determining aggregate demand, if only a subordinate one, by way of liquidity effects or real balance effects. Bank loans (assets) play no specific role at all, since other financial assets (such as bonds) are regarded as perfect substitutes.' This sort of approach can partly explain why banks could be left outside the basic analytical framework adopted in the debates on interest rates and the wealth effect.

6.4   THE DEBATE ON THE WEALTH EFFECT

In *The General Theory*, Keynes explicitly deals with the wealth effect in two chapters. In Chapter 8, 'The propensity to consume', he explicitly mentions the possibility of a wealth effect on consumption in relation to windfall changes in capital values due to unforeseen changes of the prices of securities and other assets which constitute the wealth of the upper classes (Keynes, 1936[1973], pp. 93–94). Thus, as far as consumption is concerned, Keynes

---

[37]   As we shall see in Chapter 7, Tobin (1963) criticized this mechanistic, or naive, notion of money multiplier. For a description of the money view as distinguished from the 'credit view', see Friedman (1999) and Trautwein (2000). We return to consider the credit view in Chapter 9 below.

deals with wealth effects due to speculative bubbles (or their reversal) in the prices of assets and properties, not with wealth effects on the stock of outside money. However, although he acknowledges that windfall changes in capital values can affect the propensity to consume, Keynes chooses to put aside this complication and concentrates on the basic relation between consumption and current income (Keynes, 1936[1973], p. 96).

In Chapter 19, on 'Changes in money wages', Keynes deals with the effect on nominal income of a deflation following a reduction of money wages. He points out that the consequent reduction of the transaction demand for money might bring down the rate of interest, with a positive effect on investment, which however can be offset by the negative impact of deflation on business confidence, the increased burden of debt, and the risk of insolvency. Moreover, Keynes includes a note of caution on the endogeneity of the real money stock.

> It is, therefore, on the effect of a falling wage – and price-level on the demand for money that those who believe in the self-adjusting quality of the economic system must rest the weight of their argument; though I am not aware that they have done so. If the quantity of money is itself a function of the wage- and price-level, there is indeed, nothing to hope in this direction. But if the quantity of money is virtually fixed, it is evident that its quantity in terms of wage-units can be indefinitely increased by a sufficient reduction in money-wages...We can, therefore, theoretically at least, produce precisely the same effects on the rate of interest by reducing wages, whilst leaving the quantity of money unchanged, that we can produce by increasing the quantity of money whilst leaving the level of wages unchanged. (Keynes, 1936[1973], p. 266)

The wealth-effect channel, operating through deflation on the quantity of money, is in principle equivalent to an expansionary monetary policy, and subject to the same limitations, as far as the recovery of investment is involved. A moderate wage deflation would be ineffective, just as a moderately expansionary monetary policy would be. In the case of severe deflation, the adjustment process might be self-defeating, because of the disruptive effects of deflation on the climate of social relations, business confidence and financial stability.

In the 1940s, in the wake of the debate on Keynes's *General Theory* and the ensuing controversy on the adjustment paths to restore full-employment equilibrium, wealth effects due to price deflation were discussed by various scholars. Such discussion had an impact on the way in which, in the late 1940s and early 1950s, financial markets were erased from the new Keynesian macroeconomic models, in favour of the simplified vision of the money market, as constituted by a demand for money and an exogenous supply of money.

In 1943, Pigou dealt with the wealth effect in his article 'The classical stationary state' (Pigou, 1943). A few years before, in 1936, reviewing

Keynes's *General Theory*, Pigou had interpreted the core message of Keynes's book as the dismal forecast of future stagnation due to the exhaustion of investment opportunities. He had criticized Keynes for having emphasized the tendency towards a stationary state, where, investment opportunities having vanished, income stabilizes at the very low level compatible with zero saving; the money interest rate being subject to the zero-bound constraint. Pigou ironically named such a gloomy stationary point 'Keynes's day of judgement', and the cumulative process leading to it, 'Keynes's cumulative debacle' (Pigou, 1936, pp. 129–130).[38]

Pigou, although his 1943 article is explicitly meant to criticize the stagnationist position taken by Hansen (1941), aimed to reject Keynes's analysis of the long-term convergence of advanced market economies to a stable underemployment equilibrium at zero investment. Pigou, by mixing static and dynamic analysis, argues that it is possible to reject the idea that the economy could converge, through a conjectural process of adjustment, to a stable stationary state at a less than full-employment level of income, with zero investment, zero saving, and a non negative, near zero interest rate.

Pigou is perfectly aware to be dealing with fictional cases of solely theoretical relevance. His objective is to assess the theoretical coherence of what he regards as the classical vision of the full-employment stationary state. His model is built on the assumption of a representative agent choosing between saving and consumption.[39] He maintains that in the deflationary adjustment process, real income being maintained, the representative agent will be induced to progressively cut saving to zero, because at a lower price level the real quantity of money increases. This wealth effect on *M* affects both the desired consumption expenditure, which increases with real wealth, and the equilibrium in the money market, with the money interest rate converging to zero.

> As money wage-rates fall money income must fall also and go on falling. Employment, and so real income, being maintained, this entails that prices fall and go on falling; which is another way of saying that the stock of money, as valued in terms of real income, correspondingly rises. But the extent to which the representative man desires to make savings otherwise than for the sake of their future income yield

---

[38] 'At this point the economic system comes into equilibrium. People no longer desire to save anything, and, therefore, money income no longer contracts. The stock of capital is the same as it was when the rate of interest became nothing; but employment, and therewith real income, is smaller – maybe much smaller. The situation thus reached, provided that money wage rates are still maintained, is one of stable equilibrium – the low level equilibrium that I have sometimes called Lord Keynes's Day of Judgment' (Pigou, 1947[1952], p. 186).

[39] Pigou (1947[1952], p.180) explicitly acknowledges that he is following the path opened by Ramsey (1928). Pigou's approach is an interesting anticipation of the later use of the representative agent in macroeconomics.

depends in part on the size, in terms of real income, of his existing possessions. As this increases, the amount that he so desires to save out of any assigned real income diminishes and ultimately vanishes. (Pigou, 1943, pp. 349–350)

On these grounds, Pigou holds that the classical notion of a full-employment stationary state is fully coherent when competitive conditions prevail in the labour market and money wages are flexible downward (Pigou, 1943, p. 351). Pigou, however, does not explain how and why a coherent mathematical model could be built on assuming a single representative agent, both consumer and producer, jointly with the downward pressure on flexible wages in competitive labour markets. Neither does he explain why money should have any role at all in such an economy.

Kalecki (1944) commented and rejected Pigou's thesis. For him, the wealth effect should be considered only in relation to gold money (that is to say outside money). Bank money should not be considered because deposits are compensated by corresponding private debts.[40] The wealth gain to money holders due to a lower price level would be compensated by the loss to banks' debtors, so that no net wealth effect could be effective on that part of the money stock. Thus, the wealth effect should be applied to a restricted definition of money, with a lower impact on aggregate demand. As a consequence, the net wealth effect necessary to bring the economy back to full employment might require an exceedingly large deflation, which might generate a crisis of confidence or a catastrophic financial crisis due to the bankruptcy of debtors.

Kalecki's argumentation is somewhat contradictory. On the one hand, outstanding private debts should not be considered in evaluating the net wealth effect; on the other hand, a severe deflation is regarded as having heavy real effects, because of the bankruptcies of debtors. Kalecki's second consideration follows Keynes's footsteps in warning against the risks of deflation, whereas the first opens the way to the erasing of the private debt structure and bank credit when considering the money supply.

In another article on the issue, published in 1947, Pigou takes into account Kalecki's objection; but he insists that the net wealth effect on consumption remains substantial: 'As the money rate of wages falls the money price of consumption goods falls also. ...This means that the total stock of property, as valued in consumption goods, which is held by the public becomes

---

[40]   'The increase in the real value of the stock of money does not mean a rise in the total real value of possessions if all the money (cash and deposits) is "backed" by credits to persons and firms, i.e. if all the assets of the banking system consist of such credits. For in this case, to the gain of money holders there corresponds an equal loss of the bank debtors. The total real value of possessions increases only to the extent to which money is backed by gold' (Kalecki, 1944, p. 132).

progressively larger and larger. It must be remembered, indeed, that not all the stock of money held by the public constitutes a net asset to them. Part of it is offset by debts from them to the banks in respect of advances and discounts. ...Hence the addition made to this holding of property as valued in consumption goods when prices fall is smaller than it might perhaps be thought to be at first sight. None the less, it is likely to be substantial' (Pigou, 1947[1952], pp. 186–187).

Patinkin addressed the theoretical and empirical relevance of the Pigou's wealth effect, and what he calls the Pigou's theorem, to assess it in the perspective of policy decisions. In principle, when making static comparisons of equilibrium positions, it is always possible to figure out a price level that guarantees full employment, given a certain nominal stock of money. Therefore, the Pigou's theorem is always valid in the static analysis of macroeconomic equilibrium (Patinkin, 1948, p. 556). Patinkin neatly defines the extent of the net wealth effect as related to all outstanding government debts, while excluding private debts and credits within the private sector, or any net effect of deflation on aggregate demand as related to the inside debt structure in the economy.[41]

> From the preceding analysis we can also see just exactly what constitutes the 'cash balance' whose increase in real value provides the stimulatory effect of the Pigou analysis. This balance clearly consists of the net obligation of the government to the private sector of the economy. That is, it consists of the sum of interest- and non-interest bearing government debt held outside the treasury and central bank. Thus, by excluding demand deposits and including government interest-bearing debt, it differs completely from what is usually regarded as the stock of money. (Patinkin, 1948, pp. 550–551)

Thus, in so far as the wealth effect is concerned, the role of bank money is relevant only if deposits are strictly backed by bank reserves.[42]

Patinkin derives an important implication from his analysis: open market operations affect the economy only through the liquidity preference equation (Patinkin, 1948, p. 551). The private debt structure should be ignored in the analysis of static macroeconomic equilibrium, and the effects of monetary

---

[41] 'It is obvious that a price reduction has a stimulating effect on creditors. But, restricting ourselves to the private sector of a closed economy, to every stimulated creditor there corresponds a discouraged debtor. Hence from this viewpoint the net effect of a price reduction is likely to be in the neighborhood of zero' (Patinkin, 1948, p. 549).

[42] Patinkin quotes Kalecki on this point: 'To the extent that it is backed by bank loans and discounts, the gains of deposit holders are offset by the losses of bank debtors. Thus the net effect of a price decline on demand deposits is reduced to its effect on the excess of deposits over loans, or (approximately) on the reserves of the banks held in the form of hand-to-hand currency' (Patinkin, 1948, p. 551).

policy should be analysed with exclusive attention to the liquidity preference equation.[43]

For Patinkin, Pigou was mainly interested in a purely static theoretical reasoning (Patinkin, 1948, p. 556); but when the wealth effect is evaluated from a policy perspective its impact is not significant: '...whatever evidence exists indicates that the dependence of savings on cash balances is much too weak to be of any practical use' (Patinkin, 1948, p. 557).[44] Patinkin does not endorse the self-adjusting properties of market economies,[45] but he shifts the core of the argument about persistent unemployment from static analysis to dynamic disequilibrium, which he analyses by considering processes of adjustment in the context of a real income-expenditure model with no financial sector.[46]

Patinkin's innovative dynamic vision of Keynesianism[47] loses sight of dynamic disequilibria related to financial imbalances, such as the volatility of prices in financial and property markets, credit rationing, bankruptcies or the perceived risk of bankruptcies in the economy, the collapse of banks and financial intermediaries, and so on and so forth. Patinkin, although aware of possible financial disequilibria, concentrates his effort on dynamic disequilibrium in the output and labour markets, the perspective that in his view could give strength

---

[43]	'The Pigou analysis differs also from the more sophisticated interpretations of the classical position. These present the effect of a wage decrease as acting through the liquidity preference equation to increase the real value of M_0 and thereby reduce the rate of interest; this in turn stimulates both consumption and investment expenditures – thus generating a higher level of national income. To this effect, Pigou now adds the direct stimulus to consumption expenditures provided by the price decline and the accompanying increase in real balances. Consequently, even if the savings and investment functions are completely insensitive to changes in the rate of interest (so that the 'classical' effect through the liquidity equation is completely inoperative), a wage decrease will still be stimulatory through its effect on real balances and hence on savings' (Patinkin, 1948, p. 552). Patinkin's view will enter into economic textbook as the canonical description of the wealth effect, i.e. the stimulating effect of deflation on aggregate demand.

[44]	Patinkin (1948, pp. 558–559) briefly refers also to Keynes with respect to the risk of disastrous deflationary spirals and the effect that an expected future deflation could have on decisions to postpone spending and accumulate idle cash balances.

[45]	'In other words, though the real-balance effect must be taken account of in our theoretical analysis, it is too weak – and, in some cases (due to adverse expectations) too perverse – to fulfil a significant role in our policy considerations' (Patinkin, 1959, p. 586). This is the line that Patinkin follows in answering Hicks's criticism, while maintaining that in principle even in the Keynesian case (according to Hicks) with a horizontal LM full employment equilibrium could in principle be reached due to the wealth effect on consumption in static equilibrium analysis.

[46]	For a summary exposition of Patinkin's disequilibrium model in Chapter 13 of *Money, Income and Prices*, see Barro and Grossman (1971, p. 83).

[47]	'The fundamental issue raised by Keynesian economics is *the stability of the dynamic system*: its ability to return automatically to a full-employment equilibrium within a reasonable time (say, a year) if it is subjected to the customary shocks and disturbances of a peacetime economy. In other words, what Keynesian economics claims is that the economic system may be in a position of underemployment *dis*equilibrium (in the sense that wages, prices, and the amount of unemployment are continuously changing over time) for long, or even indefinite, periods of time' (Patinkin, 1948, p. 563).

to Keynes's main contention about persistent unemployment. He bypasses the interactions of real and financial markets, and the dynamic effects of fragile financial structures. In 1951, in a later addendum to his paper, Patinkin takes into account inside debts, considering the redistribution of purchasing power due to deflation, which could hinder the debtors with a higher propensity to expenditure (Dimand, 2005).

The debate finally focussed on the aggregate wealth effect as determined by the real value of outside money, and on its direct effect on real income via real consumption expenditure. Monetary equilibrium is studied in its macroeconomic effects in terms of the variable $\frac{M}{P}$, where M is outside money controlled by the central bank. The attention to the impact on the balance sheets of specific agents or groups of agents, or of banks or other financial intermediaries in conditions of monetary instability is lost, and with it the attention to systemic risks because of bankruptcies, or the perception of systemic bankruptcy risks, which had been discussed by both Fisher and Keynes or, on different grounds, by Schumpeter when discussing the importance of sound banking in capitalist development.

6.5   TOWARDS A WALRASIAN GENERAL-EQUILIBRIUM MACROECONOMICS

A common feature of the debates on interest rates and on the wealth effect is that the critics of Keynes's theory claim that a proper macroeconomic analysis has to be carried out by taking account of all the interrelations among variables. As we shall see in the next chapter, in subsequent years these generic claims transformed themselves into attempts to set macroeconomics in a proper Walrasian general-equilibrium context, with all the implications and theoretical difficulties associated with it.

The two debates, though in different ways, have in common also that the importance and role of the banking system and financial markets is largely downplayed. Although the discussion on the two alternative theories of the interest rate obviously puts credit at the centre-stage, the analysis remains at a rudimentary level. To use Wicksell's terms, the participants in the debate are essentially concerned with a system of 'simple' rather than 'organized' credit. The banking system is mostly ignored or banks are viewed as mere intermediaries between ultimate lenders and borrowers. The 'new' view of banking might have contributed to this line of approach.

The debate on the wealth effect takes place in a context in which attention is focused on outside money. Pigou's analysis of the wealth effect is carried out without a clear-cut distinction between statics and dynamics. Patinkin, whose approach to the issue will become canonical in economics textbooks, carefully distinguishes between the static analysis of equilibrium and the dynamic analysis of disequilibrium processes. But these processes are studied only in real terms. Patinkin's approach stimulated and influenced the development of the research on 'disequilibrium micro-foundations' of macroeconomics (see Backhouse and Boianovsky, 2013), a field which however remained peripheral. Instead, Patinkin's inclination to 'forget' the possibility of major dynamic disequilibria in the financial side of the economy will be fully incorporated in the Neoclassical Synthesis of the 1960s. The neat theoretical definition of the wealth effect washed out whichever warnings Keynes and Fisher had advanced on the self-defeating effects of deflation in the light of the dramatic historical experience of the early 1930s.

PART II

From the Neoclassical Synthesis
to New Keynesian Economics

7. Finance in macroeconomics in the post-war years: the Neoclassical Synthesis

During the 1950s and 1960s, two parallel processes went on in economic theory, both of them with lasting consequences for the evolution of macroeconomics. The first was the stabilization of the general economic equilibrium theory in the form of the Arrow-Debreu model, which looked like the most coherent and advanced construction to rigorously embody the Walrasian heritage. The second was the stabilization of a comprehensive macroeconomic theory aiming to encompass both the neoclassical micro-foundations, as embedded in general equilibrium theory, and the explanation of Keynesian unemployment in the short term. In 1952 Samuelson proclaimed general equilibrium theory to be 'the peak of neoclassical economics' (Samuelson, 1952, p. 61); in the third edition of his *Economics* the term 'neoclassical economics' indicated the consensus synthesis aiming at the reconciliation of the core of theory of competitive markets with the Keynesian paradigm (Samuelson, 1955, p. 212).

The idea to build a coherent macroeconomic theory on general equilibrium foundations inspired all scholars who contributed to the 'Neoclassical Synthesis', notably Modigliani (1944) and (Patinkin, 1959).[1] In the late 1960s, the same idea inspired Friedman's definition of the natural rate of unemployment; in the 1970s it informed Lucas's research project. In the second half of the 20th century, the corpus of macroeconomics was built around the general equilibrium theory of competitive markets.

The challenge was to coherently integrate macroeconomic theory within a general equilibrium frame; but how is the modelling of competitive markets to be conceived? Which is the equilibrium model to be adopted, if any is available, and how can money and finance be integrated in the general equilibrium frame? By the early 1960s, a consensus on a refined version of the IS-LM model seemed to have been reached by the scholars working on

---

[1] For brevity, we adopt the label 'Neoclassical Synthesis' though aware of the heterogeneity of positions among the economists regarded as exponents of the synthesis (on this see, for example, De Vroey and Duarte, 2013). Under this label we put the broad line of research aiming to connect Keynesian macroeconomics to the general equilibrium approach based on optimizing behaviour.

the Neoclassical Synthesis. These new models aimed to embody aggregate behavioural functions properly micro-founded, i.e. based on the hypothesis of rational maximizing individuals. Modigliani summarized the point of arrival in 1963, in an article on the monetary mechanism and the neutrality of money. To this stabilization process we devote the first part of the chapter to argue that it had a cost: the failed integration of banks and the financial system within the Neoclassical Synthesis's standard models.[2] By the early 1960s, the new reference framework substantially erased financial markets from macroeconomic models.

This result was achieved not without resistance and attempts to maintain financial markets within a neoclassical framework. Within the broad horizon of the synthesis, the main opposition came from the research on finance and growth by Gurley and Shaw since the mid-1950s, which we examine in the second half of the chapter. Tobin, influenced by the work of Gurley and Shaw, is the heterodox Keynesian who critically focused macroeconomic research on the analysis of financial markets adopting a general equilibrium approach. We close the chapter discussing the subtleties of his views, and why his line of research remained marginal in the Keynesian mainstream. The critique of the Neoclassical Synthesis for its undervaluation of the importance of money by the exponents of the so-called 'monetarist revolution' will be considered in Chapter 8.

7.1 THE STABILIZATION OF THE THEORY OF GENERAL ECONOMIC EQUILIBRIUM IN THE 1940s AND 1950s

In the 1930s, the general equilibrium theory of competitive markets had not yet reached a consensus assessment. The importance of Walras's contribution was recognized, but Walras's *Éléments* were not well known in the English-speaking world since the book had not yet been translated. Pareto's *Manual* was available in the 1909 French edition, and not easily accessible to economists not understanding Italian. In the 1930s, Lindahl, Hayek, Hicks, Myrdal, Morgenstern and others faced the theoretical challenge to clarify the analytical model of general competitive equilibrium, and to link it to monetary theory and the theory of business cycles. These scholars addressed the distinction between statics and dynamics, uncertainty, expectations and the conditions for perfect foresight, the dynamic framing to be adopted in equilibrium theory, the market mechanism and the related stability analysis,

---

[2] We do not deal with the policy debates in the 1950s and 1960s in their wider aspects involving fiscal and monetary policy.

with the aim to develop a coherent equilibrium model of competitive markets that could stand as foundational. The question of how and if Walras's monetary theory could stand was debated. Since Walras's and Wicksell's pioneering efforts, the thorny question was still open of how to solve excess demand equations for equilibrium relative prices, and add a further equation to close the system for the price level. In 1939, the publication of Hicks's book *Value and Capital* marked a crucial step forward, not so much technically but conceptually; but throughout the 1940s, the body of general equilibrium theory was still in question.

Hicks built the logical frame to structure general equilibrium theory tracing the distinction between statics and dynamics, and defining the ideas of temporary and inter-temporal equilibrium.[3] He dealt with the modelling of expectations, addressing the controversial idea of perfect foresight within a sequential time framework of conventional 'weeks', and clarifying the requirements for perfect far-sightedness in inter-temporal equilibrium. In Chapters 9 and 10 that opened Part I on Statics, Hicks clarified the concept of temporary equilibrium within the conventional week, and he took into account expectations and change in the sequence of weeks to discuss the conditions for perfect foresight, inter-temporal equilibrium.[4] In Chapter 10, he defined the notion of Walrasian general equilibrium with perfect far-sightedness and no disappointed expectations, as being consistently realized only in the inter-temporal equilibrium of complete spot and forward markets that he named the pure Futures Economy. Hicks presented the construct of inter-temporal equilibrium as an ideal, extreme case, and not as the standard long-term state to which competitive markets converge.[5] The atemporal framework of relative prices, instantaneously set at equilibrium in the Monday of the initial week for both the first and all the future weeks to come, did not fit with the Marshallian distinction between short and long term.[6] Along the sequence of weeks, Hicks identified four sources of possible disequilibria, as arising from the inconsistent expectations held by agents, from their incompatible future plans in the absence of complete future markets, from the intervening changes in tastes or technologies in the course of time, or from the perception of uncertainty. He explained why complete future markets do not exist considering the scope and variety of goods in the markets of advanced market economies, and the evidence of innovation and change, a subject he will later develop in

---

[3] Hicks built on Pareto's definitions in the *Manual* and the Swedish economists' contributions.

[4] For a detailed examination of these chapters, see Ingrao and Israel (1990, pp. 239–241) and Ingrao (2013, pp. 568-ff).

[5] This is substantially the same position held by Hayek in 1941 (Ingrao, 2013, p. 503).

[6] Hicks dismissed Marshall's long term stationary equilibrium; he held that the Paretian frame of sequences of temporary equilibria was far superior to discuss general equilibrium in a dynamic environment.

further work. He argued that in principle complete future markets solve the first two types of disequilibria, but they cannot protect the market economy from disequilibria arising from change of tastes, innovation or productivity shocks, or the perception of uncertainty. Moreover, Hicks disliked Samuelson's tâtonnement dynamics, since he thought it betrayed the true understanding of dynamic change.

Though it appeared to be disconnected from any realistic interpretation of market economies, the 'Futures Economy' case proved to be the unique definition of Walrasian general equilibrium that permitted to circumvent the unsolvable difficulties related to expectations and change in a dynamic market environment. Arrow adopted it as the conceptual frame for the formal development of the neo-Walrasian model; it became the skeleton of the axiomatic Arrow-Debreu model. In the 1950s, Arrow and Debreu achieved the analytical stabilization of neo-Walrasian general equilibrium theory, starting from a game theoretic model of difficult interpretation, in highly technical language.[7] In 1959, Debreu's *Theory of Value* perfected the axiomatic skeleton, but the Arrow-Debreu model had still to be decoded in terms of conceptual representation, a task accomplished among controversies, since ideas of general equilibrium in economics bear multiple identities as the ideal representation of the working of competitive markets, the normative vision of welfare optimality, or the design mechanism for central planning. In the research projects since the 1940s to the 1970s, ideas of optimal control or socialist planning were ambiguously blurred with the aim to decode the working of markets.[8] Till today in dominant interpretation in macroeconomic literature the Arrow-Debreu model is claimed to be the modelling with sophisticated mathematical tools of the invisible hand idea, as embodied in an ideal system of perfectly competitive markets, with no externalities, no transaction costs and perfect far-sightedness. The possibility to adapt the model to the actual, structural characteristics of real markets, whatever those might be, was dubious to his own builders, as Arrow and Hahn (1971) recognized, though among residual ambiguities.[9]

The critical issues about dynamics that Hicks had raised in *Value and Capital* were cut out from the modelling strategy that pursued the axiomatization of general equilibrium theory, finally achieving the existence proof in 1952. After Samuelson's formalization of the auctioneer (Samuelson, 1941), for a brief span of years it seemed that neo-Walrasian scholars could prove the

---

[7] Düppe and Weintraub (2014) offer a detailed history of how Arrow and Debreu gained recognition over other scholars for the proof of the existence theorem.

[8] For the evolution of general equilibrium theory, see Ingrao and Israel (1990); Mirowski (2002). On the normative and descriptive viewpoints see notably Ingrao and Israel (1990, Chapter 12). Mirowski (2002) argues that the dream of a control economy informed research at the Cowles Foundation in the 1940s and 1950s.

[9] See also Arrow (1974, 2009); Hahn (1981).

convergence to the equilibrium by price adjustment. These hopes soon proved wishful thinking. The early 1970s saw a drastic crisis in the development of the still young neo-Walrasian research project. Less than 15 years after Debreu's comprehensive presentation of the axiomatic framework in *Theory of Value*, Sonnenschein Mantel and Debreu himself proved theorems that substantially mined all the hopes to get further results on uniqueness and stability. The theory proved to be an empty shell; because of the impossibility to significantly restrain the set of aggregate excess demand functions on meaningful micro-foundations assumptions, the neo-Walrasian apparatus could offer no strong results in terms of properties of equilibrium states or dynamic processes (Rizvi, 2006). Stability analysis metamorphosed into the search for algorithms to compute equilibria or to design mechanisms inspired by ideas of planning (Boldyrev and Ushakov, 2016; Ingrao and Israel, 1990, Chapter 12).

By the end of the 1970s, the devastating results achieved by the *crème de la crème* of mathematical economists were well known to all scholars learned in general equilibrium theory, though they were somewhat swept under the carpet, as they still are today. Even before it became clear that intractable technical difficulties plagued general equilibrium mathematical models, the conceptual difficulties of the Walrasian heritage had been clarified in the debates since the 1920s, and before. The Arrow-Debreu disincarnate image of perfect markets in an axiomatic frame emerges from the impasse and dead ends, which the earlier theoretical controversies had effectively highlighted in the effort to incorporate expectations, radical uncertainty, short-term dynamics and market imperfections into the Walrasian theoretical skeleton. Neo-Walrasian general equilibrium theory had a quickly falling trajectory, after the promising results of the 1950s; but in general economics, the Arrow-Debreu model survived well beyond the 1970s crisis. Again and again, it was referred to as the benchmark model of perfectly competitive markets in important and influential macroeconomic research.

7.2   GENERAL EQUILIBRIUM MACROECONOMICS BY THE MID-FIFTIES: PATINKIN'S *MONEY, INTEREST AND PRICES*

In the earlier debates on Keynes's *General Theory*, the reference to general equilibrium was loose, meaning the requirement to take into account the simultaneous interaction of relevant macroeconomic variables in modelling the aggregate economy, but without imposing strict requirements on the micro-foundations, the aggregation techniques, or any uniqueness or stability proofs. In 1937, Hicks's sketchy IS-LM equations built an early, macro model that seemed to satisfy these loose requirements without addressing the rigorous definition of equilibrium. Theoretically, the sketchy 'apparatus' mixed up Wicksellian with Walrasian influences. As Hicks acknowledged, it disregarded all questions of dynamic processes (Hicks, 1937, p. 158). The original IS-LM framework is inherently static, according to Hicks's later definition;[10] but the equations were open to interpretations in the long or short run perspectives, and comparative statics exercises were narrated as if they dealt with dynamic processes.

Hicks's more mature 1939 book marked the crucial turn with lasting influence. Since the early 1940s to the mid-1950s, the questions dealt with in the book came to the forefront in evaluating Keynes's message; but Hicks's contribution was misunderstood as much as it was influential. In the mid-1940s, Lange, who had been involved in debates on general equilibrium and planning, proposed a readable model connecting Keynesian results to general equilibrium in his essay *Price Flexibility and Employment* published in 1944 as a Cowles Commission Research Monograph (Lange, 1944). Lange's contribution was also crucial to the development of macroeconomics in the early 1950s. Both Hicks's and Lange's books were inspiring sources for Patinkin and Modigliani, the two scholars who built the framing of macroeconomic theory by referring to the Walrasian general equilibrium. They worked along different lines of research, both relevant to our story. We examine them by concentrating on the main subject of this chapter: how the stabilization of macroeconomic models achieved by the Neoclassical Synthesis dealt with financial intermediaries and financial markets.

In the 1940s a technical debate developed on the consistency of the general equilibrium system of equations, as it had been framed by Cassel (1932) and later revisited by Lange. Once again, the crux was the integration of value theory and monetary theory, to which both Walras and Wicksell had devoted so many efforts. The controversy over classical monetary theory versus Keynesian monetary theory revived the thorny issue in the debates over the criticism or assimilation of Keynes's *General Theory*.[11] In the 1940s, the controversy focused on the 'classical dichotomy' between the set of aggregate excess demand functions, homogeneous of degree zero in the vector of relative prices, and the quantity equation added to close the macroeconomic system and determine the general price level (Lange, 1944; Patinkin, 1948, 1949). Patinkin

---

[10] According to Hicks's definition in *Value and Capital* a model is static if the variables are not dated, and no explicit time structure is specified. In later works, Hicks substantially enriched the conceptual tools to define time dynamics in economic modelling (Hicks, 1956[1982]).

[11] For a summary of the controversy, see Johnson (1962, pp. 337–340). Patinkin included the references to the controversy in Note M of *Money, Interest and Prices* (Patinkin, 1959, pp. 477–478). He returned to the controversy in an exchange with Samuelson in 1972 (Patinkin, 1972). Whatever the flaws of Patinkin's theoretical construction, he was perfectly right about the core question he raised.

argued against the 'false dichotomy' noting that the two subsystems were disconnected, and incompatible; the added quantity equation was alien and not coherent with the 'real' equilibrium solution for relative prices, because no money balances are included in the set of excess demand functions for real goods. He summarized his argument as follows.

> Classical analysis was restricted to examining those aspects of an economy which are similar to a barter economy; or, at most, to an economy in which transactions take place with goods against goods, with money acting only as a counting unit. But it did not explain why people held actual balances. (Patinkin, 1949, p. 22)

Patinkin devoted his highly scholarly book *Money, Interest and Prices*, first published in 1956, to the effort to demonstrate the possibility of coherently including money within a general equilibrium framework of competitive markets; he aimed to arrive at a correct statement of the neutrality proposition, taking into account money balances and wealth effects properly specified within a system of general equilibrium equations depicting the economy. According to Patinkin, the elementary solution of hanging a separate quantity equation to the excess demand equations specified for all goods in terms of relative prices does not explain how, in a monetary economy, the equilibrating market forces work and make true the quantity theory. The quantity theory requires to take into account the effects of changes in money balances on the excess demand in all other markets. Patinkin unveiled what he deemed to be the 'false dichotomy' that emerged in the untenable system mixing up the 'real' equilibrium in terms of relative prices in some conventional unit of account, and the isolated, misspecified quantity equation. To properly formulate the neutrality proposition in terms of monetary prices and money balances, he insisted on the difference of merely accounting prices from the monetary prices, which is necessary to introduce when considering the wealth effects on spending and saving decisions. To this purpose, he coherently based macroeconomic analysis on four aggregate markets (goods, labour, money, bonds), having in view their simultaneous equilibrium.[12] He perfected the sketchy IS-LM skeleton, with lasting consequences on the way financial markets were elegantly erased from standard macroeconomic models for some decades.

Patinkin built his theoretical analysis of the four markets on the skeleton that Hicks had proposed; but he dealt with Hicks's temporary equilibrium with adjustments, and substantial deviations, to avoid possible dead-ends. In Chapter IV, Part I, he explicitly adopted Hicks's 'week', and a time horizon

---

[12]   The four markets equilibrium is the most complete model in the book, after more elementary models have been examined.

for optimal planning expanding to more weeks (a conventional 'month'); but in a note, he explained that in adopting such 'familiar technique', he had other purposes than Hicks (Patinkin, 1956, p. 46).[13] In the note he disposed of any disequilibrium analysis, leaving aside the clear-cut conclusions about disequilibrium that Hicks carefully underlined when defining both temporary and inter-temporal equilibrium.[14]

In the integrated four-markets macroeconomic model the main focus is on equilibrium; but dynamic reasoning is an essential component of Patinkin's criticism and reconstruction of the quantity theory in a general-equilibrium context. To such purpose, he either trusts comparative statics exercises or resorts to Samuelson's formalization of the tâtonnement process as the basic process of adjustment towards equilibrium. Patinkin carefully specifies the assumptions he makes for analytical convenience: an ad hoc transaction technology that could justify the demand for money balances;[15] a unique homogeneous representative bond with no risk of bankruptcy; the absence of redistributive effects on aggregate functions through wealth effects; the crucial stability assumption for all the dynamic processes considered. These assumptions achieved together the result to obfuscate the relevance of the inside financial structure of the economy and of all dynamic processes which might depend on it and could affect the speed of the convergence to full employment equilibrium.

Bonds are introduced in Chapter IV, Part I, to account for saving and debt. All saving is devoted to buying bonds, all dissaving takes place by selling bonds to anticipate consumption. The 'bond' is a standard good. Only a unique type of bonds exists in the economy, and all bonds are assumed to be perfect substitutes for each other. Bonds are 'just as illiquid as commodities' and they cannot substitute money in the payment technology (Patinkin, 1956, p. 49). An ad hoc transaction technology ('our model of the payment procedure') is introduced in Chapter VII to rationally account for money balances; such artificial technology is justified by referring to Friedman's methodological position on unrealistic assumptions (Patinkin, 1956, pp. 87-ff.). Patinkin aims to prove that money balances are needed even without appealing to uncertainty ('the existence of dynamic or uncertain price and interest expectations is not a sine qua non of a theory of money') and, thus, even when there is no speculative demand for money (Patinkin, 1956, pp. 87 and 95).

---

[13] 'But whereas Hicks's main purpose in devising this technique is to analyse the origin and significance of discrepancies between planned and actual behaviour, we completely ignore this fundamental problem' (Patinkin, 1956, p. 46, n. 1).

[14] In his 1940s articles, Patinkin dealt with disequilibrium states, confining the formalization to labour and good markets; see Chapter 6 above.

[15] The exact timing of payments and receipts is randomly distributed over the reference week. See Johnson (1962, p. 338) for a criticism of the artificiality of this assumption.

Two further assumptions complete the picture that substantially denies any relevance to the financial structure in the fundamentals of the basic macroeconomic model. The first one is the absence of any risk of default and thus, a priori, of any information asymmetries, which might arise in the assessment of the risk of default for different borrowers. There is no a priori risk of any break of commitments on the side of borrowers, which might plunge their creditors or other agents into illiquidity or default. By this assumption, no assets of various classes of risk exist and no financial intermediaries are needed to help savers to place their funds or investors to get financing. No effects on aggregate functions may arise in consequence of the changing perception of the risks of default in the economy by the various agents.

Agents directly and transparently buy or sell in competitive markets, the standard tickets called 'bonds', with no uncertain rating, no risk of losing income, no intermediation or information costs, no credit rationing. The complex net of financial markets is summarized as a single market where identical units of money debt are anonymously traded under perfectly competitive conditions. The final, crucial assumption is the absence of distributive effects, that is of any changes in the aggregate excess demand functions that might arise in consequence of changes in the distribution of real incomes, bond holdings or money holdings. The assumption is explicitly introduced in the opening Chapter I of Part II (Macroeconomics).

> Each of the foregoing aggregate functions is assumed to reflect absence of money illusion. Each is also assumed to remain unaffected by any change in the distribution of real income, real bond holdings, or real money balances which leaves constant the sum total of the respective item. Thus each of these functions can be represented as dependent upon among other things the real value of the *total* income, bond holdings, and money balances of the individuals or firms whose collective behaviour it describes. In brief, the assumed absence of distribution effects makes it unnecessary to consider the *arrays* of the individual incomes, holdings and balances in the economy. (Patinkin, 1956, pp. 125–126)

This last assumption amounts to erasing the patrimonial, and financial, structure of the economy as irrelevant for the macroeconomic picture. The arrays of bond holdings represent the debt-credit structure of the economy, and erasing them is tantamount to declare the irrelevance of private debts in the economy, whatever those might be. The assumption of no risk of default somewhat justifies such irrelevance, since it implies that borrowers are not affected in their borrowing capacity by the risks perceived in relation to the amount of their outstanding debts; no credit rationing due to risks of default limits the amount of credit available. In consequence, the spending decisions are not affected by credit constraints on borrowers. Patinkin is well aware of the possible distributive effects in conditions of monetary instability, and the subject is carefully dealt with in defining money illusion. He notes how the real position of the debtors' and the creditors' classes are differently affected in situations of inflation or deflation (Patinkin, 1956, p. 56). To avoid the complexities of such wealth changes in affecting aggregate spending, he decided to eliminate distributive effects out from his analysis.[16]

In Chapter XII, Patinkin explicitly discusses the relevance of his assumptions about the financial structure. In a specific paragraph he deals with the consequences of removing the simplifying assumption of homogeneous bonds and considering a more realistic financial system. Banks are added to the picture and demand deposits are included both as assets and liabilities (Patinkin, 1956, pp. 203–204). Of course, the net liquid-asset position of the private sector sums up to the amount of currency in circulation, demand deposits being cancelled in the net total of liquid assets and liquid liabilities by the cancellation of debts and credits among private units. Patinkin notes that they are irrelevant in the absence of distributive effects acting through the real wealth effects in cases of inflation or deflation (Patinkin, 1956, p. 202). Although briefly addressing the questions involved, the paragraph closes by excluding the overall consideration of the financial structure in the economy.

> More generally, the foregoing assumptions imply that the total amount of demand deposits is of no relevance for the functioning of the economy. Specifically, a parallel expansion of bank loans and deposits changes neither the net asset position of households and firms, nor consequently, their demand for commodities. This *reductio ad absurdum* merely points up the necessity of distinguishing between the degrees of liquidity and illiquidity of various types of assets and liabilities.(...) In order to take into account these and related considerations, we should actually write the aggregate demand functions as dependent upon the *arrays* of real bond holdings (classified according to their respective degrees of liquidity) and the *arrays* of real money holdings (inclusive of demand deposits). For a complete analysis we should also take account of the influence on demand of the mere availability of lines of credit. But we cannot go into these complications here. (Patinkin, 1956, p. 204)

Having put the financial 'complications' aside, Patinkin is well aware that the removal of the assumption of no distributive effects deriving from changes in the holdings of real bonds or in money balances could be devastating. He

---

[16] 'There is, nevertheless, a clear lack of analogy between individual and market-excess demand functions. Specifically, the latter does not, in general, depend upon relative prices, *total* real income of the economy, and *total* real balances. This form of dependence would be valid only under the unrealistic assumption that the distribution of neither real income nor real balances affects the amounts of market excess demand' (Patinkin, 1956, p. 30). On the absence of distributive effects see also Patinkin (1956, pp. 55 and 145), when dealing with the demand for money balances.

notes: 'By specifying the proper effects, we can obtain any desired results' (Patinkin, 1956, p. 200). If the distributive effects were taken into account, the dynamic analysis through shifting curves in comparative statics could not provide clear-cut results with respect to the equilibrium reached in the adjustment processes;[17] thus, they are dropped (Patinkin, 1956, p. 201).

Patinkin discusses at length the intertwined dynamic adjustments occurring in the four markets, since his criticism aims to bring to the fore the 'automatic, corrective market forces', which link the money market and the commodity market through the wealth effect via money balances (Patinkin, 1956, p. 101). His effort is to go beyond partial equilibrium analysis, where the market price reacts only to excess demand in the isolated market, towards the general equilibrium approach, where 'the pressure of excess demand in one market affects the price movement of all other markets' (Patinkin, 1956, p. 157). To this purpose, he evokes 'the periods of temporary disequilibrium which are necessarily inherent in the dynamic process of tâtonnement', betraying the purely virtual nature of tâtonnement that Walras had coherently perfected in the last editions of his book (Patinkin, 1956, p. 157).

Eventually, Patinkin is forced to postulate the stability of the overall process of dynamic adjustment in the aggregate economy.[18] He concludes: 'Hence the system remains stable. But this stability is now a matter of assumption – not a matter of proof' (Patinkin, 1956, p. 158). It was an honest remark, but again the assumption is dense of consequences for the representation of the financial side of the economy. It excludes, to use Fisher's metaphor, that any 'capsizing' of the ship could ever happen because of financial tempests (Fisher, 1933, p. 339). It excludes any possibility of multiple equilibria reached along alternative adjustment paths, or any vicious spiralling during severe banking or financial crises.

Patinkin's book is a specially rich source for reflecting on the open questions raised by the effort of so many scholars to connect the equilibrium of relative prices to the quantity equation and simultaneously determine the general price level. We cannot deal with Patinkin's interesting criticism of Walras, Wicksell or Fisher, but just recall that, in the Supplementary Notes, he criticizes Walras's theory of money along the lines illustrated above,[19] and notably Walras's

---

[17] 'Hence varying assumptions as to the nature of these distribution effects can shift the curves of Figure 33 in any desired way, to yield any desired equilibrium position' (Patinkin, 1956, p. 202).

[18] Stability will soon emerge as a critical issue in the evolution of neo-Walrasian general equilibrium theory.

[19] On the criticism of Walras see Patinkin (1956, pp. 392-ff). Patinkin (1956, p. 393) observes: 'Walras does not succeed in providing a conceptual framework which logically entitles him to introduce the *service d'approvisionnement* of money into the utility function.' After the detailed examination of the theory of money in the various editions of the *Éléments*, Patinkin concluded that Walras makes a serious confusion between the demand and supply of money balances and the demand and supply of money loans (Patinkin, 1956, p. 405, note 71).

tâtonnement in the money market (Patinkin, 1956, p. 404). He criticizes Walras for isolating the tâtonnement in the money market, as if it were fully independent of the tâtonnement in the goods and capital markets. For Patinkin, Walras had failed to integrate the influence of variations of the absolute price level on the goods markets.

Notwithstanding this sophisticated criticism, from an historical perspective, Patinkin's modelling provided the conceptual foundation for a subtler 'false dichotomy'. The 'complications' of banks and financial markets are left aside; the whole financial structure of the macro-economy is collapsed into the markets for outside money and government bonds. The homogeneous bond market is apparently redundant just because, according to Walras Law, it is treated as the residual market. The bond market, however, is redundant from a more substantial viewpoint: it is irrelevant by construction. Eventually, in *Money, Interest and Prices*, the basic macroeconomic model is transformed again into the simplified picture of the equilibrium equations in competitive markets for goods and labour services plus a separate quantity equation, although a more refined link is established by including aggregate wealth effects.

7.3 THE MONETARY MECHANISM WITHOUT FINANCIAL MARKETS

In 1963, Modigliani published the article 'The monetary mechanism and its interaction with real phenomena' in *The Review of Economics and Statistics*. The article draws an accurate picture of the stabilization of Keynesian macroeconomics around a comprehensive IS-LM model integrated by the explicit modelling of the labour market. In Modigliani's article the absence of distributive effects and assumptions similar to those made by Patinkin in the aggregate representation of the financial system appears again. Financial markets are explicitly dealt with, but at the same time they are substantially ignored by focusing the analysis on wage rigidities and the outside money stock. Paradoxically, the apparently detailed modelling of financial markets ended up with the *de facto* exclusion of any direct reference to banks, financial structure and private debt from the theoretical macroeconomic scenery.

In comparison with his own 1944 IS-LM model, Modigliani expounds 'a basic model of money and the economy' that, he claims, is the one currently accepted since the mid-1950s (Modigliani, 1944, 1963, p. 79). Like in Patinkin's 1956 model, the economy is dealt with 'at a highly aggregative level', including the markets for two real goods (one aggregate commodity and labour services) and two 'money-fixed claims, money and bonds' (Modigliani,

1963, p. 80). The new model is credited with an 'explicit reliance on a general equilibrium formulation', which amounts to specify supply and demand equations for each market and an equilibrium condition, one of the equilibrium conditions being redundant for the Walras Law. Modigliani focuses on the state of general macroeconomic equilibrium both in the short and the long term and he implicitly regards the overall stability assumption postulated by Patinkin as obvious.

As far as the financial sector is concerned, the model includes banks and demand deposits as well as private bonds, along lines similar to those followed by Patinkin in his book. Apparently, a quite complete, if simplified specification of the financial system is included in equations M2 to M7 with the related memos on identities well specified.[20] Soon after, however, Modigliani adds a list of assumptions that amount to eliminate such detailed additions, simply going back to the older IS-LM skeleton. The bond market equilibrium is, of course, the chosen redundant equation.

Bonds are defined as one-period loans or claims to future (next-period) money: they are assets if they are held in portfolio in a positive amount, debts if they are held in a negative amount. They are not differentiated according to the issuing borrower or to any other characteristics. Like in Patinkin's exposition they are treated as a single standard good, each unit of which is perfectly identical to any other. New substantial assumptions are added to that of no money illusion: certainty, and unit elasticity of price expectations; the banking sector is aggregated assuming the amount of bank money to be perfectly controlled by the central bank; in the bond market, the market-clearing condition cancels out all issues of bonds by private agents (that is debts) as perfectly compensated by the corresponding private credits of equal amount. The bond market equilibrium is, thus, reduced to the equilibrium conditions between the private sector's net demand for government bonds and the issue of government debt. After introducing the wealth effect in the consumption function, Modigliani adds the A_5 assumption: aggregate market demand and supply conditions for each commodity are not affected by a 'redistribution of wealth among transactors' (Modigliani, 1963, p. 84). He makes this short comment.

Note that the consumption demand – as well as labor supply – of *individual* households will generally not be homogeneous of zero degree in prices. Indeed changes in the price level affect individual wealth by determining the real value of money fixed claims and debts. However, since *aggregate* wealth is unaffected,

---

[20] Modigliani acknowledges that in his 1944 model he had failed to explicitly specify the bond market, implicitly treated as redundant and thus subject to Patinkin's criticism (Modigliani, 1963, p. 81).

such changes only result in a redistribution of wealth between households, which by A₅ does not affect *aggregate* demands and supplies. (Modigliani, 1963, pp. 84–85, n. 8)

In summary, Modigliani re-frames the complete IS-LM model, now including the explicit formalization of the labour market, the wealth effect on consumption, the distinction between short and long term. He finally excludes the financial sector by collapsing it into the single equation for the equilibrium between demand and supply of money. All financial markets become redundant because of the requirement of balanced budgets, but also by construction. The article establishes the canonical distinction between short and long term in macroeconomic theory; but it is not clear which time horizon and which assumptions on expectations and dynamics are predicated, since no dynamic structure is introduced in the model and the adjustment processes are briefly dealt with in narrative accounts. Short-term equilibrium being identified with the solution reached by imposing some price rigidity in the model, notably the nominal wage rigidity, the long-term solution is identified with general equilibrium under full price flexibility.

The distinction between short and long term, as we noted above, is not compatible with the strict neo-Walrasian definition of inter-temporal equilibrium with perfect far-sightedness; it imposes a pseudo Marshallian apparatus on a pseudo Walrasian equilibrium framework. The neo-Walrasian model of inter-temporal general equilibrium with complete future markets does not admit any notion of short-term equilibrium that eventually converges to the long-term one. None of these confusions were present in Hicks's rigorous theorizing; but they became almost standard in macroeconomics during the 1960s and 1970s. No adjustment process is specified in disequilibrium, when the convergence from the short to the long-term equilibrium should occur, whereas Patinkin had at least postulated stability along some converging path. No attention is devoted to the uniqueness of equilibrium or the possibility of multiple equilibria in the short or long term. Progressively during the 1960s, the stabilization achieved in macroeconomic modelling along these lines left in the background the theoretical construction of specific general equilibrium models. The reference became blurred, both conceptually and technically, a character that will allow the attack that in the 1970s the so-called rational expectations revolution will launch against Keynesianism.

In the poorly defined long run, price flexibility was deemed to restore full-employment equilibrium under the conventional working of the adjustment mechanism that Modigliani named the 'Pigou-Scitovsky effect mechanism' (Modigliani, 1963, p. 88). Of course, the difficulties of achieving full employment by deflation were mentioned, but this did not imply any deeper reasoning on financial markets' instability or on how financial troubles might affect real markets.[21] The empirical relevance of the wealth effect was deemed minor; but in the long run price flexibility prevailed, and with it monetary neutrality and the quantity theory of money.[22] Modigliani explicitly recognized that in such vision of the aggregate economy financial intermediaries are superfluous and capital markets are assumed as being perfectly competitive.

> The models on which we have relied so far assume, at least implicitly, a well-functioning competitive capital market in which investments are limited and brought into line with saving through the mechanism of the rate of interest or cost of capital. In such a model there exists a single short-run equilibrium rate of interest which measures both the return to lenders and the cost to borrowers, and also equals (or at least is not less than) the internal marginal rate of return to all units. There is also no need to give separate treatment to financial intermediaries: all loans may be regarded as extended directly from the lending or surplus units to the final borrowers needing funds to finance their expenditure. (Modigliani, 1963, p. 97)

Modigliani acknowledges that this picture is unrealistic, and he briefly discusses imperfect capital markets, financial intermediaries and credit rationing. To discuss specifically the so called 'availability doctrine', the attention was concentrated on the institutional rates by bank lenders, their differences from the inside rate of returns or the basic interest rate, their sluggish adjustment and the related possibility of credit rationing.[23] The conclusion is that there could be interesting novelties, as listed below, but including imperfect capital markets, financial intermediaries and credit rationing does not change the main results.[24]

> It appears from the above analysis that the recognition of the role of intermediaries and market imperfections in the guise of sluggish lending rates and of direct rationing rather than price rationing has certain significant implications. First, it helps to account for fluctuations in market lending rates which appear rather modest in relation to likely cyclical swings in the return from investment. Second, it implies

---

[21] Modigliani's comments on the issue do not call for any major change in his modelling approach (Modigliani, 1963, p. 88).

[22] 'Since in the long (and even not so long) run, rigidities can be neglected, I would conclude that neutrality and the quantity theory – in the sense of a stable relation between the money supply and the value of output at any given interest rate – is a good long-run approximation, subject, however, to the stricture that in the long run monetary institutions may gradually change' (Modigliani, 1963, p. 88).

[23] '...interest rates charged to borrowers by financial intermediaries are largely controlled by institutional forces and slow to adjust at best; and that the demand for funds is accordingly limited not by the borrowers' willingness to borrow at the given rate but by lenders' willingness to lend – or, more precisely, by the funds available to them to be rationed out among the would-be borrowers' (Modigliani, 1963, p. 97).

[24] 'It is apparent from our figure that the workings of a model with capital rationing of the type considered are not radically different from those of the original Model II' (Modigliani, 1963, p. 99).

that monetary policy may affect aggregate demand without appreciably affecting lending rates, at least in the short run. Third, it suggests that monetary policy – understood now as the control over the power of banks to create money rather than over the actual money supply – may break down under less stringent conditions than those of the original Keynesian case. Because of sticky lending rates, monetary policy may become powerless even when the value of r, corresponding to a full employment output is well above zero. (Modigliani, 1963, pp. 100–101)

Meanwhile, at a meeting of the Econometric Society in December 1956, Modigliani and Miller had presented their work on the theory of finance proving the irrelevance of a firm's leverage for the cost of raising capital. The article containing the Modigliani-Miller theorem was published in the *American Economic Review* in 1958. The theorem, although set in a partial equilibrium context, appears to be a pillar on which to justify the irrelevance of the financial structure of firms also in the aggregate economy.[25] The theorem states that 'the average cost of capital, to any firm is completely independent of its capital structure and is equal to the capitalization rate of a pure equity stream of its class' (Modigliani and Miller, 1958, pp. 268–269). The theorem excludes any effect of the leverage on the cost of investment and thus any feedback effect from the financial structure to spending decisions.

That is, *the cut-off point for investment in the firm will in all cases be* ρ_k [the average cost of capital[26]] *and will be completely unaffected by the type of security used to finance the investment*. Equivalently, we may say that regardless of the financing used, the marginal cost of capital to a firm is equal to the average cost of capital, which is in turn equal to the capitalization rate for an unlevered stream in the class to which the firm belongs. (Modigliani and Miller, 1958, p. 288, emphasis in the original)

Modigliani and Miller are cautious in drawing simplified recipes as regards the best strategies that managers should follow in planning the financial structure of firms, in consideration of a variety of other factors in their market strategies (Modigliani and Miller, 1958, p. 292). However, the theorem suggests the irrelevance of the financial structure also at the aggregate level, investment spending not being affected by the firms' leverage.

---

[25] The conditions for the validity of the theorem are the subject of extensive discussions; it is generally accepted that the theorem holds in equilibrium in perfect capital markets. For a critical appraisal, see Hellwig (1981). See also Miller's later assessment of the theorem (Miller, 1988).

[26] The variable ρ_k is the average cost of capital for firms of class k, which according to the Modigliani-Miller theorem is independent from the firm's leverage, being equal to the capitalization rate of a pure equity stream for firms in k class (Modigliani and Miller, 1958, pp. 268–269).

7.4   FINANCE IN DEVELOPMENT: GURLEY'S AND SHAW'S INNOVATIVE THESES

In 1955 John Gurley and Edward Shaw published an innovative article devoted to the role of finance in development. They noted that development processes were associated to the parallel issue of debts and the accumulation of economic assets. In short, development processes need the financing by debt, and the parallel allocation of the surplus resources that some agents are able to convert into various types of financial assets (Gurley and Shaw, 1955, p. 515). They lamented 'an inadvertent undervaluation by economists of the role that finance plays in determining the pace and pattern of growth' (Gurley and Shaw, 1955, p. 516). They underlined that, in the long-term historical perspective, the self-financing of investment was declining while external finance was correspondingly expanding, with a large part of it being not from direct but from indirect financing (Gurley and Shaw, 1955, p. 518). In development, a large part of the saving eventually allocated to investment is collected through indirect financing, that is to say finance provided through financial intermediaries, whose role is to issue indirect debts 'soliciting loanable funds from surplus spending units, and to allocate these loanable funds among deficit units whose direct debt they absorb' (Gurley and Shaw, 1955, p. 519).

Their research called attention to the variety of financial intermediaries, and the variety of products and services they provide, offering external finance for growth, on one side, and answering the needs for safe or profitable placement of savings on the other. The variety of financial products and services provided by intermediaries appears to be crucial in growth processes, to accommodate the specific channelling of savings to investment, which is adapted to the historical circumstances, or possible under the existing cultural or institutional constraints. They called the complex evolution of establishing new intermediaries and expanding product differentiation in financial markets, the 'institutionalization of savings and investment', and they noted that development is braked 'if financial intermediaries do not evolve' (Gurley and Shaw, 1955, pp. 519, 520–521).

In this vision, while the accumulation of debt is a structural aspect of development, its rate of accumulation does not necessarily stand in linear relation to the growth of income and wealth, its evolution depending on how the complex net of financial intermediaries develops, facing the changing needs of savers and investors. The variegated world of financial intermediaries plays a strategic role in accommodating the possible mismatch of these needs during growth processes, including the offer of new opportunities by strategic innovation.[27] In this respect, each country has its own financial history. On these foundations, Gurley and Shaw explicitly criticized the simplified macroeconomic approach that cancelled out private debts and indirect finance in modelling the aggregate economy.

> The familiar trichotomy in theory of goods, bonds, and money does scant justice to this complex pattern of real and financial change. By implication financial intermediaries other than the monetary system are netted out of the social accounts, their holdings of direct debt attributed to their creditor (Gurley and Shaw, 1955, p. 521)

The attack against the simplified IS-LM frame was an explicit attack against the liquidity preference approach, and the net dividing line it traced between liquid and illiquid assets as represented in theory by the opposition of money and bonds. The adoption of such a simplified frame might be justified only by a very elementary conception of the financial side of the economy, a vision that betrays the historical evolution of the financial system in the United States as in other countries.

In this picture, banks play an important and unconventional role;[28] they are represented as financial intermediaries, in direct competition with other financial intermediaries in collecting and supplying loanable funds. The monetary nature of demand deposits is recognized;[29] but the financial markets offer a continuum of assets, each with its own degree of liquidity among other characteristics.[30] No net or exclusive separation line could be traced among financial products on their character of being liquid or illiquid assets, as it was suggested along Keynesian lines in monetary theory. On the whole, the article was an outspoken attack on the Keynesian theory of money and

---

[27] 'Any complete growth model must reconcile the accumulating stock of illiquidity with the growing aversion to illiquidity at terms of lending that are suitable to the investment component of warranted income levels. The reconciliation evidently involves growth of financial intermediaries to absorb illiquid direct debt and to issue indirect debt according to the preference patterns of surplus spending units' (Gurley and Shaw, 1955, p. 530).

[28] 'We are deviating from conventional doctrine in regarding the banking system as one among many financial intermediaries, sharing with the others the functions of indirect finance' (Gurley and Shaw, 1955, p. 521).

[29] 'Banks alone have the capacity to create demand deposits and currency, to be sure, but only savings and loan associations can create savings and loan shares: both "create credit," both transmit loanable funds, both enable spending units to diversify their portfolios. Banks do have a virtual monopoly of the payments mechanism, and only claims upon monetary intermediaries embody the privilege to use this mechanism' (Gurley and Shaw, 1955, p. 521).

[30] 'Liquidity is not the only characteristic that distinguishes bonds from alternative financial assets. Each financial intermediary offers its own differentiated product for the public to hold. This product is competitive with bonds. It may be more or less liquid than bonds, but it embodies a service, perhaps insurance, that bonds do not. The product is also competitive with money narrowly defined, offering less in liquidity perhaps but offering as well security, interest, insurance, and other services' (Gurley and Shaw, 1955, p. 527).

financial markets. The Keynesian model was defined as 'not hospitable' to the financial intermediaries, which were an expanding phenomenon in the advanced economy.[31] On this account the authors were right; as we have seen above, in the 1950s the neoclassical Keynesian models were not hospitable to financial intermediaries of any kind.

In the innovative perspective proposed by Gurley and Shaw, monetary policy had to be looked at taking into account the shifting characters of liquid and illiquid assets, as far as their fluid continuum changed in consequence of financial innovation, financial differentiation, and the changing portfolio requirements by savers. All these aspects might influence the trends of interest rates and the demand for currency, or they might affect the solidity of banks and other financial institutions.[32] Credit rationing could emerge as a relevant phenomenon affecting the level of interest rates.

Gurley and Shaw published a further article in 1956 (Gurley and Shaw, 1956). In 1958 Culbertson reviewed the two articles, in very critical tones. He accused Gurley and Shaw of denying the credit-creation role of banks,[33] and he firmly criticized their concepts of direct and indirect debt as applied to discuss monetary policies. In his vision of financial intermediaries Culbertson was very conservative; he held views far away from those of Schumpeter or Fisher about the significance of financial innovation, even when it has perverse effects. Culbertson rightly affirmed that banks create credit, but he diminished the active role that financial intermediaries play in credit markets. He belittled the creative role financial managers play by promoting innovative market strategies to extend credit; he viewed them as middlemen, with no significant capacity to change the economic environment (Culbertson, 1958, p. 121). He underlined the self-adjusting nature of financial markets via price movements against the inflationary or deflationary effects of changes in the money stock.[34]

---

[31] 'This Keynesian model is inappropriate to financial aspects of growth analysis for two reasons. First, it does not permit direct debt to accumulate and affect financial determinants of spending. Second, it admits only two kinds of financial asset, money and bonds, on the assumption that the stock though not the location of bonds is fixed. The model is not hospitable to the financial intermediaries whose development in recent decades has diversified indirect finance and marked commercial banking as a relatively declining industry' (Gurley and Shaw, 1955, p. 524).

[32] 'The optimal growth in the money stock, at a given level of income, depends then on the accumulation of debt, the effect of indebtedness on deficit spending, the asset preferences of surplus units, the maturity structure of the debt and its other qualities, and the character of the banking system's portfolio' (Gurley and Shaw, 1955, 526).

[33] 'An extension of credit by a commercial bank is not preceded by or contingent upon any private act of saving or of commitment of funds to investment use. If a person saves and accumulates demand deposits, this in no way affects the ability of banks to lend. Banks (in their demand-deposit function) cannot act as a loan-fund broker' (Culbertson, 1958, p. 122).

[34] 'While an excess supply of any type of non-monetary debt or physical asset tends to depress its price and limit its creation, an excess supply of money tends rather to enlarge the spending stream, and potentially to cause inflation' (Culbertson, 1958, p. 121).

Culbertson's review missed the interesting points that Gurley and Shaw had raised, and the attention they called on regulations to be extended to financial intermediaries at large and not just to banks. Considering the recent evolution of financial markets with the emergence of shadow banking, it is quite clear that his vision was myopic, while Gurley and Shaw had well understood the plasticity of financial services, and how financial innovation could affect the capability to mobilize savings, for the good or for the bad. Gurley and Shaw (1958) replied, the substance of their answer being that their approach aimed to focus the role of finance in processes of growth. They underlined that the degree of liquidity, being just one character among many of highly differentiated financial goods, does not account either for the complex choice of assets in savers' portfolios or the explanation of the effective channels of finance for investment.

In 1960 Gurley and Shaw published the book *Money in a Theory of Finance* that marked a signpost in the debate on financial markets in macroeconomic theory in the early 1960s. The authors still argued in discursive style, but a mathematical appendix written by Enthoven was added. The approach they adopted is based on the idea that money cannot and should not be analysed separately from the general analysis of finance and financial markets. They complained that economists carried out their analyses by ignoring, or largely downplaying, financial assets, 'on the grounds that we owe domestic debt to ourselves or that the real effects of financial asset accumulation by lenders are neutralized by the real effects of debt accumulation by borrowers' (Gurley and Shaw, 1960, p. 2). They added that at the same time there had been the development of a specialistic financial literature which had become 'a descriptive-historical discipline apart from the main stream of economics' (Gurley and Shaw, 1960, p. 3).

The book was a systematic effort at the analysis of financial markets within a neoclassical frame and adopting a portfolio approach. Finance and money, for Gurley and Shaw, have to be studied as a market problem, and notably, within the framework of general equilibrium analysis. In this respect, they reaffirm the methodological approach to money and loanable funds as advocated earlier on by several critics of Keynes's theory of liquidity preference; but their criticism was far more radical than the appeal to the simultaneous consideration of all financial markets. Their theoretical aim was to provide a new assessment of the neutrality proposition including financial markets.[35] To pursue this ambitious project, their general-equilibrium analysis is carried out within the neoclassical

---

[35] 'This [Patinkin's] rarefied set of assumptions is the main object of attack in J. G. Gurley and E. S. Shaw's *Money in a Theory of Finance*, a central purpose of which is to elucidate the conditions under which money will not be neutral' (Johnson, 1962, p. 341). Johnson, following Patinkin, is critical of their conclusions on non neutrality.

framework, assuming full employment, price flexibility, no money illusion, and balanced growth, a choice due not to their unreserved belief in the neoclassical characterization of the economy, but to their purpose to show that even under such unrealistic assumptions 'money is not a veil' (Gurley and Shaw, 1960, p. 10). Although they adhere to 'neoclassical rules of static analysis', and they make the assumption of distributive effects being irrelevant in aggregate functions (Gurley and Shaw, 1960, pp. 67–68), they argue that net effects (other than distribution effects) induced by portfolio mix or diversification have to be dealt with (Gurley and Shaw, 1960, pp. 74–75).

Notwithstanding the adhesion to the neoclassical frame, Gurley and Shaw substantially deny the validity of the Modigliani-Miller theorem (Gurley and Shaw, 1960, p. 63). They underlined that business firms are chronic deficit spenders; in their table of interactions between financial and real variables in aggregate demand the debt burden in a firm's balance sheet was assigned a negative sign on investment spending (Gurley and Shaw, 1960, pp. 64, 71). Moreover, they underline that, because financial assets are not perfect substitutes, spending units might wish to hold mixed portfolios, including the issue of debts by issuing primary securities along with money balances, or they might hold variegated portfolios of financial assets, among which both heterogeneous primary securities and money balances (Gurley and Shaw, 1960, p. 113).

The most innovative aspect of the book is the way the authors portray financial markets, and notably markets for primary securities, as imperfectly competitive markets.[36] There is some Schumpeterian flavour in the analysis. In Chapter IV of the book, they go beyond the four-market economy, where financial markets are represented by a homogeneous bond that is a homogeneous primary security issued by firms and directly acquired by savers, or a government bond. They analyse the dynamics of differentiation in financial markets by 'intermediary techniques' versus the progressive standardization of security markets by 'distributive techniques'. Individual spending units differentiate the primary securities they issue.

In growth processes, finance develops by more efficient 'distributive techniques' that 'increase the breadth of markets for loanable funds', where primary securities are traded between primary issuers and savers. Financial deepening favours economies of scale, with the standardization of securities

---

[36] 'Markets for primary securities are by nature imperfectly competitive markets; they are compartmentalized markets. In and among the compartments one finds the telltale marks of imperfect competition. Many interest rates are inflexible in short periods, and excess demand for funds are resolved temporarily by rationing techniques, changes in requirements for collateral, or adjustment in other non-price terms of exchange. There are notable inequalities in bargaining power on the security markets, so that it is easy to find manifestations of monopoly or monopsony, oligopoly or oligopsony' (Gurley and Shaw, 1960, p. 117).

traded in organized markets of loanable funds. The distributive techniques enhance freedom of entry and price flexibility in large financial markets, but they have some drawbacks. Smaller firms, as much as consumers with limited wealth, may have no access to these markets. Price volatility exposes them to bubbles ('waves of bullishness and bearishness') that impact on steady growth (Gurley and Shaw, 1960, p. 125). Side by side, financial intermediaries compete by product innovation; the 'intermediary techniques' increase the variety of financial services that they create to collect saving, and channel funds to ultimate borrowers, promoting differentiation to accommodate the preferences of savers and investors (Gurley and Shaw, 1960, pp. 123-ff.). Securities are differentiated by borrower, by date, by specific issue, by a variety of other specifications; the assets and liabilities financial intermediaries trade are highly specialized (e.g. mortgages, consumer credits, insurance contracts, corporate bonds of various maturities and risk, pension equities, etc.).

Here the picture of large, organized loanable funds markets is not the image of perfectly competitive markets. Gurley and Shaw look at financial markets as operating in a risky and uncertain environment, where no agent is certain to perfectly anticipate the risks related to the debt burden, or to the uncertain real value of financial assets. Growth may proceed at unequal rates, with stagnating sectors, where creditors or debtors face the possible real depreciation of the value of their assets, or the unexpected real appreciation of the value of their debts (Gurley and Shaw, 1960, p. 118). These disequilibrium perspectives, although in contrast with the main theoretical assumptions, as the authors well understood, were taken into account in the long-term historical and institutional outlook.[37] The authors also noted significant variations in the mix of equities and bonds, or shorter versus longer term financing, during business fluctuations.

> During early recovery years, the flow of issues tends to be most heavily weighted with short-term business borrowing, and long term flotations feature bonds rather than equities. In the later phases of the upturn, corporate bond issues may decline as equities appear in heavier volume. Recession and depression minimize private short-term issues; bond financing becomes more attractive; and the federal government often succeeds state and local governments on security markets. (Gurley and Shaw, 1960, p. 122)

---

[37] 'For decades governmental units may play so large a role in economic activity that federal, state, and local government issues dominate the security markets. Over other long stretches of time the corporate business sector may be bidding for the lion share of loanable funds, so that corporate bonds, equities and short term business debt take precedence. Mortgages are issued in heavy volume during the rising phases of the building cycle, and then dry to a trickle when construction activity is at low ebb' (Gurley and Shaw, 1960, p. 122).

7.5   BANKS AS PROFIT SEEKING FINANCIAL INTERMEDIARIES IN GURLEY'S AND SHAW'S BOOK

On the whole, the financial growth supporting the real growth processes is both qualitative and quantitative (Gurley and Shaw, 1960, p. 159). Financial intermediation, far from being the mechanical transfer of savings from surplus to deficit units, or the neutral space to smooth the inter-temporal redistribution of optimal present and future consumption, is a complex industry, introducing innovation and actively channelling saving to finance growth according to the specific needs or opportunities of firms and consumers in historical context. In their book Gurley and Shaw underlined the 'creation' of credit by financial intermediaries as well as by banks, the term creation meaning the active channelling of additional saving by the incentive of appropriate financial products, or the supply of tailored financial products to satisfy the need for external finance by deficit firms investing in growth.[38] The conception of portfolio theory is, thus, richer than the static, optimal allocation of wealth among given financial assets. Financial products are imperfect substitutes tailored to the preferences of various classes of agents along the historical processes of development (see, e.g. Gurley and Shaw, 1960, pp. 222-ff.). They form a continuum, having at one end liquidity available through a set of financial goods, including money. The demand for money is affected by the variety of alternative financial assets available in the economy, and the specific 'frictions and uncertainties' to which their presence in portfolios expose investors (Gurley and Shaw, 1960, p. 188).

A specific section is devoted to banks as profit seeking firms looking for optimal portfolios on a par with other financial firms. Gurley and Shaw aimed at analysing in 'less mechanical and more behavioral' terms the expansion of money following an expansion of reserves (the money multiplier) in a general equilibrium approach, that is looking at the dynamic impact on all markets of an initial shock to reserves (Gurley and Shaw, 1960, p. 293). In the process of credit and money expansion they dealt with the single bank as a 'miniature replica' of the overall system of banks. The dynamic adjustment may proceed with shorter or longer time lags depending on how promptly both banks and spending units react to excess liquidity by adjusting their

---

[38] 'The difference between the monetary system and non monetary intermediaries in this respect, then, is not that one creates and the other does not, but rather that each creates its own unique form of debt. (...) there is nothing in these processes of creation to suggest that we should stand in awe of one to the neglect of the other' (Gurley and Shaw, 1960, p. 198).

positions in all other markets.[39] Their preoccupation is that due to the various social functions they perform under the regulations and control imposed by the central bank ('anchoring the price level, administering the payment mechanism'), private banking firms might not reach satisfactory profits on a par with other financial intermediaries and suffer as a consequence a shortage of adequate capitalization (Gurley and Shaw, 1960, pp. 289 and 299). On these views, Gurley and Shaw promoted a full range of instruments for monetary policy, including regulations of non-bank financial intermediaries, regulations of consumers' credit, and the management of the cost of refinancing for banks at the central bank. They criticized the exclusive attention paid to the minimum reserve coefficient for commercial banks, and the possible distortions that this form of direct control imposes on their portfolios (Gurley and Shaw, 1960, pp. 269–271). As an alternative they favoured a 'synthetic market in reserve balances supplied and priced by the Central Bank' (Gurley and Shaw, 1960, p. 271).

The book drew the attention of several, and the issues raised in monetary theory were at the centre of controversies, jointly with the policy recommendations. A number of reviews polemically addressed the open criticism of Keynesian monetary theory, or the unachieved balance between neoclassical assumptions and the dynamic view of financial markets. In September 1960, Kennedy placed the emphasis on the authors' criticism of 'the vice of consolidation', the point that was at the core of the stabilization of the standard neoclassical macro model of the 1960s, as far as financial markets were concerned. Kennedy pointed out Gurley's and Shaw's criticism of the tricky assumptions on which both Patinkin and Modigliani had relied; he noted how, according to the authors, consolidation 'precludes any proper analysis of the role of financial intermediaries in the economy' (Kennedy, 1960, p. 568).

In 1961, Minsky acknowledged 'the significance' of the book in signalling the need for further research 'on the relation between financial practices and the functioning of the economy' (Minsky, 1961, p. 138). While he appreciated that the authors were breaking new ground on non-monetary financial intermediaries, he criticized the emphasis they placed on equilibrium and growth at the cost of forgetting the instability issues in dealing with financial markets.[40]

---

[39] 'Expansion is propelled by both banks and spending units, not by banks alone, and the pattern of a new equilibrium is inexplicable without reference to the demand side of the money market' (Gurley and Shaw, 1960, p. 296).

[40] 'Another, not unrelated, defect of this effort is that the authors concentrate on problems of equilibrium and growth to the virtual exclusion of any consideration of the relation between financial arrangements and economic stability. Whether financial intermediation may abet growth at a price of increased susceptibility to serious economic instability is not investigated. To the extent that asset and liability diversification is undertaken in order to protect the owner or issuers of the security from uncertainty associated with the cyclical behaviour of the economy, the postulated

A related criticism pointed to the lack of attention to the role of lender of last resort of the central bank.[41]

In 1962, Lerner underlined again the criticism of the 'net-money doctrine', where private debts cancel out, 'a kind of hangover from the barter economy binge' (Lerner, 1962, p. 705). He welcomed the 'reminder that monetary problems are so fundamentally bound up with the *separateness* of people and firms from each other and the need for money or credits with the transactions between these separate entities' (Lerner, 1962, p. 707). He noted that the authors argued in favour of the benefits to be reaped from financial institutions 'in mobilizing saving for growth and in directing the savings to the most productive channels of investment' (Lerner, 1962, p. 706). The review was, however, critical. Lerner strongly defended the Keynesian and neoclassical approach placing the money stock and liquidity at the core of monetary theory, although he sympathized with the authors' effort to deal with financial markets, and 'to escape from the morass of barter economics back into the real world' (Lerner, 1962, pp. 707, 709).

The mathematical appendix of Gurley's and Shaw's book contained a specific attack to Patinkin's analysis in *Money, Interest and Prices*, which was judged to be 'static and timeless', and inadequate to properly deal with the effects of monetary policy on the allocation of resources (Enthoven, 1960, 305). Patinkin wrote a long review of the book, an important paper per se; he acknowledged the comprehensive theoretical effort by Gurley and Shaw, and notably 'the presentation of the theory of the banking system as part of a general theory of the choice of optimum portfolios of assets and debts by financial institutions of various kinds' (Patinkin, 1961, pp. 95, 97). He appreciated the authors' effort at restoring the banks as entrepreneurial firms optimizing their portfolios, with 'a purpose and a soul', as other intermediaries in the financial world (Patinkin, 1961, p. 97). On the contrary, he was sceptical about their views on monetary policy that suggested to shift the focus from the minimum reserve ratio to the regulations of the interest rate paid by the banks on their deposits at the central bank, or to the extension of the regulations to non-banking intermediaries (Patinkin, 1961, p. 99).[42] At the close of his

---

diversification effects depend, at least in part, on the existence of cyclical instability' (Minsky, 1961, p. 139).

[41] 'In considering central banking, the authors emphasize the role of the central bank as a supplier of reserves through open-market operations. The central bank's role as a lender of last resort in a world with a complex financial structure is not considered. (…) In a world of complex and ever changing financial interrelations it may very well be true that the most significant aspect of central banking is the position of the central bank as the lender of last resort' (Minsky, 1961, p. 139).

[42] Patinkin mentioned 'the possibility of imposing negative rates' on banks' deposits at the central bank; the policy has recently been adopted by the European Central Bank, much as the extension of controls on non-banking intermediaries.

review, with sharp theoretical intelligence and some malice, Patinkin pointed out to the dead end into which their analytical effort leads.

What must now be emphasized is that the assumed absence of distribution effects implies that if households' financial assets increase by the same amount that firms' decrease, then the former's increased demand for bonds is exactly offset by the latter's increased supply. That is, the absence of distribution effects implies that at the level of aggregate behavior it is only the sum total of financial assets in the economy that matters.(Patinkin, 1961, p. 104)

In cauda venenum. When Gurley and Shaw turned to modelling, the analytical difficulties had not been coherently settled; according to Patinkin, given their assumptions, in their neoclassical perspective the irrelevance of inside finance should prevail.

7.6 TOBIN: THE GENERAL-EQUILIBRIUM APPROACH TO FINANCIAL MARKETS

In the discussion of the marginalization of financial markets within the Keynesian models of the Neoclassical Synthesis in the 1960s, we left aside James Tobin, a primary figure in the debates on the financial structure and the monetary mechanism. In the 1950s, Tobin was the young, innovative scholar, whose research aimed to rebuild the behavioural aggregate equations of the Keynesian model on neoclassical micro-foundations. In those years, he reformulated the transaction demand for money, portfolio theory, and investment theory looking at them through neoclassical lenses, though without giving up the Keynesian heritage (Tobin, 1956, 1958).[43] In the 1960s and until the 1980s, the inspiring motive of Tobin's long-term research project was to coherently design models encompassing financial markets within a coherent, general equilibrium perspective (Tobin, 1969); but he again and again expressed sceptical views about the self-adjusting properties of market economies.[44] When the micro-foundations debate lighted up, he rejected the recourse to the representative agent and he ended up by proposing an eclectic approach, where the behavioural equations in macro-models are specified mixing micro-foundations with hypotheses on aggregate behaviour (Tobin, 1980, p. x). In the 1970s and 1980s, Tobin was one of the most effective critics

---

[43] 'Tobin thus added informal optimizing foundations to each component of the IS-LM model of aggregate demand: investment, saving, liquidity preference (money demand), and money supply' (Dimand, 2014, p. 142).

[44] 'The view that the market economy possesses, for unchanging settings of policy instruments, strong self-adjusting properties that assure the stability of its full employment equilibrium is supported neither by theory nor by capitalism's long history of economic fluctuations' (Tobin, 1980, p. 46).

of the so-called rational expectation revolution (Tobin, 1980, pp. 20–48). In his later career he was actively involved in the campaign for the stabilization of international financial markets through the proposed tax on speculative transactions that brings his name.

An advocate of the new framing of Keynesian theory from the general equilibrium perspective, being a sophisticated, learned theorist, Tobin never trivialized the equilibrium notion in macroeconomics, and he was perfectly aware of complex dynamic adjustment and disequilibrium paths. Tobin carefully inquired into the notion of equilibrium and its meanings according to the time frame the scholar designs for various purposes of inquiry. He did not postulate some equilibrium model in the background; on the contrary, he explored how the equilibrium concept in macroeconomics should be flexibly adjusted to the tasks at hand for analytical or policy purposes, and he faced the difficulties involved. We do not attempt here any comprehensive profile of such an accomplished scholar, nor may we account for the many nuances of his thought on financial markets in macroeconomic modelling during the years.[45] We just briefly revisit some passages of his extensive work, which are especially relevant in our story.

A student of Alvin Hansen, Tobin knew Keynes's text first hand; he had read *The General Theory* since his university years (Dimand, 2004, p. 168). He critically thought on Keynes's theory throughout his life. In 1958, in the celebrated article on liquidity preference Tobin especially criticized Keynes's discussion of liquidity preference and the speculative motive because it must necessarily assume the dispersion of expectations about interest rates among investors and it arrives at the biased conclusion that, under the fixed, conventional expectation of the future interest rate, investors choose portfolios with just one asset, either bonds or money (Tobin, 1958, p. 70). The approach that Tobin followed, inspired by Hicks's 1935 seminal paper on portfolio choices, put aside Keynes's view on liquidity as a shelter against radical uncertainty (Hicks, 1935). In Tobin's article, the portfolio of investors is restricted to the mix of money and a representative bond (consol); no other financial assets complicate the optimal choice.[46] Uncertainty on future interest rates is represented by a normal distribution of capital gains with zero expected value,[47] and investors

---

[45] In a number of essays and a book, Dimand provides a comprehensive presentation of Tobin's research (Dimand, 2014). See also Buiter (2003).

[46] 'The alternatives to cash considered, both in this paper and in prior discussions of the subject, in examining the speculative motive for holding cash are assets that differ from cash only in having a variable market yield. They are obligations to pay stated cash amounts at future dates, with no risk of default. They are, like cash, subject to changes in real value due to fluctuations in the price level' (Tobin, 1958, p. 66).

[47] 'The individual investor of the previous section was assumed to have, for any current rate of interest, a definite expectation of the capital gain or loss g (. . .) he would obtain by investing one dollar in consols. Now he will be assumed instead to be uncertain about g but to base his actions

'know the correct probability distribution for assets returns', an idea that Tobin later identified with an implicit rational expectations assumption *ante litteram* (Dimand, 2004, p. 175).

While the 1958 article accomplished the task to bury Keynes's liquidity preference, as an unorthodox Keynesian, since the early 1960s, Tobin took his distance from what he called the 'Keynes-Patinkin model', criticizing Keynes for having originally 'assumed that capital, bonds and private debts are perfect substitutes in investors' portfolios' (Tobin, 1961, pp. 30–33). The assumption implies the 'equality of yields on consols, private debts, and equity capital', account taken of appropriate risk differentials that are constant independently of the relative supplies of the various assets.[48]

> The Keynes-Patinkin model assumes that all debt instruments are perfect substitutes for capital. The interest rate to be explained is the rate common, with the appropriate constant corrections, to all assets other than money itself. What explains this rate is the supply of money relative to transactions requirements and to total wealth. Monetary policy, altering the demand debt component of government debt, can affect the terms on which the community will hold the capital stock. (Tobin, 1961, p. 33)

The macro-model, thus, focuses on a unique interest rate variable. Given the zero yield of outside money, this rate is the instrument of monetary policy to affect real capital accumulation. The alternative more advanced approach that Tobin wanted to develop differentiated from the 'Keynes-Patinkin' model as well as from approaches putting exclusive emphasis on the stock of money. He wanted to take into consideration the whole structure of interest rates.

> The price of this advance in realism and relevance is the necessity to explain not just one market-determined rate of return but a whole structure. The structure of rates may be pictured as strung between two poles, anchored at one end by the zero own-rate conventionally borne by currency (and by central bank discount rate) and at the other end by the marginal productivity of the capital stock. (Tobin, 1961, p. 34)

Tobin's richer vision of financial markets was largely inspired by the work of Gurley and Shaw, whose content we briefly expounded above. As we have seen, their approach is based on the idea that money cannot and should not be analysed separately from the more general analysis of finance and financial

---

on his estimate of its probability distribution. This probability distribution, it will be assumed, has an expected value of zero and is independent of the level of r, the current rate on consols' (Tobin, 1958, p. 71).

[48] Tobin, of course, credited Keynes with a more articulate vision than this; but he noted that both Keynes and Patinkin stick to the simplified view of asset markets in aggregate modelling (Tobin, 1961, pp. 30–31).

markets. The New View, as Tobin names it, focuses on 'the whole spectrum of assets', the linkage with the real economy being through 'the structure of interest rates, assets yields and credit availabilities' (Tobin, 1963, p. 410). These ideas affected more specifically the view Tobin developed of banks as financial intermediaries.

In a brief article Tobin (1963), criticized the idea that a single bank or the banking system as a whole creates money out of 'thin air'. Tobin's analysis downplays the importance of the distinction between money and other financial assets and, consequently, the distinction between banks and other financial intermediaries. Banks can be distinguished from other intermediaries only for the fact that they take more liquid liabilities (demand deposits); all the other alleged differences are essentially irrelevant. The first issue with which Tobin takes issue is the idea that when banks make a loan they create a liability (the newly created borrower's deposit) and an asset (the borrower's debt) simultaneously, whereas other intermediaries cannot do the same. This difference is real, but it lasts for no more than a 'fleeting moment'. From the perspective of a single bank, argues Tobin (1963, p. 413), since borrowers do not take loans to hold idle deposits but they use them to make payments to other agents, there is no guarantee that such payments will remain with the same bank in the form of deposits. Therefore, there is no guarantee that the bank can give rise to the multiplying process of deposits.

From the perspective of the banking system as a whole, banks can expand their assets (loans) either by purchasing or lending against existing assets or by lending to finance private expenditures. In the first case, the banks' expansion of their assets is not associated with any increase in private wealth; in the second case, if lending is devoted to finance investment, there is an increase in wealth as saving increases as much as investment. However, in neither case, is there an automatic increase in the savers' demand for bank deposits equal to the expansion of the banks' assets. The decision about the form in which to hold savings depends on the relative prices of alternative assets; in particular, it depends on the yields of assets alternative to deposits. Therefore, if the yield of other assets falls, profitable lending and investment opportunities available to banks decline and, eventually, the marginal return to lending will equate the marginal cost of attracting additional deposits. In this respect, there is no difference between banks and other intermediaries.

At this juncture, Tobin deals with the problem of legal reserve requirements. In a world without reserve requirements, the banks' expansion of credit and deposits is limited by the availability of assets with yields which compensate them for the cost of attracting deposits. When there are reserve requirements, the limit to the expansion of the banks' assets rises. Therefore, in such situations additional reserves made available by the central bank make it possible and profitable for banks to expand their assets (Tobin, 1963, p. 416). The expansion of reserves lowers interest rates and induces the public to demand more deposits, but the decline in the interest rates is not as large as to wipe out the banks' margin between the value and cost of additional deposits: 'It is the existence of this margin – not the monetary nature of bank liabilities – which makes it possible for the economics teacher to say that additional loans permitted by new reserves will generate their own deposits' (Tobin, 1963, p. 416).

Finally, for Tobin, the money multiplier doctrine is misleading for another, and perhaps more fundamental, reason. It is based on the assumption that banks, apart from exceptional situations, are fully 'loaned up', i.e. that they lend to the maximum extent permitted by the reserve requirement. In reality, 'the use to which commercial banks put the reserves made available to the system is an economic variable depending on lending opportunities and interest rates' (Tobin, 1963, p. 416). In conclusion, it is rather evident that, despite his intent, Tobin's criticisms do not imply a downright rejection of the banks' ability to create additional money through lending. His critique rather is a rejection of a 'naive' and simplistic version of the money multiplier. As we saw in Chapter 6, Samuelson himself had already made a number of qualifications for a correct interpretation of the process of money creation through the banking system; therefore, Tobin's and Samuelson's approaches to the problem are not radically different from one another.[49] The basic features that the two views have in common are more significant than their differences. In both cases, banks are seen as intermediaries between ultimate lenders and borrowers; in both cases, in fact, banks can lend, to a greater or lesser extent, only if they receive cash from depositors, who are the ultimate lenders. The central bank can create money, and hence reserves, by purchasing less liquid assets in exchange for (hard) money. By increasing the supply of (hard) money, the central bank allows ordinary banks to expand their loans.

As we already pointed out in Chapter 6, in such a view of the process of credit and money creation, little, if any, attention is paid to the fact that banks can borrow reserves from the central bank. In such a case the public, and their decisions to deposit or not money with the banks, play a much less significant role in the determination of the possible amount of credit (deposits) that the banks can create.[50] In so far as the central bank is ready to lend to commercial banks, deposits do not represent a constraint to lending. The role that the public

---

[49] The money multiplier can be rendered more flexible, and closer to Tobin's position, by introducing the possibility that the share of money that the public wish to hold in cash can vary or be indicative of the share of wealth that the public want to hold in forms different from bank deposits.

[50] Later on Tobin (1980, p. 91), in fact, considers the possibility for banks to borrow reserves from the central bank, but he regards deposits by the public so much more important that bank borrowing from the central bank is seen as a negative demand for base money.

play concerns the amount of loans (deposits) they demand from banks. Banks operate in the economy as lenders and borrowers.

Gurley's and Shaw's methodological stand is reflected also in a brief article by Tobin and Brainard (1963) of the same year, where they detail the reasons for financial intermediation with reference to asymmetric information, transactions costs, default or illiquidity risks, all aspects that, although present in the standard literature on banking, are absent from the 'Keynes-Patinkin model'.

> The reasons that the intermediation of financial institutions can accomplish these transformations between the nature of the obligation of the borrower and the nature of the asset of the ultimate lender are these: (1) administrative economy and expertise in negotiating, accounting, appraising, and collecting; (2) reduction of risk per dollar of lending by the pooling of independent risks, with respect both to loan default and to deposit withdrawal; (3) governmental guarantees of the liabilities of the institutions and other provisions (bank examination, investment regulations, supervision of insurance companies, last-resort lending) designed to assure the solvency and liquidity of the institution. For these reasons, intermediation permits borrowers who wish to expand their investments in real assets to be accommodated at lower rates and easier terms than if they had to borrow directly from the lenders. (Tobin and Brainard, 1963, p. 385)

7.7   HOPES, EFFORTS AND DEAD ENDS

The outspoken differentiation from Patinkin's 1956 models was the premise to Tobin's future research programme. Tobin referred to Keynes's passage in Chapter 12 that explained investment choices as influenced by the market value of existing capital assets at the Stock Exchange compared with the cost of building new equipment, by reviving its core message but also introducing important differences. Keynes's original emphasis was rooted in his notion of radical uncertainty, and the precariousness of conventional evaluations of assets prices; in Tobin's discourse, radical uncertainty being set aside, market factors account for the discrepancies between market valuation and the replacement cost of capital for individual firms (the variable qs), or in average market trends (the macro q variable). The changing q (later known as Tobin's q) becomes the link between the real and the financial side and the transmission mechanism of monetary policy.[51] The role attributed to such discrepancies shows how Tobin distanced himself from any neo-Walrasian

---

[51] 'According to this approach, the principal way in which financial policies and events affect aggregate demand is by changing the valuation of physical assets relative to their replacement costs. Monetary policies can accomplish such changes, but other exogenous events can too' (Tobin, 1969, p. 29).

conception of an auctioneer adjusting prices at infinite speed in markets that instantaneously clear. If the market valuation of capital systematically, though temporarily, diverges from its reproduction cost, this depends among other factors on the time required to design and complete investment projects, and the related adjustment costs.

In an article on the 'pitfalls' in financial modelling in macroeconomics Brainard and Tobin (1968) introduce the q variable and they argue the necessity to specify the dynamic, out-of-equilibrium adjustment of financial markets in a genuine, general equilibrium perspective including dynamic cross-adjustment effects in various markets.[52] Such dynamics adjustment effects are the most relevant to understand the effects of policies, such as the much debated effects of changes in the regulation of ceiling rates on time deposits (Brainard and Tobin, 1968, pp. 104–106).

> In our view this discussion has not paid enough attention to the general equilibrium effects of such regulatory measures and has been too preoccupied with the effects on commercial bank loans or deposits. A reduction in the ceiling may in some circumstances be deflationary, but the fact that it drives funds out of banks and forces them to contract their loans is no proof at all of this assertion. Erstwhile depositors will be looking for places to invest their funds, and they may be glad to acquire, either directly or through other intermediaries, the assets the banks have to sell and to accommodate the borrowers the banks turn away. Whether the ultimate result is to bid interest rates and equity yields down or up is a complicated question: the answer depends, among other things, on whether time deposits are in wealth-owners' portfolios predominantly substitutes for demand deposits and currency or for loans and equities. The former substitution pattern tends to make a reduction in time deposit rates deflationary, the latter pattern, expansionary. The answer depends also, of course, on what is assumed about the supply of unborrowed reserves and other instruments of monetary control. (Brainard and Tobin, 1968, pp. 104–105)

Their model details the differences between currency, reserves, time and demand deposits, equities and banks' loans, discussing their substitutability properties for savers or banks. However, in the equilibrium equations private borrowings and banks' loans simply cancel out. The authors give the variable q the primary role in the transmission mechanism of monetary policy as it affects real investment.

> In other words, the valuation of investment goods relative to their cost is the prime indicator and proper target of monetary policy. Nothing else, whether it is the quantity of "money" or some financial interest rate, can be more than an imperfect and derivative indicator of the effective thrust of monetary events and policies. (Brainard and Tobin, 1968, p. 104).

---

[52] 'We are pleading, in short, for a "general disequilibrium" framework for the dynamics of adjustment to a "general equilibrium" system' (Brainard and Tobin, 1968, p. 106).

The 1969 article 'A General Equilibrium Approach to Monetary Theory' (Tobin, 1969) was an ambitious manifesto of the New View. Tobin outlines the project to coherently include financial markets within a general equilibrium frame to be flexibly connected to the real side of the model, and manages to specify whichever number of markets to deal with the appropriate institutional details (e.g. deposit rate ceilings) relevant for monetary policy. In principle, the project aimed at encompassing the whole financial structure of the economy as well as its detailed capital structure.

> The basic framework is very flexible. It can be extended to encompass more sectors and more assets, depending on the topic under study. Other financial intermediaries can be introduced. More distinctions can be made among categories of government debts and types of private debts. Equally important, the assumption that physical capital is homogeneous can be dropped, and a number of markets, prices, and rates of return for stocks of goods introduced – distinguishing among houses, plant, equipment, consumers' durable, etc. (Tobin, 1969, p. 29)

The programme was never pursued to its full extent envisaged by Tobin, although empirical research went on for some years. The sketchy presentation in the article goes as far as to include money, government bonds, equities and the market value of real capital, banks and deposits. The main focus is again on the possible 'discrepancies' between the market valuation and the reproduction cost of capital, as in the joint contribution with Brainard a year before. In the wider, general equilibrium horizon, multiple factors drive the temporary, short term discrepancies; no single exogenous or intermediate variable (such as measures of the money stock or benchmark interest rates) captures the impact they have on aggregate demand and the real economy (Tobin, 1969, p. 29). Banks and interest rate ceilings create further ambiguities (Tobin, 1969, p. 28). In the long term, assuming the flexibility of all interest rates, the discrepancies naturally disappear; the complexities of the financial structure lose any relevance. The passage below shows the ambiguity inherent to the reference to the long-term growth equilibrium, and it is prophetical about the turn that macroeconomic theory will take in the 1970s and 1980s.

> If the interest rate on money, as well as the rates on all other financial assets, were flexible and endogenous, then they would all simply adjust to the marginal efficiency of capital. There would be no room for discrepancies between market and natural rates of return on capital, between market valuation and reproduction costs. There would be no room for monetary policy to affect aggregate demand. The real economy would call the tune for the financial sector, with no feedback in the other direction. As previously observed, something like this occurs in the long run, where the influence of monetary policy is not on aggregate demand but on the relative supplies of monetary and real assets, to which all rates of return must adjust. (Tobin, 1969, p. 26)

After having introduced the q variable in their joint article (Brainard and Tobin, 1968, pp. 103–104), Tobin and Brainard developed the subject in their later Cowles Foundation paper in 1976 (Tobin and Brainard, 1976), where they discuss divergences of market values from replacement costs in industries such as building, for technological innovations in plant and equipment, for external shocks such as the increase in oil prices, for heterogeneous risk factors or heterogeneous capital assets, and notably for the time required to build new investment goods (Tobin and Brainard, 1976, pp. 3-ff.). In their description the valuations in 'organized and efficient' securities markets are 'sensitive and volatile', while the market mechanism to absorb the discrepancies works through the completion of investment that requires time to build and adjustment costs (Tobin and Brainard, 1976, p. 4). In contrast to the Modigliani-Miller theorem, they go as far as suggesting that the valuation of capital assets may depend on the firm's financial structure (Tobin and Brainard, 1976, p. 11). Their analysis of the nexus between the financial and the real side relies on abandoning any theoretical assumption about perfect substitution between equities and riskless bonds, and on denying that arbitrage may instantaneously absorb any discrepancy arising in markets for securities (Tobin and Brainard, 1976, p. 16).

In 1975, Tobin discussed the effects of deflation on aggregate demand, building on the outline Keynes had sketched in Chapter 19 of *The General Theory*. He builds a dynamic IS-LM model, where the effects of deflation on aggregate spending result from the different propensity to spend of debtors and creditors. He argues that deflation negatively affects aggregate demand on the reasonable conjecture that debtors have a higher propensity to spend than creditors. The conjecture that the distributive effects are different from zero is a clear deviation from Patinkin's and Modigliani's assumptions; but Tobin's model was remarkably less nuanced than Keynes's or Fisher's arguing. In the model, the effects of deflation on the spending propensities of debtors and creditors are independent; they are simply added up. Although expectations of deflation are included as accelerating the deflationary effects, no account is taken of the influence of creditors' expectations as affected by the debtors' risk position. No systemic effects of bankruptcies are considered; no spreading of imitative expectations leading to panic; no bank runs due to the loss of trust in the liquidity of banks or other intermediaries; no collapse of the banking system by the erosion of safety margins. The wealth effect of deflation is assumed to directly affect, on one side, the investment demand by indebted firms and, on the other, the consumers' demand, with the possible prevalence of the negative impact on aggregate demand. The article marked an innovative turn in the debates on the macroeconomic effects of deflation; since Tobin's contribution, mathematical models of the dynamics of deflation pertain to a research niche that persists in macroeconomics. In his later essay on the issue in the Yrjö Jahnsson Lectures that he gave in 1978, Tobin effectively argued the strong reasons to conjecture that debtors have higher propensities to spend than lenders (Tobin, 1980, p. 10).

7.8   A LINE OF RESEARCH FADES OUT

A comparison between Tobin's earlier works with his fourth Yrjö Jahnsson Lectures (Tobin, 1980, pp. 73–96) and with his Nobel lecture (Tobin, 1982) is especially significant for his mature assessment of the troubled relationship between macroeconomic theory and general equilibrium theory. In both texts, a more frugal message emerges than the ambitious expectations of the earlier writings, jointly with the lucid understanding of the difficulties to fully achieve the results hoped for in the 1969 manifesto. Tobin also put a stronger accent on the possibility of 'protracted and stubborn' disequilibrium and on the damages from 'protracted underproduction' (Tobin, 1980, p. 19).

In his fourth lecture, more than twenty years after Patinkin's book, once again Tobin asks the critical question: which equilibrium are we speaking of in macroeconomic models? He critically deals with it by discussing technically the time frame to be adopted in macro-models, still a controversial issue. On the whole, he gives preference to sequential, discrete-time modelling over continuous-time modelling as more apt to capture short-term dynamics and adjustment; but he confines the proper notion of equilibrium only to stationary or balanced growth steady states (Tobin, 1980, p. 83). When introducing debt financing by firms, Tobin mentions the Modigliani-Miller theorem, underlying that it amounts to assuming that the business sector is composed by 'pure equity firms'. He comments: 'The theorem goes much too far, in my opinion, but that is a subject beyond my current scope' (Tobin, 1980, p. 90). He thus leaves the issue of private debts aside, implicitly suggesting that the leverage of firms does not create any special difficulty to the proposed theoretical structure, if not for the averaging of the qs for the different financial instruments that firms adopt. He suggests relating the market valuation of capital to the existing financial structure in the economy, but he does not discuss further how and if the qs could depend on the state of indebtedness in the economy, or on the fragility of the financial sector.

Tobin also discusses the corrections needed to include financial interme-diaries and banks in the benchmark IS-LM model; but in dealing with the issue, he falls again on the 'consolidation vice' (Tobin, 1980, pp. 85 and 91). If it is technically correct in terms of aggregate accounting procedures, once more it amounts to removing the financial sector. In short, pure equity firms in the business sector issue securities to be absorbed exclusively and directly by the ultimate savers, whose net financial accounts accommodate government bonds. Even within such a simplified frame, dynamics proves forbidding: 'The dynamic process is easy to describe in principle, but hard to analyze and implement in practice' (Tobin, 1980, p. 96).

In his Nobel lecture, Tobin insists on analysing economic processes as going on in time, and he sarcastically denies any credibility to the Walrasian auctioneer mechanism (Tobin, 1982, p. 189). After recalling the complete, future markets construction in the Arrow-Debreu model,[53] he underlines the absence of complete, contingent future markets in the real economies, pointing out that 'the financial and capital markets are at their best imperfect coordinators of saving and investment.' He credits Keynes for having pointed out such failure of coordination, judging it 'a fundamental source of macroeconomic instability' (Tobin, 1982, p. 175). After the early dreams, the scholar was aware of the disappointments in the neo-Walrasian theory: he mentions the disruptive effects of Sonnenschein's theorem on excess demand functions, and the unsolved difficulties to justify money in the neo-Walrasian framework.[54] On this sceptical view of the pitfalls in neo-Walrasian theory, Tobin distances himself from the rational expectations revolution, and from any macroeconomic modelling strategy strictly referring to the Arrow-Debreu model. In building models of the macro-economy, he proposes a middle way, not strictly rigorous on micro-foundations, in between the extremes of disaggregating the economy in a large number of markets and making recourse to a single representative agent.[55]

In discussing the macroeconomic framework he had proposed, Tobin again advocates assets' disaggregation for both analytical and policy purposes,[56] but he eventually focuses on the core of his innovative contribution to the construction of a richer IS-LM framework than the Hicksian one. He declares that 'the major conclusions of the Keynes-Hicks apparatus remain intact'(Tobin, 1982, p. 172). However, he mentions the troubles in deriving the Gross Substitutes assumption for market assets' demand functions, and in

---

[53] He mentions Arrow's 1972 Nobel Lecture as 'an elegant exposition of general equilibrium theory, recognizing both its power and its limitations' (Tobin, 1982, p. 174).

[54] Tobin mentions Hahn's 'insightful' contribution on the issue (Tobin, 1982, p. 173, n. 1). See also Tobin (1982, p. 174).

[55] 'Following an older tradition, economy-wide structural equations are an amalgam of individual behavior and aggregation across a multitude of diverse individuals. This is the pragmatic alternative to two other procedures, both with serious disadvantages. One is to preserve the diversity of agents' preferences and endowments allowed in fully general equilibrium models; the weak restrictions that optimization places on individual excess demands imply no restrictions at all on market-wide schedules. The other is to assume that all agents are alike or fall into two or three classes (old and young, for example) internally homogeneous but differing from each other in arbitrarily specified ways' (Tobin, 1982, p. 174).

[56] 'What transactions are the sources of variation of money stocks makes a difference, depending on how they alter the wealth and portfolio positions of economic agents' (Tobin, 1982, p. 173).

proving their stability in case of major changes or shocks in the economic environment (Tobin, 1982, pp.185–186). He simply trusts the stability of asset demand functions in the medium-term horizon relevant for stabilization policies. In summary, Tobin vindicated the extended IS-LM frame including equities side by side with government bonds and outside money, and dropping the 'perfect substitutes' assumption that backed the aggregation of all financial assets into homogeneous bonds, seen as alternative to outside money.[57]

> The illustrative model I wish to describe contains, I believe, the highest degree of asset aggregation compatible with analyzing the central issues of macroeconomics, in particular the workings of fiscal and monetary policy. (...) I distinguish just four assets: *equities*, titles to physical capital and its earnings, generated by investment *I*; *government bonds* and *base money*, issued to finance deficits *D*; and *foreign currency assets* (...) Representing these complex realities by four assets is a great abstraction, comparable to many others in macroeconomics. In its defence, I remind you that the common textbook macro model limits itself to two asset categories. (Tobin, 1982, p. 178)

Why Tobin's research programme, though stimulating and provocative, did not become the central line of development in macroeconomics? It has been suggested that it was hard to implement in empirical investigation because it did not produce the clear cut results which could justify the amount of resources it required. On the monetarist side, Tobin's complexity of vision was regarded a detour leading nowhere, while obfuscating aspects of monetary policy which are made more readable and visible by using the quantity equation (Brunner and Meltzer, 1971). The parallel emergence of finance as an extended, specialized sub-discipline paradoxically diverted the attention from financial markets, because of the ideological stance regarding the perfection of capital markets. If capital markets efficiently use all information, cancelling out almost instantaneously through arbitrage any difference in market yields, or any divergence of the market valuation from the rational, forward looking, discounted value of future earnings, Tobin's construction is shaken. It is difficult to argue that persistent deviations of market valuations from reproduction costs drive investment demand, or to discuss which space is left to monetary policy. As Tobin himself suggests, a coherent dynamic vision of stocks and flows finds the most satisfactory solution if looking at the steady state, where 'government policy settings are stable, real stocks and flows are growing at a common natural rate' (Tobin, 1980, p. 96). He adds: 'if one exists.'

This solution was the path that a new current in mainstream macroeconomics was taking to solve the stock and flow compatibility issue. Since the

---

[57] He proposed a four-assets model including foreign assets. For brevity, here we do not consider foreign assets.

late 1970s, the dynamic steady state became the skeleton of real business cycle models, built by refining the aggregate model of steady state growth that Ramsey (1928) conceived back in the 1920s, under the pretence that the dynamic modelling of the representative consumer's optimal, inter-temporal choices could effectively map the genuine general equilibrium of a complex market economy. Tobin's doubts on aggregation were set aside; the emphasis on the genuine diversity of agents was lost, and eventually his New View was submerged by a new family of macroeconomic models where no financial intermediation at all is included. In mainstream macroeconomics, Tobin's rich line of research faded out.[58]

7.9   DOES INSIDE FINANCE MATTER?

Patinkin and Modigliani worked on separate research lines, and their definitions of dichotomy and neutrality were not fully convergent (Modigliani, 1963, p. 84). However, by the early 1960s, their research paths converged to the stabilization of benchmark macroeconomic models with no significant role for finance and banking, which were collapsed into a homogeneous bond market by ad hoc assumptions that did the trick of deleting the network of financial intermediation from the IS-LM extended model. In turn, bonds disappeared from the view because one equation was redundant, and it was chosen to eliminate the bond market.

Such outcome was controversial. Since their articles in the 1950s, and more extensively in their 1960 book, Gurley and Shaw underlined the deep difference between what they named 'the net money doctrine' and their own effort at producing a 'gross money doctrine'. They argued that disaggregation should be at the core of monetary theory, while the net money doctrine ends up in turning macroeconomic theory into the theory of a barter economy, if some external money is not postulated by ad hoc assumptions (Gurley and Shaw, 1960, pp. 140-ff.). They criticized the ambiguous pretension to rationalize the demand for money balances in a consolidated economy, where all risks arising from debtor-creditor relationships are washed out. Interesting as their points were, in their analytical work a coherent balance between their pretence

---

[58] Dimand (2014, p. 152) suggests a sympathetic assessment balancing the core message against the shortcomings. 'So, too, with Tobin's approach: empirical implementation of models with multiple, imperfectly substitutable assets had problems with multicollinearity and with lack of explicit solutions of the nonlinear equations describing adjustment. The Tobin effect in long-run growth models depended on fine points of model specification, but there still remains the message of paying attention to stock-flow consistency, to imperfect substitution among assets, and to modelling economies that are self-adjusting for shocks up to some limit, but that do not automatically return to potential output after infrequent large demand shocks.'

to keep it within a strict neoclassical frame and their emphasis on imperfect competition, innovation and the gross money doctrine proved to be difficult to realize.

Tobin built on Gurley's and Shaw's New View trying to escape its conclusions. His research proposed a further challenge for his repeated plea to adopt a general equilibrium approach in the modelling of financial markets. Eventually, Tobin achieved the extension of the basic IS-LM frame to include three assets instead of the two customary ones, bonds and money. He added firms' equities, in view of the fact that the market valuation of capital is the crucial variable through which the financial side and the real side are linked, and monetary policy works. The market for equities was not to be swallowed by the bond market under the perfect substitution assumption, since it is the signalling market par excellence for firms' investment decisions. At the same time, Tobin downplayed the role of banks and financial intermediaries, when dealing with the feasible strategy to model the interaction of assets and goods markets in macroeconomic models. In his extended IS-LM apparatus, now including the market valuation of equities side by side with the markets for money and government bonds, he eventually returns to the procedure of cancelling out debts and loans between private units as well as the financial intermediaries marketing them.

Eventually, the 'net-money doctrine' or the 'vice of consolidation' prevailed in the debate of the 1960s. The ideological lenses that encouraged focussing exclusively on perfect capital markets and general competitive equilibrium prevented academic economists from seeing the relevant points that Gurley and Shaw had addressed. Gurley and Shaw made a prophecy about the cost of diverting the attention from the complexities of the financial structure.

> Money is supplied and demanded only in a sectored society. It is one financial phenomenon among the many that co-ordinate the activities of spending units. It is a device for communication between autonomous spending units, and a means for the self-preservation of individual spending units in a risky world. The result of consolidating spending units into a monolithic solidarity must be to eliminate money as well as other financial phenomena from aggregative economic analysis. (Gurley and Shaw, 1960, p. 140)

Their prophecy proved right. For decades finance – and, later on, money itself – disappeared from the most authoritative models of mainstream macroeconomics; an evolution that we shall examine in Chapter 8 below, which looks at the discontent with the Neoclassical Synthesis and the attacks against Keynesian economics since the early monetarist revolution.

Studies on the role of finance in development processes were mainly confined to a specialized branch of the literature, to which Shaw contributed. Aggregate indexes of financial deepening were integrated into the specialized literature on growth, losing sight of Gurley's and Shaw's attention to the qualitative aspects of the financial structure (see, e.g., Benhabib and Spiegel, 2000). Since the 1980s, almost twenty years after Gurley's and Shaw's book had been published, historical studies and a renewed interest in asymmetric information revived the attention to imperfectly competitive financial markets, and notably to credit rationing. The risks of excessive financial deepening were pointed out (Pagano, 1993, 2013). The issue of finance and growth is again hotly debated after the 2007–2008 financial crisis (Zingales, 2015; Popov, 2017).

8. The Monetarist counter-revolution: from the 'resuscitation' to the disappearance of money

Since the 1950s and during the 1960s, Milton Friedman and other scholars in the monetarist counter-revolution vindicated the relevance of money in the macro-economy against the Keynesians who – they argued – had downplayed its role in post-war years. In 1971, in his R. T. Ely Lecture, Johnson used the term 'monetarist counter-revolution' taking the cue from the expressions 'the counter-revolution in monetary theory' used by Friedman, and 'the monetarist revolution' used by Brunner (Friedman, 1970; Brunner, 1970). In his cautious assessment of the coherence and theoretical soundness of the new currents in macroeconomics that attacked the Keynesian orthodoxy, Johnson credits the new ideas with the positive effect to force economists to be 'both more conscious of monetary influences on the economy and more careful' in evaluating their importance (Johnson, 1971, pp. 8 and 13).

In the 1970s, another radical turn conquered the edge of research in macro-economics. Robert Lucas and other scholars introduced new macroeconomic models with rational expectations, inspired again by the appeal to general-equilibrium theory, but in more radical terms than those of the economists of the Neoclassical Synthesis. They explained business fluctuations as aris-ing from unexpected changes of the money stock, the so-called 'monetary surprises'. New Classical Macroeconomics launched a further frontal attack against Keynes's thought and Keynesian macroeconomics.

By the 1980s, money, whose primary role had been claimed in such major controversies among macroeconomists for thirty years, disappeared from the models of New Classical Macroeconomics and from the dominant explanations of business cycles. The controversial models with monetary surprises of the rational expectations revolution were put aside. During the 1980s to the 1990s, the economists who rejected the Keynesian heritage in macroeconomics, narrated highly fictional stories about fluctuations based on real business cycle models. The fictional worlds their mathematical models portray include no money to deal with, either as a means of exchange or as a wealth asset. In the history of economic theory, never before the 'veil' of money had been so drastically disposed of. Indeed, the label 'monetarism' does not properly apply to real business cycle models, if not as a label of convenience applied to mark a brand of the end of the century opposition to Keynesian economics. Its own promoters called it the 'transformation' of macroeconomics to emphasize the change of techniques and approach that the new programme proposed (Prescott, 2006).

Why did the monetary aspects disappear from the dominant currents in macroeconomics for such a long span of time? How did this radical change occur after the monetarist counter-revolution? This chapter is devoted to trace the path that brought from the voiced counter-revolution in monetary theory of the 1960s and 1970s to the 'monetarism without money' of the 1980s and 1990s. Without entering into the details of this complex transition, we focus exclusively on the contributions of Friedman and Lucas to explain how the emergence of a new version of the old dichotomy between the general-equilibrium equations and the quantity equation opened the way to the final erasing of money from business cycle theory. The transition to real business cycle models required the drastic change of the techniques of model building, away from the genuine general-equilibrium approach and towards aggregate growth models and the use of calibration and simulation techniques at the econometric level. This technical change bypassed the difficulties which since the 1970s had plagued the neo-Walrasian general-equilibrium models.

8.1 DOES MONEY MATTER? AN OVERVIEW OF THE MONETARIST COUNTER-REVOLUTION

A large historical literature has been devoted to the reconstruction of Monetarism and the debates in macroeconomics that involved, on one side, the neoclassical Keynesians and, on the other side, the monetarist scholars, to use for the sake of brevity this abused classification.[1]

Since the 1960s, the debate touched upon the roots of the monetarist revolution in the ideas of Chicago scholars, which Friedman had claimed, and Patinkin dismissed by suggesting that Friedman's money demand had a Keynesian flavour (Friedman, 1956; Patinkin, 1969). A major issue of contention was the dominance in the direction of causality from changes in the money stock to fluctuations of nominal income and the precise content of the monetarist analytical turn was the object of heated disputes between friends and foes. In his Ely Lecture, Johnson reminds us that the proposition that money matters

---

[1]   The group of scholars, who spread the ideas that gave substance to the monetarist counter-revolution, was not fully homogeneous in opinions and theoretical analysis and an accurate reconstruction would require taking into account major differences on a variety of issues; something that is beyond the scope of this book. For surveys on these issues, see, among others, Hoover (1984); Hirsch and De Marchi (1990); De Vroey (2016).

can be stated with a variety of nuances and that the Keynesians under attack rejected the simplistic accusation that they had totally forgotten money.[2]

Friedman himself disliked the term monetarism. He explicitly stated that he aimed at restoring the quantity theory of money, which in various passages he interprets as a causal relation going from independent changes of the aggregate money stock, the ultimate prime mover, to changes of nominal income, though without denying some feed-back mechanism from business to money that might intervene during the cycle. He restated the quantity theory in a renewed version centred on the stability of the money demand function, and notably on the income elasticity of money; but the precise form of such restatement is somewhat blurred, also because of the changing frame into which it has been expressed in different contributions along the years.

In his 1959 article 'The demand for money: Some theoretical and empirical results', Friedman puts forward his innovative theory of the demand for money as related to permanent income, drastically criticizing the Keynesian partition of the demand for money into transaction, speculative and precautionary motives (Friedman, 1959a, p. 348–349). He suggests that the increase of the money stock does not impact primarily on the rates of interest. By augmenting the real balances in the agents' portfolios, weighted in relation to their estimate of permanent income, a change in the stock of money brings about the reshaping of the whole range of assets in the consumers' wealth, including their expenditure on consumer durables. In the article, Friedman summarizes his policy indications by emphasizing the instability that the mismanagement of monetary policy might impress on the real side of the economy. He points out 'the potency of relatively small changes in the stock of money', for good or evil, and that even 'relatively small changes in the stock of money, random in timing and size' might create dangerous instability (Friedman, 1959a, p. 351).

The controversies on the monetarist views ranged from the supposed stability of the income velocity, a highly disputed issue, to the relative prevalence of real versus price effects in nominal income as a result of changes in the stock of money, to the overall plausibility of the new quantity theory to explain business fluctuations and the alleged statistical evidence supporting it. Friedman himself, in answering to various criticisms of his position, rejected any simplified interpretation of his scientific work and recalled the nuanced position he had taken on the interpretation of mild or severe fluctuations (Friedman, 1970, 1972).

---

[2] 'As James Tobin has pointed out, there is a world of difference between two alternatives to this proposition, namely, one, "money does too matter," and, two, "money is all that matters." But this difference was easily and conveniently blurred, to the benefit of the counter-revolution, by seizing on the extreme Keynesian position that money does not matter at all as the essence of the prevailing orthodoxy' (Johnson, 1971, p. 8).

Also the methodological approach championed by Friedman was questioned. In a Marshallian mode, Friedman gives priority to compact, operational theories, favouring the isolation in simplified models of 'few, key magnitudes', and looking for the key factors in short or long-run economic changes that could account for the evidence from time series, or better, not contradicted by the evidence. In this respect, Friedman fully acknowledges the validity of Keynes's approach, although he argues that his theory 'has been contradicted by evidence' (Friedman, 1972, p. 908). The strategy of modelling via simpler nexuses and key magnitudes is polemically contrasted with what he denounces as the Keynesian scholars' effort to construct all-embracing, simultaneous equations models with the pretence to provide a detailed picture of the economy, or focused mainly on the real side of it (Friedman, 1972, p. 908).

Friedman's key magnitudes are the money stock and nominal income. Although he does not reject the empirical research exploring the time series evidence on money and income in the so-called reduced form models, this is not his own approach. In his various works, Friedman explores the causal relationship between disturbances to the money stock and fluctuations of money income both in the short and the long run, both through the analysis of time series and through the detailed reconstruction of historical episodes. In drawing his conclusions, Friedman maintains a specific focus on the transmission mechanism that links independent changes in the stock of money to short and long-run variations of money income. He carefully examines the different adjustment processes during mild or severe fluctuations, possible cases of overshooting during phases of transitions as well as the eventual convergence to the long-run equilibrium.

The heated theoretical debate between monetarists and the Keynesians of the Neoclassical Synthesis came to an impasse, because of the partial convergence of milder partisans on both sides, and because of the theoretical impossibility to settle the controversy in terms of observable evidence, as Friedman predicated on the basis of his own methodological premises. In the end, the main reasons for the progressive fading of Friedman's monetarism since the late 1970s, were the poor empirical results regarding the stability of the income velocity of money and the operational difficulties to choose a satisfactory monetary aggregate, on which central bankers could base non-erratic policies (De Long, 2000, pp. 89–90).

Both the above issues impinge on the pillars of Friedman's theory. The stable money demand function is the pillar of the restatement of the quantity theory, while the money stock aggregate, which should be the variable that monetary policy stabilizes remains an unsolved puzzle in monetary management. This last issue touches upon the crucial policy recommendation. In the 1980s, Friedman attacked the Federal Reserve, for having paid just rhetorical lip-service to the monetarist rule of controlling monetary aggregates, while not really doing it (Friedman, 1982, 1984). In fact, the aim to control monetary aggregates had been abandoned, if it had ever been pursued seriously and, by the early 1990s, the established monetary policy rule, even theoretically, was based on the eclectic Taylor's rule.[3]

The transition from so-called Monetarism Mark I of the 1960s to the rational expectations revolution and New Classical Macroeconomics of the 1970s (and, since the early 1980s, to real business cycle models) has been interpreted from the perspective of the new challenges for economics (like the explanation of the coexistence of inflation and high unemployment), the changing priorities and practices in monetary policies, or even in terms of the sociology of research, for the opportunities that new technologies in mathematical modelling and econometrics offered to younger scholars, eager to publish and affirm their scientific primacy (Laidler, 2015). All these different interpretations contain a grain of salt, and help explain the tides of revolutions, or counter-revolutions, in macroeconomics. A full history of the puzzling evolution from Friedman's monetarism to real business cycle theorizing would require a reconstruction that involves both economic history and a detailed examination of the evolution of working practices, training and values in academic communities in economics. In this chapter, for brevity, the critical steps that brought to the disappearance of money from macroeconomics will be dealt with only as an episode in the history of economic ideas and ideologies.

8.2   FRIEDMAN'S PROGRAMME FOR MONETARY STABILITY

To argue his radical dissent from Keynesian economics, in the 1960s and 1970s Friedman developed a narrative of the history of macroeconomics after Keynes that underlines the disappearing of money from the explanation of macroeconomic events and policies as a consequence of the coming to dominance of radical Keynesian interpretations. His reading of early postwar Keynesianism centred on the charge that Keynesian scholars in the U.S. had given pride of place to the real side of the economy, excluding the monetary side. On the other hand, for Friedman, Keynes himself had offered a non-monetary explanation of the Great Depression, and a diagnosis of the impotence of monetary policy to cure it.

Friedman's judgement is formulated rather cryptically in the 'Summing up' of *The Monetary History of the United States*, the book that Friedman authored

---

[3]   On Taylor's rule, see Koenig et al. (2012).

jointly with Anna Schwartz in 1963.[4] In 1968, in his celebrated 'Presidential Address', where Friedman introduces the natural rate of unemployment, he formulates the charge in an outspoken attack on the American Keynesians, for whom money does not matter at all.[5] Friedman's explicit reference is to Hansen's interpretation of the Keynesian theory but also other scholars are mentioned.[6]

Friedman's own interpretation of the Great Depression imputes the severity of the contraction to the mistakes made by the Federal Reserve System in permitting a sharp contraction of the stock of money, and not providing enough liquidity to the banking system; that is to say that the Federal Reserve did not act according to its mission of lender of last resort. In 1968, summarizing the detailed historical analysis with Anna Schwartz, he expounds this view of the Great Depression by focusing on the monetary variables, and notably on the money stock: 'The Great Contraction is tragic testimony to the power of monetary policy – not, as Keynes and so many of his contemporaries believed, evidence of its impotence' (Friedman, 1968, p. 3).

In his policy message, which he expresses with a polemical stance against the early Keynesians as well as those of the Neoclassical Synthesis, Friedman argues that attention has to be concentrated on few monetary variables, mainly the stock of money and inflation, against the neoclassical suggestion that a variety of interest rates and financial variables should be considered by the economist acting as the prince's counsellor for economic policy. Looking at the bare-bones of this policy message, to regulate the steady growth of the money stock is the central banker's business, quite irrespective of possible

---

[4] 'In addition, a revolution in economic theory, having quite different origin and by no means necessarily implying the impotence of monetary policy, offered a theoretical structure that at one and the same time could rationalize the impotence of monetary policy and provide an intellectually satisfying alternative explanation of the economic debacle' (Friedman and Schwartz, 1963a, p. 691).

[5] '...Keynes believed likely in times of heavy unemployment – interest rates cannot be lowered by monetary measures. If investment and consumption are little affected by interest rates – as Hansen and many of Keynes' other American disciples came to believe – lower interest rates, even if they could be achieved, would do little good. Monetary policy is twice damned. The contraction, set in train, on this view, by a collapse of investment or by a shortage of investment opportunities or by stubborn thriftiness, could not, it was argued, have been stopped by monetary measures. (...) The wide acceptance of these views in the economic profession meant that for some two decades monetary policy was believed by all but a few reactionary souls to have been rendered obsolete by new economic knowledge. Money did not matter. Its only role was the minor one of keeping interest rates low, in order to hold down interest payments in the government budget, contribute to the "euthanasia of the rentier," and maybe, stimulate investment a bit to assist government spending in maintaining a high level of aggregate demand' (Friedman, 1968, p. 2).

[6] 'In a book on *Financing American Prosperity*, edited by Paul Homan and Fritz Machlup and published in 1945, Alvin Hansen devotes nine pages of text to the "savings-investment problem" without finding any need to use the words "interest rate" or any close facsimile thereto [5, pp. 218–227]' (Friedman, 1968, p. 4).

complications arising from the complexity of financial markets, or even from the definition of the specific monetary aggregate to control. Central bankers are perfectly able to control the relevant monetary aggregate, if they just decide to announce their firm intention to do so and are determinate to stick to it, being committed to their stabilizing mission of neutral regulators of the money stock (Friedman, 1968, p. 17).

> My own prescription is still that the monetary authority go all the way in avoiding such swings by adopting publicly the policy of achieving a steady rate of growth in a specified monetary total. The precise rate of growth, like the precise monetary total, is less important than the adoption of some stated and known rate. (...) But it would be better to have a fixed rate that would on the average produce moderate inflation or moderate deflation, provided it was steady, than to suffer the wide and erratic perturbations we have experienced. Short of the adoption of such a publicly stated policy of a steady rate of monetary growth, it would constitute a major improvement if the monetary authority followed the self-denying ordinance of avoiding wide swings. (...) But steady monetary growth would provide a monetary climate favourable to the effective operation of those basic forces of enterprise, ingenuity, invention, hard work, and thrift that are the true springs of economic growth. That is the most that we can ask from monetary policy at our present stage of knowledge. But that much – and it is a great deal – is clearly within our reach. (Friedman, 1968, pp. 16–17)

These claims are at the core of the monetarist counter-revolution. Are Friedman's drastic simplifications when dealing with policy issues coherent and consistent with his scientific and historical research? The answer to this question is nuanced, and requires a more detailed exploration of Friedman's writings, notably the way in which Friedman deals with banks and the disaggregated financial sector.

In his theoretical works, Friedman carefully examines the transmission mechanism which in principle, via wealth effects, should spread changes in the money stock on the whole spectrum of assets in the consumers' portfolios, and primarily on their demand for goods. It is necessary to take account of the full range of repercussions occurring through changes in the composition of wealth; not only in the stock exchange but also in the markets for properties and for durables, in the relative prices of services and, eventually, in current production (Friedman, 1959a, p. 349-ff., Friedman and Schwartz, 1963a, pp. 60–63). The impact on the stock exchange is just a first step in the sequence. In the complex transmission mechanism banks also play a role by adjusting their portfolios, through the reduction of excess reserves and the expansion of loans after, for example, an expansionary open market operation (Friedman and Schwartz, 1963a, p. 60). Friedman, however, does not provide a detailed analysis of the working of the transmission mechanism, but he concentrates on the immediate repercussions in financial markets. He warns against looking exclusively at the impact effects of changes in the money stock on some interest rate variables.[7] This amounts to substantially deny the relevance of the financial sector for macroeconomic forecasting. Coherently with his methodological premises, Friedman rejects the sophisticated complexity of general-equilibrium models of the financial side of the economy, such as those that Tobin had been eager to introduce.

On the contrary, in his historical reconstruction Friedman pays critical attention to the evolution of banking. He shares the anxiety about bank money that, at the end of the 19th century, had preoccupied Walras and then, in the 20th century, Wicksell, Fisher and others. In the background of Friedman's prescriptions to central bankers, there is his diagnosis of a frail structure of banks' intermediation, due to the intrinsic, structural fragility of the banking industry, after the Federal Reserve System had been established in 1913 and become operative in 1916. The vagaries of bank money, and the risk of financial crises due to the possible loss of confidence in the liquidity of banks by the public, could not be easily controlled under the regulatory framework centred on the Federal Reserve System. They could be tamed only by imposing a 100 per cent reserve requirement to all depository institutions, a measure which would spare heavy and ineffective regulations in financial markets in favour of the straightforward sterilization of any possibility for banks to create money.

Friedman formulates this diagnosis and the proposals which stem from it, in his manifesto, *A Program for Monetary Stability* (Friedman, 1959b). His suggested radical reform follows the track opened by the 1930s campaign for 100 per cent reserve banking system, to which Fisher had finally given his support. The programme required the complete separation of investment banks from deposit banks, the last ones being subject to a strict 100 per cent reserve requirement. A few years later he summarized his view as follows:

> To go much further in reforming the institutional organization of the banking system, it would be necessary to go in the radical direction of eliminating controls over individual banks, in the direction of 100% reserve banking. This move would tend to eliminate all control over the lending and investing activities of banks and would separate out the two functions of banking. On the one hand, we would have banks as depository institutions, safe-keeping money and arranging for the services of transferring liabilities by check. They would be 100% reserve banks, pure depository institutions. Their assets would be government liabilities – either pieces of paper or deposits to the credit of the bank on the books of a reserve bank or its equivalent. (Friedman, 1965, p. 12)

---

[7] Back in 1959, he had explicitly downplayed the indirect effects of variations in the money stock on investment, as far as they operate through variation of the interest rates (Friedman, 1959a, p. 351).

It is assumed that the exclusion of banks collecting deposits from any credit activity would be practicable and with no negative effects on the growth of the economy. By fixing the reserve ratio of deposit banks at 100 per cent and eliminating any fluctuation of the amount of bank money, the measure would effectively eliminate any disturbing influences on the stability of the economy via the banking industry and financial markets, due to variations of the banks' liquidity risk. Banks collecting deposits should be exclusively committed to the management of the system of payments, and the safe-keeping service for their customers.

> If 100% banking were established, our present banks would be sliced off into other branches operating like small-scale investment trusts. They would be lending and investment agencies in which private individuals would invest funds as they now do in investment trusts and other firms, and these funds would be used to make loans. Such organizations could be completely exempt from the kind of detailed control over financial activities that banks now are subject to. (Friedman, 1965, p. 12)

In this view of the financial side of the economy, the freedom of banks to expand bank money by offering new loans, or to contract it by calling back credits or by rationing credit, is the villain of the piece, jointly with the fluctuations of confidence in the stability of the banking system, which might induce major financial crises as a consequence of a severe banking crisis. A reserve ratio below 100 per cent implies the possibility of fluctuations of the money multiplier, or even of banking panics with the sudden increase of the currency/deposits ratio (De Long, 2000, p. 91). Under the 100 per cent reserve requirement – Friedman argues – the control of the money stock at a stable rate of growth would become practicable in technical terms, and the financial markets would be stabilized without the need to impose and monitor complex, financial regulations.[8]

> So I am led to suggest as a rule the simple rule of a steady rate of growth in the stock of money: that the Reserve System be instructed to keep the stock of money growing at a fixed rate, $\frac{1}{3}$ of 1% per month or 1/12 of 1% per week, or such and such a percentage per day. We instruct it that day after day and week after week it has one thing, and one thing only, to do and that is to keep the stock of money moving at a steady, predictable, defined rate in time.
>
> This is not, under our present System, an easy thing to do. It involves a great many technical difficulties and there will be some deviations from it. If the other changes I suggested were made in the System, it would make the task easier; but even without those changes, it could be done under the present System. (Friedman, 1965, p. 16)

---

[8]   Notice that in his programme Friedman does not approve of any monetary rule linked to the inflation rate: 'Many economists have been in favor of the rule that the System be instructed to keep a price level stable. I myself think it is not a good rule' (Friedman, 1965, p. 16).

Two points in Friedman's dismal picture of the banking industry in a regime of less than 100 per cent reserve requirement should be underlined. On the one hand, the role of banks in financing growth is downplayed, the real rate of growth being assumed as independent of the presence and performance of the banking industry; on the other hand, the possible instability, or malfunctioning, of financial markets is lessened as well, because the main factors of instability derive from the financial fragility of deposit banks, and their 'perverse' role in making the stock of money erratically unstable.

Both points are highly questionable. As the history of financial markets attests, 'manias, panics and crashes', to use Kindleberger's terms, existed before bank money became the dominant means of payment in market economies. The instability of financial markets was an object of study of political economy since the late 18th century (Kindleberger, 2000). The idea that financial markets work smoothly is the result of the peculiar vision prevailing in the 1960s, and not a lesson that can be learned from history. Moreover, as Schumpeter so effectively argued, in the history of market economies banks have been a powerful engine of growth, because they can provide loans, interposing the guarantee of their capital, and the monitoring capabilities of their trained staff, between final lenders and borrowers. Today, though financial markets dominate the financing channels for long term investment, banks are still essential engines for providing credit to firms, which have no access to financial markets, and to households for durable consumer goods and housing. They intermediate the retail investment markets for bonds, provide loans to finance current activities of firms, channel credit to property markets, and mix with other financial intermediaries in complex ways.

8.3   THE MONETARY HISTORY OF THE GREAT DEPRESSION

In some respects, *A Program for Monetary Stability* anticipates one of the major themes in Friedman's and Schwartz's reconstruction of the monetary history of the United States: the contraction of the money stock in the early 1930s was the result of bank runs and bank failures, with the consequent endogenous reduction of bank money.

> The decline in the stock of money was a direct consequence of the sequence of bank failures. The banking failures were not important primarily because they involved the failures of financial institutions. They were important because they forced a decline in the stock of money. (Friedman, 1965, p. 9)

In 1963, Friedman and Anna Schwartz finally published their volume *A Monetary History of the United States 1867–1960* (1963a), a piece of historical research that is highly valued for its richness even today and that remains a cornerstone for the various interpreters of the Great Depression. As far as the Great Depression is concerned, Friedman and Schwartz summarize the findings of their research by arguing that the peculiar severity in depth and duration of the 1930s depression was the result of the poor management of monetary policy by the Federal Reserve System. The informal arrangements among major banks prior to the establishment of the Federal Reserve system would have provided a more effective brake to the run on deposits. In the new institutional framework, banks relied on the Federal Reserve to stop bank runs, but the Federal Reserve did not react adequately. The financial crisis precipitated and the stock of money fell by an unprecedented amount in a few years. Friedman's and Schwartz's reconstruction of the events is rich and nuanced; it is detailed in the description of the portfolio choices by the general public and banks as well as of the conflict within the Federal Reserve System, which contributed to the paralysis of monetary policy. There is a singular disconnection between the richness of their historical reconstruction of the monetary events in the Great Depression, and the ultimate reduction of it to a renewed statement of the quantity theory that simply links variations of the money stock to variations of nominal income.

In their historical narration, two variables play a major role in the explanation of the fall of the money stock: the deposit-reserve ratio in banks' balances and the deposit-currency ratio in private portfolios. In chart 31 of the book, Friedman and Schwartz give a striking visual representation of how much the money stock fell by the de-multiplying process induced by the banking crises, notwithstanding a somewhat steady though moderate increase of high powered money from mid-1930 to early 1933 (Friedman and Schwartz, 1963a, p. 333). In opposition to what had been Fisher's primary preoccupation, they dismiss bad banking, deteriorated loans or wrong investment in the late 1920s as 'triggers' of the financial crisis on the grounds of the frail argument that bank runs and bank failures could be stopped by an injection of high powered money engineered by the Federal Reserve (see, e.g., Friedman and Schwartz, 1963a, pp. 355–356).

Although, earlier in the book, Friedman and Schwartz, in a Fisherian mood, mention the complexities of the cumulative process during a depression,[9] in their conclusions, they argue that an early intervention of the Federal Reserve could have prevented the recurring banking crises from entering their worst

---

[9] 'It happens that a liquidity crisis in a unit fractional reserve banking system is precisely the kind of event that can trigger – and often has triggered – a chain reaction. And economic collapse often has the character of a cumulative process. Let it go beyond a certain point, and it will tend for a time to gain strength from its own development as its effects spread and return to intensify the process of collapse' (Friedman and Schwartz, 1963a, p. 419).

phases after 1930, and this proves that the primary causation goes from high powered money to nominal income, even though they admit the 'influences running the other way', from money income and prices to money (Friedman and Schwartz, 1963a, p. 694).

> Changes in the money stock are therefore a consequence as well as an independent source of change in money income and prices, though, once they occur, their produce in their turn still further effects on income and prices. Mutual interaction, but with money clearly the senior partner in longer-run movements and in major cyclical movements, and more nearly an equal partner with money income and prices in shorter-run and milder movements – this is the generalization suggested by our evidence. (Friedman and Schwartz, 1963a, p. 695)

In reviewing Friedman's and Schwartz's 'magnificent book', Goodhart (1964, p. 314) effectively points out how biased it is to force their complex picture of the events into the straitjacket of the quantity theory of money. The history of the recurring financial crises in the recession years, as reconstructed by them, or other historians afterwards, should not be reduced to the straightforward causal relation from the money stock to nominal income. Crises, instead, should be seen as a cumulative process, involving both the real and the financial sides, with many stakeholders, each of them conditioned by their cultural heritage in managing business and portfolio (or policy) choices, and all of them acting within an institutional context and regulatory framework of financial markets which, later on, were drastically modified by legislation and by changes of the market structure.

Already in his 1959 article on the demand for money, Friedman considered the complexities of endogenous bank money when analysing how, during expansionary phases, banks can actively react to the favourable business climate. In dealing with the pro-cyclical expansion of bank money, he points out that the nominal supply of money is determined by the banks' prudential behaviour concerning their reserve coefficients, by their propensity to lend and by the depositors' confidence in the banking system or their desired amount of liquidity in their portfolios. Friedman signals the uncertain or even 'perverse' effects, which a simplified statement of the quantity theory does not capture.

> Throughout the period, more complicated reactions operated on the commercial banking system, sometimes in perverse fashion. For example, an attempt by holders of money to reduce cash balances relative to income tended to raise income and prices, thus promoting an expansionary atmosphere in which banks were generally willing to operate on a slenderer margin of liquidity. The result was an increase rather than a reduction in the nominal supply of money. Similarly, changes in the demand for money had effects on security prices and interest rates that affected the amount of money supplied by the banking system. (Friedman, 1959a, p. 331)

Banks, thus, do not seem to be just passive gears in the transmission mechanism going from the exogenous money stock to nominal income. The endogenous money stock could expand in response to the growth of nominal income, although Friedman concludes that despite 'these qualifications' the nominal quantity of money should be regarded as 'determined primarily by conditions of supply' (Friedman, 1959a, pp. 331–332).

In 1963, just before the book was published, Friedman and Schwartz published the long article on business cycles already mentioned (Friedman and Schwartz, 1963b). There, they explicitly take account of the 'reflex influence of business on money', but they regard it as of second-order relevance in business cycle theory, being just part of the endogenous cyclical mechanism, whereby the primary independent monetary disturbances are transmitted to the economy. They carefully discuss the problem in their effort to establish sound foundations for a proper monetary theory of business cycles, the influence running primarily from exogenous changes in the money stock to business, and not the other way round (Friedman and Schwartz, 1963b, pp. 49–50). They recognize that the vulnerability of the U.S. banking system to runs could partially explain an endogenous link from 'sizeable declines in money income' to 'sizeable declines of money', but they reject any primary independent role of investment spending in triggering fluctuations (Friedman and Schwartz, 1963a, pp. 53–54).

Yet the drastic distinction between the stock of money as the ultimate trigger and the endogenous feed-back mechanisms is slippery. Early critics of Friedman and Schwartz pointed out the dynamic complexities of macroeconomic expansion or recession, involving both real and financial variables. Minsky (1963, p. 66), commenting on their article, evokes Fisher's debt-deflation theory and criticizes the absence in their theoretical framework of 'the asset structure of the monetary authorities and the financial liabilities of other units.' For Minsky, the ultimate reasons for major changes in the money stock appear rather eclectic, as the authors themselves had recognized, while the endogenous links connecting the income-expenditure variables to the financial structure of the economy are missing in their explanation.[10] In his parallel comment, Okun (1963, p. 74), instead, points to the credit channel, viewing credit as providing resources for 'eager spenders', i.e. those economic units that at some point of time are rationed and 'hungry for more capital (or more dissaving).' The credit channel becomes relevant in later historical interpretations of the Great Depression, as we mention in Chapter 4.

The debate on the relevance of the core thesis about the causes of the Great Depression in *A Monetary History of the United States*, has proceeded until the

---

[10] Minsky (1963, p. 67, n. 5) mentions his own efforts at building a model of endogenous financial instability. On Minsky's contribution, see Chapter 9 below.

present day, with a variety of assessments (Laidler, 2013). The crucial issue in the debate about a strictly monetarist interpretation of the depression is not the contention per se that the Federal Reserve could have acted more effectively to stop the recession in its early phases. In fact, at the time of the recession, this viewpoint was shared by economists of various persuasions.[11] Many economic historians have underlined the poor performance of the Federal Reserve System, but they propose a variety of perspectives and interpretations of the crisis without exclusive emphasis on the money stock as the prime mover of all severe recessions. This latter issue is the most controversial message of the monetarist counter-revolution, which was subjected to many effective criticisms in the 1960s and 1970s. As we shall see, twenty years after the publication of *A Monetary History of the United States*, mainstream macroeconomics abandoned any monetary explanation of business cycles and reverted to real shocks as the dominant triggers of fluctuations.

8.4 IS MONEY A WAVING VEIL?

There is a point in the 'Summing up' chapter at the end of Friedman's and Schwartz's book that is crucial for solving the puzzle pointed out at the beginning of this chapter, at least as far as its theoretical core is concerned. Friedman and Schwartz hold that they have isolated the dominant (indeed almost exclusive) influence of the rate of change of the measured money stock on the rate of change of nominal income in the same way as in a controlled scientific experiment. By quoting John Stuart Mill's celebrated passage, they subscribe to the view that 'money is a veil', whereas the real forces at work are industry, ingenuity, resources, economic and political organization, 'and the like'. For Friedman and Schwartz, at the bottom, money as 'a common and widely accepted medium of exchange' is 'a social convention' and, as such, it 'is no fragile thing' (Friedman and Schwartz, 1963a, p. 696). They stress Mill's words of caution about the damages done when money gets out of order, adding that 'there is hardly a contrivance man possesses which can do more damage to a society when it goes amiss' (Friedman and Schwartz, 1963a, p. 697).

Financial markets, unless they are included in 'the like' addendum, are notably absent from their picture. They seem to dismiss any independent role of regulations, market structure, or other characteristics of financial markets and the banking industry, to explain business fluctuations in favour of the primary role of the money variable in its bare quantity dimension. They dismiss the role of varying 'monetary arrangements', in so far as they do not

---

[11] As we saw, Keynes invoked open market operations; Fisher campaigned for reflation; also Schumpeter lamented the perverse effects of the banking crisis.

affect the rate of growth of the money stock (Friedman and Schwartz, 1963a, p. 694). Thus, money as a social convention and an essential element of market economies can apparently 'go amiss' only because of its erratic quantitative variations. The real side of the economy – it is implicitly predicated – goes amiss only if money goes amiss.

Friedman's and Schwartz's 'Summing up' calls for a number of crucial questions about the dividing line between the real market forces and the monetary veil. Does the organization of credit and finance belong to the set of fundamental market institutions in the same sense as the political organization or the property rights do? Are financial institutions among the 'real forces' at work in the economy? Should they be included in the real side of the economy, so that the neat separation of real and monetary forces vanishes? If money, including bank money, is an essential social convention, a pillar and no fragile thing, do monetary arrangements belong to the core set of institutions that regulate the 'real' working of markets together with economic and political organization? Or are financial markets, together with money, part of the 'veil' and it is only when they misbehave that they deserve attention? Why should only the money stock per se matter for the smooth functioning of 'real' markets? Indeed, to understand both growth and fluctuations in market economies what matters is the complex structure of monetary institutions and financial markets. They are social conventions and market mechanisms that make the system of payments work smoothly and make it possible to finance the spending plans of a multitude of agents with different needs, balance sheets, liquidity constraints or accumulated wealth. As many historical analyses of major financial crises have shown, various aspects of this complex structure might well go wrong and have a major impact on the 'real' variables.

Despite their rich historical narration, at the theoretical level Friedman and Schwartz ignore all the questions concerning the way in which the design of monetary contracts, the frail or resilient pyramid of debt structures, the communication and safety nets in financial markets and in the banking world, which are structural components of the technology of market transactions in the absence of any fictional auctioneer, provide more or less effectively for the inter-temporal, dynamic coordination of investment, consumption and the allocation of real resources. Their 'going amiss' means that market transactions, on which the production and allocation of resources depend, are deprived of those dynamic adjustment processes which might eventually smooth disequilibria, or might open up new opportunities for welfare and growth.

The crucial emphasis that, in this and other writings, Friedman places on the mere quantitative dimension of the money stock and its variations over time betrays the best part of his research focusing on the primacy of stock adjustments over the flow dynamics of consumers' choices or banks' behaviour. The complexity of out-of-equilibrium adjustment paths, due to portfolios' changes and wealth effects, spreading from the financial to the real side of the economy, disappears. Friedman's emphasis on the adjustment of stocks disappears in his final predication of the dichotomous nature of economic forces, opposing the real ones to the monetary veil.

In his 1968 presidential address, Friedman makes a decisive step in the direction of a full restoration of money to its 'veil' status. In this celebrated work, Friedman's focus changes with respect to the detailed analysis of banks' behaviour, monetary policies and the money stock in the 1963 book. After firing at the radical Keynesians of the 1950s, for the sin of forgetting money, Friedman attacks also the Keynesians of the Neoclassical Synthesis advocating the use of monetary policy for the fine tuning of the economy. He warns his colleagues that 'the pendulum may well have swung too far' towards great expectations about what monetary policy might achieve to control unemployment and the interest rate (Friedman, 1968, p. 5). Friedman does not seem to take much notice of the fact that, in 1960, in an article on anti-inflation policy, two eminent Keynesian economists, Samuelson and Solow, although considering the possibility of a short-run trade-off between inflation and unemployment exploitable by policy, added explicit caveats. Their policy conclusions were extremely cautious as they warned that their 'menu of choice' might not stand unchanged in the long run, as it moves in consequence of the adopted policies (Samuelson and Solow, 1960, p. 193).

The substance of Friedman's position is well known, and we just remind it here. Friedman claims that, in the long run, for monetary policy there is no menu of choice between inflation and unemployment. He asserts the validity of the quantity theory in the long run and the prevalence of the tendency to long-run equilibrium over short-run deviations from the natural rate of unemployment. Monetary policy cannot control the natural rate of unemployment in the long run. Let us focus on Friedman's rhetorical trick to define the natural rate of unemployment by proposing the grand vision of a fictional Walrasian general-equilibrium system of equations, fully comprehensive of market imperfections and external shocks.[12]

> The 'natural rate of unemployment,' in other words, is the level that would be ground out by the Walrasian system of general equilibrium equations, provided there is imbedded in them the actual structural characteristics of the labor and commodity markets, including market imperfections, stochastic variability in demands and supplies, the cost of gathering information about job vacancies and labor availabilities, the costs of mobility, and so on. (Friedman, 1968, p. 8)

---

[12] The natural rate of unemployment depends on structural characteristics of markets, many of which are 'man-made and policy-made' (Friedman, 1968, p. 9).

Friedman's allusion to general equilibrium is loose but impressive. It suggests that there actually exists a well developed, theoretical model through which the natural rate can be properly and effectively defined, and in principle even measured. In reality, in the late 1960s, no satisfactory Walrasian system of equations existed that could even approximately fit Friedman's description. The Arrow-Debreu model, as perfected by Debreu in *Theory of Value* in 1959, is a highly fictional mathematical frame built on the coherence imposed by the assumption of an auctioneer that coordinates a system of complete spot and forward markets in inter-temporal equilibrium, where agents are price takers experiencing neither information costs nor liquidity constraints. It is highly implausible that such a picture of a competitive economy could be re-framed to incorporate the actual characteristics of labour and commodity markets, including market imperfections, stochastic variability in demands and supplies, information costs and so on. Friedman's assertive referring to Walrasian general-equilibrium equations to define the natural rate of unemployment, is just pie in the sky. The dreamed of Walrasian general-equilibrium equations including market imperfections, mobility, transaction and information costs, did not exist; no contemporary economist knew how to bring them to light.

It has been suggested that by mentioning Walrasian equilibrium Friedman played mere lip-service to the most authoritative tradition in economic theory, but this explanation is not fully convincing. Although Friedman was never converted to become a neo-Walrasian economist, his rhetorical allusion to general equilibrium has a cognitive function to perform: it aims at tracing a neat dividing line between the real markets' equilibrium and monetary disturbances.[13] A few years later, in 1972, Friedman appeals again to the Walrasian general equilibrium for the purpose of neatly separating the real forces from the money veil. In point of theory, he conceives the notion of long-term equilibrium as a combination of the old quantity theory with the system of Walrasian equations, under the spell of Walras's dichotomy. It is a mere logical construction, never 'attained in practice', but it is seen as the norm or trend state around which market economies fluctuate (Friedman, 1972, p. 925). In the ideal state of long-term equilibrium, the 'pervasive' presence of money, which Friedman had underlined in analysing actual economies, is relegated to the neutral quantity equation. The role of banking and financial institutions as primary players in the working of markets is erased by the very reference to Walras's general equilibrium.

If the purpose of Friedman's logical construction is to mark the neat partition between the real and the monetary sides of market economies, it is this

---

[13] Friedman writes: 'I use the term "natural" for the same reason Wicksell did – to try to separate the real forces from monetary forces' (Friedman, 1968, p. 9).

partition that has to be questioned. Friedman, like Walras, never explains why the deviations from equilibrium during dynamic cyclical paths should converge back to the natural 'norm' or 'trend' instead of generating loops, low income traps, or divergent trajectories, like in the case of the capsizing ship illustrated by Fisher. Neither is it clear why the trend equilibrium of the 'real' economy should remain unaffected by severe recessions, affecting e.g. human capital, the maintenance of properties, the renewal of infrastructures, the resources devoted to invention and innovation, international trade, or even political organization. Indeed, the focus on the dynamic adjustment of assets in consumers' wealth, which is one of the most interesting aspects of Friedman's discourse, should suggest special attention is paid to loops arising in financial crises, when the uncertain values of assets may negatively affect spending decisions and production, building up further disturbances to the financial markets, affecting the perception of uncertainty and the values of assets (Mishkin, 2011, pp. 22–23). The possibility of prolonged real effects in severe financial crises turning into depressions are well known; they have received new attention in recent literature after the global financial crisis since 2007.

Outside the fictional Arrow-Debreu world managed by the divine hand of the auctioneer, be it a fictional market economy or a planned society dominated by the benevolent dictator, it is hard to imagine any system of markets, where the mythical 'real' economy can smoothly work severed from the working of the financial structure, whatever that might be in its institutional framework and operative details. The medium-term dynamic paths of market economies certainly depend on how the real and financial aspects of the economy interact. In clearer terms, no 'real' economy exists that can be disjointed from financial and credit markets, not to speak of the system of payments, whose malfunctioning would paralyse market transactions.

8.5 LUCAS: MONEY SURPRISES IN THE THEORY OF BUSINESS CYCLES

The fascination for general equilibrium, which had captured the minds of macroeconomists since the 1930s and 1940s, seemed to promise to younger scholars new paths of research, with plenty of scientific credentials and potential advancement. Up to the end of the 1970s, the main line of research explored by Lucas is about general-equilibrium models with imperfections in information, and agents' misperceptions in distinguishing local shocks from changes of the general price level due to monetary surprises. Just as a waving veil can blur vision, the vagaries of unexpected money shocks disturb equilibrium by altering the exact perception of relative prices.

The differences between the earlier monetarist explanation and the emerging new theories and models are many, and they have been explored extensively in the historical literature on monetarism of various brands (see, e.g., Hoover, 1988). The main ones are the introduction of rational expectations as a strict requirement for rigorous macroeconomic analysis; the strict adherence to equilibrium paradigms and the assumption of continuous equilibrium with the loss of attention to the medium and short-term transition processes which still played a significant role in Friedman's analysis; the marginalization or the disappearance of wealth effects and wealth adjustments in favour of straightforward equilibrium growth models; the changed methodological approach with a radical turn towards the building of macroeconomic models conceived as artificial imitation economies; the remarkable loss of interest in economic history as a source of evidence for theory.

Since the 1980s, Lucas has claimed that theoretical mathematical models are fictional, conceptual machines, which should be framed with the purpose to mimic historical time series, and tested on the criterion of effectiveness to mimic the available statistical evidence (Lucas, 1980b, p. 697). In this overall change of perspective, at the technical and econometric levels as well as at the conceptual level in the way macroeconomic theories are built and interpreted, there remains a remarkable continuity with the Neoclassical Synthesis in the effort to set macroeconomics within the framework of the theory of general equilibrium, but with significant analytical and interpretative differences. Initially, the main change of perspective was the radical programme to directly establish macroeconomic propositions on genuine general equilibrium models of the Arrow-Debreu type, avoiding the short-cuts of the doubtful aggregative procedures of more or less refined IS-LM models. Hoover (2012) describes such objective as a 'non eliminative' micro-foundations programme, where macroeconomic theory is re-framed within the neo-Walrasian general equilibrium theory of perfectly competitive markets.[14] Macroeconomics is economic theory *tout court* as represented by the most advanced synthesis of microeconomic theory. It was the ambitious programme to eventually close the gap between 'value theory' and monetary theory and/or business cycle theory. This was the goal to achieve, to solve the Arrow's scandal that had preoccupied 'high theorists' since the early 20th century.

In 2004, in 'My Keynesian education', Lucas explains that his original inspiration was to rebuild macroeconomics on Walrasian foundations and he

---

[14] Hoover (2012, pp. 46-ff.) critically studies what he names the 'representative agent program' in opposition to the 'general equilibrium program', noting how poor the explicit arguing is to support its core simplifying assumption. In Hoover's terminology, this is an 'eliminative micro-foundations' programme.

recalls the macroeconomic debate of the 1950s and 1960s. He describes the origins and progresses of his research project in the 1970s as inspired by Patinkin's seminal book *Money, Interest, and Prices*, but along a parallel line of development.[15] Lucas was fascinated by what was the core ambition of the book: 'to unify value theory and monetary theory.' In the 1960s he thought that unifying macroeconomic theory, duly 'microeconomically founded', with 'price theory', was the 'job of our generation', as much as Hayek, in the 1930s, had thought that the main task of his generation was to unify price theory with business cycle theory (Lucas, 2004[2013], p. 511). The task that Lucas sets for himself had been quite difficult to accomplish in the more than thirty years since Hayek's statement of intentions. The problem of the real effects of monetary instability had not yet found any solution, although being generally seen as an open question in macroeconomics (Lucas, 2004[2013], pp. 514–515).

In Lucas's narration, Patinkin, however, had somewhat failed to realize his 'high aspirations' because he had anchored his project to a technically primitive version of the general-equilibrium theory, acquired from Lange; he was not aware of the technical improvement introduced by Arrow and Debreu (Lucas, 2004[2013], p. 507).[16] Although paying due tribute to Patinkin's pathbreaking research, Lucas specifies that, in facing the same task, he refers to the Arrow-Debreu neo-Walrasian version of general equilibrium, a framework that he regards as the most sophisticated available representation of the working of a system of perfectly competitive markets.[17] This argumentation is related to his epistemological idea that progress in economic theory is substantially, if not exclusively, advancement by the adoption of more powerful instruments in mathematization or statistical testing (Lucas, 1980b, p. 700; Lucas, 2004[2013], p. 513).

Lucas makes the point that it is possible to incorporate any sort of dynamics into the Arrow-Debreu model of contingent claims. He champions a vision of the technical perfection of the Arrow-Debreu model, which goes beyond the static image of competitive markets, but in this vision all substantial questions of what dynamics means in economics, and if and how it deals with change, are put aside (Lucas, 2004[2013], p. 514). Lucas is apparently unaware

[15] Lucas reasserts his evaluation of Patinkin's reading of macroeconomics with Walrasian lenses already advanced in his 1996 Nobel lecture.

[16] 'That was the objective Patinkin had stated in his subtitle: to unify value theory and monetary theory. I liked his high aspirations. They were inspiring to me. But the book doesn't quite come off, does it? I mean, the theory is never really solved' (Lucas, 2004[2013], p. 506).

[17] 'I think Patinkin was absolutely right to try and use general equilibrium theory to think about macroeconomic problems. Patinkin and I are both Walrasians, whatever that means. (...) Patinkin's problem was that he was a student of Lange's, and Lange's version of the Walrasian model was already archaic by the end of the 1950s. Arrow and Debreu and McKenzie had redone the whole theory in a clearer, more rigorous, and more flexible way ...' (Lucas, 2004[2013], p. 507).

of the advanced literature that, since the 1970s, had radically questioned
the uniqueness and stability results that could be achieved in neo-Walrasian
models, and pointed out the indeterminacy that undermines the neo-Walrasian
system of equations (Rizvi, 2006). The technical requirements of mathematical
tractability were soon to provide major restrictions to the original project of
'non eliminative' micro-foundations, with a change of perspective towards
simplified models with a representative agent in place of models with multiple,
heterogeneous agents and goods.

Quite beyond the technical pitfalls, which go unnoticed by Lucas, it is
clear that conceptually the neo-Walrasian model of complete spot and forward
markets in inter-temporal equilibrium cannot offer a theory of business cycles.
Some imperfections have to be added to allow for fluctuations that could
simulate the historical business cycles observed in capitalist economies. As
we have seen, already in 1968 Friedman had suggested to look at Walras's
equilibrium plus imperfections and frictions. Lucas plays with a new kind
of frictions, looking at local versus general information instead of looking at
market imperfections in competition. In 1973, he expresses the issue neatly in
his well known paper on the output-inflation trade-off:

> All formulations of the natural rate theory postulate rational agents, whose decisions
> depend on *relative* prices only, placed in an economic setting in which they cannot
> distinguish relative from general price movements. Obviously, there is no limit to
> the number of models one can construct where agents are placed in this situation of
> imperfect information; the trick is to find tractable schemes with this feature. (Lucas,
> 1973, p. 327).

One of these schemes is the island metaphor already introduced by Phelps,
with the related local imperfections in deciphering monetary signals (Phelps,
1969). The new, technical apparatus is based on the crucial assumptions of
rational expectations and continuous market equilibrium, considering different
states of nature and contingent claims (Lucas, 1980b, p. 707). In fact, a very
long line of thought since the 19th century had linked fluctuations, however
interpreted, to misperceptions of some nature in forecasting or perceiving
crucial economic variables, be they interest rates, profit expectations on
investment, future flows of incomes or costs. The assumption of rational expectations, or better the imposition of the formal discipline of rational expectations
in the practice of modelling, substantially reduces the range of misperceptions
allowed in modelling business cycles. The admitted misperceptions, which do
not violate the dogma of far-sighted rationality and optimal forecasts, are non
systematic and regard price signals.

The assumption of continuous equilibrium is not only in line with the
Walrasian tradition but it is essential to elaborate a 'tractable scheme'; it avoids
the intricacies of out-of-equilibrium dynamics that according to Lucas had

spoilt Patinkin's theoretical construction, as much as they mined the Keynesian models of the Neoclassical Synthesis (Lucas, 1980b, pp. 702-ff.). It eliminates ad-hockeries and the free parameters indiscipline from model building.

As we saw, since 1948 Patinkin had looked at Keynes's message essentially through disequilibrium lenses. Lucas rejects this aspect of the Keynesian heritage because, in his opinion, Patinkin's effort at building disequilibrium dynamics in macroeconomics had failed to achieve definite solutions.[18] He makes the continuous equilibrium assumption, being aware of the technical intricacies of the dynamics of out-of-equilibrium price or quantity adjustments. Lucas looks for tractable models with definite solutions. These technical requirements substantially influence his research agenda, along with the more ambitious aspiration to introduce optimizing micro-foundations into macroeconomic models. It is a major break with the previous monetarist agenda, where Friedman had again and again dealt with adjustment processes jointly with reference to long-term equilibrium.

8.6   FROM MONETARY SURPRISES TO REAL BUSINESS CYCLES

By the early 1980s, the project to unify value theory and monetary theory disappears from the frontier of research in macroeconomics. The line of research that emphasized monetary surprises as the causes of macroeconomic fluctuations becomes out-dated and fades away. On the one hand, poor empirical results killed it, on the other hand it was hard to conceive of major monetary surprises in a world in which data on the money stock are public and readily available to everybody.

Historians of economic thought, who have explored how models with rational expectations and monetary misperceptions left the scene of macroeconomic research, tell us that the turn took place at the end of the 1970s. In his recollections, Lucas dates the turn at the Bald Peak conference organized by the Federal Reserve Bank of Boston in 1978 (De Vroey, 2016, p. 262). He reminds that then he understood that he had to abandon his previous research project, and turn his hopes to a new family of models, which seemed to promise rich technical results, while claiming a better fit to data with new econometric techniques.[19] At the beginning of the 1980s, at the frontier of macroeconomics,

---

[18] 'What are the predictions of Patinkin's model? The model is too complicated to work them out. All the dynamics are the mechanical auctioneer dynamics that Samuelson introduced, where *anything* can happen' (Lucas, 2004[2013], p. 506).

[19] At the end of his 1996 Nobel Lecture, Lucas recognizes with remarkable honesty the poor success of rational-expectations models with monetary surprises to explain business cycles. These models have provided important insights on the distinction between anticipated and

new advanced research had moved to real business cycle models, whose first satisfactory version was presented by Kydland and Prescott (1982). The analytical focus moved from monetary surprises to technology shocks, in the context of models in which money, not to speak of finance, had disappeared.

Friedman had distinctively seen random shocks to the money supply as the main cause of fluctuations of nominal income, and the primary cause of macroeconomic instability. In the new family of real business cycle models, money is absent and the explanation of business cycles is based only on real, so-called 'technology' shocks. These shocks, of a rather unexplored nature, impress the business cycle motion on otherwise steady, optimal, paths of growth determined by the optimal choices of a representative agent. It is the extreme development of the 'academic exercises' that Pigou had explored in his models of the stationary state inspired by Ramsey.

Lucas, however, was never fully satisfied with the absence of money in macroeconomic models. In various passages he insists on hopes to incorporate monetary aspects into macro-modelling.[20] In the effort to put money into the inhospitable environment in which he chose to work, since the 1980s Lucas pursued the idea of building models with a transaction technology that could force fictional rational agents to make recourse to a means of payment. The transaction technology invented is an ad-hockery, as it imposes arbitrary restrictions on how agents can behave in transactions or how different household members specialize in receiving or spending income. It is the same strategy that Patinkin had adopted in 1956 but, for Lucas, this is an unusual line of approach as he so often attacked the alleged ad-hockeries that vitiate Keynesian models and claimed that all ad-hockeries are spurious and should be strictly avoided.

In 1980, Lucas builds a model in which the decision unit (the household) is split into two fictional agents: the wage-earner and the shopper, who spends the income received by the wage-earner in non-simultaneous transactions (Lucas, 1980a). In this pure currency economy, the demand for cash is justified by the ad-hoc cash-in-advance restrictions imposed on traders. Trying to figure out the ad-hoc transaction technology that can justify the existence of a medium of exchange, Lucas, however, underlines that money is a 'second-rate

---

unanticipated monetary changes, but they offer no satisfactory theory of the business cycles (Lucas, 1996, pp. 679–680). Lucas then simply suggests directing the research towards the new class of real business cycle models. This turn was made easier by the fact that, meanwhile, his methodological views had moved towards the conception of mathematical modelling as fictional thought experiments (Ingrao, 2018).

[20] For the evolution of Lucas's position, see the critical reconstruction offered by Sargent in his review of Lucas's *Collected Papers on Monetary Theory* (Sargent, 2015). Sargent (2015, p. 49) reminds us that Wallace (1998) radically criticized Lucas's cash-in-advance approach for not being a satisfactory foundation for monetary theory.

asset', whose only role is that of 'a means of *approximating* some idealized "real" resource allocation', or 'an aid in *approximately* attaining real general equilibrium' (Lucas, 1980a, p. 219). In conclusion, in the same article, Lucas argues that the absence of money does not severely harm the explicative power of macroeconomic models.[21] In short, the absence of money, banks and the financial structure in macroeconomic models is justified by the belief that the pure barter economy of general-equilibrium theory conveys the core theoretical knowledge that economists need for the evaluation of what occurs in actual monetary economies. Thus, even this work conveys the basic message that, in core macroeconomic theory, the focus on the institutional structure of the system of payments, the banking industry or the financial system and the complex structure of debts within the private sector, is superfluous for the understanding of the working of free markets, a view which still is the conceptual hard core of many currents in contemporary macroeconomics, although somewhat disguised.

During the same period, there were other attempts to find a theoretical justification for the existence of money, both as a medium of exchange and as a store of value. Models with money in the utility or production functions and overlapping-generation models with money were developed.[22] These attempts, however, have not been too successful. After a survey of a number of these models, Heijdra (2017, p. 364) concludes: 'Despite the fact that every layman knows what money is (and what it can do) it has turned out to be difficult to come up with a convincing model of money.'

8.7   THE IRRELEVANCE OF MONEY IN REAL BUSINESS CYCLE MODELS

The roots of the new research programme on real business cycles that Kydland and Prescott started in the 1980s are in the article that in the early 1930s Ragnar Frisch had written on propagation and impulse problems in business cycles (Frisch, 1933).[23] In the real business cycle research the impulses are predicated to be shocks to productivity, which are persistent enough to impress on the fictional model cyclical fluctuations, which mimic those observed in

---

[21]   The ideal model of a barter economy can convey all the useful insights that are needed, since 'the theoretical "barter" economy is a tractable, idealized model which approximates well (is well approximated by) the actual, monetary economy' (Lucas, 1980a, p. 219).

[22]   See, for example, Kareken and Wallace (1980) for a collection of representative monetary models of the period.

[23]   See Young (2014) for a detailed history of the development of this research programme and the various intellectual influences, which inspired it. On Frisch's influence in particular, see pp. 8–10.

time series. The novelty is to imagine an isolated household that has to optimally allocate work and leisure and invest capital on an infinite horizon being exposed to random productivity shocks. The exogenous real shocks are defined by borrowing the notion of Solow residual; the propagation mechanism is assured by the time to build new capital.

If Frisch provided the inspiration, the conceptual core of the new models is Ramsey's model of growth (Ramsey, 1928). In 1928 Ramsey had accepted the challenge to determine the optimal rate of saving in the national community posed by Pigou in welfare economics (Pigou, 1920). As we saw in Chapter 6, Ramsey inspired Pigou's analysis of the convergence to the stationary state. The intellectual influence of Ramsey's approach proved to be lasting. The model of optimal growth was modified to include random shocks to which the rational household reacts optimally by adapting its resource allocation in time. In the early 1970s, along this line of research, Brock and Mirman (1972) reached an innovative assessment, building the optimal, stochastic growth model that constitutes the skeleton of real business cycle models. The academic exercises, whose explanatory value Pigou was so cautious to assert, are expanded to depict both growth and fluctuations as autistic phenomena in the fictional world of the isolated national household.

The ambitious project to rebuild macroeconomics within the framework of the Arrow-Debreu model gives way to the dominant modelling technique based on a representative household, whose microeconomic behaviour is the appropriate 'artificial' device to mimic the macroeconomic time series effectively. The representative agent model is the artificial engineering device to model fictional business cycles, with the advantage of tractable mathematics, straightforward steady-state dynamics and micro-foundations based on optimization and rational expectations. This shortcut is the death of the micro-foundations programme inspired by the Walrasian general equilibrium; but again and again it is predicated to be in continuity with it and even its culmination.

The 'transformation' in macroeconomic theory, as it came to be called, was also inspired by Lucas's strong critique of the econometric procedures in macroeconomics, and by the time consistency debate that followed, after the earlier rules-versus-discretion controversy and in continuation of it.[24] The new message is that fluctuations are Pareto optimal reactions to exogenous shocks, and unemployment is the result of the reallocation in time-consistent optimal plans of work and leisure. In this extreme vision, there is no possibility to mitigate cycles, as they are Pareto-optimal movements.

---

[24]   As is well known, Kydland and Prescott (1977) gave an essential contribution to the time consistency literature.

In 2004, addressing the Nobel audience in Stockholm, Prescott argues that there are more important problems than business cycles, and no public intervention is needed to improve welfare during economic fluctuations, as they are just Pareto-optimal responses to real shocks.

> We learned that business cycle fluctuations are the optimal response to real shocks. The cost of a bad shock cannot be avoided, and policies that attempt to do so will be counterproductive, particularly if they reduce production efficiency. During the 1981 and current oil crises, I was pleased that policies were not instituted that adversely affected the economy by reducing production efficiency. This is in sharp contrast to the oil crisis in 1974 when, rather than letting the economy respond optimally to a bad shock so as to minimize its cost, policies were instituted that adversely affected production efficiency and depressed the economy much more than it would otherwise have been. To summarize, concern has shifted away from business cycle fluctuations toward more important things. (Prescott, 2006, p. 14)

In this 'transformation' of advanced macroeconomic modelling, there are no unanticipated monetary shocks, no money, no finance, no banking to be technically embodied within the neo-Walrasian framework, with or without misperceptions. Even the Neo-Walrasian framework is no longer there. The environment of multiple markets, with a competitive multitude of diverse agents and firms, which had originally imbued Walras's or Pareto's ideas of general equilibrium, disappears. It is predicated that the new models are general-equilibrium models, on the assumption that a single-agent economy can perfectly depict and summarize the larger world of multiple markets with a variety of goods, consumers and firms. In these models, the invisible hand is conceived as erratically trembling, because the very core of the equilibrium in the real barter economy is, so to speak, disturbed by a permanent flow of erratic real shocks, whose ultimate origin remains obscure, apart from reference to the Solow residual. The economists pursuing the new research programme broadly follow Lucas's methodological statements. To test the models, they apply the techniques of computable simulations to generate paths of the relevant variables, which they think mimic with reasonable approximation the actual time series of major macroeconomic variables. Adopting the method of calibration, the parameters to apply in simulations are 'manufactured' by the model builders, who freely choose from various sources the micro-data assessed as reliable. This idea of 'evidence' breaks with the traditional econometric techniques of fitting to data.

The irrelevance of money finds a logical foundation in the representative agent assumption on which real business cycle models are built; the fictional 'real' economy they portray is not even a barter economy based on exchanges. The representative agent 'barters' present versus future goods in the isolation of his/her mind, by applying shadow prices as if they were market prices. The autistic player in real business cycle models can be thought of as being the standard type of many identical agents, each one adopting the best profile of optimal flows of consumption and saving over a infinite horizon. Prices are introduced by some spurious device of shadow pricing; but these models do not stage bilateral transactions taking place by the intermediation of a means of exchange. Proper markets do not exist in this merely mental world, where the representative hermit rationally chooses the optimal growth path under the sudden sunshine or rain of productivity shocks. And then, why not completely dismiss the money veil?

In December 1987, in his Nobel Lecture, Solow explained the essence of the new approach lucidly.

> The idea is to imagine that the economy is populated by a single immortal consumer, or a number of identical immortal consumers. (...) This consumer does not obey any simple short-run saving function, or even a stylized Modigliani life-cycle rule of thumb. Instead she, or the dynasty, is supposed to solve an infinite-time utility-maximization problem. (...) The next step is harder to swallow in conjunction with the first. For this consumer every firm is just a transparent instrumentality, an intermediary, a device for carrying out intertemporal optimization subject only to technological constraints and initial endowments. Thus any kind of market failure is ruled out from the beginning, by assumption. ...The end result is a construction in which the whole economy is assumed to be solving a Ramsey optimal-growth problem through time, disturbed only by stationary stochastic shocks to tastes and technology. To these the economy adapts optimally. Inseparable from this habit of thought is the automatic presumption that observed paths are equilibrium paths. So we are asked to regard the construction I have just described as a model of the actual capitalist world. What we used to call business cycles – or at least booms and recessions – are now to be interpreted as optimal blips in optimal paths in response to random fluctuations in productivity and the desire for leisure' (Solow, 1988, p. 310)

Major events of historical relevance in capitalist economies in so far as macroeconomic instability is concerned are explained by exogenous although autocorrelated shocks. There is a drastic split between steady growth and exogenous shocks falling from above for unexplained reasons, and affecting productivity. It is a vision opposite to Schumpeter's, in which highly correlated waves of innovations appear in swarms, with major innovations driving a whole family of minor ones, all of them rooted in the new social atmosphere of competitive capitalism.[25] The absence of money and credit, and the absence

---

[25] From a long-term historical perspective, it is like ignoring that in the British textile industry the invention of the spinning jenny was related to the previous development of the flying shuttle in weaving, or that it was related to the later development of the spinning mule, and that historically the emergence of the industrial revolution, far from being a random exogenous shock, was rooted in the economic, institutional, and intellectual environment of the times.

of banks, suggest that these institutional frameworks are seen as irrelevant for technology shocks of macroeconomic relevance.

This idea of technical change is plainly wrong in terms of whatever evidence we have, statistical and historical, on how there emerged innovations that affected productivity and radically changed the existent structure of the economy. In the history of technology, new inventions giving rise to productivity shocks are highly correlated with previous innovation and their mode of adoption as well as with the long-term evolution of education and training, scientific knowledge, institutions, political organization. Even the most basic technological shocks, such as climatic changes affecting crops, can be related to the long-term efforts for the maintenance of the environment, not to speak of the major shocks eventually correlated to global environmental mismanagement.

Without entering into a more general discussion of the notion and use of shocks in economics, to which we return in Chapter 9, here it will suffice to point out that the recourse to exogenous technology shocks as the main triggers of macroeconomic changes amounts to a declaration of cognitive powerlessness. The 'impulses' or 'triggers' of fluctuations cannot be accounted for by economists; they do not belong, apparently, to their sphere of inquiry and explanation. Shocks are postulated and measured, but they are not properly investigated and explained. 'Shocks' refer to a variety of phenomena, such as for example the oil crises mentioned by Prescott in the passage of his Nobel lecture quoted above. These oil crises, far from being unexplained exogenous occurrences, were historical episodes resulting from both the political and the economic evolution; they were related to changes of the market structure or the trends of supply and demand in energy markets. In the wider horizon of historical research, 'exogenous' shocks such as the oil crises have been the object of interpretation, and active policies in the international scenery have been implemented to tackle them.

8.8 THE 'HARDER QUESTIONS' OF MONETARY ECONOMICS

Another implicit claim of the real business approach is that in the larger world of markets, which the representative hermit is assumed to portray, the system of payments is perfectly smooth, to the point that it becomes wholly irrelevant and can be erased from the theoretical picture, like in the Arrow-Debreu model. A perfectly smooth system of payments means that no disequilibrium in the flows of payments can threaten the optimal equilibrium of the macroeconomic system and its stability. There are no voluntary or involuntary break of contracts, no uncertain speculation on price trends, no liquidity risk, no bankruptcy, no necessity to coordinate in time the unequal flows of the anticipated costs with the future flows of sales, as it happens in the long-term investment activity and in the current business of all firms. The malfunctioning of the system of payments and credit is admitted as a major cause of disturbance only in exceptional conditions, notably because of a poor management of the money stock by central bankers. The ultimate cause of the severity of the Great Depression is located not in any malfunctioning, or imperfect functioning, of the financial system, but it is imputed to the poor abilities of central bankers of the 1930s (Lucas, 2013, p. xxiii).

The Great Depression is classified as an exceptional event, which eludes the economists' ability to analyse business cycle fluctuations with their mathematical models. There are a few, abnormal financial disasters that rarely hit the economy, though with severe damages. They are 'black swans', a sort of unexpected Tsunami hitting the economy.[26] According to such interpretations, the shocks have a time-invariant Gaussian distribution, and their extreme tails are of exceedingly low probability. Under more sophisticated and realistic hypotheses, on the contrary, the disturbances may have non-Gaussian distributions, and their tails exhibit 'excess kurtosis, that is, tail risk', i.e. the probability of negative, severe shocks can be far more relevant (Mishkin, 2011, p. 24). Whichever the statistical description of shocks may be, financial crises of various severity had been accounted for by less sophisticated economists for more than two hundred years. They have been recognized by the historical and statistical literature as recurring, if irregular, events which involve banks and financial flows, with the possibility that they are nurtured within the economy as a consequence of bubbles, financial innovations and excessive financial disequilibria.[27]

Sargent observes that Prescott explicitly downplayed the role of monetary influences in business cycle theory by recommending to work with 'an entirely real Arrow-Debreu model' (Sargent, 2015, p. 49), but Lucas, as we saw, did not abandon the hope to merge monetary theory and business cycle theory on the grounds of sound micro-foundations. In 1996, at the end of his Nobel lecture, he suggests that in due time future research might incorporate monetary features into real business cycles models (Lucas, 1996, p. 680). In 2004, he suggests that 'certain kinds of monetary variations' had been introduced 'with success' in real business cycles macro-models based on the Arrow-Debreu general-equilibrium model (Lucas, 2004[2013], p. 514), even though this line

---

[26] Alan Greenspan defined the financial crisis starting in 2007 as a 'once-in-a-century credit tsunami' (Mishkin, 2011, p. 2).

[27] Unfortunately, the scholarly knowledge of past economists' ideas is not the point of force of the new theorists of Pareto-optimal cycles without money. In Prescott's Nobel lecture, Jevons is barely mentioned in a footnote, by referring to Frisch's authority: 'Frisch (1970, p. 12) reports that the English mathematician and economist Jevons (1835–1882) dreamed that we would be able to quantify neoclassical economics' (Prescott, 2006, p. 18).

of research was not as successful as he hoped. In 2013, Lucas points again to the real business cycle theory as the central interpretation of fluctuations and money now is left out of the picture. Quite paradoxically, in the introduction to the collection of his monetary essays, Lucas declares that macroeconomists have been unable to produce models that could successfully replicate, simulate or explain fluctuations in monetary economies, with whatever reference to the existence of money, or the workings of financial markets. In this later assessment of the state of the art in macroeconomics, Lucas notes that money plays no role, or a very limited one, in both real business cycle models and New Keynesian models.

The authoritative scholar, who had introduced rational-expectations models with misperceptions in the 1970s, with neither repentance for the failures of past theorizing nor doubts about the difficulties to be encountered in future research, writes

> On the harder questions of monetary economics – the real effects of monetary instability, the role of outside and inside money, the instability of fractional reserve banks- this volume may contribute some useful theoretical examples but little in the way of empirical successful models. It is understandable that in the leading operational macroeconomics models today – real business cycle models and new Keynesian models – money as a measurable magnitude plays no role at all, but I hope we can do better than this in the models of the future. (Lucas, 2013, pp. xxvi–xxvii)

In the early 21st century, the models mentioned above, in which for Lucas money plays no role, were still largely dominant in macroeconomics, transmitted by academics as the core theoretical framework of the discipline. Since in these models money plays no role, it would seem that taking money into account makes no crucial difference for successful macroeconomic forecasting or for policy guidelines. Such is the conclusion that should be reached by logical deduction, but policy makers and central bankers do not strictly follow the logic embodied in such models. They persist in being worried by money and finance, and the more so after the 2007–2008 financial crisis and the European sovereign debt crisis. However, as Laidler notes, 'by the late 1990s the dominant theory of monetary policy had come to focus on the central bank's control of interest rates rather than monetary – or indeed credit – aggregates of any description, and was supported by equilibrium macroeconomic models whose account of the transmission mechanism completely bypassed the institutional complications presented by the monetary and financial system' (Laidler, 2013, p. 13).[28]

---

[28] Mishkin (2011, pp. 2–3) lists the nine principles that guided central banks' strategies around 2007, soon before the financial crisis. According to the last one, 'financial frictions' are relevant

8.9 CONCLUSION

In the early 1960s, in their article on 'Money and business cycles' Friedman and Schwartz (1963b, p. 63) argued their 'strong case' about the rate of change of the money stock being the prime mover to account for the path of nominal income. They proposed a monetary theory of business fluctuations based on their interpretation of the evidence from time series and the obvious idea that 'money is a pervasive element in the economy', and economic activity is carried out through monetary transactions.[29] If in his historical explanation Friedman was very attentive to the peculiar role of the banking sector in the evolution and timing of events, especially during the Great Depression, in the new quantity theory of money, banks appear as troubling gears in the transmission mechanism to account for how changes in the money stock turn into changes in nominal income. In Friedman's simplified macroeconomic models, and in his core policy message as well, banks and finance disappear. Banks in principle are 'domesticated' thanks to the 100 per cent reserve requirement or the stable monetary rule adopted by the central bank. Financial markets are ambiguously disposed of thanks to an implicit, smooth equilibrium assumption.

After the short phase during which misperceptions of general price movements were seen as the main cause of fluctuations, New Classical Macroeconomics totally forgot not only finance and banking, but even money itself, to explain fluctuations, not to speak of long-term growth trends. By the early 1990s, thirty years later, in 'counter-revolutionary', non-Keynesian, macroeconomic theory, money, far from being 'pervasive' or 'all that matters', had been wiped off, with the exception of a few models, where it was reduced to a sort of embellishment. Money was no longer one of the variables employed to explain business cycles; a step that not even the most radical Keynesians criticized by Friedman had conceived of in the 1950s. With money, as the baby with the bathwater, credit, banks and inside debt had been thrown away as inessential complications to understand economic fluctuations or growth. A large body of literature continued to exist on finance, banks and financial markets but, notes Laidler, 'these developments took place in isolation from mainstream macroeconomics, which continued on its way without help from the analysis of monetary and financial institutions and assets markets' (Laidler, 2015, p. 20).

---

in business cycles. He notes: 'The last principle that financial frictions play an important role in business cycles was not explicitly part of models used for policy analysis in central banks, but was well understood by many, although not all central bankers.'

[29] Friedman and Schwartz (1963b, p. 49) quote Mitchell on this point, which they clearly consider as self-evident to all economists.

In conclusion, abandoning the earlier vindication by Friedman and other monetarist scholars of the crucial importance of the money stock, and monetary policy, the 1980s and 1990s mainstream rejected the relevance of unanticipated monetary shocks to explain business fluctuations. Their research agenda moved to develop macroeconomic models with rational expectations in which money is totally absent. Even accounting for the evidence of monetary transactions and of monetary stocks held by private agents or created by banks became a theoretical puzzle. The fictional world portrayed could not even be described as barter economy, since it stages the inter-temporal optimal choices of a representative agent having no need to trade with other agents.

At the beginning of the 21st century, this was the state of macroeconomic theory in so far as the most authoritative theoretical currents were concerned. The prevailing mainstream models totally ignored the financial side of the economy as crucially intertwined with the real side. This was the set of ideas that the best theoreticians and Nobel Prize winners of New Classical Macroeconomics were teaching in universities, publishing in academic journals, spreading as their scientific credentials to the larger audience of learned communities outside economics. In principle, models are just fictional devices, but on many occasions the model builders were very vocal about the policy recommendations derived from their theoretical apparatus and simulations. They warned colleagues, students and policy makers about the risks of active policies. Friedman did the same, but with a less radical attitude since, for example, he had defended the classical lender of last resort role of the Federal Reserve.

Prescott, emphasizing the necessity to follow good monetary rules, claims that the fundamental message of his theories had illuminated central bankers and prevented the adoption of bad, discretionary policies (Prescott, 2006, p. 6). These views were proudly expounded just three years before the eruption of one of the worst financial crises of the world economy in the last two centuries. In the United States, the worst was avoided by the coordinated effort of the Federal Reserve and the Treasury and massive bail-outs. A few years later, during the sovereign debt crises in Europe, the worst was avoided by the 'whatever it takes' stance that the European Central Bank adopted. In the following years, the adoption of the quantitative easing programmes, as limited or late as they might have been, helped mitigate the recession. The financial crisis forced a rethinking of both theory and policy, including central banks' strategies.

We conclude by quoting Eichengreen's comments on the experts' and outstanding economists' misperceptions of the risks in the U.S. financial system till 2005. They reassured the general public by holding that financial institutions were effectively hedging and diversifying risk, and financial markets and financial intermediaries were now resilient to shocks. On the contrary, in his historical reconstruction, Eichengreen (2015, p. 171) shows that the peculiar structure of housing finance exposed the mortgage markets, linked to the intricate structure of the financial system as a whole, to price shocks. After all, the forgetting of the financial structure by mainstream macroeconomics had heavy welfare and policy costs, as the course of events in the first decade of the 21st century forcefully and dramatically demonstrates.

9. Credit and finance in today's mainstream

In the 1970s and 1980s, the New Classical Macroeconomics and the real business cycles approaches undoubtedly were the dominant streams in macroeconomics. But, in the 1980s, there emerged a new approach, known as New Keynesian Economics, which expressed dissatisfaction with the dominant paradigm. This school can be characterized for the crucial role that market imperfections play in the determination of the equilibrium and dynamics of the economy. The abandonment of the hypothesis of perfect markets allowed exponents of the New Keynesian Economics to make some advancements in the analysis of credit markets even though, for quite a long time, the main focus remained on the real side of the economy.[1]

In the same years, in a relatively independent way, there emerged also a novel approach to the analysis of financial markets based on the rejection of the typical New Classical hypothesis of fully rational agents, largely accepted also by New Keynesians. This line of research, known as behavioural finance, brings back to the fore aspects and features of financial markets that had been identified by Keynes.

In this chapter we look, in a highly selective way, at some of the above-mentioned recent contributions by pointing out their advancement with respect to the NCM/RBC approach as well as the problems and issues that remain still unsolved and in need of further developments.

9.1 IMPERFECTION ENTERS THE SCENE

At the end of the 1980s, the New Classical Macroeconomics and the real business cycle line of research and the emerging New Keynesian approach were at 'war': macroeconomics looked like a 'battlefield' (Blanchard, 2008). About thirty years later, however, it looked as if that war had finished for good; so much so that two important macroeconomists, Blanchard (2008) and Woodford (2009), could hold that a significant process of convergence

---

[1] For a brief reconstruction of how imperfect competition came to macroeconomics, see Dixon and Rankin (1995b).

on a number of relevant topics and issues had occurred. Goodfriend and King (1997) called the outcome of this process of convergence the 'New Neoclassical Synthesis'.

It is not possible to enter into a detailed and thorough examination of either the New Keynesian Economics or the debates with exponents of the New Classical Macroeconomics and the real business cycle approach that led to the convergence to a large consensus on the basic features that macroeconomic analysis must have.[2] Here, it will suffice to recall a few aspects that are more relevant for the macroeconomic analysis of credit and finance. From this perspective, a point of central importance is the key role that 'imperfections' and 'frictions' have come to play in macroeconomics in general and, more specifically, in the analyses of credit and finance.

In the New Keynesian narration and reconstruction of how macroeconomics evolved over time, it is their merit to have brought the problem of imperfections in macroeconomic analysis to the fore. New Keynesian Economics, though composed by people with different views and positions on quite a wide spectrum of topics, characterizes itself for two major points: i) the conviction that market imperfections play a key role in the understanding of the functioning of the economy; ii) the rejection of the 'classical dichotomy' (Mankiw and Romer, 1991a). Market imperfections imply the non-perfect flexibility of prices and wages, something which, according to this interpretation, was simply assumed by the 'old' Keynesian whereas New Keynesians want to provide such rigidities with rigorous micro-foundations, based on the assumption of rational maximizing agents.[3] NKE, thus, is not a return to the Keynesianism of the 1950s and 1960s; it tries to obtain 'Keynesian results' by taking account of and accepting some basic features of the anti-Keynesianism of the 1970s and 1980s.

The New Keynesian historical reconstruction is problematic in several respects. The importance of market imperfections for macroeconomic analysis has a long history: Marshall's analysis of inertia in monetary wage settings,

---

[2]   For a good summary of the main features of the NKE, the differentiations among its exponents and its relationship with other traditions of thought in macroeconomics see, for example, Goodfriend and King (1997), Snowdown and Vane (2005, pp. 357–432), Blanchard (2008) and Woodford (2009). For a critical comparison of the new synthesis to the old one, see De Vroey and Duarte (2013).

[3]   Snowdown and Vane (2005, p. 366) express this point clearly: 'Both orthodox and new Keynesian approaches assume that prices adjust slowly following a disturbance. But, unlike the Keynesian cross or IS-LM approaches, which arbitrarily assume fixed nominal wages and prices, the new Keynesian approach seeks to provide a microeconomic underpinning for the slow adjustment of both wages and prices. In line with the choice-theoretical framework of new classical analysis, the new Keynesian approach assumes that workers and firms are rational utility and profit maximizers, respectively.' For a brief reconstruction of how imperfect competition came to contemporary macroeconomics, see also Dixon and Rankin (1995a).

Pigou's analysis of the labour market in the 1920s, or Keynes's sociological explanation of the wage rigidity are just a few examples. As for the 'old' Keynesians, it is not correct to hold that they were not at all concerned with the problem of providing micro-foundations to wage or price stickiness. Their micro-foundations simply were different from the assumption of Olympian rationality that largely prevailed in the 1970s and 1980s. We shall return to this issue in the final section 9.7; for now we proceed with the exposition of the New Keynesian positions, with particular attention to credit and financial markets.

It is thanks to the New Keynesian characteristics mentioned above that the convergence to a new Neoclassical Synthesis could occur. The key theoretical and analytical features of the new synthesis can be summarized as follows: i) macroeconomic analysis must be based on coherent inter-temporal general-equilibrium foundations; ii) agents are forward-looking and their expectations are rational; iii) the economy is characterized by imperfections and frictions and in such an environment policies (monetary policy especially) can be effective, at least in the short-medium term; iv) the most advanced and rigorous analytical tool is dynamic stochastic general equilibrium (DSGE) models.[4] The New Keynesian contribution to the realization of the new synthesis is represented by the role that imperfections, rigidities and frictions play within a general framework earlier developed by the New Classical Macroeconomics and the RBC approach.[5] The new Neoclassical Synthesis, however, has not been exempted from criticisms. Eminent economists have criticized DSGE models at the theoretical level (for example Solow, 2010; Stiglitz, 2018) as well as at the empirical/econometric level (for example Hendry and Muelbauer, 2018). We shall return to some of these criticisms later on (section 9.7).

Initially, during the 1980s and 1990s, the New Keynesian concern for imperfections was essentially focused on the goods and labour markets.[6] Although with exceptions, some of which are considered below, New Keynesian economists did not pay much attention to financial and monetary issues. As for monetary policy, most models were based on the assumption that the

---

[4] For a useful presentation and introduction to the basic features of dynamic stochastic models, see Heijdra (2017, pp. 669–796).

[5] For Blanchard, attempts at explaining important aspects of the real world 'through exotic preferences or exotic segmented-market effects of open market operations, while maintaining the assumption of perfectly competitive markets and flexible prices, have proven unconvincing at best. This has led even the most obstinate new-classicals to explore the possibility that nominal rigidities matter. Present nominal rigidities, movements in nominal money lead to movements in real money, which lead in turn to movements in the interest rate, and the demand for goods and output' (Blanchard, 2008, pp. 5–6).

[6] Mankiw and Romer (1991b) includes 55 chapters, of which only four are concerned with monetary and financial issues. Dixon and Rankin (1995c) contains 16 chapters, of which only two are devoted to such topics.

policy interest rate is fixed by the central bank, which implements an inflation-targeting policy by using some version of the Taylor rule.[7] Later on, especially after the 2007–2008 crisis, the research on imperfect credit and financial markets has grown significantly thanks to the work of several economists, not always definable as strictly New Keynesians. In dealing with these topics the crucial imperfection is the asymmetry of information. The asymmetric distribution of information between lenders and borrowers gives a more solid rationale to the existence of banks and other intermediaries in credit markets.

The contemporary literature on the relationship between macroeconomic analysis and credit markets has reached by now considerable dimensions and here it is not possible to carry out any extensive survey of it.[8] We restrict ourselves to consider a number of issues and the way they have been tackled by some selected authors. Trautwein (2000, pp. 158–159) puts most of the literature that we examine in this chapter under the label 'credit view', within which he discerns three main streams of research: i) on the problem of credit rationing; ii) on the problem of the non-perfect substitutability between bank loans and securities; iii) on the so-called financial accelerator. In all these fields of research Stiglitz and Bernanke with several co-authors have produced a large number of important contributions, some of which we consider here.

In the next section we concentrate on the relationship between informational imperfections, the nature of credit markets and credit rationing. Section 9.3 deals with the problem of the so-called financial accelerator.

9.2   IMPERFECT INFORMATION AND CREDIT RATIONING

In looking at the problems of the nature of credit markets and the possibility of rationing, a good point of reference is the work of Stiglitz who, on his own or in collaboration with others, has provided many important contributions on these topics.[9] For Stiglitz, market imperfections in credit and financial markets are essentially due to two crucial factors: i) the special nature of information; ii) the existence of informational asymmetries. As a consequence, equilibrium

---

[7]   Woodford (2003), for example, considers a cashless economy in which the central bank is always able to fix the interest rate which affects the agents' decision making.

[8]   There are however several useful collections of works and surveys. For a good selection of pre-crisis contributions see, for example, Bhattacharya et al. (2004). Brunnermeier and Eisenbach (2012) survey the literature on frictions in financial markets. Morley (2016), looks at recent literature by paying most attention to empirical issues. Christiano et al. (2017), more specifically, look at the DSGE literature on credit produced before and after the 2007–2008 crisis.

[9]   In 2001, Stiglitz, together with Akerlof and Spence, was awarded the Nobel Prize for his analysis of markets with asymmetric information. See Stiglitz (2002) for an illustration of his research leading to the prize.

in the markets for loans cannot be thought of as similar to equilibrium in real markets.

For Stiglitz, a large part of economic theorizing has been founded on the hypothesis that agents are perfectly informed. A market economy with perfect information is able to produce optimal Paretian outcomes without the need for external interventions. But the hypothesis of perfect information is inadequate to understand important aspects of the real world where informational imperfections are pervasive. Moreover, even small imperfections can have significant implications (Stiglitz, 2000, pp. 1443–1444).

The fundamental imperfection in the market for information, which has many of the properties of public goods (Stiglitz, 2000), is asymmetry which has implications for the analysis of the nature and working of credit and financial markets. Stiglitz and Weiss (1981), in their pioneering work on asymmetric information in credit markets demonstrate the possibility of equilibria with credit rationing, i.e. equilibria with a persistent excess demand for loans. Lenders need information about the creditworthiness of potential borrowers, but such information is costly and not necessarily always possible to acquire. The lender does not know with certainty the riskiness of the project for which a loan is demanded; therefore the lender does not know the probability with which the borrower will repay the debt. The existence of financial intermediation, and in particular of banks, can reduce the risk of lending, but the information that banks can acquire remains imperfect (Stiglitz and Weiss, 1981, p. 393).

Suppose that the equilibrium between supply and demand for credit can be obtained at the interest rate r^*, but banks believe that at such a rate a significant proportion of borrowers would be highly risky.[10] As a consequence, it is not necessarily true that banks maximize their expected returns by lending at the rate r^*; they can maximize their returns, and hence the expected value of their net worth, by lending at a rate $\bar{r} < r^*$, which implies credit rationing. The equilibrium interest rate cannot be regarded simply as the market-clearing price of loans.

Stiglitz and Greenwald (2003) develop and extend the analysis of banking under imperfect and asymmetric information.[11] All banks invest resources on screening the applicants for loans. Banks are risk neutral provided that they do not go bankrupt. Bankruptcy has a high cost c, which banks want to avoid (Stiglitz and Greenwald, 2003, pp. 54–55). On the grounds of their analysis, Greenwald and Stiglitz argue for a new approach to monetary economics. The key feature of such new monetary theory is the analysis of the demand

---

[10] Borrowers who are ready to take large risks, and hence, with a high probability of default.

[11] They consider both banks that take deposits (depository institutions) and banks that do not (investment banks).

and supply of loanable funds, which in turn requires the understanding of the importance of informational imperfections and the consequent behaviour of lenders (Stiglitz and Greenwald, 2003, p. 2).[12] The interest rate is not the price that clears the market for loans. In the determination of the supply and demand for loans, several other factors play a crucial role. Such factors mostly are of an individual and specific nature (Stiglitz and Greenwald, 2003, p. 30).

In symbols, Greenwald's and Stiglitz's notion of equilibrium in the credit market can be expressed as follows. The banks' function to maximize is

$$E(a_{t+1}) - cF(\hat{\theta}) \qquad (9.1)$$

s.t.

$$N \leq N^d(r,e)$$

where $E(a_{t+1})$ is the banks' expected net worth at $(t + 1)$; $F(\hat{\theta})$ is the probability of bankruptcy whose cost is c; N is the amount loaned; N^d is the demand for loans at the interest rate r and e is the screening cost. When $N^d > N$ there is credit rationing. If the constraint is not binding the interest rate is determined by supply and demand for loans.

Informational asymmetries also play an important role in financial markets and can give rise to 'equity rationing': firms operate in an environment in which they cannot raise any desired quantity of equity capital. Equity rationing applies also to banks, which therefore cannot augment their capital indefinitely. If there is equity rationing banks cannot fully diversify their risk and, hence, reduce their probability of bankruptcy. The reasons for equity rationing are various. First, issuing of additional equity can have a negative effect on the firm's net worth because the issuing of new shares conveys a negative signal to the market with the consequence of a negative effect on their price.[13] This is one of the reasons why there is non-perfect substitutability between borrowing from banks and issuing new shares.

9.3　IMPERFECT INFORMATION AND THE FINANCIAL ACCELERATOR

Other important contributions have not been so concerned with credit rationing as with economic fluctuations and the propagating effects of credit (the

---

[12]　Stiglitz and Greenwald (2003, pp. 45–46) see their theoretical approach as a generalized version of the loanable funds theory of the 1930s, which we examined in Chapters 5 and 6.

[13]　The information conveyed by firms which sell shares is that they are willing to do so because they believe that the market is overpricing their shares. See Stiglitz and Greenwald (2003, pp. 34–35) for other factors that can induce firms not to issue equity for their financing.

financial accelerator). The research carried out by Bernanke and several co-authors is largely representative of this strand of literature.[14] The analysis has been carried out in several different analytical frameworks, ranging from an IS-LM model (Bernanke and Blinder, 1988) to an overlapping-generation model and a New Keynesian DSGE model. Bernanke and Gertler (1989) employ a model with overlapping generations, where generations denote the entry and exit of firms from credit markets. Bernanke et al. (1999a) use a New Keynesian DSGE model, in which households with infinite life work, consume, save and lend to financial intermediaries; entrepreneurs buy physical capital goods by financing them with entrepreneurial wealth (net worth) and by borrowing from intermediaries. Entrepreneurs are risk-neutral and households are risk-adverse, so that loan contracts establish that any aggregate risk is absorbed by entrepreneurs.

In all the models mentioned above the financial sector is characterized by the existence of imperfections and frictions, which imply the necessity to reject the Modigliani-Miller theorem (Modigliani and Miller, 1958), which relies on the assumption of perfect financial markets. Both New Classical models and the 'old' Keynesian models – though with exceptions like in the case of Tobin – explicitly or implicitly, accept the theorem and, for this, they ignore the conditions in financial and credit markets and their effects on the real economy. In the environment considered by Bernanke et al. the informational asymmetry between lenders and borrowers implies the existence of verification costs *à la* Townsend (1979). The consequence is that external finance is more costly than internal finance, i.e. there exists an external finance premium. In this context, the borrowers' net worth becomes crucial as it affects the external finance premium: the cost and amount of lending are decreasing functions of the discounted value of the borrower's net worth used as collateral (for further details, see, e.g, Trautwein, 2000, pp. 162–163).

The macroeconomic implications of this sort of approach are significant: i) since the borrowers' net worth has a pro-cyclical dynamics, agency costs have a counter-cyclical dynamics; ii) shocks to the borrowers' net worth, which are independent of the dynamics of aggregate output, are an initial source of real fluctuations. This is sufficient to obtain investment fluctuations and cyclical persistence: when the economy is, for example, in a recessive phase the net worth is low and agency costs high, so that also the cost of investment financing is high with further depressive effects. Credit has accelerating effects on business fluctuations as the counter-cyclical external finance premium generated by agency costs enhances 'the swings in borrowing and thus in investment, spending, and production' (Bernanke et al., 1999a, p. 1345).

---

[14] The theoretical research carried out by Bernanke and others is influenced also by historical research, in particular on the Great Depression (see Chapter 4).

Kiyotaki and Moore (1997) construct a model of the cycle in which credit plays a propagating role. More recently, Christiano et al. (2014) draw on Bernanke et al. (1999a). Although not considering financial intermediation, Eggertsson and Krugman (2012) look at the economic effects of debt limits for the agents in the economy. They consider two representative agents: a patient agent and an impatient one. The impatient agent borrows from the patient one, but there is a limit to the amount that can be borrowed. A decrease of the debt limit forces borrowers to de-leverage and determines a fall in the interest rate, which can become negative if the decrease of the limit is large enough (Eggertsson and Krugman, 2012, p. 1477).[15]

In their analysis, Bernanke et al. do not explicitly consider banks but only generic financial intermediaries. Only when outlining possible developments and extensions of their work do they mention the possibility to introduce banks in a non-trivial way. More in particular, they refer to the possibility to consider the existence of frictions for banks which are due to constraints on their ability to raise funds to lend to borrowers. In this sort of analytical framework, the net worth of the banking sector would also become relevant (Bernanke et al., 1999a, p. 1379). Woodford (2010) looks at this latter aspect by using a model in which it is the limited amount of capital available to intermediaries that produces an accelerating effect when the economy is hit by a positive or negative shock. If there is an increase in economic activity, the values of the intermediaries' assets and their net worth rises, so that they can further increase their borrowing and lending. The opposite occurs in the case of a negative shock. Moreover, the effects of shocks on the intermediaries' capital tend to persist over time, with obvious repercussions on the economy as a whole.

9.4   THE COMPLEXITY OF THE BANKING SYSTEM AND THE FINANCIAL SECTOR

Most of the models cited above do not pay particular attention to, or do not consider at all, the complex nature of the modern banking system in which different types of institutions operate. More in particular, these models do not make a precise distinction between traditional banks (depository institutions) and investment banks (including shadow banks), which do not collect deposits. But the process of financial innovation, characterized by the emerging and growing importance of non-traditional forms of intermediation and new types

---

[15] Eggertsson and Krugman see their analysis of the process of recovery from the recession, which depends on the debtors repaying their liabilities, as similar to Koo's notion of a protracted balance sheet recession developed by mainly referring to the Japanese experience (Koo, 2008, 2015).

of financial assets which have played a decisive role in the recent financial crisis, has sparked off the production of numerous works which take into explicit consideration the complexity of the financial sector in contemporary economies and the emerging of new types of financial firms.

The works of Adrian and Shin represent important contributions in this direction (Adrian and Shin, 2010, 2011; Shin, 2010). For example, Adrian and Shin (2011) show how the pervasiveness of leveraged intermediaries, which are different from ordinary banks and drive the financial cycle, implies a different working of the transmission process of monetary policy and, in particular, of how variations of the short-term rate affect the whole economy. Gertler et al. (2016) argue that wholesale banking is at the centre-stage of financial crises, while retail banks remain substantially stable. Wholesale banks lend to non-financial agents and borrow from retail banks, which use their deposits to lend to them and to the non-financial sector. The size of the wholesale sector is determined endogenously as it depends on the advantage of wholesale over retail banks in managing assets and on the advantage of retail over wholesale banks in dealing with agency problems (Gertler et al., 2016, p. 14).[16]

Carlin and Soskice (2015, pp. 149–261) offer a good synthesis of the most recent research on the interaction between the financial and real sectors, financial cycles and crises. They consider both retail and investment banks.[17] Households and firms borrow from banks. Retail banks provide core services (running the payment system and mortgage lending) and collect savers' deposits; investment banks, which do not take deposits, trade in various financial instruments and their assets are marked-to-market. Investment banks buy mortgages from retail banks and use them as raw material to produce financial assets (securitized assets). Investment banks as well as savers invest in financial assets, but savers are risk averse whereas banks are risk neutral. The leverage of investment banks is the key variable, which works as a financial accelerator both in the upswings and downswings of the cycle.[18]

The upswing ends, and the downswing starts, when, for some reasons (for example, a fall in the prices of houses that underlie the asset F), the risk $\bar{z}$ increases. As a consequence, the demand for assets declines and so do their prices. If the fall of prices is significantly large, some investment banks might become insolvent, because of the fall in the value of their equity. The

---

[16] See also Gertler and Kiyotaki (2011, 2015).

[17] Carlin and Soskice (2015) is the new edition of their intermediate macroeconomics textbook. It is interesting to refer to the book also to evaluate the extent to which the more recent research on finance and macroeconomics is trickling down to the teaching level. See Carlin and Soskice (2015, pp. 600–610) for a comparison between their model, RBC and New Keynesian DSGE models.

[18] The investment bank's leverage is $\lambda = \frac{F}{e} = \dfrac{1}{\bar{z} - (1 + r - P)}$, where e is the bank's equity; F denotes assets, whose price is P; $\bar{z}$ is the risk of F, and r is the expected rate of return from F. λ is decreasing in $\bar{z}$ and increasing in the expected return to the bank, i.e. $(1 + r - P)$.

effects on the whole banking system, where retail and investment banks are interconnected, are significant: 'the crash reduces the willingness and ability of banks to make new loans. Banks will sell assets and call in loans in order to strengthen their weakened balance sheets' (Carlin and Soskice, 2015, p. 212). As a result aggregate demand decreases, with further negative effects on the banks' positions. But even if no bank becomes insolvent, the systemic effects remain important: the fall in the prices of assets causes capital losses for investment banks and the worsening of their balance sheets, which induces them to reduce the demand for assets with a consequent fall in their prices, a further worsening of the balance sheets and so on.

Carlin and Soskice (2015, pp. 214–217) describe what they call a 'balance sheet recession', which involves both banks and non-banking borrowers (households and firms). The triggering event is a decrease in house and asset prices. The major effects of such a decrease are: i) a loan-to-value effect; ii) a collateral effect; iii) the banks' calling of loans; iv) the increase in the borrowers' propensity to save. When there is a fall in asset prices, banks reduce their loan-to-value ratio,[19] with a negative effect on aggregate demand. The reduction of the house prices makes the value of the households' collateral decrease and, hence, their demand for loans for consumption decreases too, with negative effects on aggregate demand. Another important effect is that banks call in loans already made because the value of their corresponding collateral has fallen and become lower than the loan itself. If borrowers are credit-constrained, the repayment of their debt implies a corresponding reduction in their demand for consumption. Finally, borrowers increase their propensity to save and reduce expenditures in the attempt to rebuild their net worth.

9.5   ON THE OLD AND NEW VIEWS OF BANKS AGAIN

All the models cited in the previous sections, with one exception, share the view of banks as mere intermediaries. Banks in general (depository institutions and investment banks) intermediate between ultimate savers and borrowers. Banks must first borrow from somebody before being able to lend.[20] Stiglitz and Greenwald (2003) is the exception mentioned above: they take a different position on the nature of banks, which is closer to the 'old view', according to

---

[19]   The ratio of the banks' loan to the value of the borrowers' collateral.

[20]   Gertler and Kiyotaki (2011, p. 555), for example, state: 'To finance lending in each period, banks raise funds in a national financial market. Within the national financial market, there is a retail market (where banks obtain deposits from households) and a wholesale market (where banks borrow and lend amongst one and another)'. On the prevailing view of the nature of banks in recent macroeconomics, see also Bianco and Sardoni (2018).

which banks can create additional money *ex nihilo*. Stiglitz and Greenwald (2003, pp. 104–136) emphasize the essential differences between a 'corn' (non-monetary) economy and a monetary economy. In a corn economy, banks necessarily are intermediaries between savers and borrowers.[21] The representative bank has a certain capital K; it pays an interest rate ρ to savers and receives an interest rate r from borrowers. If the bank wants to lend more seeds than those deposited with it, it can raise the interest rate paid to depositors to attract additional funds or it can augment its capital. The amount of loans made can be either smaller or equal to the amount demanded by borrowers, that is to say there can be or not credit rationing.[22]

When we turn to consider credit markets in a monetary economy, banks do not actually give 'seeds' to borrowers; they lend to borrowers by creating deposits (money) *ex novo*, which will be then used to buy 'seeds'. The creation of deposits certifies the creditworthiness of the borrowers (Stiglitz and Greenwald, 2003, p. 117). In the context of a monetary economy, the banks' ability to lend is no longer constrained by their capital plus deposits even though, if bankruptcy is costly, banks want to keep a certain amount of 'money on hand' (reserves).[23]

Stiglitz's and Greenwald's view of banks is still in the minority within the mainstream, but recently a renewed interest in the 'old' view of banks has re-emerged even though, so far, invitations to rethink the nature of banks mainly come from economists who are not in academia but work in other economic and/or financial institutions. Werner (2014a,b) espouses the view that the banks' ability to lend and create money is not constrained by their ability to collect deposits. Banks are essentially different from other financial intermediaries, which must first borrow to lend.[24] To support empirically his position, Werner (2014a) conducts an experiment with a bank, which confirms the idea that 'banks individually create money out of nothing'. In articles published in the *Quarterly Bulletin* of the Bank of England, McLeay et al.

---

[21] 'Those with excess corn seed bring their excess seed down to such a specialized institution, the bank, which promises a particular rate of return. The bank in turn lends to many different borrowers' (Stiglitz and Greenwald, 2003, p. 105).

[22] The equilibrium is also affected by the bank's capital K: the larger is K, the more the bank is willing to lend and the more the savers are willing to deposit with the bank (Stiglitz and Greenwald, 2003, p. 109).

[23] '…there may be an imbalance between what individuals would like to save (at full employment) and what other individuals or firms would like to invest. (…) As a result, unlike the corn model, if their willingness to supply certifications exceeds the supply of seed, banks are not forced to adjust the interest rates they pay depositors or charge borrowers. Rather, the problem in the banking market becomes reflected as a problem in the goods market, with an excess demand for goods (seed)' (Stiglitz and Greenwald, 2003, pp. 119–120).

[24] See Werner (2014b) for a detailed analysis of the differences between banks which are depository institutions and other intermediaries, included investment banks, which do not take deposits. On the topic see also Kashyap et al. (2002).

(2014a,b) reject the idea that the amount of loans (money) generated by banks is strictly constrained by their deposits. In modern economies deposits are largely created by commercial banks by making new loans (McLeay et al., 2014a, pp. 15–16), although this does not mean that the banks' ability to lend and create money has no limits.[25]

Similar positions have been taken by Borio, Head of the Monetary and Economics Department at the Bank for International Settlements (BIS), and Turner, a former chairman of the UK Financial Services Authority (FSA). Borio (2014) proposes a novel approach to the problem of financial cycles and argues that a most important step in such a direction is changing the view of the nature of banks, which do not simply transfer resources from one sector to another but generate nominal purchasing power anew. Turner (2016), who sees excessive private credit creation as the fundamental reason of the 2007–2008 crisis and the following recession, bases his analysis on the rejection of the view of banks as mere intermediaries. The new purchasing power created by banks through credit can be channelled towards investment and promote growth, but it can also be 'skewed' towards asset speculation. Therefore, how much credit (money) is created and how it is used are problems of crucial importance, which cannot be dealt with through the exclusive use of interest rates (Turner, 2016, p. 58).[26]

Finally, Jakab and Kumhof (2015), at the IMF, criticize the view of banks as intermediaries of loanable funds (ILF) as well as the notion of deposit multiplier, or fractional reserve approach. They adopt, instead, the view that banks create money through credit (financing through money creation – FMC). They introduce their FMC view of banks into a DSGE model and compare its results and predictions with other DSGE models with similar features but with banks acting as intermediaries (see also Jakab and Kumhof, 2014). The models, which consider retail and wholesale banks, households and firms, are subjected to several shocks to observe their different results and their ability to represent a number of stylized facts. The authors regard their FCM model as more consistent with empirical observation. Policies based on their model would significantly differ from those derived from models based on a view of banks as mere intermediaries (Jakab and Kumhof, 2015, p. 39).

Similarly to Stiglitz and Greenwald, Jakab and Kumhof criticize the ILF approach because it can apply only to a non-monetary economy (Jakab and

---

[25] The limits to lending (and money creation) are set by: i) banks themselves for profit and risk considerations; ii) the behaviour of household and firms, which might make transactions that immediately or very rapidly destroy deposits; iii) the central bank that affects the demand for loans through the interest rate (McLeay et al., 2014a, pp. 17–21).

[26] Turner draws inspiration from Wicksell's view of banks and credit and criticizes Woodford's 'Wicksellian' theory (Woodford, 2003) for its exclusive concentration on interest rates rather than on the volume of credit.

Kumhof, 2015, pp. 9–10). The fractional reserve approach is criticized because it is based on the idea that the creation of hard money by the central bank must precede the creation of broad money by banks, whereas in the real world the process of money creation is just the reverse (Jakab and Kumhof, 2015, pp.13–14).

For the authors, their model is able to forecast larger and faster changes in the size of banks' balance sheets, with larger effects on the real economy. The basic reason for this is that in the ILF approach the additional savings required to allow the banking system to expand lending can be created either through increases in output and income or through the foregoing of consumption of existing goods and both these processes are 'slow and continuous'. Instead, banks which are not simply intermediaries can create purchasing power 'instantaneously and discontinuously' (Jakab and Kumhof, 2015, pp. 4–5), even though the banks' ability to create money does not imply that they can do so without any limit.[27]

The above-mentioned contributions might differ from one another in several respects, but they all share a view of banks as active and crucial actors that significantly affect the dynamics of the economy as a whole. The view of banks as essentially passive agents, explicitly or implicitly accepted by most of the macroeconomic literature at least since the 1950s, is rejected. This alternative view of the banking system has also another implication. By insisting on the capacity of banks to create money *ex nihilo*, monetary analysis is set in a stock-flow context, as opposed to an only-stock context associated with the view of banks as mere intermediaries, for which, ultimately, the central bank is the only institution able to vary the supply of money. Financial intermediaries different from traditional banks certainly play a larger and growing role in contemporary economies, but it remains true that only traditional banks can create money through lending, i.e. make the money stock vary endogenously, and that they still play a significant role in lending to households and small-medium firms.

9.6   ARE FINANCIAL MARKETS ALWAYS RATIONAL (EFFICIENT)?

The literature considered in the previous section focuses on credit markets, while less attention is paid to the functioning of stock markets. As we saw, this was not the case with Keynes, who devoted considerable attention to the working of stock markets, their inherent instability and their effects on the rest of the economy. Instead, at least until recently, the belief that financial markets,

---

[27]   The main constraint on the banks' creation of money through credit is to be found in the parameters that enter their profit maximization problem (Jakab and Kumhof, 2015, p. 14).

populated by rational agents, work in an essentially smooth and orderly way was dominant among economists. There were, of course, exceptions and here we briefly consider those represented by Kindleberger's and Minsky's contributions.

We start by considering Kindleberger's historical critique of the rationality of markets or, more precisely, of the idea that markets always work rationally. In his masterful book on manias, panics and crashes (Kindleberger, 2000), Kindleberger criticizes the idea that markets always work and behave in a smooth and fully rational way. He gives a long and detailed historical description of the many financial crises experienced by market economies at least since 1600 and the differing objects of speculation which characterized them. Prolonged phases of price rises (manias) have been followed by crises characterized by panic and sharp price falls. The economic model underlying Kindleberger's historical reconstruction is significantly influenced by Minsky's theoretical contribution, which belongs to a long tradition of thought – including Mill, Wicksell and Fisher among others – where debt structures and their evolution over time play a crucial role in the explanation of financial cycles (Kindleberger, 2000, pp. 13–22).[28]

The scope of Minsky's analysis, however, is wider than stock markets as, more in general, he is concerned with the variations of the structure of credit and debt relations over the cycle. Minsky expounded the essential features of his approach to financial instability already in his book on Keynes (Minsky, 1975), where he explicitly relates to Chapter 12 of *The General Theory*. In a subsequent work (Minsky, 1986[2008]), his views are expressed in a more extensive and detailed way. For brevity, we look only at these two works.[29] The fundamental reason why modern capitalist economies are subject to recurrent changes in their behaviour and, more in particular, to experiencing booms, busts and recessions is that, over time, financial practices and the structure of credit and debt relations vary (Minsky, 1986[2008], p. 219). Changes in the behaviour of the economic system as a whole are strictly related to such changes.

For the understanding of how financial commitments affect the economy, it is necessary to analyse the behaviour over time of the cash flows of all the agents that operate in it and that have to be considered 'as if they were banks' (Minsky, 1986[2008], p. 221). Cash flows are originated by three kinds of economic activity: i) income cash flows, which result from productive

---

[28] Minsky was an important exponent of the so-called heterodoxy in economics, but he is also one of the few non-mainstream economists who have been taken into a certain consideration by the mainstream, especially after the 2007–2008 crisis. See, e.g., Lahart (2007) and Eggertsson and Krugman (2012).

[29] For more comprehensive surveys of Minsky's other contributions, see, e.g., Mehrling (1999) and Papadimitriou and Wray (1998, 1999).

activities; ii) balance-sheet cash flows, which derive from the payment of interests, dividends, rents, etc.; iii) portfolio cash flows, which derive from trading in capital assets and financial instruments (Minsky, 1986[2008], p. 223). As we shall see presently, income cash flows are the foundation on which the whole financial system rests (Minsky, 1986[2008], p. 226).

It is the emerging of unsustainable imbalances among the agents' cash flows that is the fundamental cause of crises. The origins of such imbalances are to be found in the phase during which the economy experiences a boom. A positive shock to the economy generates an improvement in confidence that is accompanied by an increase in the demand and supply of credit. Changes in the state of confidence that affect the firms' decisions to borrow to finance investment also affect the financing of the ownership of shares, i.e. borrowing to acquire shares, with the consequent increase in their prices. The financing of such operations comes from two sources: money creation and wealth owners' portfolio choices. Therefore, the evolving of the boom brings with it the evolving of liabilities at three levels: firms expand their debt; households and firms reduce their holding of more liquid assets relatively to their debt; banks increase their loans at the expense of their holdings of securities and government debt. Correspondingly, speculation takes place at three different levels: i) the owners of capital assets speculate by debt-financing their investments and positions in the stock of capital assets; ii) banks and other financial firms speculate on their portfolios of assets and liabilities; iii) non-financial firms and households speculate on their financial assets and the way they finance their positions (Minsky, 1975, pp. 119–121).

The increased agents' indebtedness generates an increase in their payment commitments that, at a certain juncture, can exceed their cash receipts. Income cash flows become insufficient for the fulfilment of the payment commitments.[30] When the agents involved can fulfil their cash payment commitments only by selling their assets or their liabilities (i.e. borrowing), they carry out a 'position making'. For industrial firms, the position to finance is in productive capital assets; for financial firms the position is in assets with poor secondary markets (Minsky, 1975, p. 122). As the boom develops, agents are forced to undertake an increasingly 'adventuresome position-making activity'. When, because of such activities, the agents' ability to borrow from somebody to repay somebody else reaches its limit, they must either sell some positions or stop, or slowdown, their asset acquisitions. This causes a fall in the prices of assets, which can lead to a Fisherian debt-deflation crisis which, though it

---

[30] Minsky, at least in the works considered here, does not devote much attention to the reasons why, at a certain point, income cash flow declines but, given his Keynesian views, it is easy to deduce that such a decline is mainly due to an insufficient growth of aggregate demand with respect to the expansion of the productive capacity.

will eventually come to a halt in consequence of various stabilizing factors, is associated with a period of low income and high unemployment (Minsky, 1975, p. 125).

The process described above can be better analysed by considering the different types of financing that Minsky contemplates: hedge, speculative and Ponzi finance.[31] Agents that engage in speculative and Ponzi financing must undertake portfolio transactions, i.e. selling assets or debt, and therefore they depend on the prevailing conditions of financial markets, whereas hedge agents are not affected by the conditions of such markets.

Minsky sees as inevitable the occurring of processes that make the economy move from a robust situation (in which hedge finance dominates) to a fragile one, in which speculative and Ponzi finance dominate. The working and structure of modern financial markets and the rationale of industrial investment are crucial factors for the explanation of such processes. As for financial markets, the interest rates structure is an important factor. In a robust economy, with hedge finance dominant and with short-term interest rates sensibly lower than long-term rates, there arise profit opportunities for speculative arrangements (Minsky, 1986[2008], p. 235). Moreover, in a robust economy, payment commitments on longer-term debts are low relatively to expected and realized quasi-rents. In this context, it is possible to finance 'positions in capital assets by long- and short-term debts, and positions in long-term financial assets by short-term, presumably liquid, debts. Hence a double set of profit opportunities exists' (Minsky, 1986[2008], p. 235).

In modern capitalist economies, the financing of investment as well as of portfolio positions is significantly determined by the banks' own portfolio decisions. When it is profitable for them to do so, banks use the set of already available financial instruments, and possibly new ones, to fund investment and portfolio positions. The endogenous increase in money and in liquid assets determines an increase in the prices of capital assets, which makes the difference between capital-asset and investment-good prices larger. Investment then will rise and bring about new demand for finance. It is the success of the various techniques used that leads towards an increasingly imprudent behaviour of borrowers as well as lenders. However, this does not necessarily mean that the economy immediately moves from a robust to a fragile situation. There exist various limits and barriers to the economy's movement towards fragility. First of all, the predominant lender's and borrower's risk sets a limit to

---

[31] We have hedge financing when the expected and realised income cash flows are sufficient to meet all the commitments on the agents' liabilities. When this is not the case, commitments can be met either by rolling over part of the debt (speculative finance) or by increasing debt (Ponzi finance). For a detailed description of the three types of financing, see Minsky (1986[2008], pp. 230–238).

the rapidity with which the profit opportunities mentioned above are exploited (Minsky, 1986[2008], pp. 235–237).

Firms' investment plays a crucial role. Investment projects must be financed and the debts so created can be paid by using either internal funds (the firms' gross profits after tax) or external funds (new issued equities and new debts). An increase in the ratio of investment to internal funds leads to growing fragility and instability.[32] Firms that finance investment with external funds have two safety margins: the amount of liquid assets in their portfolio and the excess of the present value of their expected stream of quasi-rents over the cost of their investment projects (the firms' safety margins determine their creditworthiness). If, for an increase in interest rates, the firms' safety margins decline, their financing costs rise and the present value of their quasi-rents decreases. The reaction of financial markets to lower safety margins brings about their further decrease and a consequent increase in costs. These, for Minsky, are the outcomes of the sort of financing relations that are established during an investment boom (Minsky, 1986[2008], p. 242).[33]

The transition of the economy from robustness to fragility can be described in terms of Keynes's conventions and their breaking. Keynes refers to the convention that 'the existing state of affairs will continue indefinitely'. During a boom, the convention is that asset revaluations and capital gains will keep on going indefinitely; during debt deflation and recession, the convention is 'debts are to be avoided, for debts lead to disaster'. In both cases conventions will be disproved by facts: neither booms nor deflationary phases last indefinitely (Minsky, 1975, pp. 125–126).

Kindleberger's and Minsky's views of the working of financial markets evidently are radically different from the positions taken by those who believe in the smooth functioning of markets. In the post-war era, such a belief translated itself into the hypothesis of efficient financial markets (EMH), according to which the working of financial markets is determined by the rational maximizing behaviour of all, or even part of, the agents that operate in them.[34]

Under the assumption of efficient markets, rational investors evaluate each asset at its fundamental value, i.e. the expected present value of its future

---

[32] Moreover, the demand for the financing of investment projects is highly inelastic with respect to interest rates. An investment has no value unless it is completed; therefore the steps to complete the projects must be made and financed, even though interest rates rise and make the cost of the project increase (Minsky, 1986[2008], p. 241).

[33] For an interesting formalization of several aspects of Minsky's analysis, see Bhaduri (2011).

[34] Samuelson (1965, 1973) gave important contributions to the development of the idea of efficient financial markets. Also, Friedman's work on arbitrage is regarded as an important contribution to the development of the EMH (see Friedman, 1953). For more detailed and technical discussions of the efficient markets hypothesis, see for example Fama (1970), Shleifer (2000, pp. 1–27), Sornette (2003, pp. 27–48), Malkiel (2003) and Shiller (2003).

cash flows conditional on the information available at that time.[35] At t, the equilibrium price of a certain asset therefore is

$$p_t = E_t [PV_t] \qquad (9.2)$$

E_t is the expectation of the present value PV_t of the asset conditional on the information available at t. Whenever the available information at t varies, prices rapidly adjust.

Therefore, price variations can be explained only by changes in information. Whatever is the nature of the information that is embodied into prices, it follows that, over time, prices must move randomly.[36] Prices follow a random walk, because new information necessarily accrues randomly. If it were not so, information would not be new at all as it would be predictable.

The reasoning above is conducted under the assumption that all the operators in the market are fully rational, but the EMH can stand even if the assumption is removed and non-fully rational investors (noise traders) are assumed to exist along with rational fully informed traders. If noise traders, i.e. agents who do not use rationally all the available information to evaluate securities, follow non-correlated strategies the effects of their trades balance each other out and prices remain at their fundamental values. If the non-rational strategies are correlated, the EMH still holds because of arbitrage, which keeps prices at their fundamental values. When, for example, the correlated behaviour of noise traders determine the underpricing of a security (or an index), rational traders can make a profit through arbitrage: they would buy the underpriced security and sell some other security, rationally priced, which is a close substitute for the underpriced one. Profits realized in this way, however, would be quickly eliminated because the rational traders' purchases would determine a price rise for the initially underpriced security, which will quickly return to its fundamental value. Security prices do not diverge from their 'true' value for long.

At least until the end of the 1970s, the efficient markets hypothesis appeared to be largely supported by empirical observation; so much so that it was claimed that no other proposition in economics had more robust empirical support than EMH (Jensen, 1978). But, in the following years, the hypothesis has been subjected to severe criticisms both at the theoretical and empirical

---

[35] Adherents of the EMH differ among them for the discount rate that they use to determine the present value of cash flows. See, e.g., Fama (1970) and Shiller (2003).

[36] The EMH takes three forms according to different hypotheses on information: i) weak; ii) semi-strong; iii) strong. A market is weakly efficient when the available information is just historical prices. The market efficiency is semi-strong if prices efficiently adjust to the emerging of new publicly available information. Finally, market efficiency is strong if prices reflect information which can be gathered privately (inside information).

level.[37] Tobin (1984) discusses and criticizes the notion of market efficiency and makes a number of considerations on the determination of the fundamental values and arbitrage that have been followed and developed by others. Shiller (2003) deals with equilibrium prices as defined by the EMH. If the hypothesis of efficient markets holds and 9.2 above is true, it must be

$$PV_t = P_t + \epsilon_t \tag{9.3}$$

where ϵ_t is the forecast error that necessarily is uncorrelated with the information available at t and embodied into the price P_t. Therefore, the variance of PV_t is equal to the sum of the variance of P_t plus the variance of ϵ_t and hence

$$\text{Var}\,[PV_t] \geq \text{Var}\,[P_t] \tag{9.4}$$

because the variance of ϵ cannot be negative. In other words, the forecast P_t must be less variable than the variable forecasted, PV_t.

Shiller refers to several empirical analyses that, though carried out by adopting different methodologies and using different discount rates for the calculation of the present value of future cash flows, disprove 9.3: the variability of stock prices is significantly larger than the variability of the present value regardless of how it is calculated (see, e.g., Figure 1 in Shiller, 2003, p. 86). Thus he concludes that the volatility of stock markets cannot be explained by any variant of the EMH model (Shiller, 2003, p. 90).[38]

When noise traders are introduced and it is also admitted that their trades are correlated, the validity of the EMH depends on the existence of arbitrage which in turn requires the existence of close substitutes. Shleifer (2000, pp. 13–15) holds that in some cases arbitrage is not possible at all and in all cases it remains a very risky and, hence, limited activity. The possibility of arbitrage depends on the existence of close substitutes that in many cases do not exist, but even if they exist,[39] arbitrage remains highly risky. If substitutes are not perfect, arbitrage is based on the statistical probability rather than the certainty that prices will eventually converge. If substitutes are perfect, the risk of arbitrage lies in the fact that there is uncertainty about the timing of the elimination of mispricing. The prices of two securities perfectly substitutable for one another will eventually converge, but the arbitrageur

---

[37] Quite naturally, after the eruption of the 2007–2009 financial crisis such criticisms gained momentum. See, e.g., the proceedings of the 34th annual conference of the International Organization of Security Commissions (Tel-Aviv, 8–11 June 2009) at www.iosco.org.

[38] Analogous considerations were made by Tobin (1984) who refers to previous works of Shiller. See also Shleifer (2000, pp. 16–23) for the discussion of other empirical challenges to the EMH.

[39] Which is more likely for single securities than for the market as a whole.

can suffer losses during the process of convergence. If he/she is unable to maintain his/her position through such losses, arbitrage is limited (Shleifer, 2000, pp. 14–15).

While the efficient markets hypothesis appears to be largely incapable to offer a convincing explanation of how financial markets actually work, for behavioural financial economists a better understanding of these markets can be gained by recourse to the works of a number of psychologists, in particular Kanheman and his collaborators, who have devoted quite a lot of attention to the behaviour of financial investors and to decision making under uncertainty (Kahneman and Tversky, 1973; Tversky and Kahneman, 1974; Kahneman and Tversky, 1979; Kahneman and Riepe, 1998). By following these works, Shleifer indicates three areas in which the behaviour of individual agents deviates from the rational behaviour predicated by the EMH: i) in the estimation of risky gambles people, who are loss-averse, tend not to be concerned with the final wealth that they can get but with gains and losses relative to some reference point that varies from situation to situation and this can give rise to non-fully rational choices; ii) individuals do not follow the Bayes rule in making predictions of uncertain outcomes; iii) people make different choices depending on how a certain problem is presented to them (framing) (Shleifer, 2000, pp. 10–11). The behaviour of noise traders can be described by referring to these psychological characteristics of human behaviour, but Shleifer argues that they can be applied to rational 'investors' as well, who after all are people themselves (Shleifer, 2000, p. 12).

Also Shiller (2003) takes account of psychological factors, those already mentioned and others, but he also points out the importance of historical, institutional and social factors. In his book on irrational exuberance (Shiller, 2000) he enumerates various factors that could explain the prolonged boom of the stock market in the 1990s. Among these factors, there are institutional and historical events like the expansion of pension funds and mutual funds or the end of the Cold War (Shiller, 2000, pp. 17–43). Pension and mutual funds tend to stimulate the demand for stocks and have vested interests in keeping their prices high. The optimistic climate created by the end of the Cold War had amplifying effects: investors were induced to increase their demand for shares, which determined a rise in their prices and induced more investors to enter the market with a further price rise, and so on (Shiller, 2000, p. 44). This is what Shiller calls 'feedback effect' (see also Shiller, 2003). Finally, Akerlof and Shiller (2015, pp. 23–40) describe the role played by rating agencies in conveying 'wrong' information to the market and in inducing investors to buy highly risky assets.

In their analyses of the working of financial markets, the exponents of behavioural finance describe and deal with a number of phenomena that are similar to those already considered by Keynes, Fisher, Minsky and others.[40] Behavioural finance, however, takes a step further. Such phenomena are not explained by irrational factors, 'false beliefs' or by uncertainty in general. The human nature, as theoretical and empirical psychological research shows, is such that the normal behaviour of people does not conform with the traditional hypothesis of rationality predicated by the believers in the efficient markets hypothesis. Manias and panic are not deviations from normality, but rather phases in which certain features of the human nature become dominant and prevalent. Certainly this does not imply that markets are totally chaotic all the time. In certain periods, even significantly long, markets behave in ways that resemble full rationality, but the possibility that these states of quiet come to an end is always present. In this perspective, the widespread uneasiness of economists with waves of irrationality and false beliefs could be solved.[41] Waves of 'irrationality' or 'false beliefs' should not be factors introduced ad hoc to describe the market dynamics; they are inherent features of the 'normal' agents' behaviour over the cycle. In the economy of model building, it may be acceptable to deal with such waves by treating them as exogenous shocks; but, in a more general perspective, they need an explanation based on the knowledge of economic, social, psychological and historical factors which extends beyond the mere technical features of the model.

9.7 THE CURRENT STATE OF THE ART: SOME CRITICAL REMARKS

The hypothesis of non-perfect markets has come to significantly bear on mainstream macroeconomics. The initial conflict between the New Keynesian and the New Classical Macroeconomics has evolved into the establishment of a new synthesis, in which the analysis of credit and financial markets, based on hypotheses of some forms of imperfections and frictions, is a significant factor for the explanation of economic fluctuations, crises and recessions. Asymmetric information is the kind of imperfection that plays the most important role. The asymmetric distribution of information between lenders and borrowers makes it possible to develop the analysis of the credit and financial sector and the rationale for the existence of banks and other intermediaries in a clearer and more systematic way. It also produces analytical

---

[40] 'Keynes's *General Theory* was the progenitor of the modern behavioral finance view of asset markets' (Akerlof, 2002, p. 424).

[41] Carlin and Soskice (2015, p. 213) express well this sense of uneasiness: 'A question that may spring to mind is whether it is satisfactory to model the economy in such a way that in the upswing of the financial cycle everyone is swept up in the belief that risk has fallen – permanently. Economists do not generally like models based on "false beliefs".'

results: credit markets are intrinsically different from goods markets and interest rates are not the only significant variable for the determination of their equilibrium; the form of financing chosen by borrowers, which is contingent on their net worth, is relevant and it has important implications for the dynamics of financial cycles and their impact on the economy as a whole; the net worth of lenders too is important for the understanding of financial cycles. The importance of the net worth derives from the asymmetry of information.

Although the introduction of imperfections in general, and informational imperfections in particular, allowed macroeconomics to make some significant steps forward, it is the very notion of imperfection in economics that requires more careful consideration; something that appears to be largely missing in the current debate and that we regard as important for the possibility of further progress. That the introduction of imperfections allowed macroeconomics to make some steps forward is hardly surprising, since an imaginary, perfectly competitive economy, like that assumed by the Arrow-Debreu model, certainly is far from depicting the world in which we live. From this point of view, introducing imperfections might appear as a legitimate analytical 'stratagem', especially when concerned with policy implications. The main difficulty with such a stratagem resides in the ambiguity of the very notion of 'imperfections', which can give rise to serious misunderstandings if not properly clarified and correctly interpreted. To make our point clearer, it is useful to start from considering the way in which 'imperfections' and 'frictions' came to be introduced into macroeconomic analysis by the New Keynesians.

The New Keynesian approach to macroeconomics has its origin in the debate on the micro-foundations of macroeconomics, which developed from the question whether the 'old' Keynesian results at the macro level were compatible with the traditional hypotheses at the micro level.[42] New Classical Macroeconomics, in the wake of Monetarism, reacted to the alleged contradiction between micro and macroeconomic theory by developing micro-founded models under the assumption of maximizing agents operating in conditions of perfect competition. It has been effectively argued (for example, Solow, 1988; Hoover, 2012) that, in reality, the New Classical approach to the issue was not an attempt to give macroeconomics its missing micro-foundations, but an attempt to found macroeconomics on the corpus of a specific microeconomic theory, characterized by fully rational and omniscient agents and perfectly competitive markets.[43] Micro-foundations were not absent before; they were

---

[42] On the debate on the micro-foundations of macroeconomics, which started in the 1970s, see, for example, Harcourt (1977), Weintraub (1979), Duarte and Lima (2012), Backhouse and Boianovsky (2013) and Sardoni (2015b).

[43] See also Chapter 8, where we dealt with the issue of non eliminative micro-foundations.

present also in Keynes's *The General Theory*, but they were of a different nature.

The way in which the 'quest' for the microeconomic foundations of macroeconomics has evolved has created some ambiguities. A subtle ambiguity is about how and if the mathematical models built to design artificial 'imitation economies' in thought experiments or in computer simulations can be claimed to be images of the working of real economies. A further ambiguity is about whether these artificial economies are to be trusted to advise policy makers and central bankers on economic policies in the real world. The New Classical results might be logically consistent, but they are largely unable to give an acceptable account of the behaviour of actual economies. The New Keynesian approach, which was the reaction to the failures of New Classical Macroeconomics, is characterized by its rejection of the hypothesis of perfect competition. In these alternative models agents still operate in a fully rational way, but they face an environment with market as well as informational imperfections, which are explicitly introduced. The 'old' Keynesian models of the Neoclassical Synthesis too were contingent on the existence of imperfections, but it is pretended that in the New Keynesian models the agents' behaviour in imperfect markets is explained through coherent micro-economic foundations rather than being simply assumed (see, e.g., Blanchard, 2000, 2008). The perfectly competitive case, however, is not regarded as a hypothesis to reject and discard altogether, but as the benchmark to which the 'imperfect' case is contrasted.[44] The model that should be adopted as the conceptual instrument to study the real world is constructed by divesting the perfectly competitive, artificial benchmark of some of its characteristics (price flexibility, perfect information, etc.).

If, from an historical perspective, the New Keynesian methodological choices derive from the need to criticize the previous paradigm, in a more general perspective, the idea to compare some 'imperfect' imitation economy to a 'perfect' artificial benchmark has no solid grounds on which to rest. Even Blanchard, one of the most authoritative New Keynesian macroeconomists, has expressed his perplexity about using the perfectly competitive benchmark, but he justifies it on the grounds of easiness of communication.[45] Blanchard may be right to hold that the use of the conventional benchmark can facilitate

---

[44] The structure and organization of Blanchard and Fischer (1989) is perhaps the clearest example of this type of approach followed by New Keynesians.

[45] The 'utterly' unrealistic case of perfect competition is given the status of benchmark 'because most current research is organized in terms of what happens when one relaxes one or more assumption in that model. This may change one day. But for the time being, this approach provides a common research strategy and makes for easier communication among macroeconomic researchers' (Blanchard, 2000, p. 580n).

communication, but he underrates the conceptual difficulties and ambiguities that such a choice encounters, notably when dealing with financial markets.

Another problematic aspect of the current macroeconomic consensus is the implicit view of the basic nature of economic processes, centred on the conceptual representation of an equilibrium steady state and the deviations from it. The standard DSGE methodology is designed to study temporary divergences from the steady state equilibrium considering an 'economy' subjected to a flow of positive or negative exogenous random shocks, that is an imitation economy 'trembling', so to speak, in the vicinity of its equilibrium path. This line of approach is consistent with the belief that in the real economies of this world, as much as in the artificial economies of DSGE models, there are effective forces at work ensuring that people and markets normally are in equilibrium along steady state-trajectories. More precisely, in the background there is some entrenched idea that, in their historical evolution, the market economies normally proceed along the kind of equilibrium contemplated by these models, with minor and temporary divergences due to random disturbances that do not alter the prevailing trends. If this were the case, to regard deviations from equilibrium as due to random, essentially unpredictable, events, could be considered as an acceptable analytical stratagem. Unfortunately, there is no historical evidence to support such contention. Although market economies are not chaotic and, in fact, they experience more or less long periods of relative stability, they are prone to the recurring occurrence of serious turbulence, like during financial crises or major recessions and even during phases of 'great moderation', not to speak of the radical changes induced by historical processes such as the first industrial revolution, colonization and post colonization, automation and mass production, phases of rapid globalization and the likes.

The methodology just recalled raises two other important issues, which concern the New Classical and the real business approaches as well: i) if divergences from equilibrium depend on random exogenous shocks, macroeconomics is substantially unable to elaborate a satisfactory theory of business cycles, be a financial sector introduced or not into the model; ii) the very notion of exogenous shock is not properly defined and it certainly requires critical consideration.[46] It is quite evident that if shocks are random, there is no possibility to have a proper theory of economic fluctuations, i.e. phenomena occurring with a certain recurrence and some regularity. The problem concerning the nature and origin of shocks is even more relevant and has many implications. The basic point is that economic shocks cannot be regarded as similar to shocks (disturbances) that occur in scientific experiments. Some

---

[46] On theoretical and empirical problems connected to the use of shocks in macroeconomic models, see Duarte and Hoover (2012).

explanation of why they might occur is in order. If we exclude catastrophic shocks due to natural phenomena (earthquakes, tsunamis, etc.), other shocks, even though not strictly economic, require an explanation of their origin and role in relation to the economic context, and some insights of why and how they affect the economy's functioning. Often the phenomena defined with the ambiguous label of 'shocks' arise within the economic sphere (e.g. technological change or financial fragility), or at the junction of economic activity with other aspects of social life, and notably in connection with sociological and political evolution. Good theoretical explanations require an effort to explain 'shocks', i.e. to make them endogenous, rather than take them as something coming from a mysterious outside.

Another major issue concerns the policy advice provided on the basis of DSGE models. Recently, Stiglitz, criticizing the use of DSGE models for the implementation of monetary policy by central banks, has held that, for good policies, we need people like Stanley Fischer as a central banker rather than the use of a DSGE model. Christiano et al. (2017), commenting on Stiglitz, argued that central banks need both good DSGE models and good central bankers like Stanley Fischer. This polemic could be translated into more general terms. Models, and not necessarily DSGE models only,[47] doubtless are indispensable economists' tools for rigorous coherent reasoning and for providing quantitative estimates of the working of the economy, but in the economists' toolbox there should be other cognitive tools, equally indispensable, and not to be forgotten.

Finally, problems are raised also by the view of banks and their nature that is usually adopted in most models. A large part of the macroeconomic literature on credit shares the view that all banks are intermediaries between ultimate lenders and borrowers; a view that has been recently criticized, and a return to the 'old view' of banks as able to create additional money through credit has been advocated. The debate on this topic has not yet gained momentum, but the topic deserves more attention, as it can have important analytical and policy implications. If banks are 'active players of the game', and not just institutions that merely make the relations between ultimate savers and borrowers smoother, their impact on the economy is not only larger but also more prone to rapid and discontinuous changes.

Since the beginning of the debate that eventually led to the new Neoclassical Synthesis, a number of hypotheses and assumptions were shared by all the protagonists. In particular, all agreed on the hypothesis of fully rational and forward-looking agents. As we saw, the hypothesis of full rationality is being

---

[47] We do not enter into a thorough examination of the criticisms addressed to DSGE models. On this see, for example, the issue 1–2, Volume 34 (2018) of the *Oxford Review of Economic Policy*, Duarte (2013) and Christiano et al. (2017).

questioned by a growing number of economists, who can be defined as behavioural economists. They argue that the actual behaviour of agents can hardly be represented by the traditional assumption of rationality. Behavioural finance rejects the efficient markets hypothesis and describes the working of financial markets in a way that is not too far from Keynes's. The novelty is that behavioural analyses of markets and the agents operating in them finds support in psychological research and a large number of empirical analyses and tests. So far, however, the interaction between behavioural economics and macroeconomics has not been particularly effective, even though there are some interesting contributions that go in this direction. De Grauwe (2012), for example, develops a macroeconomic model which embodies several features of behavioural economics and, in particular, gives an important role to play to changes of the 'animal spirits' endogenously generated.[48] The next concluding chapter is devoted to exploring alternative and more satisfactory approaches to the analysis of the role played by banks and other financial institutions in their interrelation with the real sector.

---

[48] For general considerations on the relation between macroeconomics and behavioural economics, see Akerlof (2002). Also the mainstream is devoting some attention to the construction of models that are not necessarily based on the traditional hypothesis of rational expectations (see, e.g., Woodford, 2013).

10. Conclusions

In looking at how the treatment of banks and finance in a macroeconomic perspective evolved during the 20th century to the present, several have divided this span of time into three periods: the period until the mid-1930s when banks and credit relations were at the core of many major economists' theories and analyses; the period between the publication of Keynes's *General Theory* and the 1980s, when credit and financial markets ceased to be at the centre-stage of macroeconomic analysis, if they did not disappear completely; the period from the late 1980s to the present, characterized by a renewed interest in the interrelations between the real and financial sectors of the economy. In the book we have adopted the same temporal subdivision and tried to explain why macroeconomics evolved in such a way. The main results of our attempt are briefly summarized in this concluding chapter, which also offers some suggestions and indications for further developments.

10.1 BANKS UNTIL THE 1930s: TWO APPROACHES

Although until the 1930s most economists put banks at the centre-stage of their analyses, they did so for different theoretical reasons. We have singled out two major lines of approach to the problems of credit and debt relations. On the one hand, there was the attempt to develop and generalize the quantity theory of money in the context of well developed market economies, where banks played a growing role both in the management of the system of payments and in the financing of productive activities. Wicksell and Fisher, considered in Chapter 2, two eminent representatives of this line of analysis. Wicksell introduced the notion of a pure credit economy in which banks operate in such a way that their lending is not constrained by their deposits. The banks' behaviour represents a major driver of his cumulative processes. Fisher firmly restated the quantity theory of money as a scientific proposition, with much attention to credit and endogenous bank money. He analysed the transition periods after a monetary shock, considering the banks' strategic behaviour, the variability of the reserve coefficient and the ratio of currency to deposit.

The other line of approach to credit and banks is well represented by the positions taken by Schumpeter and Robertson. Neither of them was particularly interested in the determination of the price level per se. Their main concern was the analysis of the role of credit and banks in dynamic processes of change and both saw banks as central and indispensable actors in such processes. Banks, with their ability to create purchasing power *ex nihilo*, are the agents that make it possible for the economy to undergo dynamic processes of change, be they a long-period process of growth or short-period economic fluctuations.

Schumpeter's and Robertson's view of the banking system, which was close to Wicksell's, was at the time prevailing among economists; but there already existed an alternative position, which will become dominant later on. According to this different view, the individual banks' ability to lend and create money is strictly constrained by the amount of deposits that they can collect. It is the banking system as a whole that can create additional money with respect to the currency issued by the central bank (the money multiplier). In this perspective, banks are given a significantly less important role to play and are regarded as mere intermediaries between savers and borrowers. It is the central bank that ultimately determines the amount of money in circulation.

In 1930, in *A Treatise on Money*, which might be regarded as another attempt to provide a more satisfactory version of the quantity theory of money, Keynes, on the one hand, carried out his general analysis of banks by following an approach not dissimilar from Wicksell's, Schumpeter's and Robertson's; but, on the other hand, in carrying out his analysis of the determination of the general price level, he ended up to regard banks as mere intermediaries between savers and borrowers: they lend what they have borrowed from savers. In this framework, although the existence of banks makes the determination of the general price level more complex, it does not imply any fundamental difference from the results that would be obtained in a world without banks.

We argued that Keynes's choice was essentially motivated by his urge to stress the crucial importance of the economy's degree of bearishness (liquidity preference) expressed as demand for idle money. In *The General Theory*, Keynes further developed his notion of liquidity preference by grounding his theory of the interest rate on it and by stressing, more strongly than in *A Treatise*, the relation between liquidity and defence from uncertainty. Keynes's analysis was now carried out without considering banks, seen as a complication that can be ignored to convey the importance of more fundamental ideas and novelties with respect to his previous works. Moreover, with Keynes's abandonment of the dynamic approach adopted in *A Treatise* in favour of the equilibrium method of *The General Theory*, banks and credit became even less analytically relevant.

However, in his earlier writings, and notably in the early 1930s, Keynes, in considering the destabilizing effect of severe deflation, was well aware of the impact that it has on the financial sector and the consequent negative effects on the economy as a whole. Keynes's deep distrust of price deflation as an adjustment mechanism for the maintenance of full employment is in the background of his mature vision of involuntary unemployment. In the recession years, Fisher shared the same distrust. In his debt-deflation theory he pointed to out-of-equilibrium dynamic paths that can push the economy into a severe recession, which further deflation aggravates instead of curing. Both Fisher and Keynes were worried about financial fragility and the risk to have financial crises turning into severe deflationary spirals.

10.2 FROM *THE GENERAL THEORY* TO REAL BUSINESS CYCLES

In the history of macroeconomics and, more generally, in the history of economics, the publication of *The General Theory* represents a watershed from several different viewpoints; we have concentrated on those aspects that are more relevant to our research project. In this sense the debate on the theory of the interest rate, which saw the contrast between Keynes's liquidity preference theory and the loanable funds theory, is relevant for several reasons, both theoretical and methodological.

The advocates of the loanable funds theory criticized and rejected Keynes's emphasis on money as a special asset as the demand for idle money represents the economy's aversion to spend. As an alternative, they argued in favour of a theory of the interest rate based on the demand and supply of credit. The debate, which went on until the 1950s, led to a somewhat paradoxical eventual outcome. The dispute on liquidity preference vs loanable funds eventually ended with the appeal to carry out the analysis within a general-equilibrium framework, where the two approaches to the determination of the interest rate appear to be interchangeable with one another. In this context, however, the loanable funds theory was analysed and illustrated by referring only to the market for bonds and ignoring banks as well as other forms of financial intermediation. Keynes's underrating of banks and financial intermediation, criticized for example by Robertson and Ohlin in the 1930s, remained unchallenged.

The general-equilibrium approach soon came to be regarded as the framework in which proper macroeconomic analysis should be carried out; the IS-LM model itself was nothing but a simplified version of a general-equilibrium model. At the same time, the difficulties to introduce money, banks and finance into a Walrasian environment became evident. Patinkin, who was the earliest and most representative scholar to propose the general-equilibrium approach to macroeconomics, perceived these difficulties clearly. The solution he offered in his major work *Money, Interest and Prices*, sanctioned an approach to the financial side of the economy as collapsed into a single perfectly competitive market for bonds.

The critical debate on Keynes's liquidity preference did not only 'forget' banks; it also essentially overlooked another important concern of Keynes's, which was the main reason for his concentration on liquidity preference, that is to say, the problem of uncertainty and how economic agents cope with it. In a way which we regard as a possible alternative to his liquidity theory, Keynes offered a lucid analysis of how financial markets work and affect the real economy in a world characterized by ineliminable, or radical, uncertainty. For a very long time, this aspect of Keynes's analysis was ignored by the mainstream by making the assumption that financial markets cannot work other than smoothly.

We single out two main approaches that defied this dominant line of development in macroeconomics: Gurley's and Shaw's attempt to build an articulate theory of finance and Tobin's efforts to go beyond what he named the 'Keynes-Patinkin model'. Tobin, influenced by Gurley and Shaw, tried to develop the analysis of financial markets in a genuine general equilibrium framework, where they interact with the real sector, namely through investment decisions. His line of research was not successful and, on the whole, remained at the margin of the mainstream.

The subsequent developments of macroeconomics kept on ignoring banks altogether, or regarding them as merely passive agents, which 'multiply', in a mechanistic way, the currency created by the central bank. This sort of attitude towards the financial sectors of the economy was shared by most macroeconomic models, including those of the Keynesians, the anti-Keynesian monetarists and those of the New Classical Macroeconomics. Their analytical focus was on the central bank's decisions about the supply of (hard) money. But in dealing with money itself the same difficulties encountered in the original Walrasian models emerged in the new Arrow-Debreu framework, even though they were largely underrated, or ignored altogether. The eventual outcome essentially was the abandonment of any pretence to give money a significant role to play in standard macroeconomic models. From Lucas's initial recourse to 'monetary surprises' to explain deviations from equilibrium, macroeconomics arrived at ignoring money altogether and arguing that, after all, money is not so important to understand the fundamental features of economic dynamics. In the real business cycle approach, technological shocks are seen as the fundamental drivers of the economy's fluctuations.

10.3 FROM MARKET IMPERFECTION TO THE NEW NEOCLASSICAL SYNTHESIS

Both monetary surprises and technological shocks proved unable to give a reasonable account of economic fluctuations in the world in which we live. The failure of such attempts to explain fluctuations gave impetus to the emerging of a new approach to macroeconomics, based on the abandonment of the hypothesis of perfectly competitive markets and, in particular, of perfect and complete information, which is of particular importance for the analysis of credit and financial markets. The adoption of the hypothesis of imperfect and asymmetric information is more congenial to the analysis of banks and finance and their interaction with the real sector of the economy.

The imperfect information hypothesis, along with the urge generated by the world financial crisis of the late 2000s, favoured the flourishing of many works concerned with the macroeconomic interactions between the financial and real sectors of the economy. In contrast to what happened in post-war macroeconomics, nowadays it is hard to find mainstream macroeconomic models that do not incorporate, in one way or another, some form of financial intermediation. Credit rationing, the accelerating effects of the financial sectors on the economy's fluctuations, some attention to the complexity of the financial sector characterize most of the current macroeconomic literature which mainly deals with such topics by using DSGE models, generally regarded as the most adequate available analytical tool.

The need for considering 'imperfect' economies, initially championed by the New Keynesian Economics, after a period of conflict with the previously dominant macroeconomic paradigm, has led to the emerging of the so-called new Neoclassical Synthesis, which can be defined as the previous New Classical and real business cycles approaches with the addition of market and informational imperfections. The general theoretical environment within which the analysis is carried out is still a general-equilibrium inter-temporal world, populated by maximizing agents, who respond rationally to shocks in markets that now are imperfect and incomplete.

The introduction of 'imperfections' and 'frictions' allowed macroeconomics to make some steps forward in the analysis of the actual functioning of the economy. Something that is hardly surprising, since an imaginary, perfectly competitive economy, like that assumed by the Arrow-Debreu model, certainly is far from depicting the world in which we live. Credit and financial markets are no longer totally absent from macroeconomic models. The interaction between the financial and real sectors can be dealt with less uneasily than in the past. Introducing imperfections may appear as a legitimate analytical 'stratagem', especially when dealing with policy implications. These results, however, should not be contemplated with complacency. Important crucial issues are still open and in need for further reflection and developments to arrive at a more satisfactory theoretical and analytical capacity to deal with finance in market economies. We argue in Chapter 9 that the main difficulties encountered by the current mainstream essentially derive from its still strong connection to the previously dominant paradigm and the excessively simplistic approach to issues like the very notion of imperfections and the use of exogenous shocks to explain phenomena that require deeper and richer analyses.

10.4   SOME CONCLUDING CONSIDERATIONS

Our historical reconstruction of the evolution of macroeconomics does not aim to have a mere antiquarian value. Our objective essentially is to call attention to a number of critical issues and problems raised by the way in which the discipline evolved over time. In this sense, the insights from the history of economic ideas are relevant. They evoke aspects such as the sequential nature of monetary transactions and the role of the standard of value; the role of finance in economic growth; the role of institutions in financial markets and financial innovation; banks and other financial intermediaries as strategic actors in market economies; the dynamic paths which do not converge towards equilibrium trajectories; the episodes of severe crises or periods of low growth; the non conventional aspects of economic choices, when people face radical uncertainty and incomplete information.

In this perspective, a crucial issue is the 'troubled marriage' of macroeconomics with general equilibrium theory since Patinkin's early efforts in the 1950s. The model of a perfectly competitive economy keeps on being regarded as the benchmark for 'imperfect' models. Even Stiglitz (2018), though strongly polemical with the current mainstream, makes recourse to this benchmark. However, the very notion of a perfectly-competitive benchmark raises questions. Is it still the Arrow-Debreu model of the late 1950s? Or should it be the later model of Brock and Mirman, which is not a general equilibrium model since it does not include heterogeneous agents and multiple goods? Why should a representative-agent model be considered equivalent to a general equilibrium one and how may it stage competition if its fictional agents do not compete with each other but are isolated hermits with no need to trade? Why should such fictional economy be adopted as the standard in building explanations and suggesting policy advice?

In any attempt to answer these questions in a rigorous way it appears perfectly clear that the Arrow-Debreu model is plagued by both analytical and conceptual difficulties. It does not provide a unique solution and it cannot provide demonstrations of converging dynamics towards equilibrium. It cannot support the presence of money other than as a numeraire; it cannot include financial markets. The auctioneer assumption on which it is built cannot be removed. On further inquiry it appears that the representative agent model is not equivalent to the multi-agents, multi-goods general equilibrium model, unless very restrictive assumptions are made. It is well known that aggregation is a very difficult technical issue, and no equivalence theorem can be reasonably proven.[1] An assessment of the current situation should then conclude that in economic theory there is no satisfactory benchmark model of perfectly competitive markets, which may stand as the polar star.

As far as the Arrow-Debreu world is concerned, imperfections and frictions cannot be added to it. It is a delicate castle of cards and removing perfect information, farsighted rationality, the auctioneer, and so on makes it immediately collapse. As historical inquiry teaches, the perfect equilibrium world of the Arrow-Debreu model is the result of a selection of assumptions to isolate its conceptual skeleton from any contamination, so that no addition of imperfections can be made if it has to stand. The Arrow-Debreu model is the result of the quest for the conceptual coherence of the Walrasian theory started in the 1920s and 1930s, but Walras himself had carefully refined his model to this purpose in the various editions of the *Éléments*. If one wants to go beyond conceptual coherence and address the problem of the credibility of images of perfect competition in relation to competition in the actual world, it is important to acknowledge that, in the history of economics, the idea of perfect competition belongs to the sphere of normative rather than positive economics. In Walras's theory, notably, it corresponds to the normative ideal of justice in trade as distinguished from the normative ideal of distributive justice.

To state that something is 'imperfect', or behaves imperfectly, implies that it differs, at least in some respect, from something else that is 'perfect', or it behaves perfectly. And then, it would be necessary to explain how the alleged perfect economy morphed to an imperfect one. How could, for example, small independent price-taker firms that react to market signals in a purely passive way become large market-maker firms, which behave strategically and 'make' the market? Or, how could the agents's perfect information become imperfect? If anything, the agents' degree of information should have increased rather than diminished.

The problem is that there does not exist, and never existed, a perfect economy to contrast to the imperfect economy of our experience. In fact, it cannot even be argued that sometime in the past, market economies operated in a competitive regime that resembled the perfect-competition abstraction to a significant extent. Competitive markets were never perfect in an Arrow-Debreu sense. Even the more or less freely competitive markets, as they might be characterized for example by the existence of many independent agents, too small to influence prices or other variables, cannot be legitimately depicted as perfectly competitive markets at the theoretical level.

---

[1]   On the problem of aggregation, see for example Martel (1996), and Forni and Lippi (1997).

The way out of these dead ends is, in our opinion, to follow a radically alternative approach to the problem of competition. It is the line that can be traced back to Classical Political Economy, Marx, Schumpeter and Hayek.[2] In this tradition, free competition is not the static world of the neoclassical perfect competition; it is a dynamic environment in which firms operate strategically to maximize profits and gain market shares, first of all through all sorts of innovations. As Hayek observed, competition is a discovery procedure in a dynamic environment. It is this dynamic environment that eventually produces large firms that directly affect prices and control markets; firms themselves create 'imperfections' and 'differentiations' for the purpose of gaining a better market position and larger profits. 'Imperfections' are not the result of 'subtractions' from the perfectly competitive benchmark; they rather are the outcome of the competitive process itself. On the grounds of this notion of the competitive process, for Schumpeter, the 'imperfect' case should be regarded as the general one and the perfectly competitive case as well as that of pure monopoly should be considered as limiting cases (Schumpeter, 1954[2006], pp. 938–951).

What is more relevant in the present context is that the competitive dynamic process is inherently related to the existence of banks, and possibly other financial institutions, which are themselves strategic firms operating for the purpose to maximize their profits. If this is the case, credit, banks, and other forms of financial intermediation are not something that is introduced into the analytical framework only after some forms of imperfection are admitted. They are an essential element for the working of the competitive engine. Banks, far from being mere intermediaries between savers and borrowers, are active strategic agents (a visible hand) which, through the creation of money, represent a crucial element of the process of change and growth as well as of the phases of crisis, when they may contribute to accelerate and worsen the negative dynamics of the economy.

Another radical question revolves around the vision of dynamics as a steady-state equilibrium at the exclusion, or marginalization, of out-of-equilibrium dynamic adjustment processes. The conceptual structure of dynamic models in contemporary macroeconomics has its technical roots in Frisch's formalization of the rocking chair idea. It has, more in general, its cultural roots in the Walrasian heritage of equilibrium economics. The use of models based on the equilibrium-plus-shocks dyad is only apparently methodological. Models are, so it seems, engineering devices to deal with simulations and statistical evidence; in fact, the dyad has become a hypostasis: a property attributed to

---

[2] See Sardoni (2011, pp. 132–137) for some considerations about the differences between the Marxian-Schumpeterian and the New Keynesian approaches to perfect and imperfect competition. See Ingrao (2013, pp. 509–511) for Hayek's idea of competition.

the underlying structure of the economic processes in market economies on the basis of an almost metaphysical vision. Models are regarded as if they were the essence of the economic world more than a technical tool to be used within proper limits. The dyad can blind economists, blocking their search for more satisfactory explanations of the complex phenomena of finance, growth and fluctuations.

Again, a possible way out from such difficulties can be found in a different and alternative interpretation of the fundamental nature of the capitalist economic process, which is not seen as an essentially orderly and smooth process, episodically disturbed by unpredictable events, but as a process taking place in an environment in which disequilibria, which exist and may persist, are the outcome of endogenous forces at work. The nature of the behaviour of the main agents in the economy is such that they endogenously produce out-of-equilibrium phenomena in their market interaction, as much as in their social interaction at large. In this respect, various theoretical lines appear relevant: the Keynesian tradition, the Fisherian tradition, Schumpeter's emphasis on innovation and change, or the more recent behavioural approach to economics.

Keynes's analysis and the line of approach represented by the work of Minsky, considered in Chapter 9, explain the inherent instability of capitalist economies by recourse to the radically uncertain environment in which they operate: agents try to cope with uncertainty through the adoption of conventions, which however are fragile and doomed to break. The behavioural approach goes further in the analysis of the economic agents by using psychological, but sometimes also social and historical, explanations of why they behave in such a way that markets, and the economy as a whole, are subject to phases of booms and busts. In both approaches, the succession of waves of optimism and pessimism plays a crucial role as an explanatory factor of the economy's dynamics. The phases of 'optimism' create the conditions for subsequent phases of 'pessimism'. For example, excessive indebtedness due to a fall in the agents' risk aversion that leads to crises of liquidity or solvency.

Authoritative economists like Fisher and Hicks, even though studying business cycles, deny the existence of proper cycles in the historical experience; they suggest to look at episodes of recession in their historical complexity. Schumpeter looks at business cycles within the sociological perspective of the long-term evolution of market economies. Thanks to all these insights, economists should be aware of the complexity of historical explanation when addressing monetary instability, financial fragility, or financial crises.

In the light of our inquiry, here we sketch a few specific themes, which emerge as of major relevance for macroeconomic research. The first one is the link between stocks and flows out of steady states and in dynamic change. Along out-of-equilibrium trajectories, the disequilibrium of stocks affects the income flows. The perception of the volatile valuations of assets and debts in private wealth, or in the portfolios of financial intermediaries, affects consumption and investment choices, as much as it influences expectations and portfolio choices. When agents in the economy perceive the burden of private debts or the market value of wealth assets as in severe disequilibrium, or anticipate severe disequilibrium, the related adjustment processes have persistent effects on balance sheets and, consequently, on the macro-economy. Complex interactions of the value of stocks with flow dynamics cannot be cancelled under simplified aggregation assumption or smooth equilibrium theorems. In this respect, the contributions coming from Tobin and Minsky are important.

As a second and related subject, the temporal frame of macroeconomic analysis should be thoroughly revisited. The conventional distinction between short and long period of Marshallian descent is inadequate to take into account the more complex interactions of the real and the financial sides. This distinction is as inadequate as the dyad steady-state plus shocks. The dynamic paths which involve money and finance together with real changes create phenomena of path dependency and hysteresis. Short-period disequilibria may turn into low growth traps affecting human and physical capital, capacity for innovation, institutional stability, international relations or trade specialization. When the economic 'ship' capsizes, there is no easy going back to a postulated steady state. The ship may perhaps not sink, but it may be wearing because its full-employment capacity is not restored to its previous levels. Cases of path dependency and hysteresis characterize most economic phenomena; in the book we have naturally concentrated on those more directly related to recession and financial crises by referring especially to the contributions of Fisher and Keynes.

In historical processes of change, the short and the long period are not so neatly distinguished; their times slide and merge. Crucial passages may turn the immediate events into long-term radical rupture, or the long, progressive erosion of institutional roots may evolve into drastic breaks and changes. In the history of nations the real forces of 'industry', 'ingenuity', 'resources', 'economic and political organization' are certainly affected by major financial disasters, by the paralysis of the system of payments or the collapse of financial institutions, by prolonged inflationary or deflationary spirals, by long periods of persistent unemployment.

As an additional reflection on the same set of issues, it has to be stressed the importance of taking into account the institutional aspects of monetary regimes and financial markets, with due attention to detailed institutional structure, the practices embedded in the way financial institutions work. The expectations about other people's behaviour or about policy makers' stance are of major relevance in the dynamic evolution of the economy during financial crises. Monetary regimes and the financial structure belong to the political and institutional structure, on which opportunities of real growth depend. They should be of primary interest in macroeconomics not just insofar they are portrayed in more or less fictional models, but in the direct knowledge of their networks and market structure, their strategies for innovation and their standards of behaviour. From this point of view, Schumpeter's analysis of banks as well as Friedman's and Schwartz's monetary history of the U.S. are examples to follow.

The last, but not least, crucial theme is the analysis of actual economic behaviour versus micro-foundations constructed under the assumption of Olympian rationality. The alternative to the perfect rationality of far-sighted agents optimizing over infinite horizons is not irrationality *tout court*. It is neither madness nor stupidity: it is bounded rationality, interpreted as the intelligent human response in an environment of radical uncertainty and limited information. Incomplete, asymmetric information, far from being a 'friction' to be added, is intrinsic to human knowledge and action. As Hayek underlined, Reason with a capital R does not exist in human societies; the division of knowledge is a central characteristic of market economies against the pretence of knowledge that nurtures totalitarian dreams. Both for Hayek and for Schumpeter incomplete information is the incubator of innovation through the operation of competition. Uncertainty if recognized suggests the adoption of intelligent strategies to face the possible failures of our best plans; strategies that may fail or succeed. Current developments in behavioural economics seem to move in the same direction.

The main problem with the lines of research which these themes suggest is that it is difficult to translate and embody historical change, the intricacies of human intelligent response and initiative, the formation of expectations in conditions of radical uncertainty, into analytical models. The ambition to capture these complexities into some simplified formal scaffolding would be a further, dangerous pretence of knowledge. This difficulty is not a minor one given the current state of affairs in macroeconomics, which essentially considers models as the only proper way to approach economic problems. It is a matter of convincing a significant part of the profession that a more satisfactory analysis of the dynamics of the economy cannot be looked for only through models, although they may be very sophisticated, but it requires a variety of intellectual tools and combined efforts to explore the complex reality at various and different levels. If it is true that, for example, it is arduous to elaborate a fully endogenous explanation of waves of optimism and pessimism, or the change over time of the 'animal spirits', this does not mean that it is impossible to provide acceptable and rigorous explanations of such waves by recourse to other instruments, like analyses that take advantage of historical, social, or political knowledge.

The understanding and explanation of money and finance in their complex links to phases of growth or recurring fluctuations, to booms and busts or severe crises call for the integrated set of learned knowledge at the disposal of the economist. In light of these considerations, let us conclude by observing that one tool that economists should put in their box should be a good knowledge of the way in which economic ideas have evolved and changed over time, to understand the roots of the present state of affairs, the dead ends emerging in research programmes, the reasons why, in certain periods, views alternative to the dominant paradigm did not prevail. Despite their failure, their insights may be important and still worth consideration today. Our book, we hope, can be a contribution in this direction.

Bibliography

Adrian, T. and Shin, H. S. (2010), 'The changing nature of financial intermediation and the financial crisis of 2007–2009,' *Annual Review of Economics*, **2010** (2), 603–618.

Adrian, T. and Shin, H. S. (2011), 'Financial intermediaries and monetary economics,' in B. M. Friedman and M. Woodford (eds.), *Handbook of Monetary Economics*, Amsterdam: North Holland, vol. 3A, pp. 601–650.

Akerlof, G. A. (2002), 'Behavioral macroeconomics and macroeconomic behavior,' *American Economic Review*, **92** (3), 411–433.

Akerlof, G. A. and Shiller, R. J. (2015), *Phishing for Fools*, Princeton: Princeton University Press.

Arrow, K. J. (1967), 'Samuelson Collected,' *Journal of Political Economy*, **75** (5), 730–737.

Arrow, K. J. (1974), 'Limited knowledge and economic analysis,' *American Economic Review*, **64** (1), 1–10.

Arrow, K. J. (2009), 'Some developments in economic theory since 1940: An eyewitness account,' *Review of Economics*, **1** (1), 1–16.

Arrow, K. J. and Hahn, F. H. (1971), *General Competitive Analysis*, San Francisco: Holden-Day Inc.

Backhouse, R. E. and Boianovsky, M. (2013), *Transforming Modern Macroeconomics*, Cambridge: Cambridge University Press.

Baranzini, M. (2005), *Léon Walras e la moneta senza velo*, Torino: UTET.

Barro, R. J. and Grossman, H. I. (1971), 'A general disequilibrium model of income and employment,' *American Economic Review*, **61** (1), 82–93.

Benhabib, J. and Spiegel, M. (2000), 'The role of financial development in growth and investment,' *Journal of Economic Growth*, **5** (4), 341–360.

Bernanke, B. S. (1983), 'Nonmonetary effects of the financial crisis in the propagation of the Great Depression,' *American Economic Review*, **73** (3), 257–276.

Bernanke, B. S. (1995), 'The macroeconomics of the Great Depression: A comparative approach,' *Journal of Money, Credit and Banking*, **27** (1), 16–29.

Bernanke, B. S. and Blinder, A. S. (1988), 'Credit, money, and aggregate demand,' *American Economic Review*, **78** (2), 435–439.

Bernanke, B. S. and Gertler, M. (1989), 'Agency costs, net worth, and business fluctuations,' *American Economic Review*, **79** (1), 14–31.

Bernanke, B. S., Gertler, M. and Gilchrist, S. (1999a), 'The financial accelerator in a quantitative business cycle framework,' in J. Taylor and M. Woodford (eds.), *Handbook of Macroeconomics*, Amsterdam: North Holland, pp. 1341–1393.

Bernanke, B. S., Laubach, T., Mishkin, F. S. and Posen, A. S. (1999b), *Inflation Targeting*, Princeton and Oxford: Princeton University Press.

Berti, L. and Messori, M. (eds.) (1996), *Trattato della moneta capitoli inediti*, Napoli: Edizioni Scientifiche Italiane.

Bhaduri, A. (2011), 'A contribution to the theory of financial fragility and crisis,' *Cambridge Journal of Economics*, **35** (6), 995–1014.

Bhattacharya, S., Boot, A. W. A. and Thakor, A. V. (eds.) (2004), *Credit, Intermediation, and the Macroeconomy*, New York: Oxford University Press.

Bianco, A. and Sardoni, C. (2018), 'Banking theories and macroeconomics,' *Journal of Post Keynesian Economics*, https://doi.org/10.1080/01603477.2017.1408418, 1–20.

Blanchard, O. J. (2000), 'What do we know about macroeconomics that Fisher and Wicksell did not?' *De Economist*, **148** (5), 571–601.

Blanchard, O. J. (2008), 'The state of macro,' Working Paper 14259, National Bureau of Economic Research, Cambridge Ma.

Blanchard, O. J. and Fischer, S. (1989), *Lectures on Macroeconomics*, Cambridge Ma.: MIT Press.

Boianovsky, M. (1995), 'Wicksell's business cycle,' *European Journal of the History of Economic Thought*, **2** (2), 375–411.

Boianovsky, M. (2013), 'Fisher and Wicksell on money: A reconstructed conversation,' *European Journal of the History of Economic Thought*, **20** (2), 206–237.

Boianovsky, M. (2018), 'Cambridge anticipations of the natural rate hypothesis? Robertson and Champernowne revisited,' CHOPE Working Paper 2018–09, Center for the History of Political Economy at Duke University, Durham.

Boldyrev, I. and Ushakov, A. (2016), 'Adjusting the model to adjust the world: Constructive mechanisms in postwar general equilibrium theory,' *Journal of Economic Methodology*, **23** (1), 38–56.

Borio, C. (2014), 'The financial cycle and macroeconomics: What have we learnt?' *Journal of Banking and Finance*, **45** (12), 182–198.

Borio, C., Erdem, M., Filardo, A. and Hofmann, B. (2015), 'The costs of deflations: A historical perspective,' *BIS Quarterly Review*, March, 31–54.

Brainard, W. C. and Tobin, J. (1968), 'Pitfalls in financial model building,' *American Economic Review*, **58** (2), 99–122.

Bridel, P. (1987), *Cambridge Monetary Thought*, New York: Palgrave Macmillan.

Bridel, P. (1997), *Money and General Equilibrium Theory: From Walras to Pareto (1870–1923)*, Aldershot: Edward Elgar Publishing.

Brock, W. and Mirman, L. (1972), 'Optimal economic growth and uncertainty: The discounted case,' *Journal of Economic Theory*, **4** (3), 479–513.

Brunner, K. (1970), 'The "monetarist revolution" in monetary theory,' *Review of World Economics*, **105** (1), 1–30.

Brunner, K. and Meltzer, A. H. (1971), 'The uses of money: Money in the theory of an exchange economy,' *American Economic Review*, **61** (5), 784–805.

Brunnermeier, M. K. and Eisenbach, T. M. (2012), 'Macroeconomics with financial frictions: A survey,' Working Paper 18102, NBER, Cambridge Ma.

Buiter, W. H. (2003), 'James Tobin: An appreciation of his contribution to economics,' *Economic Journal*, **113** (491), 585–631.

Cannan, E. (1921), 'The meaning of bank deposits,' *Economica*, (1), 28–36.

Carlin, W. and Soskice, D. (2015), *Macroeconomics. Institutions, Instability and the Financial System*, Oxford: Oxford University Press.

Cassel, G. (1932), *The Theory of Social Economy*, London: E. Benn Ltd, new revised edition, translated by S. L. Barron.

Chiodi, G. (1991), *Wicksell's Monetary Theory*, New York: Palgrave Macmillan.

Christiano, L. J., Motto, R. and Rostagno, M. (2014), 'Risk shocks,' *American Economic Review*, **104** (1), 27–65.

Christiano, L. J., Eichenbaum, M. S. and Trabandt, M. (2017), 'On DSGE models,' Manuscript.

Colander, D., Holt, R. P. F. and Rosser, J. B., Jr (2004), 'The changing face of mainstream economics,' *Review of Political Economy*, **16** (4), 485–499.

Costabile, L. (2005), 'Money, cycles and capital formation: von Mises the "Austrian" vs. Robertson the "Dynamist",' *Cambridge Journal of Economics*, **29** (5), 685–707.

Crick, W. F. (1927), 'The genesis of bank deposits,' *Economica*, (20), 191–202.

Culbertson, J. M. (1958), 'Intermediaries and monetary theory: A criticism of the Gurley-Shaw theory,' *American Economic Review*, **48** (1), 119–131.

Dal-Pont Legrand, M. and Hagemann, H. (2016), 'Business cycles, growth and economic policy: Schumpeter and the Great Depression,' Working Paper 2016–16, GREDEG.

De Grauwe, P. (2012), *Lectures on Behavioral Macroeconomics*, Princeton, N.J.: Princeton University Press.

De Long, J. B. (2000), 'The triumph of Monetarism?' *Journal of Economic Perspectives*, **14** (1), 83–94.

De Vroey, M. (2016), *A History of Macroeconomics from Keynes to Lucas and Beyond*, New York: Cambridge University Press.

De Vroey, M. and Duarte, P. G. (2013), 'In search of lost time: The neoclassical synthesis,' *B. E. Journal of Macroeconomics*, **13** (1), 965–995.

Debreu, G. (1959), *Theory of Value. An axiomatic analysis of economic equilibrium*, Cowles Foundation for Research in Economics at Yale University. Monograph. no. 17, New York: John Wiley & Sons.

Dimand, R. W. (2003), 'Irving Fisher on the international transmission of booms and depressions through monetary standards,' *Journal of Money, Credit and Banking*, **35** (1), 49–90.

Dimand, R. W. (2004), 'James Tobin and the transformation of the IS-LM model,' *History of Political Economy*, **36** (Suppl_1), 165–189.

Dimand, R. W. (2005), 'Fisher, Keynes, and the corridor of stability,' *American Journal of Economics and Sociology*, **64** (1), 185–199.

Dimand, R. W. (2014), *James Tobin*, London: Palgrave Macmillan.

Dixon, H. and Rankin, N. (1995a), 'Imperfect competition and macroeconomics: A survey,' in H. Dixon and N. Rankin (eds.), *The New Macroeconomics*, Cambridge: Cambridge University Press, pp. 34–62.

Dixon, H. D. and Rankin, N. (1995b), 'Introduction,' in H. D. Dixon and N. Rankin (eds.), *The New Macroeconomics*, Cambridge: Cambridge University Press, pp. 1–11.

Dixon, H. D. and Rankin, N. (eds.) (1995c), *The New Macroeconomics. Imperfect markets and policy effectiveness*, Cambridge: Cambridge University Press.

Domar, E. D. (1946), 'Capital expansion, rate of growth and employment,' *Econometrica*, **14** (2), 137–147.

Duarte, P. G. (2013), 'Recent developments in macroeconomics: the DSGE approach to business cycles in perspective,' in J. B. Davis (ed.), *The Elgar Companion to Recent Economic Methodology*, Cheltenham: Edward Elgar Publishing, pp. 375–403.

Duarte, P. G. and Hoover, K. D. (2012), 'Observing shocks,' *History of Political Economy*, **44** (Winter Supplement), 226–249.

Duarte, P. G. and Lima, G. T. (eds.) (2012), *Microfoundations Reconsidered*, Cheltenham: Edward Elgar Publishing.

Düppe, T. and Weintraub, E. R. (2014), *Finding Equilibrium. Arrow, Debreu, McKenzie and the Problem of Scientific Credit*, Princeton: Princeton University Press.

Eggertsson, G. B. and Krugman, P. (2012), 'Debt, deleveraging, and the liquidity trap: A Fisher-Minsky-Koo approach,' *Quarterly Journal of Economics*, **127** (3), 1469–1513.

Eichengreen, B. (2015), *Hall of Mirrors. The Great Depression, the Great Recession and the Uses – and Misuses – of History*, Oxford and New York: Oxford University Press.

Enthoven, A. C. (1960), 'Mathematical appendix: A neo-classical model of money, debt and economic growth,' in J. C. Gurley, and E. S. Shaw, *Money in a Theory of Finance*, Washington: The Brooking Institution, pp. 303–359.

Fama, E. F. (1970), 'Efficient capital markets: A review of theory and empirical work,' *Journal of Finance*, **25** (2), 383–417.

Festré, A. (2002), 'Money, banking and dynamics: Two Wicksellian routes from Mises to Hayek and Schumpeter,' *American Journal of Economics and Sociology*, **61** (2), 439–480.

Festré, A. and Nasica, E. (2009), 'Schumpeter on money, banking and finance: an institutionalist perspective,' *European Journal of the History of Economic Thought*, **16** (2), 325–356.

Fisher, I. (1896), *Appreciation and Interest*, vol. XI-4 of *Publications of the American Economic Association*, New York: Macmillan.

Fisher, I. (1922), *The Purchasing Power of Money*, New York: Macmillan, 2nd edn., first edition 1911.

Fisher, I. (1930a), *The Stock Market Crash – And After*, New York: Macmillan.

Fisher, I. (1930b), 'The stock market panic in 1929,' *Journal of the American Statistical Association*, **25** (169), 93–96.

Fisher, I. (1932), *Booms and Depressions: Some First Principles*, New York: Adelphi Company.

Fisher, I. (1933), 'The debt-deflation theory of great depressions,' *Econometrica*, **1** (4), 337–357.

Forni, M. and Lippi, M. (1997), *Aggregation and the Microfoundations of Dynamic Macroeconomics*, Oxford: Clarendon Press.

Friedman, B. (1999), 'The future of monetary policy: The central bank as an army with only a signal corps?' *International Finance*, **2** (3), 321–338.

Friedman, M. (1953), 'The case for flexible exchange rates,' in *Essays in Positive Economics*, Chicago: University of Chicago Press, pp. 157–203.

Friedman, M. (1956), *Studies in the Quantity Theory of Money*, Chicago: University of Chicago Press.

Friedman, M. (1959a), 'The demand for money: Some theoretical and empirical results,' *Journal of Political Economy*, **67** (4), 327–351.

Friedman, M. (1959b), *A Program for Monetary Stability*, New York: Fordham University Press.

Friedman, M. (1965), 'A program for monetary stability,' in M. D. Ketchum and L. T. Kendall (eds.), *Readings in Financial Institutions*, Boston: Houghton Mifflin, pp. 189–209. Quotations from the digital edition at https://miltonfriedman.hoover.org/.

Friedman, M. (1968), 'The role of monetary policy,' *American Economic Journal*, **58** (1), 1–17.

Friedman, M. (1970), 'The counter-revolution in monetary theory,' Occasional paper, Institute of Economic Affairs, London.

Friedman, M. (1972), 'Comment on the critics,' *Journal of Political Economy*, **80** (5), 906–950.

Friedman, M. (1982), 'Monetary policy: Theory and practice,' *Journal of Money, Credit and Banking*, **14** (1), 98–118.

Friedman, M. (1984), 'Lessons from the 1979–82 monetary policy experiment,' *American Economic Review*, **74** (2), 397–400.

Friedman, M. and Schwartz, A. J. (1963a), *A Monetary History of the United States 1867–1960*, Princeton: Princeton University Press.

Friedman, M. and Schwartz, A. J. (1963b), 'Money and business cycles,' *Review of Economics and Statistics*, **45** (1, Part 2, Supplement), 32–64.

Frisch, R. (1933), 'Propagation problems and impulse problems in dynamic economics,' Publikasjon 3, Universitetets Økonomiske Institutt, Oslo, reprinted from *Economic Essays in Honour of Gustav Cassel*.

Frisch, R. (1970), 'From utopian theory to practical applications: The case of econometrics.' Lecture to the memory of Alfred Nobel, 17 June 1970, https://www.nobelprize.org/prizes/economics/1969/frisch/lecture/.

Gertler, M. (1988), 'Financial structure and aggregate economic activity: An overview,' *Journal of Money, Credit and Banking*, **20** (3, Part 2), 559–588.

Gertler, M. and Kiyotaki, N. (2011), 'Financial intermediation and credit policy in business cycle analysis,' in B. M. Friedman and M. Woodford (eds.), *Handbook of Monetary Economics*, Amsterdam: North-Holland, vol. 3A, pp. 547–599.

Gertler, M. and Kiyotaki, N. (2015), 'Banking, liquidity, and bank runs in an infinite horizon economy,' *American Economic Review*, **105** (7), 2011–2043.

Gertler, M., Kiyotaki, N. and Prestipino, A. (2016), 'Wholesale banking and bank runs in macroeconomic modelling of financial crises,' Working Paper 21892, National Bureau of Economic Research, Cambridge Ma.

Goetz, P., von (2005), 'Debt-deflation. Concepts and a stylised model,' Working Paper 176, BIS, Basel.

Goetzmann, W. N. (2016), *Money Changes Everything. How Finance Made Civilization Possible*, Princeton: Princeton University Press.

Goodfriend, M. and King, R. G. (1997), 'The New Neoclassical Synthesis and the role of monetary policy,' Working Paper 98–05, Federal Reserve Bank of Richmond, Richmond.

Goodhart, C. A. E. (1964), 'Review of Friedman M., Schwartz A. J. *A Monetary History of the United States 1867–1960*,' *Economica*, **31** (123), 314–318.

Goodhart, C. A. E. (1992), 'Dennis Robertson and the real business cycle,' in J. R. Presley (ed.), *Essays in Robertsonian Economics*, Basingstoke: Macmillan, pp. 8–34.

Goodhart, C. A. E. (2005–2006), 'What can academics contribute to the study of financial stability?' *Economic and Social Review*, **36** (3), 189–203.

Goodhart, C. A. E. (2007), 'Whatever became of the monetary aggregates?' *National Institute Economic Review*, (200), 56–61.

Gurley, J. C. and Shaw, E. S. (1955), 'Financial aspects of economic development,' *American Economic Review*, **45** (4), 515–538.

Gurley, J. C. and Shaw, E. S. (1956), 'Financial intermediaries and the saving-investment process,' *Journal of Finance*, **11** (2), 257–276.

Gurley, J. C. and Shaw, E. S. (1958), 'Intermediaries and monetary theory: A criticism of the Gurley-Shaw theory: Reply,' *American Economic Review*, **48** (1), 132–138.

Gurley, J. C. and Shaw, E. S. (1960), *Money in a Theory of Finance*, Washington: The Brooking Institution.

Hagemann, H. (2015), 'Introduction,' in L. A. Hahn, *Economic Theory of Bank Credit*, Oxford: Oxford University Press, pp. v–xxiv.

Hahn, F. H. (1965), 'On some problems of proving the existence of an equilibrium in a monetary economy,' in F. H. Hahn and F. P. R. Brechling (eds.), *Theory of Interest Rates*, London: Macmillan, pp. 126–135.

Hahn, F. H. (1981), 'Reflections on the Invisible Hand,' *Lloyds Bank Review*, (144), 1–21.

Hahn, F. H. (1982), *Money and Inflation*, Oxford: Basil Blackwell.

Hahn, F. H. (1987), 'The foundations of monetary theory,' in M. De Cecco and J. Fitoussi (eds.), *Monetary Theory and Economic Institutions*, London: Palgrave Macmillan, pp. 21–43.

Hahn, L. A. (2015[1920]), *Economic Theory of Bank Credit*, Oxford: Oxford University Press, English translation of 1st and 3rd German edn., with an introduction by H. Hagemann.

Handa, J. (2000), *Monetary Economics*, London and New York: Routledge.

Hansen, A. H. (1941), *Fiscal Policy and Business Cycles*, New York: W. W. Norton & Company Inc.

Hansen, A. H. (1951), 'Classical, loanable-fund, and Keynesian interest theories,' *Quarterly Journal of Economics*, **65** (3), 429–432.

Harcourt, G. C. (ed.) (1977), *The Microeconomic Foundations of Macroeconomics*, London: Macmillan.

Harrod, R. F. (1936), *The Trade Cycle*, Oxford: Oxford University Press.

Harrod, R. F. (1939), 'An essay in dynamic theory,' *Economic Journal*, **49** (193), 14–33.

Hawtrey, R. G. (1913), *Good and Bad Trade*, London: Constable & Company Limited.

Hawtrey, R. G. (1919), *Currency and Credit*, London: Longmans, Green and Co.

Hayek, F. A., von (1933), *Monetary Theory and the Trade Cycle*, New York: Sentry Press.

Hayek, F. A., von (1933[1939]), 'Price expectations, monetary disturbances, and malinvestments,' in F. A. von Hayek, *Profits, Interest and Investment*, London: Routledge & Sons, pp. 135–156.

Hayek, F. A., von (1939), *Profits, Interest and Investment*, London: Routledge & Sons.

Heijdra, B. J. (2017), *Foundations of Modern Macroeconomics*, Oxford: Oxford University Press, 3rd edn.

Hellwig, M. F. (1981), 'Bankruptcy, limited liability, and the Modigliani-Miller theorem,' *American Economic Review*, **71** (1), 155–170.

Hendry, D. F. and Muelbauer, N. J. (2018), 'The future of macroeconomics: macro theory and models at the Bank of England,' *Oxford Review of Economic Policy*, **34** (1–2), 287–328.

Hicks, J. R. (1935), 'A suggestion for simplifying the theory of money,' *Economica*, **2** (5), 1–19.

Hicks, J. R. (1937), 'Mr. Keynes and the "Classics": A suggested interpretation,' *Econometrica*, **5** (2), 147–159.

Hicks, J. R. (1939[1965]), *Value and Capital. An Inquiry into some Fundamental Principles of Economic Theory*, Oxford: Oxford University Press, 2nd edn.

Hicks, J. R. (1942), 'The monetary theory of D. H. Robertson,' *Economica*, **9** (33), 53–57.

Hicks, J. R. (1956[1982]), 'Methods of dynamic analysis,' in *Money, Interest and Wages. Collected Essays on Economic Theory*, Oxford: Oxford University Press, vol. 2 of *Collected Essays on Economic Theory*, pp. 219–235.

Hicks, J. R. (1966), 'A memoir,' in *Sir Dennis Robertson – Essays in Monetary Theory*, Manchester: Fontana Library, pp. 9–22.

Hicks, J. R. (1967a), *Critical Essays in Monetary Theory*, Oxford: Clarendon Press.

Hicks, J. R. (1967b), 'The two triads. Lecture I,' in *Critical Essays in Monetary Theory*, Oxford: Clarendon Press, pp. 1–16.

Hicks, J. R. (1979), *Causality in Economics*, Oxford: Basil Blackwell.

Hicks, J. R. (1989a), 'LF and LP,' in M. Kohn (ed.), *Finance Constraints and the Theory of Money. Selected Papers of S. C. Tsiang*, New York: Academic Press, pp. 351–358.

Hicks, J. R. (1989b), *A Market Theory of Money*, Oxford: Clarendon Press.

Hiltzik, M. (2011), *The New Deal. A Modern History*, New York: Free Press.

Hirsch, A. and De Marchi, N. (1990), *Milton Friedman: Economics in Theory and Practice*, Ann Arbor: The University of Michigan Press.

Hoover, K. D. (1984), 'Two types of Monetarism,' *Journal of Economic Literature*, **22** (1), 58–76.

Hoover, K. D. (1988), *The New Classical Macroeconomics: A Sceptical Inquiry*, Oxford: Basil Blackwell.

Hoover, K. D. (2012), 'Microfoundational programs,' in P. G. Duarte and G. T. Lima (eds.), *Microfoundations Reconsidered*, Cheltenham: Edward Elgar Publishing, pp. 19–61.

Ingrao, B. (2013), *Portraits of European Economists*, Rome: Aracne.

Ingrao, B. (2018), 'Models in economics. Fables, fictions and stories,' *Annals of the Fondazione Luigi Einaudi*, **52** (1), 113–135.

Ingrao, B. and Israel, G. (1990), *The Invisible Hand. Economic Equilibrium in the History of Science*, Cambridge, Ma: MIT Press.

Jakab, Z. and Kumhof, M. (2014), 'Models of banking: Loanable funds or loans that create funds?' (31 July 2014). Available at SSRN:https://ssrn.com/abstract=2474759 or http://dx.doi.org/10.2139/ssrn.2474759.

Jakab, Z. and Kumhof, M. (2015), 'Banks are not intermediaries of loanable funds – and why this matters,' Working Paper 529, Bank of England, London.

Jensen, M. C. (1978), 'Some anomalous evidence regarding market efficiency,' *Journal of Financial Economics*, **6** (2–3), 95–101.

Johnson, H. G. (1962), 'Monetary theory and policy,' *American Economic Review*, **52** (3), 335–384.

Johnson, H. G. (1971), 'The Keynesian revolution and the Monetarist counter-revolution,' *American Economic Review*, **61** (2), 1–14.

Kahn, R. F. (1954[1972]), 'Some notes on liquidity preference,' in *Selected Essays on Employment and Growth*, Cambridge: Cambridge University Press, pp. 72–102.

Kahn, R. F. (1984), *The Making of Keynes' General Theory*, Cambridge: Cambridge University Press.

Kahneman, D. and Riepe, M. (1998), 'Aspects of investor psychology,' *Journal of Portfolio Management*, **24** (4), 52–65.

Kahneman, D. and Tversky, A. (1973), 'On the psychology of prediction,' *Psychological Review*, **80** (4), 237–251.

Kahneman, D. and Tversky, A. (1979), 'Prospect theory: An analysis of decision under risk,' *Econometrica*, **47** (2), 263–292.

Kaldor, N. (1939), 'Speculation and economic stability,' *Review of Economic Studies*, **7** (3), 1–27.

Kaldor, N. (1940), 'A model of the trade cycle,' *Economic Journal*, **50** (197), 78–92.

Kaldor, N. (1960a), 'Introduction,' in *Essays on Economic Stability and Growth*, London: Duckworth, vol. 1 of *Collected Economic Essays by Nicholas Kaldor*, first edn., pp. 1–15.

Kaldor, N. (1960b), 'Keynes' theory of the own-rates of interest,' in *Essays on Economic Stability and Growth. Collected Economic Essays by Nicholas Kaldor*, London: Duckworth, vol. 1, first edn., pp. 59–74.

Kaldor, N. (1960c), 'Speculation and economic stability,' in *Essays on Economic Stability and Growth. Collected Economic Essays by Nicholas Kaldor*, London: Duckworth, vol. 1 of *Collected Economic Essays*, first edn., pp. 17–58.

Kaldor, N. (1989a), 'The new Monetarism,' in F. Targetti and A. P. Thirlwall (eds.), *The Essential Kaldor*, London: Duckworth, pp. 474–494.

Kaldor, N. (1989b), 'Origins of the new monetarism,' in *Further Essays on Economic Theory and Policy. Collected Economic Essays by Nicholas Kaldor*, New York: Holmes & Meyer, vol. 9, pp. 160–177.

Kalecki, M. (1943[1991]), 'Studies in economic dynamics,' in J. Osiatyński (ed.), *Capitalism. Economic Dynamics*, Oxford: Clarendon Press, vol. 2 of *Collected Works of Michal Kalecki*, pp. 117–202.

Kalecki, M. (1944), 'Professor Pigou on "the classical stationary state" – a comment',' *Economic Journal*, **54** (213), 131–132.

Kalecki, M. (1954[1965]), *Theory of Economic Dynamics*, London: Allen and Unwin, 2nd edn.

Kareken, J. H. and Wallace, N. (eds.) (1980), *Models of Monetary Economics*, Minneapolis: Federal Reserve Bank of Minneapolis.

Kashyap, A. K., Rajan, R. G. and Stein, J. C. (2002), 'Banks as liquidity providers: An explanation for the coexistence of lending and deposit-taking,' *Journal of Finance*, **57** (1), 33–73.

Kennedy, C. (1948–49), 'Period analysis and the demand for money,' *Review of Economic Studies*, **16** (1), 41–49.

Kennedy, C. (1960), '*Money in a Theory of Finance*. By J. G. Gurley and E. S. Shaw,' *Economic Journal*, **70** (279), 568–569.

Keynes, J. M. (1919[1971]), *The Economic Consequences of the Peace*, vol. 2 of *The Collected Writings of John Maynard Keynes*, London: Macmillan.

Keynes, J. M. (1923[1971]), *A Tract on Monetary Reform*, vol. 4 of *The Collected Writings of John Maynard Keynes*, London: Macmillan.

Keynes, J. M. (1930[1971]), *A Treatise on Money. The Pure Theory of Money*, vol. 5 of *The Collected Writing of John Maynard Keynes*, London: Macmillan.

Keynes, J. M. (1931[1972]a), 'The consequences to the banks of the collapse of money values,' in *Essays in Persuasion*, Macmillan, vol. 9 of *Collected Writings of John Maynard Keynes*, pp. 150–158.

Keynes, J. M. (1931[1972]b), 'The economic consequences of Mr. Churchill,' in *Essays in Persuasion*, London: Macmillan, vol. 9 of *Collected Writings of John Maynard Keynes*, pp. 207–230, originally published in 1925.

Keynes, J. M. (1931[1972]c), *Essays in Persuasion*, vol. 9 of *Collected Writings of John Maynard Keynes*, London: Macmillan.

Keynes, J. M. (1931[1972]d), 'The great slump of 1930,' in *Essays in Persuasion*, London: Macmillan, vol. 9 of *Collected Writings of John Maynard Keynes*, pp. 126–134.

Keynes, J. M. (1931[1973]), 'An economic analysis of unemployment,' in D. E. Moggridge (ed.), *The General Theory and After. Part I, Preparation*, London: Macmillan, vol. 13 of *The Collected Writings of John Maynard Keynes*, pp. 343–367.

Keynes, J. M. (1933[1973]), 'A monetary theory of production,' in D. E. Moggridge (ed.), *The General Theory and After. Part I, Preparation*, London: Macmillan, vol. XIII of *Collected Writings of John Maynard Keynes*, pp. 408–411.

Keynes, J. M. (1936 [1973]), *The General Theory of Employment Interest and Money*, vol. 7 of *The Collected Writings of John Maynard Keynes*, London: Macmillan.

Keynes, J. M. (1937a), 'Alternative theories of the rate of interest,' *Economic Journal*, **47** (186), 241–252.

Keynes, J. M. (1937b), 'The "ex-ante" theory of the rate of interest,' *Economic Journal*, **47** (188), 663–69.

Keynes, J. M. (1937c), 'The general theory of employment,' *Quarterly Journal of Economics*, **51** (2), 209–223.

Keynes, J. M. (1973), *The General Theory and After. Part II, Defence and Development*, vol. 14 of *The Collected Writings of John Maynard Keynes*, London: Macmillan.

Kindleberger, C. P. (2000), *Manias, Panics, and Crashes*, New York: Wiley, 4th edn., first edition 1978.

King, M. (1994), 'Debt deflation: Theory and evidence,' *European Economic Review*, **38** (3–4), 419–445.

King, R. A. and Levine, R. (1993), 'Finance and growth: Schumpeter might be right,' *Quarterly Journal of Economics*, **108** (3), 717–737.

Kirman, A. P. (1992), 'Whom or what does the representative agent represent?' *Journal of Economic Perspectives*, **6** (2), 117–136.

Kirman, A. P. (2006), 'Demand theory and general equilibrium: From explanation to introspection, a journey down the wrong road,' *History of Political Economy*, **38** (annual supplement), 246–280.

Kiyotaki, N. and Moore, J. (1997), 'Credit cycles,' *Journal of Political Economy*, **105** (2), 211–248.

Koenig, E. F., Leeson, R. and Kahn, G. A. (eds.) (2012), *The Taylor Rule and the Transformation of Monetary Policy*, Stanford: Hoover Institution Press.

Koo, R. (2008), *The Holy Grail of Macroeconomics: Lessons from Japan's Great Recession*, New York: Wiley.

Koo, R. (2015), *The Escape from Balance Sheet Recession and the QE Trap*, Singapore: Wiley.

Kydland, F. E. and Prescott, E. C. (1977), 'Rules rather than discretion: The inconsistency of optimal plans,' *Journal of Political Economy*, **85** (3), 473–491.

Kydland, F. E. and Prescott, E. C. (1982), 'Time to build and aggregate fluctuations,' *Econometrica*, **50** (6), 1345–1370.

Lagos, R., Rocheteau, G. and Wright, R. (2017), 'Liquidity: A new monetarist perspective,' *Journal of Economic Literature*, **55** (2), 371–440.

Lahart, J. (2007), 'In time of tumult, obscure economist gains currency,' *Wall Street Journal*, 18 August.

Laidler, D. E. W. (1991), *The Golden Age of the Quantity Theory*, Princeton: Princeton University Press.

Laidler, D. E. W. (1995), 'Robertson in the 1920s,' *European Journal of the History of Economic Thought*, **2** (1), 151–174.

Laidler, D. E. W. (1999), *Fabricating the Keynesian Revolution*, Cambridge: Cambridge University Press.

Laidler, D. E. W. (2013), 'Reassessing the thesis of the monetary history,' Working paper no. 2013–5, Economic Policy Research Unit, London, ON.

Laidler, D. E. W. (2015), 'Three revolutions in macroeconomics: their nature and influence,' *European Journal of the History of Economic Thought*, **22** (1), 1–25.

Lange, O. (1942[1959]), 'Say's Law: A restatement and criticism,' in *Papers in Economics and Sociology*, Oxford and New York: Oxford University Press, pp. 149–170.

Lange, O. (1944), *Price Flexibility and Employment*, Bloomington: Principia Press.

Leijonhufvud, A. (1973), 'Effective demand failures,' *Swedish Journal of Economics*, **3** (1), 27–48.

Leijonhufvud, A. (1981), 'The Wicksell connection: Variations on a theme,' in *Information and Coordination. Essays in Macroeconomic Theory*, Oxford and New York: Oxford University Press, pp. 131–202.

Leijonhufvud, A. (1997), 'The Wicksellian heritage,' *Economic Notes*, **26** (1), 1–10.

Lerner, A. P. (1938), 'Alternative formulations of the theory of interest,' *Economic Journal*, **48** (190), 211–230.

Lerner, A. P. (1944), 'Interest theory – supply and demand for loans or supply and demand for cash,' *Review of Economics and Statistics*, **26** (2), 88–91.

Lerner, A. P. (1962), '*Money in a Theory of Finance*, by John G. Gurley, Edward S. Shaw,' *Journal of the American Statistical Association*, **57** (299), 704–709.

Lindner, F. (2015), 'Does saving increase the supply of credit? A critique of loanable funds theory,' *World Economic Review*, (no. 4), 1–26.

Lucas, R. E., Jr (1972), 'Expectations and the neutrality of money,' *Journal of Economic Theory*, **4** (1), 103–124.

Lucas, R. E., Jr (1973), 'Some international evidence on output-inflation tradeoffs,' *American Economic Review*, **63** (3), 326–334.

Lucas, R. E., Jr (1977), 'Understanding business cycles,' *Carnegie-Rochester Conference Series on Public Policy*, **5**, 7–29.

Lucas, R. E., Jr (1980a), 'Equilibrium in a pure currency economy,' *Economic Inquiry*, **18** (2), 203–220.

Lucas, R. E., Jr (1980b), 'Methods and problems in business cycle theory,' *Journal of Money, Credit and Banking*, **12** (4), 696–715.

Lucas, R. E., Jr (1981), *Studies in Business Cycle Theory*, Oxford: Basil Blackwell.

Lucas, R. E., Jr (1996), 'Nobel lecture: "monetary neutrality",' *Journal of Political Economy*, **104** (4), 661–682.

Lucas, R. E., Jr (2004[2013]), 'My Keynesian education,' in *Collected Papers in Monetary Theory*, Cambridge Ma.: Harvard University Press, pp. 503–516.

Lucas, R. E., Jr (2013), 'Introduction,' in M. Gillman (ed.), *Collected Papers on Monetary Theory*, Cambridge Ma.: Harvard University Press, pp. xvii–xxvii.

Machlup, F. (1965), 'The cloakroom rule of international reserves: Reserve creation and resources transfer,' *Quarterly Journal of Economics*, **79** (3), 337–355.

Malkiel, B. G. (2003), 'The efficient market hypothesis and its critics,' *Journal of Economic Perspectives*, **17** (1), 59–82.

Mankiw, N. G. and Romer, D. (1991a), 'Introduction,' in N. G. Mankiw and D. Romer (eds.), *New Keynesian Economics*, Cambridge Ma.: MIT Press, vol. 1, pp. 1–26.

Mankiw, N. G. and Romer, D. (eds.) (1991b), *New Keynesian Economics*, vol. 1 and 2, Cambridge Ma.: MIT Press.

Marshall, A. (1923), *Money, Credit and Commerce*, London: Macmillan.

Martel, R. J. (1996), 'Heterogeneity, aggregation, and a meaningful macroeconomics,' in D. Colander (ed.), *Beyond Microfoundations: Post Walrasian Macroeconomics*, Cambridge: Cambridge University Press, pp. 127–144.

McLeay, M., Radia, A. and Thomas, R. (2014a), 'Money creation in the modern economy,' *Bank of England Quarterly Bulletin*, **54** (1), 14–27.

McLeay, M., Radia, A. and Thomas, R. (2014b), 'Money in the modern economy: An introduction,' *Bank of England Quarterly Bulletin*, **2014** (Q1), 4–13.

Mehrling, P. (1999), 'The vision of Hyman P. Minsky,' *Journal of Economic Behavior & Organization*, **39** (2), 129–158.

Meltzer, A. H. (2010), *A History of the Federal Reserve, 1913–1951*, vol. 1, Chicago: Chicago University Press.

Messori, M. (1996), 'Nota ai testi,' in M. Messori and L. Berti (eds.), *Trattato della moneta capitoli inediti*, Napoli: Edizioni Scientifiche Italiane, pp. xi–xlvi.

Messori, M. (1997), 'The trials and misadventures of Schumpeter's Treatise on Money,' *History of Political Economy*, **29** (4), 639–673.

Miller, M. H. (1988), 'The Modigliani Miller proposition after thirty years,' *Journal of Economic Perspectives*, **2** (4), 99–120.

Minsky, H. P. (1961), '*Money in a Theory of Finance* by J. G. Gurley, E. S. Shaw, Alain C. Enthoven,' *Journal of Finance*, **16** (1), 138–140.

Minsky, H. P. (1963), 'Comment on Friedman's and Schwartz' Money and the Business Cycles,' *Review of Economics and Statistics*, **45** (1, Part 2, Supplement), 64–72.

Minsky, H. P. (1975), *John Maynard Keynes*, New York: Columbia University Press.

Minsky, H. P. (1986[2008]), *Stabilizing an Unstable Economy*, New York: McGraw-Hill.

Mirowski, P. (2002), *Machine Dreams: Economics Becomes Cyborg Science*, New York: Cambridge University Press.

Mishkin, F. S. (2011), 'Monetary policy strategy: Lessons from the crises,' Working Paper 16755, NBER, Cambridge Ma.

Modigliani, F. (1944), 'Liquidity preference and the theory of interest and money,' *Econometrica*, **12** (1), 45–88.

Modigliani, F. (1963), 'The monetary mechanism and its interaction with real phenomena,' *Review of Economics and Statistics*, **45** (1), 79–107.

Modigliani, F. and Miller, M. (1958), 'The cost of capital, corporation finance and the theory of investment,' *American Economic Review*, **48** (3), 261–297.

Moggridge, D. E. (1992), *Maynard Keynes. An Economist's Biography*, London and New York: Routledge.

Morley, J. (2016), 'Macro-finance linkages,' *Journal of Economic Survey*, **30** (4), 698–711.

Myrdal, G. (1939), *Monetary Equilibrium*, New York: Augustus M. Kelley.

Ohlin, B. (1937a), 'Alternative theories of the rate of interest: Three rejoinders,' *Economic Journal*, **47** (187), 424–427.

Ohlin, B. (1937b), 'Some notes on the Stockholm theory of savings and investment I,' *Economic Journal*, **47** (185), 53–69.

Ohlin, B. (1937c), 'Some notes on the Stockholm theory of savings and investment II,' *Economic Journal*, **47** (186), 221–240.

Okun, A. M. (1963), 'Comment on Friedman's and Schwartz' Money and the Business Cycles,' *Review of Economics and Statistics*, **45** (1, Part 2, Supplement), 72–77.

Pagano, M. (1993), 'Financial markets and growth: An overview,' *European Economic Review*, **37** (2–3), 613–622.

Pagano, M. (2013), 'Finance: Economic lifeblood or toxin?' Working Paper 9, EIEF, Rome.

Papadimitriou, D. B. and Wray, L. R. (1998), 'The economic contributions of Hyman Minsky: Varieties of capitalism and institutional reform,' *Review of Political Economy*, **10** (2), 199–225.

Papadimitriou, D. B. and Wray, L. R. (1999), 'Minsky's analysis of financial capitalism,' Working Paper 275, The Levy Economics Institute of Bard College, Annandale-on-Hudson, N.Y.

Patinkin, D. (1948), 'Price flexibility and full employment,' *American Economic Review*, **38** (4), 543–564.

Patinkin, D. (1949), 'The indeterminacy of absolute prices in classical economic theory,' *Econometrica*, **17** (1), 1–27.

Patinkin, D. (1956), *Money, Interest, and Prices*, Evanston and White Plains: Row, Peterson and Company, 1st edn.

Patinkin, D. (1958), 'Liquidity preference and loanable funds: Stock and flow analysis,' *Economica*, **25** (100), 300–318.

Patinkin, D. (1959), 'Keynesian economics rehabilitated: A rejoinder to Professor Hicks,' *Economic Journal*, **69** (275), 582–587.

Patinkin, D. (1961), 'Financial intermediaries and the logical structure of monetary theory. A review article,' *American Economic Review*, **51** (1), 95–116.

Patinkin, D. (1969), 'The Chicago tradition, the quantity theory and Friedman,' *Journal of Money, Credit and Banking*, **1** (1), 46–70.

Patinkin, D. (1972), 'Samuelson on the neoclassical dichotomy: A comment,' *Canadian Journal of Economics*, **5** (2), 279–283.

Patinkin, D. (1982), *Anticipations of The General Theory?*, Chicago: Chicago University Press.

Pavanelli, G. (1997), 'Non-neutrality of money and business cycles in Irving Fisher's work,' *Rivista Internazionale di Scienze Economiche e Commerciali*, **44** (2), 269–298.

Pavanelli, G. (1999), 'Il problema della stabilizzazione nel pensiero di Irving Fisher,' *Rivista Internazionale di Scienze Sociali*, **107** (1), 49–84.

Pavanelli, G. (2004), 'The Great Depression in Irving Fisher's thought,' in I. Barens, B. Caspari and B. Schefold (eds.), *Political Events and Economic Ideas*, Cheltenham: Edward Elgar Publishing, pp. 289–305.

Phelps, E. S. (1969), 'The new microeconomics in inflation and employment theory,' *American Economic Review*, **59** (2), 147–160.

Phillips, C. A. (1921), *Bank Credit*, New York: Macmillan.

Pigou, A. C. (1920), *The Economics of Welfare*, London: Macmillan, 1st edn.

Pigou, A. C. (1943), 'The classical stationary state,' *Economic Journal*, **53** (212), 343–351.

Pigou, A. C. (1946), 'Mr. J. M. Keynes' General Theory of Employment, Interest and Money,' *Economica*, **3** (10), 115–132.

Pigou, A. C. (1947[1952]), 'Economic progress in a stable environment,' in F. A. Lutz and L. W. Mints, (eds.), *Readings in Monetary Theory*, London: George Allen and Unwin Ltd, vol. 5 of *Blakiston Series of Republished Articles on Economics*, chap. 12, pp. 241–283.

Pigou, A. C. (1950), *Keynes's General Theory: A Retrospective View*, London: Macmillan.

Popov, A. (2017), 'Evidence on finance and economic growth,' Working Paper 2115, European Central Bank, Frankfurt.

Prescott, E. C. (2006), 'The transformation of macroeconomic policy and research,' *American Economist*, **50** (1), 3–20.

Presley, J. R. (1978), *Robertsonian Economics*, London: Macmillan.

Ramsey, F. P. (1928), 'A mathematical theory of saving,' *Economic Journal*, **38** (152), 543–559.

Rauchway, E. (2015), *The Money Makers*, New York: Basic Books.

Rizvi, S. A. T. (2006), 'The Sonnenschein-Mantel-Debreu results after thirty years,' *History of Political Economy*, **38** (Suppl. 1), 228–245.

Robertson, D. H. (1913), 'Review of *Good and Bad Trade: An Inquiry into the Causes of Trade Fluctuations*, by R. G. Hawtrey,' *Cambridge Review*, **35**, 162–163.

Robertson, D. H. (1915), *A Study of Industrial Fluctuations*, Westminster: P. S. King & Son, Ltd.

Robertson, D. H. (1926[1949]), *Banking Policy and the Price Level. An Essay in the Theory of the Trade Cycle*, Fairfield, NJ: Augustus M. Kelley Publishers, 4th edn.

Robertson, D. H. (1928[1962]), *Money*, Chicago: University of Chicago Press, 4th edn.

Robertson, D. H. (1928[1966]), 'Theories of banking policy,' in *Essays in Money and Interest*, London: Fontana Books, pp. 23–42, originally published in *Economica*, no. 23, 1928.

Robertson, D. H. (1934), 'Industrial fluctuation and the natural rate of interest,' *Economic Journal*, **44** (176), 650–656.

Robertson, D. H. (1937), 'Alternative theories of the rate of interest: Three rejoinders-II,' *Economic Journal*, **47** (187), 428–436.

Robertson, D. H. (1940), 'Mr. Keynes and the rate of interest,' in *Essays in Monetary Theory*, Staple Press, pp. 1–38.

Robertson, D. H. (1952), 'Some notes on the theory of interest,' in D. H. Robertson (ed.), *Utility and All That*, London: George Allen & Unwin Ltd, pp. 97–115.

Robertson, D. H. and Keynes, J. M. (1938), 'Mr. Keynes and "finance",' *Economic Journal*, **48** (190), 314–322.

Robinson, J. V. (1951), 'The rate of interest,' *Econometrica*, **19** (2), 92–111.

Samuelson, P. A. (1939), 'Interactions between the multiplier analysis and the principle of acceleration,' *Review of Economics and Statistics*, **21** (2), 75–78.

Samuelson, P. A. (1941), 'The stability of equilibrium: Comparative statics and dynamics,' *Econometrica*, **9** (2), 97–120.

Samuelson, P. A. (1948), *Economics*, New York: McGraw-Hill.

Samuelson, P. A. (1952), 'Economic theory and mathematics – an appraisal,' *American Economic Review*, **42** (2), 56–66.

Samuelson, P. A. (1955), *Economics*, New York: McGraw-Hill, 3rd edn.

Samuelson, P. A. (1965), 'Proof that properly anticipated prices fluctuate randomly,' *Industrial Management Review*, **6** (2), 41–49.

Samuelson, P. A. (1973), 'Proof that properly discounted present values of assets vibrate randomly,' *Bell Journal of Economics and Management Science*, **4** (2), 269–374.

Samuelson, P. A. and Solow, R. M. (1960), 'Analytical aspects of anti-inflation policy,' *American Economic Review*, **50** (2), 177–194.

Sardoni, C. (1989–90), 'Chapter 18 of the General Theory. Methodological issues,' *Journal of Post Keynesian Economics*, **12** (2), 293–307.

Sardoni, C. (1996), 'Prices, expectation and investment,' in S. Pressman (ed.), *Interactions in Political Economy*, London and New York: Routledge, pp. 93–109.

Sardoni, C. (2007), 'Kaldor's monetary thought: A contribution to a modern theory of money,' in M. Forstater, G. Mongiovi and S. Pressman (eds.), *Post Keynesian Macroeconomics*, London and New York: Routledge, pp. 129–146.

Sardoni, C. (2011), *Unemployment, Recession and Effective Demand*, Cheltenham: Edward Elgar Publishing.

Sardoni, C. (2015a), 'The functions of money and the demand for liquidity,' Working Paper 3, Dipartimento di Scienze Sociali ed Economiche, Rome.

Sardoni, C. (2015b), 'Searching for the microfoundations of macroeconomics,' *History of Economic Ideas*, **23** (1), 173–180.

Sardoni, C. (2017), 'Circuitist and Keynesian approaches to money. A reconciliation?' *Metroeconomica*, **68** (2), 205–227.

Sargent, T. (2015), 'Robert E. Lucas, Jr *Collected Papers in Monetary Theory*,' *Journal of Economic Literature*, **53** (1), 43–64.

Schumpeter, J. A. (1917–1918[1956]), 'Money and the social product,' *International Economic Papers*, **6**, 148–213, traslated into English by A.W. Marget.

Schumpeter, J. A. (1927), 'The explanation of the business cycle,' *Economica*, **21**, 286–311.

Schumpeter, J. A. (1928), 'The instability of capitalism,' *Economic Journal*, **38** (151), 361–386.

Schumpeter, J. A. (1931), 'The present world depression: a tentative diagnosis,' *American Economic Review*, **21** (1), 179–182.

Schumpeter, J. A. (1934[1983]), *The Theory of Economic Development. An Inquiry into Profits, Capital, Credit, Interest, and the Business Cycle*, New Brunswick and London: Transaction Publishers.

Schumpeter, J. A. (1935), 'The analysis of economic change,' *Review of Economic Statistics*, **17** (4), 2–10.

Schumpeter, J. A. (1939), *Business Cycles. A Theoretical, Historical, and Statistical Analysis of the Capitalist Process*, vol. 1 and 2, New York and London: McGraw-Hill.

Schumpeter, J. A. (1946), 'The decade of the Twenties,' *American Economic Review*, **36** (2), 1–10.

Schumpeter, J. A. (1947), 'The creditive response in economic history,' *Journal of Economic History*, **7** (2), 149–159.

Schumpeter, J. A. (1950[1994]), *Capitalism, Socialism and Democracy*, London and New York: Routledge, 3rd edn.

Schumpeter, J. A. (1954[2006]), *History of Economic Analysis*, Abingdon: Taylor & Francis.

Shiller, R. J. (2000), *Irrational Exuberance*, New York: Broadway Books.

Shiller, R. J. (2003), 'From efficient markets theory to behavioral finance,' *Journal of Economic Perspectives*, **17** (1), 83–104.

Shin, H. S. (2010), *Risk and Liquidity*, New York: Oxford University Press.

Shleifer, A. (2000), *Inefficient Markets. An Introduction to Behavioral Finance*, Clarendon Lectures in Economics, Oxford: Oxford University Press.

Skidelsky, R. (1992), *John Maynard Keynes*, vol. 2: The Economist as a Saviour, London: Macmillan.

Snowdown, B. and Vane, H. R. (2005), *Modern Macroeconomics. Its Origins, Development and Current State*, Cheltenham: Edward Elgar Publishing.

Solow, R. M. (1988), 'Growth theory and after,' *American Economic Review*, **78** (3), 307–317.

Solow, R. M. (1998), *Monopolistic Competition and Macroeconomic Theory*, Federico Caffè Lectures, Cambridge: Cambridge University Press.

Solow, R. M. (2010), 'Statement of Robert M. Solow,' Hearing before the Subcommittee on investigations and oversight, Committee on Science and Technology, House of Representatives of the United States.

Sornette, D. (2003), *Why Stock Markets Crash*, Princeton and Oxford: Princeton University Press.

Stiglitz, J. E. (2000), 'The contributions of the economics of information to twentieth century economics,' *Quarterly Journal of Economics*, **115** (4), 1441–1478.

Stiglitz, J. E. (2002), 'Information and the change in the paradigm in economics,' *American Economic Review*, **92** (3), 460–501.

Stiglitz, J. E. (2018), 'Where modern macroeconomics went wrong,' *Oxford Review of Economic Policy*, **34** (1–2), 70–106.

Stiglitz, J. E. and Greenwald, B. (2003), *Towards a New Paradigm in Monetary Economics*, Cambridge: Cambridge University Press.

Stiglitz, J. E. and Weiss, A. (1981), 'Credit rationing in markets with imperfect information,' *American Economic Review*, **71** (3), 393–410.

Swedberg, R. (1991), *Schumpeter–A Biography*, Princeton: Princeton University Press.

Thirlwall, A. P. (1987), *Nicholas Kaldor, Grand Masters in Economics*, Brighton, Sussex: Wheatsheaf Books.

Tichy, G. (1984), 'Schumpeter's monetary theory: An unjustly neglected part of his work,' in C. Steindl (ed.), *Lectures on Schumpeterian Economics*, Berlin: Springer-Verlag, pp. 125–138.

Tobin, J. (1956), 'The interest-elasticity of transactions demand for cash,' *Review of Economics and Statistics*, **38** (3), 241–247.

Tobin, J. (1958), 'Liquidity preference as behavior towards risk,' *Review of Economic Studies*, **25** (2), 65–86.

Tobin, J. (1961), 'Money, capital and other stores of value,' *American Economic Review*, **5** (2), 26–37.

Tobin, J. (1963), 'Commercial banks as creators of "money",' Paper 205, Cowles Foundation, New Haven.

Tobin, J. (1969), 'A general equilibrium approach to monetary theory,' *Journal of Money, Credit and Banking*, **1** (1), 15–29.

Tobin, J. (1975), 'Keynesian models of recession and depression,' *American Economic Review*, **65** (2), 195–202.

Tobin, J. (1980), *Asset Accumulation and Economic Activity*, Oxford: Basil Blackwell.

Tobin, J. (1982), 'Money and finance in the macroeconomic process,' *Journal of Money, Credit, and Banking*, **14** (2), 171–203.

Tobin, J. (1984), 'On the efficiency of the financial system,' *Lloyds Bank Review*, (153), 1–15.

Tobin, J. and Brainard, W. C. (1963), 'Financial intermediaries and the effectiveness of monetary controls,' *American Economic Review*, **53** (2), 383–400.

Tobin, J. and Brainard, W. C. (1976), 'Asset markets and the cost of capital,' Discussion Paper 427, Cowles Foundation, New Haven.

Townsend, R. M. (1979), 'Optimal contracts and competitive markets with costly state verification,' *Journal of Economic Theory*, **21** (2), 265–293.

Trautwein, H. (2000), 'The credit view, old and new,' *Journal of Economic Surveys*, **14** (2), 155–189.

Tsiang, S. C. (1956), 'Liquidity preference and loanable funds theories, multiplier and velocity analyses: A synthesis,' *American Economic Review*, **66** (4), 539–564.

Turner, A. (2016), *Between Debt and the Devil*, Princeton and Oxford: Princeton University Press.

Tversky, A. and Kahneman, D. (1974), 'Judgment under uncertainty: Heuristics and biases,' *Science*, **185** (4157), 1124–1131.

Wallace, N. (1998), 'A dictum for monetary theory,' *Federal Reserve Bank of Minneapolis Quarterly Review*, **22** (1), 20–26.

Walras, L. (1900), *Éléments d'Économie Politique Pure ou Théorie de la Richesse Sociale*, Lausanne: F. Rouge, 4th edn.

Weintraub, E. R. (1979), *Microfoundations*, Cambridge: Cambridge University Press.

Werner, R. A. (2014a), 'Can banks individually create money out of nothing? The theories and the empirical evidence,' *International Review of Financial Analysis*, **36** (C), 1–19.

Werner, R. A. (2014b), 'How do banks create money, and why can other firms not do the same? An explanation for the coexistence of lending and deposit-taking,' *International Review of Financial Analysis*, **36** (C), 71–77.

Wicksell, K. (1898[1936]), *Interest and Prices*, London: Macmillan, first German edition 1898.

Wicksell, K. (1901[1934]), *Lectures on Political Economy*, vol. 1, London: Routledge & Sons, first Swedish edition 1901.

Wicksell, K. (1906[1935]), *Lectures on Political Economy*, vol. 2, London: Routledge & Sons, first Swedish edition 1906.

Wicksell, K. (1907), 'The influence of the rate of interest on prices,' *Economic Journal*, **17** (66), 213–220.

Wicksell, K. (1907[2001]), 'A new theory of crises,' *Structural Change and Economic Dynamics*, **12** (3), 335–342.

Woodford, M. (2003), *Interest and Prices*, Princeton and Oxford: Princeton University Press.

Woodford, M. (2009), 'Convergence in macroeconomics: Elements of the new synthesis,' *American Economic Journal: Macroeconomics*, **1** (1), 267–279.

Woodford, M. (2010), 'Financial intermediation and macroeconomic analysis,' *Journal of Economic Perspectives*, **24** (4), 21–44.

Woodford, M. (2013), 'Macroeconomic analysis without the rational expectations hypothesis,' *Annual Review of Economics*, **5** (1), 303–346.

Young, W. (2014), *Real Business Cycle Models in Economics*, London and New York: Routledge.

Zingales, L. (2015), 'Presidential address: Does finance benefit society?' *Journal of Finance*, **70** (4), 1327–1363.

Index

Adrian, T. 221
Akerlof, G. A. 216, 232–3, 238
'animal spirits' 238, 249
arbitrage 231–2
Arrow, K. J. 12–13, 143, 175, 198–9
Arrow-Debreu model 12–13, 15, 21, 140,
    143–4, 175, 196, 198–9, 204, 207–9,
    234, 242–5
asymmetric information
    bank role in world of 18, 86
    financial institutions existing in world
      of 17
    between financial promoters and
      savers 83
    as intrinsic to human knowledge and
      action 249
    between lenders and borrowers 216,
      233–4
    Stiglitz's pioneering work on 216–17
auctioneer
    Arrow-Debreu model 196–7, 244–5
    consequences of removal 19
    formalization of 143
    neo-Walrasian conception of 170–71
    and smooth working of markets 16
    Tobin's denial of credibility of 175
Austrian school 8, 56, 88
'availability doctrine' 154

Backhouse, R. E. 138, 234
balances
    active 107–8
    real 131, 136, 149, 182
bank runs 72–3, 82, 173, 189–90
banking
    mystery of 32–5, 84–5
banking system
    complexity of 220–22
    in trade cycle 62–6
bankruptcy
    of banks 72, 217–18, 223

consequences of 39
domino effects 4, 81–2
relevance of 19
risk of 73, 86, 137, 147
banks
    as active players/agents 10, 237
    in deflationary spiral 81–5
    in *General Theory* 91, 98–101
    new view of 137, 168, 172, 177–8,
      222–5
    old view of 127–8, 130–31, 222–5, 237
    as passive agents 8, 11, 114, 192, 225,
      242
    pre-1930s approaches 239–41
    as profit seeking financial
      intermediaries 162–5,
      228–9, 246
    and quantity theory 24–41
    retail 221, 224
    in *Treatise on Money* 92–5
    wholesale 221, 224
Baranzini, M. 5
Barro, R. J. 136
barter economy
    classical analysis 146
    general equilibrium theory 5–6, 203
    ideal models of 49, 203
    neoclassical theory 7
    and net-money doctrine 164, 177
    Schumpeter's analysis 44
bearishness 95, 97, 161, 240
bears 123
behavioural economics 238, 247–9
behavioural finance 213, 232–3, 238
Benhabib, J. 179
Bernanke, B. S. 10, 72, 85–7, 219–20
Berti, L. 42–43
Bhaduri, A. 229
Bhattacharya, S. 216
Bianco, A. 222
'black swans' 75, 207